# Unemployment, Inequality and Poverty in Urban China



Although the Chinese economy is growing at a very high rate, there are massive social dislocations arising as a result of economic restructuring. These problems include urban unemployment resulting from labour retrenchment, the rural–urban migration, and increasing poverty as the social benefits that went with employment in state-owned enterprises are curtailed.

The scale of these problems is huge, and worsening income distribution has generated concern from the Communist Party about the quality of Chinese growth. Observation of the political trends from the 16th Party Congress reveals that the ruling circle has begun to care about income distribution-related issues much more than it did in the past. However, very few studies have presented results on the changes in income inequality in the late 1990s because of a lack of comprehensive microdata.

Based on extensive original research, this book redresses this imbalance and explores many aspects of unemployment, inequality and poverty in urban China. It examines the market outcomes in post-reform urban China, focusing on the relationships between unemployment, inequality and poverty. Part I provides a picture of the relationships between unemployment, inequality and poverty in urban China at the end of the 1990s. Part II provides analyses on the emerging urban labour market, focusing on its stratified structure, job mobility, profit sharing and the role of social capital. Empirical analyses are supported by rich data from nationally representative urban household and rural migrant surveys. This volume aims to draw the latest picture of the widening inequality in Chinese urban society.

**LI Shi** is Professor of Economics at the School of Economics and Business, Beijing Normal University. He has done research as a visiting scholar at the University of Oxford and Göteborg University, has taught as a professor at Hitotsubashi University and is the co-editor of *China's Retreat from Equality* (M. E. Sharpe, 2001).

**Hiroshi SATO** is Professor of Chinese Economy and Society at the Graduate School of Economics, Hitotsubashi University, Tokyo. He is the author of *The Growth of Market Relations in Post-Reform Rural China* (Routledge, 2003).

## Routledge Studies on the Chinese Economy

Series Editor
Peter Nolan, *University of Cambridge*

Founding Series Editors
Peter Nolan, *University of Cambridge* and Dong Fureng, *Beijing University*

The aim of this series is to publish original, high-quality, research-level work by both new and established scholars in the West and the East, on all aspects of the Chinese economy, including studies of business and economic history.

1 **The Growth of Market Relations in Post-Reform Rural China**
A Micro-Analysis of Peasants, Migrants and Peasant Entrepreneurs
*Hiroshi Sato*

2 **The Chinese Coal Industry: An Economic History**
*Elspeth Thomson*

3 **Sustaining China's Economic Growth in the Twenty-First Century**
*Edited by Shujie Yao and Xiaming Liu*

4 **China's Poor Regions**
Rural–Urban Migration, Poverty, Economic Reform and Urbanisation
*Mei Zhang*

5 **China's Large Enterprises and the Challenge of Late Industrialization**
*Dylan Sutherland*

6 **China's Economic Growth**
*Yanrui Wu*

7 **The Employment Impact of China's World Trade Organisation Accession**
*A.S. Bhalla and S. Qiu*

8 **Catch-Up and Competitiveness in China**
The Case of Large Firms in the Oil Industry
*Jin Zhang*

9 **Corporate Governance in China**
*Jian Chen*

10 **The Theory of the Firm and Chinese Enterprise Reform**
The Case of China International Trust and Investment Corporation
*Qin Xiao*

11 **Globalisation, Transition and Development in China**
The Case of the Coal Industry
*Huaichuan Rui*

12 **China Along the Yellow River**
Reflections on Rural Society
*Cao Jinqing, translated by Nicky Harman and Huang Ruhua*

13 **Economic Growth, Income Distribution and Poverty Reduction in Contemporary China**
*Shujie Yao*

14 **China's Economic Relations with the West and Japan, 1949–79**
Grain, Trade and Diplomacy
*Chad J. Mitcham*

15 **China's Industrial Policy and the Global Business Revolution**
The Case of the Domestic Appliance Industry
*Ling Liu*

16 **Managers and Mandarins in Contemporary China**
The Building of an International Business Alliance
*Jie Tang*

17 **The Chinese Model of Modern Development**
*Edited by Tian Yu Cao*

18 **Chinese Citizenship**
Views from the Margins
*Edited by Vanessa L. Fong and Rachel Murphy*

19 **Unemployment, Inequality and Poverty in Urban China**
*Edited by Li Shi and Hiroshi Sato*

20 **Globalisation, Competition and Growth in China**
*Edited by Jian Chen and Shujie Yao*

21 **The Chinese Communist Party in Reform**
*Edited by Kjeld Erik Brodsgaard and Zheng Yongnian*

22 **Poverty and Inequality among Chinese Minorities**
*A.S. Bhalla and Shufang Qiu*

# Unemployment, Inequality and Poverty in Urban China

*Edited by*
**Li Shi and Hiroshi Sato**

Routledge
Taylor & Francis Group
LONDON AND NEW YORK

First published 2006
by Routledge
2 Park Square, Milton Park, Abingdon, Oxon OX14 4RN

Simultaneously published in the USA and Canada
by Routledge
711 Third Avenue, New York, NY 10017

*Routledge is an imprint of the Taylor & Francis Group*

First issued in paperback 2012



Typeset in Times by Keyword Group Ltd, Wallington
Printed and bound in Great Britain by Antony Rowe Ltd, Chippenham, Wiltshire



*British Library Cataloguing in Publication Data*
A catalogue record for this book is available from the British Library

*Library of Congress Cataloging in Publication Data*
A catalog record for this book has been requested

ISBN13: 978-0-415-65466-1 (pbk)
ISBN13: 9-78-0-415-33872-1 (hbk)

# Contents

# Figures

# Tables

# Contributors

**Appleton, Simon**
School of Economics, University of Nottingham, Nottingham

**Gustafsson, Björn**
Department of Social Work, Göteborg University, Göteborg

**Knight, John**
Department of Economics, University of Oxford, Oxford

**Li, Shi**
School of Economics and Business, Beijing Normal University

**Meng, Xin**
Research School of Asian and Pacific Studies, The Australian National University, Canberra

**Sato, Hiroshi**
Graduate School of Economics, Hitotsubashi University, Tokyo

**Song, Lina**
School of Sociology and Social Policy, University of Nottingham, Nottingham

**Wei, Zhong**
Institute of Economics, Chinese Academy of Social Sciences, Beijing

**Xia, Qingjie**
School of Economics, Beijing University, Beijing

**Xue, Jinjun**
Department of Economics, Oita University, Oita

**Yueh, Linda**
Pembroke College, University of Oxford, Oxford

**Zhao, Yaohui**
China Center for Economic Research, Beijing University, Beijing

# Foreword

China's urban state-led system of employment and welfare has been radically restructured, involving a transformation that is globally unprecedented in scale and speed. The penetration of market forces into the worker's state has destroyed the iron rice bowl and created massive lay-offs, while cracks in the household registration system have unleashed waves of rural migrants seeking work in cities. These well-documented forces have contributed to the emergence of a more competitive urban labour market, with greater job choice, mobility and market-determined rewards for many employees. For others, however, they have generated vulnerability, insecurity of employment and declining entitlements to social security, and thus given rise to new social and economic problems in China's cities – poverty, unemployment and highly visible inequalities.

While these trends have been the subject of interest and research by scholars and policy makers over the past two decades, much scholarly economic analysis has focused on the relatively narrow question of how far China has moved towards a market-driven system of labour allocation, and on assessing how competitive the labour market has become. Some studies have gone beyond these questions to explore the welfare and distributional outcomes of labour market and social security system reform, and the growing problems of urban poverty and inequality. Few studies have delved more deeply to understand the institutional underpinnings that shape the process of labour market transition and determine both its efficiency and distributional outcomes.

The major contribution of this volume lies in explicitly using a lens of welfare outcomes – unemployment, inequality and poverty – to view and assess labour market transformation. In the introductory chapter, the editors highlight the inevitable risks as well as opportunities that accompany the process of marketization, and locate these in the wider institutional and policy context. The speed, pattern and consequences of labour market transition in China have been heavily shaped by the underlying structure of the economy and political and institutional legacies of the pre-reform era. Labour market change has been piecemeal and incremental, and many barriers to mobility, as well as forms of discrimination (by gender and other characteristics), remain. The new set of policies starting in 1998 under the then newly appointed Premier Zhu Rongji put enterprise, employment and welfare reform at the centre of the policy agenda, but new social problems – including increasing urban poverty and marginalization of those laid off from essentially bankrupt enterprises – were quick to emerge and a series of responses, including the development of new social security and social assistance mechanisms, put in place. The studies in this volume make an important contribution to understanding these complex trends and policy responses.

Edited by leading scholars of China's income distribution, inequality and labour market institutions, and including contributions from several of the most prominent economists working on China's labour markets, the chapters make use of data from a series of household surveys covering much of the 1990s. These large and comprehensive surveys enable the authors to address empirically a series of questions about labour market trends and outcomes, and their impact on different population groups. Such analyses are important both for scholars and other observers trying to understand China's reform process, and – perhaps more so – for policy makers who need to react quickly to ongoing changes in the economic environment and their implications for sustainable job creation and for social stability. China's phenomenal growth rates improve welfare for the majority only in so far as those who are relatively disadvantaged can be incorporated into the economy through the labour market. Providing decent employment, with adequate social security, and guarantees of safety nets or other assistance, will remain a central challenge for the leadership well into the future.

The Ford Foundation is proud to have been associated with this project through its support for data collection, analysis and workshops that have led to this, and an accompanying Chinese, volume.

Sarah Cook
*The Ford Foundation*
*Beijing*
*February 2005*

# Acknowledgements

This book is the fruit of an international joint research project conducted during 1999–2000, although many of the chapters have been revised subsequently. The aim of the project was to investigate unemployment, inequality and poverty in urban China in the 1990s through original household surveys.

In the process of completing this study, we received wonderful support from many people. Above all, we would like to express our sincere gratitude to many Chinese urban residents and rural–urban migrants, who kindly cooperated in the survey. Needless to say, this study could not have been accomplished without the cooperation of these people. The survey was conducted through the Urban Socioeconomic Survey Team of the National Bureau of Statistics (USST/NBS). We wish to thank all the staff of the team for their cooperation throughout the survey. In particular, we are grateful to Mr Huang Langhui, Director of USST/NBS, for his firm support and Mr Wang Youjuan, Director of the Division of Household Survey, USST/NBS, for his efficient organization of the survey and helpful advice.

The project received enormous assistance from Professor Zhang Ping, Professor Wei Zhong, Ms Xie Yanhong and Ms Zhang Fan in the process of data entry and data cleaning. We are very grateful for their contributions and efforts.

This project was possible owing to generous financial support from the Ford Foundation ('Urban poverty and unemployment in China', 1999–2000, Principal Investigator: Li Shi). We should like to express our appreciation to Dr Sarah Cook, Program Officer of the Ford Foundation's Beijing Office, for her interest in and enthusiasm towards the project. In addition, financial support from the Masayoshi Ohira Memorial Foundation, the Grant in Aid for Scientific Research from the Japan Society for the Promotion of Science (JSPS), the UK Department for International Development (DFID), the CCK Foundation, the George Webb Medley Fund, the International Centre for the Study of East Asian Development (ICSEAD) and Hitotsubashi University is gratefully acknowledged.

Most of the chapters in this book were presented and discussed at an international workshop held at St Edmund Hall, University of Oxford, 22–23 August 2001. We are grateful to all the participants, especially Dr Gong Xiaodong (IZA, Germany), Dr Sarah Cook (the Ford Foundation and University of Sussex), Professor Yao Shujie (Middlesex University) and Dr Dai Erbiao (ICSEAD) for their helpful comments. We should like to thank Ms Ann Gibson for her help in organizing the workshop.

Colleagues in the Chinese Academy of Social Sciences (CASS), such as Professor Zhao Renwei and Professor Zhu Ling, are acknowledged for their support and encouragement of the project.

Finally, it is gratefully acknowledged that the publication of this study was made possible by the understanding and encouragement of Professor Peter H. Nolan, University of Cambridge, and Mr Peter Sowden, our editor at Routledge.

# 1 Introduction

*Li Shi and Hiroshi Sato*

## 1.1 Setting the agenda

Marketization offers both opportunities and risks. People who seize the opportunities in a timely fashion can improve their economic situation. On the other hand, risks are bound to have a negative impact on the welfare of those who respond slowly to changes in the marketization process. This duality of marketization is especially meaningful for a transition economy like China. This volume, the product of an international joint study, examines the market outcomes in post-reform urban China, focusing on the relationships between unemployment, inequality and poverty. Empirical analyses are supported by rich data from nationally representative urban household surveys. Cutting-edge studies on specific topics are combined with broader, informative studies.

Concerning the relationship between economic growth and income distribution, the governing party has so far emphasized that growth will solve distribution problems, i.e. it has depended on economic growth producing a trickle-down effect across the regions and social strata, rather than directly targeting income distribution. However, the trickle-down effect has not occurred automatically. In fact, Chinese income inequality widened throughout the 1990s and, as a result, China has changed from an egalitarian society to one of the most unequal societies among the Asian countries (World Bank 1997; Riskin, Zhao and Li 2001).

Worsening income distribution generated concern from the governing party about the quality of Chinese growth. Observation of the political trends from the 16th Party Congress reveals that the ruling circle has begun to care about income distribution-related issues much more than it did in the past. For example, Secretary General Jiang Zemin's report in the 16th Party Congress of November 2002 addressed various issues related to income inequality – such as slumping peasant income and heavy tax burdens in rural areas, the expansion of rural–urban income disparity, the fact that a considerable portion of the population still lives in poverty, and increasing urban unemployment – as one of the main challenges facing the party, and declared the intention of enhancing the government's ability to redistribute income and to develop social safety nets. Zhu Rongji, who reported on government activities for the last term of his service as the Prime Minister in the National People's Congress in March 2003, emphasized the critical importance of policies related to employment, income distribution, poverty reduction and social security. It is obvious that the party/government recognizes that income distribution-related issues tend to retard growth and may even lead to social instability. In addition, recently there has been an increase in the research and publications arguing for a more equitable society for China (Lu 2003; Li, Li and Sun 2004; World Bank 2004; Yao 2004).

Overall income inequality can be decomposed into three components: rural–urban disparity, inequality within rural areas, and inequality within urban areas. Urban inequality is a newly emerging topic with many issues to be investigated. Until the mid-1990s, changes in the economic environment of urban households were moderate, and 'staff and workers' (*zhigong*) of the public sector remained protected by 'work-unit socialism', i.e. the system of income distribution, social security and governance based on work units (*danwei*) in urban areas and other urban-biased institutional policy arrangements.[1] The increase in urban income inequality was caused mainly by those who enjoyed a larger share of growth. However, deepening economic reforms in urban areas, especially the restructuring of state-owned enterprises and the promotion of labour mobility, led to an unexpected increase in persons losing their economic status. A large percentage of these fell into poverty. Chinese urban households have faced difficult challenges since the mid-1990s. A number of studies – for example, Gustafsson and Li (2001) and Zhao and Li (1997) – showed rising income inequality in urban China in the early 1990s. However, very few studies have presented results on the changes in income inequality in the late 1990s because of lack of microdata of household income. This volume aims to draw the latest picture of the widening inequality in urban society.

## 1.2 *Xiagang*, migration and labour market formation

As suggested above, the marketization of labour relations lies behind the great changes in urban inequality and poverty. The labour market did not exist in China until the end of the 1980s because many institutional obstacles restricted regional and inter-firm job mobility of urban workers and rural–urban migration. However, from the mid-1990s onwards, the formation of the urban labour market accelerated.

First, the *xiagang* policy, the labour restructuring policy, was implemented, and millions of workers were forced to leave their work units and thrown into the labour market. *Xiagang* is a Chinese variant of unemployment compensation that is used to soften the shock of massive unemployment to urban society (on the *xiagang* policy, see Yu 2000, Duojicairang 2001, Li et al. 2001). *Xiagang* workers lost their positions but maintained their labour relationships with the work units to which they originally belonged and kept the right to receive 'basic living expenses for *xiagang* workers' (*xiagang daigong renyuan jiben shenghuofei*). *Xiagang* workers were required to register at the Re-employment Service Centres (*zaijiuye fuwu zhongxin*) that took charge of economic assistance, social security-related services, and training and vocational guidance for re-employment. *Xiagang* status could be maintained for up to three years. If a *xiagang* worker failed to get a new job within this term, then his or her status changed to 'unemployed' (*shiye*) and he or she received unemployment benefits, instead of 'basic living expenses', for up to two years.[2] Because of the *xiagang* policy, the number of retrenched workers jumped sharply in the latter half of the 1990s. However, the official unemployment statistics do not include *xiagang* workers, so urban unemployment is seriously underestimated. To find out precisely how large a proportion of urban workers are actually unemployed and to examine the economic conditions of households with unemployed/*xiagang* workers, it is necessary to collect original individual- and household-level data on labour market outcomes. There are few such studies and this volume is one of them.[3]

The second factor behind the accelerating formation of the urban labour market is that the flow of rural–urban migration has increased, and millions of migrant workers of rural origin have entered into the lower stratum of the urban labour market. Migrant workers are naturally isolated from the 'work-unit socialism', and their labour relations with employers are purely market-based, with various uncertainties and risks. At the same time, many rural migrants engage in various kinds of self-employment activities. Most of the existing surveys on rural–urban migration are village- or factory-based (see, e.g., Cook and Maurer-Fazio 1999 and West and Zhao 2000). This volume utilizes original household-based surveys on migrants and, in doing so, increases understanding of the actual situation of migrants, including self-employed migrants, who 'settled' in urban areas.

The formation of a labour market forces urban people to change their attitude towards work and life, which is one of the most difficult and arduous processes in economic transition. Thus, it would be very interesting to investigate labour mobility, factors relating to wage and employment status, the determinants of unemployment/*xiagang*, job search channels, the economic outcomes of re-employment, and other labour market behaviour.

## 1.3 New poverty

Absolute poverty was perceived as solely a rural phenomenon until the mid-1990s. However, it has become a vital issue in China. Two factors lie behind this 'new poverty' (Knight 2000). First, the ability of central/local governments to give financial assistance to the unemployed/*xiagang* workers is limited, resulting in large numbers of retrenched workers who cannot get their entitlements from the government (Institute of Labour Science 2000). As clearly shown in this volume, the new urban poor population overlaps considerably with the unemployed/*xiagang* workers and their family members. Second, the massive flow of rural–urban migration is, in a sense, the export of rural poverty to urban areas. Migrants have formed a new peripheral stratum of urban society in terms of income and housing poverty. Few studies have focused on this new incidence of poverty to date.

Although researchers can examine poverty, ordinary people, who naturally have a greater knowledge of their own living conditions than anyone else, also perceive it. Recently, a new approach, the subjective poverty approach, has emerged and been applied to many countries. This volume provides a case study showing that the approach can be applied to urban China.

## 1.4 Surveys and data

The main data sources of this volume come from a series of household surveys conducted by the Chinese Income Distribution Project Team, the Institute of Economics, the Chinese Academy of Social Sciences (CASS) in cooperation with several foreign research institutions. The reference years of the surveys are 1999, 1995 and 1988 (hereinafter referred to as the 1999 CASS survey, the 1995 CASS survey and the 1988 CASS survey, respectively). The CASS surveys are nationally representative household surveys that are based on the sampling frame of the official household survey conducted by the National Bureau of Statistics of China (NBS).

Table 1.1 shows the structure of the three surveys. The 1995 and 1988 surveys covered households with urban household registration (*feinongye/chengzhen hukou*). The 1999 CASS survey, which is the main data source of this entire volume, covered not only urban households, but also migrant households with rural household registration (*nongye/nongcun hukou*). Thirteen cities located in six province-level administrative units are covered in the 1999 CASS survey. The six province-level administrative units are Beijing (chosen to represent the four province-level cities), Liaoning (representing the north-east region), Henan (representing the central interior), Gansu (representing the north-west region), Jiangsu (representing the eastern coastal region) and Sichuan (representing the south-west region).[4]

Three questionnaires were employed in the 1999 CASS survey. The main questionnaire includes: basic information on individual/household characteristics, employment situations, job history, individual/household income, household consumption, household assets, housing conditions and work-related subjective questions. The second questionnaire is for household members who have experienced retrenchment, including those who are currently unemployed/*xiagang* and those who are re-employed after retrenchment. It contains detailed questions on the situation of unemployment/*xiagang* and re-employment. The third questionnaire is for migrant households with rural household registration. It contains basic questions equivalent to the main questionnaire, and specific questions on the process of migration and job search.

As shown in Table 1.2, the designated sample size of the 1999 CASS survey is 5,300 households and includes three types of samples. Type A households (4,000 households) are subsamples of the NBS's household survey. Type A-1 is the subsample of the NBS's account-keeping households (*jizhanghu*) in 1999. The account-keeping households were chosen using a stratified random sampling method.[5] More specifically, 200 to 500 households were randomly drawn at the first stage in each district (*qu*), street (*jiedao*) or neighbourhood committee (*jumin weiyuanhui*). Then, after the households were ranked by income, 10 to 20 households were selected upon the principle of 'equal distance'. The account-keeping

*Table 1.1* Structure of CASS surveys

| | *1988 survey* | *1995 survey* | *1999 survey* |
|---|---|---|---|
| Urban household (household with urban household registration) | | | |
| Number of samples (household)[1] | 9,009 | 6,931 | 3,977 (4,471)[2] |
| Number of samples (person) | 31,827 | 21,694 | 12,060 (13,571) |
| Average household size (persons per household) | 3.5 | 3.1 | 3.0 |
| Number of provinces covered | 10 | 11 | 6 |
| | Beijing, Shanxi, Liaoning, Jiangsu, Anhui, Henan, Hubei, Guangdong, Yunnan, Gansu | Beijing, Shanxi, Liaoning, Jiangsu, Anhui, Henan, Hubei, Guangdong, Yunnan, Gansu and <u>Sichuan</u>[3] | Beijing, Liaoning, Jiangsu, Henan, Sichuan, Gansu |
| Migrant household (household with rural household registration who lives in urban area) | | | |
| Number of samples (household) | | | 790 |
| Number of samples (person) | | | 1,785 |
| Average household size (persons per household) | | | 2.3 |
| Number of provinces covered | | | 6 |
| | | | Beijing, Liaoning, Jiangsu, Henan, Sichuan, Gansu |

Sources: Zhao and Griffin (1994). Zhao, Riskin and Li (1999), Riskin, Zhao and Li (2001), Khan and Riskin (2001) and the data sets of the CASS surveys.

Notes:
1 Numbers in parentheses include an additional sample of unemployed persons.
2 Number of effective samples.
3 The underlined province is not included in the 1988 CASS survey.

*Table 1.2* Allocation of sample households, the 1999 CASS survey

| *Province* | *City* | *A: Basic sample* | | *B: Additional sample of households with unemployed and xiagang workers* | *C: Migrant households* |
|---|---|---|---|---|---|
| | | *A-1* | *A-2* | | |
| Beijing | Beijing | 400 | 200 | 70 | 100 |
| Liaoning | Shenyang | 300 | 150 | 40 | 70 |
| | Jingzhou | 100 | 100 | 40 | 60 |
| Jiangsu | Nanjing | 300 | 150 | 40 | 70 |
| | Xuzhou | 100 | 100 | 40 | 60 |
| Henan | Zhengzhou | 200 | 100 | 40 | 60 |
| | Kaifeng | 100 | 100 | 30 | 50 |
| | Pingdingshan | 100 | 100 | 30 | 50 |
| Sichuan | Chengdu | 300 | 100 | 40 | 70 |
| | Zigong | 100 | 100 | 30 | 50 |
| | Nanchong | 100 | 100 | 30 | 50 |
| Gansu | Lanzhou | 300 | 100 | 40 | 60 |
| | Pingliang | 100 | 100 | 30 | 50 |
| Total | | 2,500 | 1,500 | 500 | 800 |
| Sampling methods | | Stratified random sampling by income class (subsample of NBS's account-keeping households) | | Random sampling from NBS's account-keeping households | Random sampling based on temporary residence registration |
| Questionnaires | | Main questionnaire and questionnaire for household members who have experienced retrenchment | | Main questionnaire and questionnaire for household members who have experienced retrenchment | Questionnaire for migrant households |
| Method of data collection | | Interview and account book kept by the households | Interview | Interview | Interview |

households kept detailed records of income and daily expenditures. Note that this sample includes only households with urban household registration. Type A-2 households are subsamples of NBS's large sample that was compiled by a concise survey conducted in 1999 to establish the new sampling frame for the official annual household survey from 1999 onwards. This sample of households is more representative because households with rural household registration are included. However, daily records of income and consumption are not available for this type of household because detailed account keeping was not required in the survey.

Type B is an additional sample of households with members that have been retrenched in the past five years. This type is an independent subsample from the type A-2 households and was chosen from the unofficial lists of retrenched workers compiled by the neighbourhood committees.

Type C households are migrant households with rural household registration, and are a subsample drawn from the NBS's large sample (type A-2). This sample can be seen as most representative of 'settled' migrants who have lived in an urban area for a certain period. In other words, migrant workers who lived in communal housing (dormitories, construction sites or workplaces) were not included.

Table 1.3 lists the general characteristics of the thirteen cities that were included in the 1999 CASS survey. Shenyang, Nanjing, Zhengzhou, Chengdu and Lanzhou are provincial capital cities. Jinzhou City is located in the south-western part of Liaoning Province. Its major industries include petroleum, chemistry, metallurgy and paper manufacturing. Xuzhou City is the central city in the northern part of Jiangsu Province. Kaifeng City in Henan Province is an ancient city located on the east side of the provincial capital. Pingdingshan, also situated in Henan, specializes in coal-mining industries. Zigong City in Sichuan Province is a city that has been known for its salt industry throughout the ages. Nanchong City is located at the north-eastern edge of the Sichuan basin and has an industrial structure centred on light manufacturing, such as spinning, apparel and food processing. Pingliang City is a county-level city in the eastern part of Gansu Province, the main mining and manufacturing industries of which are coal, cement and wool processing (Wang 1989).

## 1.5 Overview of the study

This volume is divided into two parts. Chapters 2 to 8 in Part I provides pictures of the relationships among unemployment, inequality and poverty in urban China at the end of the 1990s. Part II, consisting of Chapters 9 to 13, provides analyses on the emerging urban labour market, focusing on its stratified structure, job mobility, profit sharing and the role of social capital.[6]

Chapter 2, written by Simon Appleton, John Knight, Lina Song and Qingjie Xia, analyses the determinants of labour retrenchment. This chapter examines the individual-level determinants and consequences of the *xiagang* policy, using the 1999 CASS survey. The authors' analysis shows that as many as 11 per cent of

*Table 1.3* Characteristics of surveyed cities, 1999

| *Province* | *City* | *Total population at year-end 1999 (thousand)* | *Population with urban household registration (feinongye renkou) at year-end 1999 (thousand)* | *Number of staff and workers belonging to work units (danwei congye renyuan) (thousand)* | *Number of self-employed workers (geti laodongzhe) (thousand)* | *Proportion of staff and workers of secondary industries (%)* | *Proportion of staff and workers of tertiary industries (%)* | *GDP per capita of total population (yuan)* | *Annual average wage of staff and workers (yuan)* |
|---|---|---|---|---|---|---|---|---|---|
| Beijing | Beijing | 10,527 | 6,997 | 4,059 | 198 | 37 | 63 | 17,332 | 14,255 |
| Liaoning | Shenyang | 4,815 | 3,896 | 3,354 | 285 | 40 | 48 | 17,500 | 8,770 |
| | Jinzhou | 822 | 667 | 226 | 69 | 53 | 43 | 10,036 | 7,187 |
| Jiangsu | Nanjing | 2,823 | 2,472 | 973 | 83 | 49 | 50 | 23,916 | 12,624 |
| | Xuzhou | 1,524 | 1,055 | 432 | 48 | 60 | 39 | 16,778 | 9,909 |
| Henan | Zhengzhou | 2,096 | 1,515 | 625 | 102 | 49 | 50 | 13,782 | 8,825 |
| | Kaifeng | 769 | 575 | 221 | 50 | 56 | 44 | 7,077 | 5,805 |
| | Pingdingshan | 867 | 636 | 301 | 25 | 71 | 29 | 10,186 | 7,639 |
| Sichuan | Chengdu | 3,303 | 2,212 | 932 | 281 | 50 | 50 | 18,933 | 9,592 |
| | Zigong | 1,053 | 468 | 185 | 32 | 55 | 45 | 7,763 | 6,605 |
| | Nanchong | 1,791 | 410 | 141 | 15 | 36 | 61 | 3,396 | 6,093 |
| Gansu | Lanzhou | 1,781 | 1,455 | 591 | 140 | 56 | 44 | 12,253 | 8,359 |
| | Pingliang | 441 | 135 | 202 | 15 | — | — | 3,908 | — |

Source: National Bureau of Statistics (2001b).

Note: All figures are for downtown areas and inner suburbs (*shiqu*). Other suburbs (*jiaoqu*) and rural areas (*jiaoxian*) are not included. Figures for Pingliang (a county-level city) are for the whole area of the city.

urban workers were retrenched, and 53 per cent of these remained unemployed. Furthermore, the risk of retrenchment was higher for women, the less educated, those with few skills, the middle-aged, and those employed by local government or urban collectives. In addition, the authors calculated the re-employment rates, which are low and imply long-term unemployment. The duration of unemployment is longer for the unhealthy, the less educated, and women with young children. More interestingly, the analysis provides no evidence that unemployment benefits have had any effect on the duration of unemployment. It is not surprising that the income losses from retrenchment stem largely from the loss of earnings while unemployed. However, re-employed workers are paid less than those who were never retrenched.

In Chapter 3, by Jinjun Xue and Wei Zhong, the relationships among unemployment, poverty and income disparity in urban China are described. This chapter attempts to deal with three important issues: a robust estimation of the urban unemployment rate, a precise calculation of poverty incidence including rural migrant households, and an analysis of the effects of unemployment and migration on urban income distribution. Utilizing various data from official and unofficial sources, the authors calculate a much higher unemployment rate than the one officially published. Moreover, as the chapter indicates, regarding rural migrant households as urban residents would increase the urban poverty incidence because the rural households were more likely to fall into poverty. In regard to income distribution in urban China, the chapter finds that unemployment is one of the main factors behind rising income inequality and poverty. In addition, rural–urban migration contributes to rising income inequality and poverty.

Chapter 4, by Xin Meng, examines the relationship between economic restructuring and income distribution. The economic transition from a planned to a market-oriented economy is often associated with a widening of income inequality. However, the nature of this change may vary during the different stages of the economic transition. This chapter investigates the increase in income inequality in urban China during two phases of economic reform: a moderate reform era (1988–1995) and a radical reform era (1995–1999). It is found that the nature and causes of the increase in inequality are different during both stages. In the first stage, the main cause of the inequality is regional income dispersion. However, in the second stage, income reductions at the lower end of the distribution are observed, and are mainly due to the large-scale unemployment generated by labour reallocation. The group of households whose incomes were severely reduced by the radical economic reform are identified as those with one or more household members unemployed.

Chapter 5, also by Xin Meng, focuses on consumption smoothing and precautionary saving by urban households. Economic shocks occur in all economies, especially in China as a developing and transition economy. Many individuals and households will experience difficult periods in facing such shocks. Whether governments should finance income support for households that face transitory shocks is an important policy issue. The permanent income hypothesis and the richer life-cycle models, which allow for precautionary saving, suggest that individual households may be able to smooth their consumption by saving during normal periods or when facing high-income flow and dissaving when adverse economic shocks occur. If so, governments in the developing world may better use scarce resources by supporting the most needy. The chapter attempts to test these hypotheses using the 1999 CASS survey, which showed that unemployment and future income uncertainty were a reality for many urban households. Meng's findings indicate that Chinese urban households are capable of smoothing their consumption and that they have a strong motivation for precautionary saving. Hence, a government-financed income support scheme for the unemployed may not be necessary in general. However, there is strong evidence of an inability to smooth educational consumption. Thus, educational subsidies for the poor may be needed if further increases in income inequality are to be prevented in the next generation.

In Chapter 6, Li Shi and Yaohui Zhao attempt to answer the question of why in-kind payments in urban areas declined over time. They use the three-round surveys from 1988, 1995 and 1999. In-kind payments, one of the special characteristics in China's transition period, were a very common phenomenon in the 1980s, but gradually declined over the 1990s. As the chapter shows, approximately 70 per cent of workers received payments in kind in the 1988 sample, but this figure fell to only 10 per cent in the 1999 sample. The authors propose two alternative hypotheses and empirically test each of them. One hypothesis is related to market shortages whereby individuals have difficulty acquiring some consumer goods. The second hypothesis is that firms evade government controls on wages to raise workers' real wages. The paper provides empirical evidence from three-round surveys that supports the second hypothesis. The policy implication resulting from Li and Zhao's analysis is that hard budget constraints are the key to inducing rational behaviour from public enterprises.

Chapter 7, by Li Shi, presents a detailed picture of the rising urban poverty and analyses its causes. The chapter shows that there is a large regional variation in the incidence of urban poverty, partly due to the difference in economic circumstances and partly due to the disparity in local governments' abilities to promote employment and social security policies. The author's analysis of the causes of poverty indicates the vital importance of unemployment/*xiagang* for poverty incidence in urban China. A probit estimation demonstrates that individuals being unemployed/*xiagang* or households with unemployed/*xiagang* heads have a predicted probability of falling into poverty three to six times higher than the average person. In addition, health conditions, educational attainments and skills are important determinants of poverty. Further, the chapter presents the results for a simulation analysis of the impact of the government's anti-poverty policy. The simulation analysis demonstrates that promoting employment is a sound solution to alleviating poverty in urban China.

Chapter 8, by Björn Gustafsson, Li Shi and Hiroshi Sato, attempts to apply the subjective poverty line approach to urban China. Recently, this approach has attracted more attention in poverty studies. The chapter derives a national poverty line and city poverty lines using information on households' perceptions of income adequacy and household characteristics. In the case of the national poverty line, the subjective approach yielded estimates of poverty that were close to those obtained using the official poverty line. However, in the case of the city lines, the subjective approach indicates a different picture from the official one of the poverty profile of the cities studied. The reason is that perceptions on income adequacy vary greatly across cities. As indicated in the chapter, a provincial capital city has a higher poverty incidence when the city line is applied than that indicated when the national line is applied. This indicates the need to apply, not only a national urban poverty line, but also local poverty lines, which can be useful for evaluating policies at the sub-national level. The chapter also finds that the highest poverty rates and comparatively high rates of registered unemployment are correlated in medium-sized cities and that poverty status in urban China greatly depends on the educational level of the household head, labour market status and health status. Being jobless involves a high poverty risk, whereas those employed in a state-owned enterprise or old-age pensioners face a low poverty risk. Finally, the chapter recommends the Chinese government be more concerned with people's perception of poverty in large cities.

Chapter 9, by Hiroshi Sato, describes the transformation of the basic institutional framework of urban society, which has seen the decline of the 'work-unit socialism' and the emergence of a stratified labour market. In particular, three major issues are discussed. First, institutional and policy changes that relate to labour market formation since the 1980s are described, and a framework for stratifying urban society is presented. Second, people in urban society are classified into six strata according to their socio-economic status and degree of marketization, in terms of wage determination and work-related behaviour. These six strata are: (1) a 'public core' stratum, composed of urban workers employed in the central/provincial-level public sector; (2) a 'non-public' stratum, composed of urban workers employed in the non-public sector; (3) a 'public job-turnover' stratum, composed of urban workers employed in the public sector who have changed their work units; (4) a 'public peripheral' stratum, composed of urban workers employed in local state-owned/urban collective work units; (5) urban workers who have experienced retrenchment, including those who are re-employed; and (6) a rural migrant stratum. Third, this pre-identified hierarchical structure is clarified by the following objective and subjective factors: a description of income disparity among strata and inequality within each stratum, an analysis of income determinants, and analyses of factors relating to the probability of retrenchment, the sense of hierarchy of urban workers and migrants, and urban workers' sense of discrimination towards migrants.

Chapter 10, contributed by Simon Appleton, John Knight, Lina Song and Qingjie Xia, focuses on the formation of the labour market in urban China. There have been alternative judgments on the nature of the labour market in China. Is it more competitive or more segmented? Different researchers have provided different answers to this question. As indicated in Meng and Zhang (2001), a two-tier labour market existed in urban China, with urban workers favoured over rural–urban migrants. One of the most interesting findings of this chapter is that, from the late

1990s, new developments such as retrenchment policy have aimed to create a three-tier labour market. To prove their argument, the authors compare wage structures across three groups of worker: never-retrenched workers, re-employed workers, and rural–urban migrant workers. Their comparison indicates that the highest-paid group is those urban workers who were never retrenched even after controlling for their personal characteristics. In regard to the other two groups, although they have quite similar wage rates, the authors find that they have different wage structures. Thus, it is difficult to conceive of re-employed workers and rural–urban migrant workers as working in a single labour market. From these findings, the authors conclude that urban China is creating a more segmented labour market with three tiers.

Chapter 11, by John Knight and Linda Yueh, investigates the job mobility of urban residents and migrants. The large-scale reform of the state-owned sector and the development of a private sector in the 1990s changed the nature of employment in urban China. Under state planning, the 'iron rice bowl' (*tie fanwan*) system, involving allocated, lifelong jobs, had prevailed. However, this system was eroded, permitting more labour turnover and mobility. The degree of mobility of urban workers in China does not appear to have been investigated, no doubt because there was so little mobility until recently. Using the 1999 CASS survey, this chapter provides a first analysis of inter-firm mobility in the urban labour market, its evolution and its causes. A distinction is made between the institutionally favoured urban residents and the rural–urban migrants. The mobility rate of migrants greatly exceeds that of urban residents. For both groups the extent, patterns, determinants and consequences of mobility are explored.

In Chapter 12, John Knight and Li Shi describe how profitability affects wages in urban enterprises. China has accelerated its reform of state-owned enterprises in urban areas since the mid-1990s. The reform is expected to strengthen the linkage between the wages of workers and the performance and profitability of their firms. This chapter attempts to ascertain the significant of the linkage for the development of labour market, using the 1995 and 1999 CASS surveys. Knight and Li's analysis suggests that labour market segmentation among firms was strong and became stronger over the period from 1995 to 1999. In addition, the authors find that profits were distributed to workers in different ways in the two survey years. In 1995, the workers who gained the most from employment in profit-making firms were those with longer tenure, and those in state-owned and private firms. It appears that more experienced, longer-serving workers were particularly rewarded. This relationship had disappeared by 1999. In the 1999 wage function, only the intercept term was important, implying that all workers received roughly the same proportionate increases in wages from profit-making employers. This development suggests that managers chose to adopt a more neutral, less discriminating stance in sharing profits, consistent with the need to satisfy and motivate all of their workers. Finally, the chapter analyses the relationship between profit sharing and wage inequalities during the period of study. Not only were the employees of loss-making firms paid less than those of profit-making firms in 1995, but also their wages grew less rapidly over the subsequent four years.

Chapter 13, by Linda Yueh, applies an investment model of social capital to an empirical analysis of women's labour market outcomes. There is evidence that the shift to a more market-oriented economy is associated with increased inequality in earned income in urban China. One factor in determining success in the labour market could be *guanxi*, the Chinese variant of social capital. She develops an approach in which investment in *guanxi* is conceptualized as a function of the time and resources expended by an individual over a lifetime. The chapter's measures of social capital are created from a sample of persons who have experienced unemployment drawn from the 1999 CASS survey. Yueh finds that there are gender differences in the stock of social capital and economic returns. Women have less social capital than men and lower economic returns, in terms of earned income and probability of re-employment once unemployed. These findings suggest another dimension to gender inequality in urban China. *Guanxi* generates opportunities, but does so differently for men and women. It is suggested that social capital reduces friction in an underdeveloped labour market and will cause equally productive individuals to have different labour supply elasticities to a firm.

## Notes

1 In regard to 'work-unit socialism', see Womack (1991) and Li and Li (2000).
2 If a person remains under low-income conditions after they have ceased to be eligible for unemployment benefits, they will be covered by the welfare system at the local level, which is the Urban Minimum Cost-of-Living Assistance Programme (*chengshi jumin zuidi shenghuo baozhang zhidu*).
3 Several chapters in this volume apply the term 'laid-off' or 'lay-off' to *xiagang*.
4 For a detailed description of the 1988 and 1995 CASS surveys, see Griffin and Zhao (1993), Zhao and Griffin (1994), Riskin, Zhao and Li (2001) and Zhao, Li and Riskin (1999).
5 A more detailed introduction to the method can be found in the National Bureau of Statistics (2001: 311–32, 2004: 352–4).
6 The sister edition of this volume has been published in China (Li and Sato 2004).

## References

Cook, S. and Maurer-Fazio, M. (eds) (1999) *The Workers' State Meets the Market: Labour in China's Transition*, London: Frank Cass.

Duojicairang (2001) *Zhongguo Zuidi Shehui Baozhang Zhidu Yanjiu yu Shixian* (Theory and Practice in the Urban Minimum Cost-of-Living Assistance Program in China), Beijing: People's Press.

Griffin, K. and Zhao, R. (eds) (1993) *The Distribution of Income in China*, London: Macmillan.

Gustafsson, B. and Li, S. (2001) 'A more unequal China? Aspects of inequality in the distribution of equivalent income', in Riskin, C., Zhao, R. and Li, S. (eds), *China's Retreat from Equality: Income Distribution and Economic Transition*, Armonk, NY: M.E. Sharpe.

Institute of Labour Science (2000) 'Shenyang he wuhan xiagang zhigong zhuangkuang fenxi baogao' (Analytical report of situation of *xiagang* workers in Shenyang and Wuhan), *Yanjiu Luntan* (Research Forum), 19.

Khan, A.R. and Riskin, C. (2001) *Inequality and Poverty in China in the Age of Globalization*, Oxford: Oxford University Press.

Knight, J. (2000) 'Trends in poverty, inequality and the achievement of international development targets in China', paper prepared for the DFID China Programme.

Li, L. and Li, H. (2000) *Zhongguo de Danwei Zuzhi* (The Chinese Work Unit Organization), Hangzhou: Zhejiang People's Press.

Li, P., Li, Q. and Sun, L. (2004) *Dangdai Zhongguo Fenceng* (Social Stratification in Contemporary China), Beijing: Publisher of Social Science Literature.

Li, Q., Hu, J. and Hong, D. (2001) *Shiye Xiagang Wenti Duibi Yanjiu* (Comparative Study on *Xiagang* and Unemployment), Beijing: Qinghua University Press.

Li, S. and Sato, H. (eds) (2004) *Jingji Zhuanxing de Daijia: Zhongguo Chengshi Shiye Pinkun Shouru Chaju de Jingyan Yanjiu* (Price of Economic Transition: An Empirical Analysis on Urban Unemployment, Poverty, and Income Inequality), Beijing: Publishing House of Chinese Finance and Economy.

Lu, M. (2003) 'Jingji gaige yu shehui gongping' (Economic reform and social equity), in Wang, M. (ed.), *Gaige Gongjian Sanshiti: Wanshan Shehui Zhuyi Shichang Jingji Ttizhi Tansuo* (30 Tough Topics for Reforms: Searching for Perfect System of Socialist Economy), Beijing: China Development Press.

Meng, X. and Zhang, J. (2001) 'The two-tier labour market in urban China: occupational segregation and wage differentials between urban residents and rural migrants', *Journal of Comparative Economics*, 29: 485–504.

National Bureau of Statistics (2001a) *Urban Statistical Yearbook of China 2000*, Beijing: China Statistics Press.

National Bureau of Statistics (2001b) *Guojia Tongji Diaocha Zhidu 2001* (National Statistical Survey System 2001), Beijing: National Bureau of Statistics.

National Bureau of Statistics (2004) *China Statistical Yearbook 2004*, Beijing: China Statistics Press.

Riskin, C., Zhao, R. and Li, S. (eds) (2001) *China's Retreat from Equality: Income Distribution and Economic Transition*, Armonk, NY: M.E. Sharpe.

Wang, S. (ed.) (1989) *Zhongguo Shixian Jingji Fazhan Gaikuang* (Review on Economic Development of Chinese Counties and Cities), Beijing: Economic Science Press.

West, L.A. and Zhao, Y. (2000) *Rural Labour Flows in China*, Berkeley: Institute of East Asian Studies, University of California, Berkeley.

World Bank (1997) *Sharing Rising Incomes: Disparities in China*, Washington, DC: The World Bank.

World Bank (2004) *Zhongguo: Tuidong Gongping de Jingji Zengzhang* (China Country Economic Memorandum: Promoting Growth with Equity), Beijing: Qinghua University Press.

Womack, B. (1991) 'Transfigured community: neo-traditionalism and work-unit socialism in China', *The China Quarterly*, 126: 313–32.

Yao, Y. (2004) 'Jianli yige zhongguo de shehui gongping lilun' (Building up a theory of social justice for China), in Yao, Y. (ed.), *Zhuangui Zhongguo: Shehui Gongzheng yu Pingdeng* (China Transition: Social Justice and Equality), Beijing: People's University of China Press.

Yu, F. (ed.) (2000) *Xiagang Zhigong Laodong Guanxi Toushi* (Clarification of the Labour Relations of *Xiagang* Workers and Staffs), Beijing: Economic Science Press.

Zhao, R. and Griffin, K. (eds) (1994) *Zhongguo Jumin Shouru Fenpei Yanjiu* (Studying Income Distribution of Chinese Households), Beijing: China Social Sciences Press.

Zhao, R. and Li, S. (1997) 'Zhongguo jumin shouru chaju kuoda jiqi yuanyin fenxi' (Analysis on increasing income inequality and its causes in China), *Jingji Yanjiu* (Economic Research), March.

Zhao, R., Li, S. and Riskin, C. (eds) (1999) *Zhongguo Jumin Shouru Fenpei Zai Yanjiu* (Re-examination of Income Distribution of Chinese Households), Beijing: Publishing House of Chinese Finance and Economy.

# Part I

# Unemployment, inequality and poverty

# 2 Labour retrenchment in China

## Determinants and consequences

*Simon Appleton, John Knight, Lina Song and Qingjie Xia*

### 2.1 Introduction

The Chinese urban radical reform known as *xiagang*, first on trial in 1994 and finally launched in 1997, was intended to resolve the problem of inefficiency of the state sector by laying-off a quarter or more of its workers within four years (1997–2000). By the end of 1999, the official figure of the accumulated laid-off workers exceeded 24.4 million, representing 20.7 per cent of the 'staff and workers' at risk and 13.2 per cent of the urban labour force.[1] At that date, those who remained *xiagang* numbered 9.4 million. To this must be added the registered unemployed (5.7 million) to obtain the true measure of urban unemployment (then 8.2 per cent of the urban labour force). The sharp fall in urban employment by 5.6 per cent in the five quarters after the end of 1999 implies that the accumulated number of lay-offs and the true unemployment rate will have continued to rise.[2] These developments have ended the 'win-win' phase of economic reform, and have brought it into a phase in which there are clear losers, at least in the short term.

Who were the losers? In this chapter, we use household survey data for 1999–2000 to identify what kinds of urban worker were most likely to have suffered retrenchment. Given that the administered earnings in state-owned enterprises (SOEs) were unlikely to match productivity, we hypothesize that those most at risk were the least productive. These include those in unprofitable firms, the unskilled and those in poor health. However, we also examine the importance of other characteristics not necessarily connected to productivity – characteristics such as gender, Communist Party membership and minority (non-Han) ethnicity.

The extent of the private loss from retrenchment depends heavily on how long the retrenched workers remain unemployed. We identify the determinants of the duration of unemployment using a semi-parametric model, testing for omitted heterogeneity. Among the hypothesized determinants we include variables for receipt of unemployment benefits and methods of job search. Our analysis of the duration of unemployment is the first that we know of for China. Indeed, such work is rare for developing countries in general; the only two applications we know of are for the construction sector in Egypt (Tunali and Assaad 1992) and for men in urban Ethiopia (Serneels 2001).

How much did retrenched workers lose as a result of redundancy? The loss is mainly due to earnings forgone while unemployed, but there may also be an additional cost in earnings if workers are only able to find re-employment at a lower wage. We quantify these losses for the year of our survey, under assumptions about counterfactual wages, i.e. what retrenched workers would have been paid had they not been dismissed. Again, this work is novel for China and indeed developing countries more generally. There is a growing literature on the consequences of worker displacement but the research is confined to the US and a few European countries. A consistent finding of the US literature is that worker displacement leads to a large and persistent wage loss upon re-employment of the order of 10–25 per cent (Burda and Mertens 2001). Interestingly, a recent study of the UK has found weaker 'scarring' (estimated at 3.4 per cent) from redundancies than from unemployment due to other reasons (Arulampalam 2001).

The structure of the chapter is as follows. Section 2.2 explains the data set used and the econometric methods of analysis. Section 2.3 employs a probit model for the probability of retrenchment. Section 2.4 presents a duration model for the length of unemployment spells. Section 2.5 investigates whether retrenchment leads to lower wages following re-employment. Section 2.6 concludes.

## 2.2 Methods

### *2.2.1 Data*

The data come from a nationally representative urban household survey, referred to as the 1999 CASS survey, covering 4,000 households of thirteen cities in six provinces.[3] In order to obtain a sufficiently large sample of retrenched workers, the representative sample in this survey was enlarged by an additional group of 503 households who had experienced retrenchment since the end of 1994. For the regression analysis, we work with the enlarged sample of 4,503 households. We focus on urban resident workers, that is to say, those with urban *hukou* (residence registration) who are either employed or unemployed. Within the 4,503 households in the sample, there were 6,929 people aged 18–59 who were either in employment or were unemployed.[4] We classify these workers into three categories:

1. *Non-retrenched urban workers*: 5,770 workers in our sample were both currently employed and have not been laid off since 1992.[5]
2. *Retrenched urban workers*: 1,159 workers in our sample have been laid off since 1992.
3. *Re-employed urban workers*: 433 workers in our sample have been laid off since 1992 but were back in employment by the time of the survey. Note that (3) is a subset of (2).

Table 2.1 provides a description of the different groups. Non-retrenched urban workers are the most educated group, with an average of 11.4 years of education compared with 10 years for the retrenched workers. The re-employed workers are

*Table 2.1* Descriptive statistics: means and percentages by type of worker

| | *(1)* *Never-retrenched urban worker* | *(2)* *Retrenched urban worker* | *(3)* *Of (2), still unemployed* | *(4)* *Of (2), re-employed* |
|---|---|---|---|---|
| No. of observations | 5,770 | 1,159 | 726 | 433 |
| Wages (yuan per eight-hour period of work) | 33.49 (27.13) | 17.24* (8.51) | — | 25.17 (20.43) |
| Male (%) | 56.8 | 38.7 | 35.5 | 43.9 |
| Working experience (in years) | 21.8 (9.83) | 20.9 (8.55) | 20.8 (8.70) | 23.5 (8.29) |
| Education (in years) | 11.4 (2.7) | 9.96 (2.2) | 9.94 (2.29) | 9.98 (2.2) |
| Ethnic minority (%) | 3.9 | 4.4 | 3.4 | 6.0 |
| Party membership (%) | 28.8 | 9.3 | 8.5 | 10.6 |
| Not generally healthy (%) | 3.8 | 8.4 | 9.9 | 5.8 |
| Ownership (%) | | | | |
| State-owned by central government | 36.8 | 12.1 | 13.8 | 12.0 |
| State-owned by local government | 40.9 | 47.8 | 46.1 | 44.1 |
| Urban collective | 9.9 | 31.1 | 31.1 | 27.0 |
| Urban private | 1.1 | 1.1 | 1.1 | 2.1 |
| Urban individual | 3.0 | 2.2 | 2.2 | 8.3 |
| Joint venture and foreign investment | 2.2 | 0.6 | 0.8 | 0.2 |
| Listed firms with the majority of state shares | 2.4 | 2.2 | 2.1 | 1.6 |
| Other shareholding | 1.8 | 0.8 | 0.8 | 1.4 |
| Rural private business or individual | 0.1 | 0.1 | 0.0 | 0.2 |
| Other ownership | 1.3 | 1.2 | 1.2 | 2.3 |
| Occupation (%) | | | | |
| Professional or technical | 23.2 | 9.5 | 10.1 | 9.7 |
| Administrative | 13.5 | 4.5 | 4.3 | 4.8 |
| Clerical | 18.4 | 8.5 | 8.1 | 10.6 |
| Industrial worker | 33.0 | 59.1 | 57.7 | 55.9 |
| Commercial staff | 5.1 | 9.2 | 10.6 | 9.0 |
| Service worker | 4.9 | 7.3 | 7.6 | 6.5 |
| Others | 1.5 | 1.6 | 1.4 | 2.1 |
| City (%) | | | | |
| Beijing | 15.3 | 10.4 | 11.4 | 8.5 |
| Shenyang, Liaoning | 11.9 | 7.8 | 7.3 | 8.5 |

(Continued)

*Table 2.1* (Continued)

| | *(1) Never-retrenched urban worker* | *(2) Retrenched urban worker* | *(3) Of (2), still unemployed* | *(4) Of (2), re-employed* |
|---|---|---|---|---|
| Jinzhou, Liaoning | 4.8 | 10.2 | 5.1 | 18.7 |
| Nanjing, Jiangsu | 10.6 | 7.9 | 5.1 | 12.5 |
| Xuzhou, Jiangsu | 5.0 | 6.9 | 5.8 | 8.8 |
| Zhengzhou, Henan | 7.3 | 5.3 | 6.3 | 3.5 |
| Kaifeng, Henan | 4.4 | 6.1 | 8.0 | 3.0 |
| Pingdingshan, Henan | 6.2 | 3.7 | 5.4 | 0.9 |
| Chengdu, Sichuan | 10.1 | 10.1 | 11.4 | 7.9 |
| Zigong, Sichuan | 4.6 | 7.1 | 9.5 | 3.0 |
| Nanchong, Sichuan | 5.1 | 6.6 | 6.6 | 6.5 |
| Lanzhou, Gansu | 9.5 | 11.0 | 11.8 | 9.7 |
| Pingliang, Gansu | 5.1 | 7.1 | 6.2 | 8.5 |

Source for this and all subsequent tables: the 1999 CASS survey.

Note: *Earnings in previous job, updated to allow for price inflation.

Standard deviation for continuous variables in parentheses.

oldest, averaging 23.5 years of potential work experience compared to 21.8 years for the non-retrenched workers.[6] The incidence of retrenchment was higher among women, non-party members, industrial, commercial and service workers, and urban collective and local government but not central government SOEs.

### 2.2.2 Econometric specification

Our first research question is what kinds of individual suffered retrenchment. Although the simple descriptive statistics in Table 2.1 provide some insights into this question, multivariate analysis is required in order to isolate the contribution of particular factors. We model whether an individual $i$ has ever been retrenched ($R_i = 1$) using a binary probit:

$$R_i^* = \alpha' \boldsymbol{X}_i + U_i \qquad \text{where } U_i \sim N(0, 1)$$
$$\Pr(R_i = 1) = \Pr(R_i^* > 0) = \Phi(\alpha' \boldsymbol{X}_i) \tag{2.1}$$

where $\boldsymbol{X}_i$ is a vector of explanatory variables and $\alpha$ a vector of associated coefficients.

A number of factors are likely to be relevant to retrenchment decisions. Some concern the enterprise in which the worker is employed: in the worst case, an entire enterprise may be closed and all workers retrenched regardless of their personal characteristics. More commonly, however, retrenchment is selective, with some workers in an enterprise being laid off and others retained. When selecting workers for retrenchment, employers concerned with minimizing costs are likely to take into account their productivity relative to their wages. We cannot estimate worker productivity from our household data, so we adopt a reduced form approach, including in the vector of explanatory variables, $\boldsymbol{X}_i$, those variables such as education and occupation likely to affect wages and/or productivity. Given that wages were largely set by the state sector, we hypothesize that they are unlikely to fully reflect productivity and so the least productive workers may be at most risk of being retrenched.

Our second research question is what determines the length of time for which re-employed workers remained unemployed. This depends on both the demand and supply sides of the labour market: the frequency of job offers received and the worker's willingness to accept these offers (Nickell 1980). Since we are reliant on household data, the available explanatory variables are mainly characteristics of the workers and their jobs. All the determinants of retrenchment identified above may a priori affect the frequency of job offers, but may also have an impact on the supply side. For example, more educated workers may attract more job offers but may also have higher reservation wages. However, some additional variables are likely only to affect the supply side: for example, household demographics may affect the willingness of unemployed workers to accept job offers, but should not directly affect the frequency of such offers (or the probability of retrenchment).

When analysing the length of unemployment spells, it is appropriate to work with a duration model. These models allow for pervasive 'right censoring': most retrenched workers in our sample are still unemployed at the time of the survey and so the completed duration of their unemployment is not known. To deal with censoring, duration models focus on modelling the determinants of the 'hazard rate', $h_i(t)$; in this context, the probability of exiting unemployment at time $t$, conditional upon being unemployed up to time $t-1$. If $T_i$ is time until re-employment, the hazard for individual $i$ at time $t$ is defined as:

$$h_i(t) = \lim_{\delta \to 0^+} \frac{\Pr[t + \delta > T_i \geq t | T_i \geq t]}{\delta} \tag{2.2}$$

We use aproportional hazards model, so that the explanatory variables, $\mathbf{Z}_i$, raise the 'baseline' hazard, $h_0(t)$, by a given proportion:

$$h_i(t) = h_0(t) \exp\{\beta' \mathbf{Z}_i\} \tag{2.3}$$

where $\mathbf{Z}_i$ is a vector of explanatory variables and $\beta$ a vector of associated (non-time-varying) coefficients to be estimated.

When estimating the model in equation (2.3), a key issue is whether to assume a particular distribution for the duration data, and hence a specific form for the baseline hazard, or to allow the baseline hazards to be estimated more flexibly.

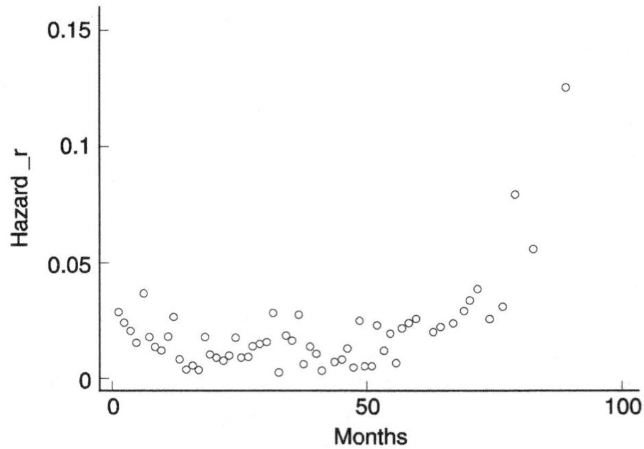


*Figure 2.1* Empirical hazard: the conditional probability of re-employment.

In our case, it was evident from inspecting the data that the empirical hazard followed an erratic pattern with multiple peaks (see Figure 2.1 discussed later in the chapter).[7] This made it unlikely that the data will be well fitted by the kind of simple baseline hazard functions implied by the distributions commonly used to model duration data. Most such hazards are either monotonic (e.g. from the exponential and Weibull distributions) or imply increasing then decreasing duration dependence (e.g. from the lognormal and log-logistic distributions). If anything, our data imply first decreasing then increasing duration dependence, that is to say, the empirical hazards first fall and then rise with the number of months. Consequently, we adopted a duration model that does not assume a particular distribution for the duration data.

We use the Prentice–Gloeckler (1978) grouped duration model; this starts from an instantaneous hazard rate function of the form in equation (2.3) but then divides the timeline into intervals.[8] Conceptualizing the duration data as being grouped into intervals is natural in our case, since recorded unemployment spells in our data set are reported in intervals of a month. The baseline hazard is assumed to be a step function that can change its value freely across (but not within) intervals. No specific functional form is assumed for this function, but instead a separate parameter (a log-integrated baseline hazard) is estimated for each interval. This approach allows for complete flexibility in estimating the effect of the baseline hazards – what is conventionally described as fully non-parametric estimation.[9]

We follow Meyer (1990) in extending the Prentice–Gloeckler model to allow for unobserved heterogeneity. This is often argued to be important for survival analysis (Lancaster 1979; Heckman and Singer 1984): some of the unemployed may be more likely to find re-employment early owing to favourable unobservable characteristics. In particular, Meyer proposes assuming a term for multiplicative random heterogeneity, $\varepsilon_i$, so that the hazard becomes:[10]

$$h_i(t) = \varepsilon_i h_0(t) \exp\{\beta' \mathbf{Z}_i\} \tag{2.4}$$

where $\varepsilon_i$ follows a gamma distribution with mean one (a normalization) and variance $\sigma^2$.

In Section 2.5, we consider the income losses of retrenched workers. Much of this loss is due to the absence of earned income while unemployed. However, we focus on whether there is a further 'scarring' effect, whereby retrenched workers who find re-employment earn less than they would if they had never lost their original jobs. This is an example of a general type of problem known in the econometric literature as that of 'treatment effects'. We wish to know what are the effects on an outcome (in this case, wages) of a particular 'treatment' (in this case, retrenchment). The central underlying problem is that we cannot observe counterfactual wages: what retrenched workers would have earned if they had not lost their jobs. We assume that they would be paid in a like manner to workers are who have never been retrenched. Consequently, we estimate wage functions for the never retrenched and predict what re-employed workers would earn, given their observed characteristics, if paid like the never retrenched. The use of wage functions allows us to control for possible differences in the observed characteristics (education, experience, etc.) of the re-employed compared to the never retrenched workers. More problematic is the possibility that the re-employed differ in characteristics that are not observed in the data – for example, ability, ambition, and so forth. We allow for this sample selectivity using the methods pioneered by Heckman (1979).

Following Mincer (1974), we use a semi-log wage function whereby log wages, $\ln Y_i$, are determined as:

$$\ln Y_i = \gamma_k' \boldsymbol{W}_i + \nu_{ki} \tag{2.5}$$

where $k$ denotes the type of worker (never retrenched or re-employed), $\boldsymbol{W}_i$ denotes a vector of explanatory variables, $\gamma$ a vector of associated coefficients, and $\nu$ are stochastic terms. The explanatory variables included: years of education, a quadratic for experience, occupation, ownership sector and control variables such as dummy variables for sex, ethnicity, Communist Party membership, poor health and location.

For never retrenched workers ($k=1$), we used the now standard Heckit model, selecting on the retrenchment probit (equation 2.1):

$$\begin{aligned} E(\ln Y_i | R_i = 0) &= \gamma_1' \boldsymbol{W}_i + E(\nu_{1i} | R_i^* \leq 0) \\ &= \gamma_1' \boldsymbol{W}_i + \gamma_\lambda \lambda_{1i} \end{aligned} \tag{2.6}$$

where $\lambda_{1i} = -\phi(\alpha' \boldsymbol{X}_i)/(1-\Phi(\alpha' \boldsymbol{X}_i))$. Consistent estimates of this model can be obtained using Heckman's two-stage method by regressing the log wage for the never retrenched upon the determinants of wages, $\boldsymbol{W}_i$, and a variable to correct for selectivity, $\lambda_{1i}$, computed from the results of the probit for retrenchment.

For the re-employed workers ($k=2$), the issue is complicated by double selectivity: not only must the workers be retrenched, they must also be re-employed.

To allow for this, we estimated a probit for re-employment from the sample of retrenched workers:[11]

$$E_i^* = \pi'\mathbf{Z}_i + \eta_i \qquad \text{where } \eta_i \sim N(0, 1)$$
$$\Pr(E_i = 1) = \Pr(E_i^* > 0) = \Phi(\pi'\mathbf{Z}_i) \tag{2.7}$$

For re-employed workers, expected log wages are:

$$E(\ln Y_i | R_i = 1, E_i = 1) = \gamma_2'\mathbf{W}_i + \gamma_{\lambda_1}\lambda_{1i} + \gamma_{\lambda_2}\lambda_{2i} \tag{2.8}$$

where $\lambda_{1i} = \phi(\alpha'\mathbf{X}_i)/\Phi(\alpha'\mathbf{X}_i)$ and $\lambda_{2i} = \phi(\pi'\mathbf{Z}_i)/\Phi(\pi'\mathbf{Z}_i)$.

Note that this correction assumes that the probabilities of retrenchment and re-employment are independent, an assumption that we tested and could not reject (Maddala 1983: 282).[12]

The above approach to sample selectivity raises issues of identification. Although the sample selectivity corrections are identified purely by functional form, this is not persuasive. Instead some identifying variables need to be included among the determinants of retrenchment, $\mathbf{X}$, and the determinants of re-employment, $\mathbf{Z}$, but excluded from the direct determinants of wages, $\mathbf{W}$. To identify the correction for the selectivity of re-employment, we include variables for the demographic composition of the household in $\mathbf{Z}$. These variables may affect labour supply decisions, particularly of women. In particular, where there are a number of young children in the household, one might expect female labour supply to be reduced. The presence of older household members – possibly retired – may offset this effect. To capture such interactions, we explored various specifications in preliminary regressions. Identifying the correction for the selectivity of retrenchment was more problematic, but one instrument did suggest itself. Official policy during retrenchment has been to take account of whether a worker has a fellow household member employed in the state sector and not to sack both of them. If this policy were implemented, one would expect that an SOE worker would have less chance of being retrenched from an SOE if their spouse was retrenched from an SOE. Consequently we included in $\mathbf{X}$ a 0/1 dummy variable that equals 1 if the individual was employed in an SOE and is married to a spouse who had been employed in an SOE but was retrenched.[13] This variable is hypothesized to have a negative coefficient in the probit for retrenchment but to have no direct effect on earnings.

## 2.3 The probability of retrenchment

We model the probability that an urban resident in the labour force has been retrenched since the start of 1992. We exclude those who have never been employed, such as new entrants to the labour market looking for work. From our sample of 6,929 urban workers, 1,159 people (16 per cent) had been retrenched between 1992 and the survey in early 2000. Since the survey over-sampled households with retrenched workers, these raw figures overstate the rate of retrenchment. Within the subsample of 6,102 urban workers from the nationally representative group of 4,000 households, the retrenchment rate was 11.4 per cent. Clearly, there has been widespread implementation of the government's policies for compulsory lay-offs from SOEs.

What kinds of worker were most at risk of retrenchment? The results of the probit are given in Table 2.2. Since our data over-samples households with retrenched workers, we correct for this by estimating the probit with weights.[14] The model identifies a number of determinants of the probability of retrenchment; most hypothesized explanatory variables are statistically significant. The goodness of fit, measured by the likelihood ratio (0.18) or the percentage of correct predictions (84 per cent), is respectable. Since most explanatory variables are dummy variables, one way of showing their quantitative importance is by reporting the predicted probabilities of the model evaluated at the means of the other explanatory variables. We use the means of our sample, after applying weights to offset the over-sampling of households with retrenched workers. The base probability of retrenchment at the mean of the explanatory variables is 22.9 per cent. This is higher than the actual 11.4 per cent urban retrenchment rate among the nationally representative sample.[15] Consequently, the predicted probabilities presented in Table 2.2 should be used to assess the relative effect of explanatory variables rather than to provide measures of the absolute risk of retrenchment faced by individuals with particular characteristics.

When considering the impact of explanatory variables, we begin with the controls for ownership. The default category is employment in local government SOEs. Such workers faced above-average risks of being retrenched, estimated at 26 per cent at the mean of the other explanatory variables. Workers in urban collectives faced an even greater risk, calculated at 34 per cent. The lowest risk of retrenchment was faced by workers employed by the central government, including those employed in centrally run SOEs. The probability of such workers being retrenched was 16 per cent. Similarly low risks were faced by workers in micro-enterprises (less than eight employees), in enterprises listed on the stock market and in enterprises benefiting from foreign investment.

Within enterprises, retrenchment risks were substantially higher for certain occupation categories. The default occupation category is technical and professional. This category and the administrative and clerical categories all faced low probabilities of retrenchment, estimated at 19 per cent. By contrast, the retrenchment risks faced by other workers were in the range 25–30 per cent.

Now consider the personal characteristics of the workers. Men were significantly less likely to be retrenched, with a 20 per cent risk compared to 26 per cent for women. Education reduced the risk of being retrenched. The estimated marginal effect of each year of education on the probability of being retrenched was −0.0076, evaluated at the mean of the explanatory variables, so that ten years of education would reduce the risk by eight percentage points.[16] The risk of being retrenched had an inverse-U relationship with potential experience (defined as years since education was completed), peaking at 26 years of experience. The

*Table 2.2* Probit model for the probability of retrenchment

| | *Coefficients* | *t-ratio* | *Predicted probability of retrenchment at mean of other explanatory variables* |
|---|---|---|---|
| Constant | −1.043 | −5.06*** | 22.9 |
| Male | −0.306 | −7.24*** | 20.4 |
| Female (default) | | | 25.9 |
| Education in years | −0.043 | −3.93*** | |
| Experience | 0.036 | 3.81*** | |
| Experience squared | −0.001 | −3.35*** | |
| Minority ethnicity | 0.081 | 0.78 | 24.2 |
| Han Chinese (default) | | | 22.8 |
| Party member | −0.348 | −5.48*** | 18.6 |
| Non-party member (default) | | | 24.5 |
| Bad health | 0.252 | 2.95*** | 27.4 |
| Good health (default) | | | 22.7 |
| Central SOE | −0.608 | −10.90*** | 16.3 |
| Local SOE (default ownership sector) | | | 26.4 |
| Urban collective | 0.357 | 6.56*** | 33.8 |
| Urban private | −0.056 | −0.30 | 25.3 |
| Urban individual | −0.431 | −3.39*** | 18.9 |
| Foreign invested | −0.615 | −2.96*** | 16.2 |
| State listed | −0.125 | −0.99 | 24.0 |
| Other listed | −0.528 | −2.84*** | 17.4 |
| Rural enterprises | 0.355 | 0.54 | 33.8 |
| Other ownership | −0.118 | −0.65 | 24.1 |
| Administrative | 0.047 | 0.49 | 19.7 |
| Professional/technical (default occupation) | | | 18.9 |
| Clerical | −0.027 | −0.34 | 18.5 |
| Low-skill industrial | 0.584 | 7.45*** | 29.5 |
| High-skill industrial | 0.386 | 5.09*** | 25.6 |
| Unskilled industrial | 0.525 | 6.81*** | 28.3 |
| Commercial worker | 0.503 | 5.35*** | 27.8 |
| Service worker | 0.411 | 4.19*** | 26.0 |
| Other occupation | 0.342 | 2.05** | 24.7 |
| Beijing (default city) | | | 20.9 |
| Shenyang, Liaoning | −0.122 | −1.41 | 18.9 |
| Jinzhou, Liaoning | 0.392 | 4.19*** | 28.1 |
| Nanjing, Jiangsu | −0.110 | −1.24 | 19.2 |
| Xuzhou, Jiangsu | 0.243 | 2.44*** | 25.2 |
| Zhengzhou, Henan | −0.086 | −0.82 | 29.5 |
| Kaifeng, Henan | 0.285 | 2.76*** | 26.0 |
| Pingdingshan, Henan | −0.140 | −1.25 | 18.7 |
| Chengdu, Sichuan | 0.237 | 2.76*** | 25.1 |
| Zigong, Sichuan | 0.247 | 2.44*** | 25.3 |
| Nanchong, Sichuan | 0.266 | 2.60*** | 25.7 |
| Lanzhou, Gansu | 0.244 | 2.89*** | 25.3 |

*Table 2.2* (Continued)

| | *Coefficients* | *t-ratio* | *Predicted probability of retrenchment at mean of other explanatory variables* |
|---|---|---|---|
| Pingliang, Gansu | 0.540 | 5.33*** | 31.2 |
| Dummy for SOE workers married to retrenched SOE workers | −0.090 | −0.98 | 22.9 |
| Spouse not retrenched (default) | | | 21.4 |
| Log-likelihood | −2500.22 | | |
| Restricted log-likelihood | −3128.64 | | |
| Likelihood ratio index | 0.18 | | |
| No. of observations | 6,929 | Predicted | |
| | | 0 | 1 |
| Actual | 0 | 5,658 | 112 |
| | 1 | 1,018 | 141 |

Note: For this and all subsequent tables, *** = significant at 1%, ** = significant at 5%, * = significant at 10%.

mean years of experience were 22, so at face value, the probit results imply that both younger and older workers faced lower risks of retrenchment. This result should be regarded with caution since the risks of retrenchment may increase with age if older workers are forced into early retirement but not reported as retrenched in the survey.[17] However, it is notable that the finding contrasts strongly with the pattern in OECD countries, where there is typically a U-shaped relationship between age and the incidence of unemployment (see, e.g., Nickell 1980). Being in poor health increased the probability of retrenchment by five percentage points. Membership of the Communist Party reduced the risk by six points. The dummy for belonging to a minority ethnic group had only an insignificant effect.

Finally, consider the dummy variable for whether the individual had a spouse who had been retrenched from the state sector. Since the government encouraged employers to ensure that married couples were not both laid off, we expected an individual to be less vulnerable to dismissal from the state sector if their spouse had been retrenched from the state sector. As predicted, the variable has a negative effect, consistent with implementation of the government's wishes. However, it is not statistically significant. This imposes a technical limitation on our later estimates of wage functions, since we had hoped to use this variable to identify the correction for the possible selectivity of retrenchment.

## 2.4 The duration of unemployment

How long a spell of unemployment do retrenched workers face in China? Over half (55 per cent) of the re-employed found their new job within a year of being sacked. Among these re-employed workers, the duration of unemployment was heavily skewed: the median spell was 10 months, but the mean was 18 months (the inter-quartile range was 4 to 28 months). However, since mass unemployment is relatively recent in urban China, looking only at completed spells of unemployment is likely to be very misleading. The majority (63 per cent) of the retrenched workers in our sample had not found re-employment by the time of our survey.[18] The mean spell of unemployment for the combined sample of the re-employed and unemployed is 24 months (the median is 19 months). This statistic underestimates the expected duration of unemployment because the observed unemployment spells for the still unemployed are incomplete. To obtain a more meaningful figure, we need to allow for the censoring of unemployment durations using the concepts of survival analysis.

Figure 2.1 uses data from the enlarged sample to plot the empirical hazard rates for re-employment. These are the proportions of workers who found re-employment in a given month after previously being unemployed. One feature to note is that the hazard rates are generally low; the chance of an unemployed person finding work in any given month is typically below 3 per cent. Taken together, these empirical hazard rates imply very long durations of unemployment. Given the empirical hazard rates plotted in Figure 2.1, the expected duration of unemployment would be 47 months (almost four years).[19] Such long spells of unemployment contrast with what is observed in industrialized countries, but are not unprecedented. The mean observed duration of unemployment in urban Ethiopia in 1994 was found to be 48 months, without controlling for censoring (Serneels 2001).[20] The long unemployment durations observed in China imply that retrenchment has had serious consequences, entailing a substantial loss of wages.

It is clear from Figure 2.1 that the baseline hazard does not follow any simple pattern such as that implied by the distributions commonly used to model duration data. The empirical hazard proves to be very ‘spiky’, although this may be partly due to noise. The hazard falls after the first year of unemployment and rises at very long durations; beyond that, it is hard to discern a pattern. Most studies of industrialized countries find negative duration dependence: hazard rates fall as unemployment spells lengthen. This is usually interpreted as depreciation of human capital: skills may become obsolete or even forgotten owing to lack of practice. This explanation could apply here to explain the fall in hazard rates after a year of unemployment. Hazard rates may nonetheless ultimately increase with time if very prolonged unemployment erodes savings and makes unemployed workers willing to take on any kind of work, however low-paid or unpleasant. Figure 2.2 plots the baseline hazards from the Prentice–Gloeckler model and shows that they follow the irregular pattern of the empirical hazard.[21]

In selecting the explanatory variables to be included in the duration model, we were constrained by computational cost. There are a large number of nuisance parameters to be estimated in the Prentice–Gloeckler model (one for every month a person may be unemployed, with some unemployed for five years or more).[22] In preliminary work, we included the same explanatory variables as were entered into the probit for retrenchment together with variables for household demographics,

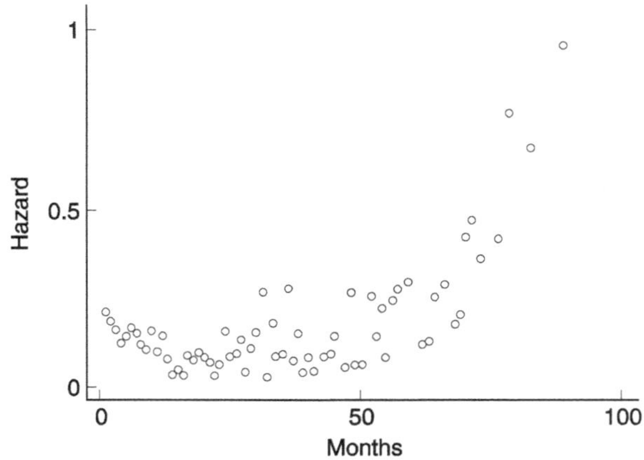


*Figure 2.2* Baseline hazard from the Prentice–Gloeckler semi-parametric model: the conditional probability of re-employment abstracting from the effects of the covariates.

receipt of unemployment benefit and indicators of the main form of job search. Likelihood ratio tests revealed that two whole blocks of variables – those for occupation and type of ownership – were statistically insignificant, and since these were not of particular a priori interest, they were not retained in the final model. Controlling for other factors, we cannot reject the hypothesis that their occupation has no effect on how long workers remain unemployed. Similarly, whether they were previously employed in centrally run SOEs, local collectives or other forms of enterprise seems irrelevant.

Table 2.3 reports the estimates of the final Prentice–Gloeckler model for the duration of unemployment without heterogeneity.[23] When the model was estimated with multiplicative gamma heterogeneity, the variance of the gamma distribution was not different from zero at any conventional level of statistical significance and hence we were not able to reject the hypothesis that there was no omitted heterogeneity.[24] The finding that unobserved heterogeneity does not matter is surprising given the literature on industrialized countries, where those who are unemployed for longer are commonly found to have unobservable characteristics that lower their probability of re-employment (Keifer 1988).[25]

Positive coefficients indicate explanatory variables that raise the hazard of re-employment and so reduce the duration of unemployment. Considering first the personal characteristics of the workers, those measuring aspects of human capital – education and health – are all statistically significant. More educated workers are more likely to be re-employed quickly: each year of education increases the hazard by 6 per cent.[26] Workers reporting themselves to be in poor health are estimated to be 40 per cent less likely to re-employed in any given month, *ceteris paribus*. These results match those found in studies of the duration of unemployment in transitional Central European economies in the 1990s, where the least educated and the handicapped were found to have a harder time than others obtaining jobs

(Svejnar 1999). Age is estimated to have a U-shaped effect on the hazard rate, with the turning point coming quite early at 32 years of age. Sex, ethnicity and party membership are all statistically insignificant.

Household demographic composition influenced the duration of unemployment. In preliminary work, we included a full set of variables for numbers of household members of particular ages and sexes. We then experimented with a variety of interaction terms, dropping insignificant variables until we obtained the final form presented here. Table 2.3 includes the number of children aged under 7, both on its own and as part of two interaction terms. The first interaction term is with a dummy for the individual worker being female. The second interaction term is with both the dummy for the individual worker being female and a variable for the number of older household members (aged 60 or over) in the household. On its own, the number of young children is insignificant, implying that it does not affect the duration of unemployment for male workers. The interaction with the dummy for being a female worker is significant and negative. Taken together with the coefficient on the number of young children, the term implies that having a young child reduces the re-employment probability of a female worker by 23 per cent if there are no older people in the household. The second interaction is significant and positive, implying that the negative effects of young children on women's re-employment chances are negated if there were older people in the household. We interpret this as elder, possibly retired, household members freeing women from the constraints of child rearing.

We included in the duration model a dummy variable for whether the individual ever received unemployment benefits, i.e. institutional support on account of their unemployment. The variable is wholly insignificant, with a near-zero coefficient. Just over half (56 per cent) of the workers in our sample reported ever receiving unemployment benefit. Workers who entered the labour market after 1984 were not entitled to government redundancy benefits. They could be paid by an unemployment benefit scheme, run by semi-private insurance companies, provided that they had happened to join the scheme before their job contracts were terminated. Other *xiagang* retrenched workers have been entitled to redundancy payments, supposed to be paid in equal parts by the state via local government, the work unit and semi-private insurance companies (usually run by the local government insurance agents).[27] However, in reality, enterprises and insurance companies may not have had sufficient funds to contribute their share of the benefit while even the government's share of the benefit may sometimes not have been paid.

The result that unemployment benefits do not appear to affect the duration of unemployment is contrary to what is typically found in the West. Estimates for other transitional economies typically found only 'modest' effects (Svejnar 1999). The finding that unemployment benefits do not affect the duration of unemployment could be explained in several ways. First, it may be that unemployment is purely involuntary: workers would take any available jobs offered, regardless of their benefits. However, the significance of household demographics raises a question mark over such an explanation for at least some retrenched workers.

*Table 2.3* Prentice-Gloeckler semi-parametric model for the duration of unemployment

| | *Coefficients* | *t-ratio* |
|---|---|---|
| Male | 0.155 | 1.37 |
| School years | 0.057 | 2.40** |
| Age | −0.102 | −1.93** |
| Age squared | 0.002 | 2.22** |
| Minority ethnicity | −0.275 | −1.28 |
| Party member | −0.201 | −1.20 |
| In bad health | −0.507 | −2.39** |
| Ever received unemployment benefit | −0.003 | −0.03 |
| Job search: via market | −1.015 | −7.22*** |
| Job search: using social network | −2.654 | −12.97*** |
| Job search: self-employed | −1.480 | −6.43*** |
| Others forms of job search | −1.476 | −5.28*** |
| Beijing | −0.620 | −2.55*** |
| Jinzhou | −0.293 | −1.39 |
| Nanjing | 0.250 | 1.09 |
| Xuzhou | −0.406 | −1.61 |
| Zhengzhou | −0.921 | −2.95*** |
| Kaifeng | −1.188 | −3.63*** |
| Pingdingshan | −1.469 | −2.77*** |
| Chengdu | −0.530 | −2.13** |
| Zigong | −0.672 | −2.04** |
| Nanchong | 0.548 | 2.11** |
| Lanzhou | −0.207 | −0.88 |
| Pingliang | −0.247 | −1.03 |
| No. of children under 7* female worker | −0.540 | −1.82* |
| No. of children under 7* female worker * no. of old people | 0.417 | 2.51*** |
| No. of children under 7 | 0.276 | 1.32 |

Note: The default method of job search is "through government".

Nuisance parameters (log integrated baseline hazards) not reported.

Log-likelihood (−0.5*Deviance) = −1931.7.

Cf. log-likelihood for intercept-only model (Model 0) = −2215.3.

Chi-squared statistic for Model (1) vs. Model (0) = 567.3.

Prob. > chi2(94) = 9.506 e–69.

Second, it may be that the unemployment benefits are not sufficiently large to affect behaviour. For those who received them, the benefit averaged 210 yuan per month in 1999–2000. This can be compared to the average monthly wages of re-employed retrenched workers of 544 yuan per month. Clearly, there remains a substantial financial incentive for unemployed workers to find re-employment, even if they are fortunate enough to be among those receiving unemployment benefits. The finding that unemployment benefits do not affect the duration of unemployment implies that the government could provide compensation for retrenched workers so as to mitigate the social and political consequences of the reform without worsening the problem of mass unemployment. However, since

*Table 2.4* Number of workers using different means of job search

| | *Re-employed* | *Still unemployed* |
|---|---|---|
| Government (previous work unit; employment agency) | 300 | 110 |
| Network | 28 | 357 |
| Starting own business | 22 | 64 |
| Search on one's own | 69 | 149 |
| Other | 14 | 43 |

Note: For re-employed workers, the responses are to the question: "How did you get your current job?" For unemployed workers, the responses are to the question: "What is the main way in which you look for work?"

the survey, the government has taken steps to reduce benefits because of the large fiscal burden they impose.[28]

The final set of variables that we include as determinants of the duration of unemployment describe the means by which individuals sought jobs or, in the case of the re-employed, found jobs. The default category was job search through the government, whether through an employment agency or the previous work unit. Other alternatives were: search using one's social network such as friends and family; seeking work by setting up one's own business; or search on one's own, including using newspapers or sitting open competitive examinations for posts. The government continues to be the main means of obtaining employment: of the 433 retrenched workers who found re-employment, 300 did so through job centres or their previous work unit (Table 2.4). Workers who were still unemployed tended to rely more on networks and searching on their own. As a result, means of job search other than going through the government have significant negative effects on the re-employment hazard.

It is interesting to examine why some re-employed workers were able to find jobs through the government when others were not. Table 2.5 addresses this question, modelling the probability that re-employed workers found their new jobs from government sources, whether employment agencies or their previous work units. One of the most important contributory factors is whether the re-employed ever received unemployment benefit. At the mean of the other explanatory variables, the probability of having obtained re-employment through the government is 67 per cent for those who ever received unemployment benefit compared to 59 per cent for those not so fortunate. A plausible explanation is that the government is keen on reducing the cost to it of retrenched state workers and uses its administrative power to help the recipients of this state aid to regain employment.

## 2.5 Income losses from redundancy

On average, retrenched workers face prolonged periods of unemployment. We have already noted that the low proportions of unemployed workers who are

*Table 2.5* Probit regression for the probability of regaining jobs from government agent: subsample of those who are re-employed after retrenchment

| | *Coefficient* | *Probability of re-employment via government agent (%)* |
|---|---|---|
| Constant | 0.2078<br>(0.34) | |
| Male | 0.0274<br>(0.19) | 64 |
| Female | 0 | 63 |
| Education (in years) | 0.021<br>(0.57) | |
| Experience (in years) | −0.0546<br>(1.54) | |
| Experience squared | 0.0006<br>(0.68) | |
| Han Chinese | 0 | 65 |
| Minority ethnicity | −0.0560<br>(0.18) | 64 |
| Non-party member | | 63 |
| Party member | −0.1112<br>(0.45) | 66 |
| Good health reported | 0 | 64 |
| Bad health reported | 0.4969<br>(1.75)* | 52 |
| Duration of unemployment (in years) | −0.1403<br>(2.84)*** | |
| Non-recipient of unemployment benefit (default) | 0 | 59 |
| Recipient of unemployment benefit | −0.3395<br>(2.26)** | 67 |
| Currently working in the state sector | 0.4082<br>(1.45) | 64 |
| Currently working in the non-state sector (default) | 0 | 54 |
| No. of children in household | 0.3351<br>(1.59) | |
| Liaoning (default) | 0 | 67 |
| Beijing | 0.5322<br>(2.03)** | 55 |
| Jiangsu | 0.0208<br>(0.10) | 67 |
| Henan | −0.1852<br>(0.48) | 71 |

(Continued)

*Table 2.5* (Continued)

| | *Coefficient* | *Probability of re-employment via government agent (%)* |
|---|---|---|
| Sichuan | 0.5161<br>(2.57)*** | 55 |
| Gansu | 0.1635<br>(0.82) | 64 |

Note: The dependent variable takes a value of 1 if the worker was re-employed via a government agent and 0 if the worker was re-employed by some other means.

Number of observations 433.

Log-likelihood function −240.1873.

Restricted log-likelihood −267.0783.

Chi-squared 53.78197.

Significance level 0.00000.

Actual distribution of dependent variable: 0 = 300, 1 = 133.

Predicted distribution of dependent variable: 0 = 375, 1 = 58.

Probabilities of the model 0 = 0.636*100; 1 = 0.364*100.

re-employed in any one month (the empirical hazard rates plotted in Figure 2.2). These imply a long expected duration of unemployment of about four years. Given the very incomplete coverage and low level of unemployment benefits, unemployment leads to a pronounced loss of personal income. However, in this section we consider whether the re-employed workers are 'scarred' by the effect of unemployment. Specifically, do they receive lower wages upon re-employment than they would have received had they never been retrenched?[29]

Appendix 2.A reports wage functions estimated separately for workers who have never been retrenched and for re-employed workers. We are interested in what these wage functions imply about the effects of retrenchment on wages. We do not discuss the estimated effects of the explanatory variables in detail – this is done in a companion paper (Appleton *et al.* 2001). The corrections for selectivity were statistically insignificant at the 5 per cent level.[30] The insignificance of the corrections for the selectivity of retrenchment is perhaps not surprising given that our only hypothesized instrument for the selectivity of retrenchment – whether SOE workers had spouses who had been retrenched from SOEs – had proved to be insignificant in the probit for retrenchment. The signs of the coefficients on the corrections for the selectivity of retrenchment were perverse in both functions. They imply that the unobservables that raise the probability of retrenchment are positively correlated with the unobservables that raise wages. We were able to find statistically significant identifying instruments for the selectivity of re-employment, and although the correction itself was insignificant, it had the anticipated positive sign. Given that the selectivity corrections were insignificant and often poorly identified, we relied on OLS wage functions to obtain predictions of wages. If we had used the selectivity corrected wage functions, we would have obtained even larger estimates of the scarring from retrenchment.[31]

Does retrenchment leave workers 'scarred', that is to say, does it lower their wages upon re-employment? This is suggested by the descriptive statistics: the mean log wage of re-employed workers is 3.009 compared with the figure of 3.340 for those workers who have never been retrenched. However, as we have noted, the re-employed tend to have less productive observed characteristics. To standardize for this, we take the mean observed characteristics of the re-employed and use the wage function for the never retrenched to predict the log wage. This gives a figure of 3.127, implying that the re-employed workers would receive 12 per cent higher wages than they actually get (3.127−3.009=0.118) if they were paid in a like manner to workers who had never been retrenched. This degree of scarring from unemployment is within the 10–25 per cent range estimated for the US. However, it is greater than the 3 per cent scarring from redundancy (as opposed to other causes of unemployment) found in one study for the UK (Arulampalam 2001). Note that our estimates of scarring are for the year of the survey only. We do not know how long the wage differential between the re-employed and the non-retrenched urban workers will be maintained.

## 2.6 Conclusions

The state enterprise sector in China has been widely regarded as inefficient and in need of reform. The impetus to reform has come from the declining profitability of state enterprises in the face of growing market competition, both from rural industry and internationally. The state could no longer afford the loss of tax revenue and the burden of rising subsidies. One of the problems of state-owned enterprises is their overmanning – the consequence of the long-standing policy to ensure that all urban residents were securely employed. Hence the programme of requiring state enterprises to shed their 'surplus labour', a policy that began in the early 1990s, accelerated in the late 1990s, and continues apace.

The last decade has seen widespread redundancies in urban China: from a survey of 13 cities in 1999–2000, we estimate that 11 per cent of urban workers had been retrenched since 1992. The threat of redundancy has not affected all types of worker equally. Certain personal characteristics are associated with a greater risk of redundancy; these include having little education, being female and being middle-aged. Particular kinds of employment have also suffered more retrenchment, notably employment by local government or urban collectives, and manual and/or unskilled occupations. Some of these risk factors, such as lack of education, are consistent with retrenchment of less productive labour. However, others – notably being a woman – are more suggestive of discriminatory retrenchment policies.

Retrenched workers typically remain unemployed for a long period of time. We estimate that 53 per cent of those dismissed since 1992 remained unemployed at the time of the survey in early 2000. The pervasive censoring in the data complicates estimates of the average duration of unemployment: for a majority of the retrenched, their spell of unemployment has not yet ended. However, the empirical hazard rates for re-employment are low and imply that the typical retrenched worker in our sample can be expected to remain without a job for about four years. This estimate may, of course, prove invalid if labour market conditions change dramatically. Certain individual characteristics reduce the duration of unemployment. The young, the old, the healthy and the educated are likely to have to endure shorter spells of unemployment. Women with young children are likely to be unemployed for longer, although not if there are older people in the household who can care for the children. Although receipt of unemployment benefits has no effect on the duration of unemployment, it appears that government gives priority to finding jobs for those unemployed workers for whom it has some financial responsibility.

Although the main source of hardship for retrenched workers is the direct loss of earnings while unemployed, they also appear to be re-employed for lower wages than if they were never retrenched. We used wage functions to calculate the extent of such 'scarring' during 1999. If the re-employed could have been paid according to the same standards as those urban workers who did not lose their jobs, their wages would be 12 per cent higher.

The redundancies have no doubt contributed to an improvement in the efficiency of state enterprises. However, there have been costs, at least in the short term, and these have been borne unevenly. Some of the redundancy criteria are consistent with efficiency objectives but others look to be discriminatory. Redundant workers generally suffer a long and uncertain period of unemployment and bear a heavy loss of income, and possession of certain characteristics – not all of them related to efficiency – appears to impede re-employment. The urban redundancy programme is a potent source of poverty, insecurity and discontent. Its speed and extent require a delicate weighing and balancing of considerations in the political economy of China.

## Notes

The authors are grateful to the Department for International Development, United Kingdom, for their funding of the project (Escor grant R7526), to the CCK Foundation for a research grant (RG019-U-01) and the Ford Foundation for their support of data collection. We are grateful to Stephen Jenkins for his STATA programme to estimate the Prentice–Gloeckler–Meyer model and for his advice on several technical issues. Useful comments were provided by an anonymous referee, Xiaodong Gong, Peter Wright, and participants at seminars at Oxford and Nottingham. This chapter is reprinted from *China Economic Review*, Vol. 13, Simon Appleton, John Knight, Lina Song and Qingjie Xia, 'Labor retrenchment in China: determinants and consequences', 252–275, 2002, with permission from Elsevier.

1 Only annual *net* lay-offs are reported prior to 1998.
2 Derived from the National Bureau of Statistics (2001a, 2001b, 2001c).
3 The survey was designed by an international team that included the authors. Data collection took place at the start of 2000 by a joint team from the Department of Economics, University of Oxford, the Chinese Academy of Social Sciences, and the National Statistics Bureau of PR China.
4 Given our focus on redundancy, we excluded from the analysis first-time job seekers – those unemployed who had never worked. We also excluded employees with earnings below 8 yuan per day, as it was thought likely that these were either part-time workers or errors in the data.

5 This year was chosen because it marked the appointment of a new Prime Minister and the beginnings of significant moves to reform the SOE sector. The number of sample workers laid off in 1992 was 25, compared to 9 in the year before and 55 in 1993. The ten-year SOE restructuring programme began officially in 1994, when 127 sample workers were laid off. 1998 saw the largest number of redundancies in our sample, with 305 workers losing their jobs.

6 We define potential work experience as the number of years since a person finished full-time education.

7 From inspecting the figure, there may be an appearance of a U-shaped pattern to the baseline hazards. However, regressing the baseline hazards against a quadratic term for months produced a wholly insignificant result (an $F$-test on the quadratic terms had a $p$-value of 0.45).

8 A related alternative semi-parametric method is that proposed by Cox (1972). However, the Cox method encounters severe difficulties in the presence of heavy ties in the duration data (Cox and Oates 1984). The Prentice–Gloeckler model is more reliable in the presence of heavy ties. In preliminary work, we estimated both models and found similar estimates for the effects of the covariates.

9 Some argue that it is a misnomer to describe the baseline as non-parametric since the model requires estimation of one parameter for each interval.

10 Note that the omitted heterogeneity terms ($\varepsilon_i$) vary neither within nor across intervals for a given person.

11 An alternative approach would be to use a model for the duration of unemployment to compute a correction for the selectivity of re-employment. This was straightforward using an ordered probit model for the duration of unemployment. Such a model corresponds closely to the Prentice–Gloeckler grouped duration model. However, the coefficients on determinants of wages of the re-employed workers did not change noticeably when using this model to compute a correction for selectivity and so we focused instead on the model selecting on a binary probit, since this gave a slightly better fit to the data.

12 We tested this restriction by estimating a more general model, a bivariate probit, which allows for a correlation between the two error terms, $\eta_i$ and $U_i$. A bivariate probit was estimated in LIMDEP using the option for estimation with sample selectivity, the sample selectivity being that re-employment is not observed for those never retrenched. However, the estimate of the covariance between $\eta_i$ and $U_i$ was not statistically significant at the 5 per cent level, so we could not reject independence. Given that the corrections for the sample selectivity of earnings are much simpler under independence, we imposed this restriction.

13 Specifically, the variable is 1 if the individual (a) works in an SOE or worked in an SOE (and was retrenched since 1992), and (b) has a spouse who worked in an SOE and was retrenched since 1992.

14 Within the nationally representative sample of 4,000 urban households, 747 (18.7 per cent) had experienced redundancy. We enlarge this with the additional sample of 503 households that had experienced redundancy. To keep the proportion of households experiencing redundancy at 18.7 per cent, we gave all households experiencing redundancy a weight of 0.6 (since 0.6*(747 + 503)/(3253 + 0.6*(747 + 503)) = 0.187).

15 The discrepancy is partly because of the non-linearity of the probit model. Furthermore, the rates of individual worker retrenchment are higher in the additional sample of 503 households experiencing retrenchment than in the 747 similar households in the representative sample of 4,000 households.

16 Marginal effects are given by $\alpha P(1-P)$, where $\alpha$ is the relevant coefficient and $P$ is the probability at which the effect is being evaluated.

17 There are 118 people who reported having been made redundant through early retirement and these are included in our definition of the retrenched. Of these 118, 70 were

defined as being currently unemployed and the rest had found re-employment. However, these people are only a subset of all those who had taken early retirement. A total of 198 people in the survey reported currently being in early retirement.

18 Within the subsample from 4,000 nationally representative urban households, 53 per cent had not found re-employment.

19 These figures should be regarded with some caution, since they are based on empirical hazard rates and these may be misleading predictors for future hazard rates of the still unemployed. In particular, the still unemployed may differ in observed and unobserved characteristics from the re-employed, and labour market conditions may change in the future. Furthermore, most retrenchment occurred less than four years before the survey. Only 178 out of 1,159 retrenched workers in the sample had experienced unemployment spells lasting over 47 months. This fact, which reflects the relatively high incidence of censoring in our data, implies that our results are of limited reliability in making inferences about what happens towards the end of relatively long spells of unemployment.

20 Although very different contexts, a comparison between Ethiopia in 1994 and China in 1999–2000 may be justified on the grounds that in both cases the state was the dominant employer in urban areas. However, it should be noted that unemployment in urban Ethiopia was concentrated among first-time job seekers whereas we have excluded such cases here.

21 A referee comments that we should not allow our parameterization of the baseline hazard to approximate the empirical pattern but should smooth it out using wider intervals. Following this comment, we estimated the model with two- and three-month intervals. However, the findings about the explanatory variables were robust to this decision: the coefficients typically did not alter when expressed with two decimal places and the same ones remained statistically significant at the 5 per cent level.

22 When heterogeneity was allowed for, estimation took over a day on a standard office PC.

23 The Prentice–Gloeckler–Meyer models were estimated in STATA using the pgmhaz command of Jenkins (1997).

24 The estimated gamma variance was $6.246 \times 10^{-6}$ with a standard error of 0.000603 and $z$-score of 0.01.

25 It might be supposed that the finding of no heterogeneity is partly the result of our allowing for a flexible form for the baseline hazard. However, when we estimate a Weibull duration model, omitted heterogeneity is still statistically insignificant with a $p$-value of 0.24.

26 From equation (2.3), the percentage effect of a unit change in the explanatory variable on the hazard rate is $\exp(\beta)-1$, where $\beta$ is the relevant coefficient.

27 The system was later changed in 2001, with the onus being on requiring enterprises to insure their existing workers against the possibility of unemployment.

28 As per the previous footnote, newly redundant workers will not be entitled to the *xiagang* redundancy payments provided to those previously retrenched.

29 Another aspect of 'scarring' is that those with a history of unemployment may be more likely to be unemployed in the future (see, e.g. Arulampalam 1998). Given how recent the *xiagang* reforms are, it is not possible to explore this empirically.

30 We report only the OLS results. The coefficient on the correction for the selectivity of retrenchment was 0.144 ($p$-value 0.19) in the wage function for the never retrenched. For the re-employed, the coefficients were 0.231 ($p$-value 0.09) for the correction for the selectivity of retrenchment and 0.453 ($p$-value 0.07) for the correction for the selectivity of re-employment.

31 Using the selectivity corrected wage functions, we estimate that re-employed workers with average (mean zero) unobservable characteristics would earn 87 per cent more if paid like never retrenched workers.

## References


Appleton, S., Knight, J., Song, L. and Xia, Q. (2001) *Towards a Competitive Labour Market in China?*, Nottingham: Institute for Contemporary China Studies, University of Nottingham.

Arulampalam, W. (1998) 'State dependence in unemployment incidence: evidence for British men, 1991–1995', mimeo, Department of Economics, University of Warwick, Warwick.

Arulampalam, W. (2001) 'Is unemployment really scarring?', *Economic Journal,* 111: 585–606.

Burda, M.C. and Mertens, A. (2001) 'Estimating wage losses of displaced workers in Germany', *Labour Economics*, 8: 15–41.

Cox, D.R. (1972) 'Regression models and life tables', *Journal of the Royal Statistical Society Series B*, 34: 186–220.

Cox, D.R. and Oakes, D. (1984) *Analysis of Survival Data*, London and New York: Chapman & Hall.

Heckman, J. (1979) 'Sample selection bias as a specification error', *Econometrica*, 47: 153–61.

Heckman, J. and Singer, B. (1984) 'A method for minimizing the distributional assumptions in econometric models for duration data', *Econometrica*, 52(2): 271–320.

Jenkins, S.P. (1997) 'Discrete time proportional hazards regression.' *STATA Technical Bulletin*, 39: 22–32.

Keifer, N. (1988) 'Economic duration data and hazard functions', *Journal of Economic Literature,* 26: 646–79.

Lancaster, T. (1979) 'Econometric methods for the duration of unemployment', *Econometrica*, 47(3): 939–56.

Maddala, G.S. (1983) *Limited Dependent and Qualitative Variables in Economics*, New York: Cambridge University Press.

Meyer, B. (1990) 'Unemployment insurance and unemployment spells', *Econometrica,* 58: 757–82.

Mincer, J. (1974) *Schooling, Experience and Earnings*, Chicago: Chicago University Press.

National Bureau of Statistics (NBS) (2001a) *China Statistical Yearbook 2000*, Beijing: China Statistics Press.

National Bureau of Statistics (NBS) (2001b) *China Labour Statistical Yearbook 2000*, Beijing: China Statistics Press.

National Bureau of Statistics (NBS) (2001c) *China Monthly Economic Indicators July 2000*, Beijing: China Statistics Press.

Nickell, S. (1980) 'A picture of male unemployment in Britain', *Economic Journal*, 90(363): 776–94.

Prentice, R. and Gloeckler, L. (1978) 'Regression analysis of grouped survival data with application to breast cancer data', *Biometrics*, 34: 57–67.

Serneels, P. (2001) 'Unemployment duration in urban Ethiopia', mimeo, Centre for the Study of African Economies, University of Oxford.

Svejnar, J. (1999) 'Labor markets in transitional Central European economies', Chapter 42 of Orley Ashenfelter and David Card (eds), *Handbook of Labor Economics*, Vol. 3B, pp. 2809–58, Amsterdam: Elsevier.

Tunali, I. and Assaad, R. (1992) 'Market structure and spells of employment and unemployment: evidence from the construction sector in Egypt', *Journal of Applied Econometrics,* 7: 339–67.

## Appendix 2.A: Wage functions

| | *Non-retrenched urban workers* | | *Re-employed workers* | |
|---|---|---|---|---|
| | *Coefficient* | *t-ratio* | *Coefficient* | *t-ratio* |
| Constant | 2.850 | 44.42*** | 2.778 | 8.72*** |
| Male | 0.135 | 9.75*** | 0.313 | 5.11*** |
| Education in years | 0.034 | 10.61*** | 0.007 | 0.44 |
| Experience | 0.037 | 12.13*** | 0.052 | 3.99*** |
| Experience squared | −0.001 | −9.40*** | −0.001 | −3.67*** |
| Minority ethnicity | 0.051 | 1.54 | −0.131 | −1.24 |
| Party member | 0.074 | 4.68*** | −0.038 | −0.23 |
| Bad health | −0.085 | −2.05** | −0.056 | −0.55 |
| Central SOE | 0.156 | 10.77*** | 0.057 | 0.60 |
| Urban collective | −0.169 | −6.86*** | −0.129 | −1.83* |
| Urban private | 0.104 | 1.26 | −0.117 | −0.55 |
| Urban individual | −0.031 | −0.59 | 0.125 | 1.42 |
| Foreign invested | 0.347 | 6.35*** | −0.380 | −3.09*** |
| State listed | 0.085 | 2.35** | 0.000 | 0.00 |
| Other listed | 0.064 | 1.21 | 0.187 | 0.83 |
| Rural enterprises | −0.257 | −2.40** | −0.624 | −6.50*** |
| Other ownership | −0.023 | −0.36 | −0.181 | −1.04 |
| Administrative | 0.000 | −0.02 | 0.016 | 0.12 |
| Clerical | −0.068 | −3.43*** | −0.327 | −2.34** |
| Industrial worker | −0.239 | −12.68*** | −0.173 | −1.72* |
| Commercial worker | −0.226 | −6.57*** | −0.123 | −1.04 |
| Service worker | −0.254 | −7.46*** | −0.346 | −2.18** |
| Other occupation | −0.346 | −5.24*** | 0.124 | 0.56 |
| Shenyang, Liaoning | −0.477 | −17.64*** | −0.252 | −1.61 |
| Jinzhou, Liaoning | −0.445 | −11.80*** | −0.520 | −4.12*** |
| Nanjing, Jiangsu | −0.136 | −5.23*** | −0.162 | −1.21 |
| Xuzhou, Jiangsu | −0.341 | −10.67*** | −0.207 | −1.46 |
| Zhengzhou, Henan | −0.431 | −14.09*** | −0.478 | −2.47** |
| Kaifeng, Henan | −0.692 | −19.88*** | −0.636 | −3.32*** |
| Pingdingshan, Henan | −0.477 | −15.69*** | −0.379 | −1.55 |
| Chengdu, Sichuan | −0.404 | −14.86*** | −0.231 | −1.70* |
| Zigong, Sichuan | −0.527 | −15.53*** | −0.754 | −4.41*** |
| Nanchong, Sichuan | −0.585 | −17.31*** | −0.511 | −3.90*** |
| Lanzhou, Gansu | −0.456 | −16.08*** | −0.336 | −2.54** |
| Pingliang, Gansu | −0.642 | −21.16*** | −0.691 | −4.53*** |
| No. of observations | 5,770 | | 433 | |
| Mean of dependent variable | 3.340 | | 3.009 | |
| Adjusted $R^2$ | 0.330 | | 0.151 | |
| Standard error of equation | 0.486 | | 0.595 | |

Note: *t*-ratios are calculated by using White's heteroscedasticity-consistent standard errors.

# 3 Unemployment, poverty and income disparity in urban China

*Jinjun Xue and Wei Zhong*

## 3.1 Introduction

Urban poverty has become a crucial issue in China while rural poverty has reduced dramatically in recent years. There have been a few studies on urban poverty in which some estimates of poverty and analyses of the factors causing it have been conducted. In the analysis of poverty, many studies have stressed differences in non-wage income and money in kind, housing and education, size of family, and so on.[1] However, some recent and vital subjects have been ignored in these studies, such as: (1) the relationship between unemployment and poverty, namely, whether urban unemployment has become a novel factor causing the increase in urban poverty; (2) the income inequality and poverty of rural migrants[2] and its influence on urban poverty and income distribution; and (3) the relationship between poverty and income inequality, explicitly, the effect of unemployment and poverty on income distribution. These issues are worth examining not only for their theoretical value but also for their policy implications.

This chapter will focus analysis on the above issues and make estimates of unemployment and poverty in urban China by using the 1999, 1995 and 1988 CASS surveys. It will also study income disparities among urban registered households, households with unemployed people, and rural migrant households, and their effects on the distribution of income in urban China.

The chapter is organized as follows. Section 3.2 estimates urban unemployment and its trend. Section 3.3 calculates urban poverty rates by groups and specifies the effects of unemployed and rural migrant households on poverty. Section 3.4 analyses the effects of unemployment, migration and poverty on urban income distribution. Section 3.5 presents the main findings and conclusions.

The 1988 CASS survey was conducted in the spring of 1989, and contains a large sample of 9,008 urban households and 31,827 individuals, 10,258 rural households and 51,352 individuals covering 28 provinces. This was the first microeconomic survey of income distribution in China conducted using international standards and statistical methodology. It enables us to do research based on reliable data available at the micro-level. The aims of the survey were to measure inequality and to consider its causes. The overall result was that the Gini coefficient, a measure of income distribution, was 0.233 for urban households, 0.338 for rural households and 0.382 overall (Khan and Riskin 1998). It illustrated that although there had been a great achievement in economic reform and growth, inequality of income distribution had worsened since the early 1980s (for which there was a World Bank estimate; World Bank 1985). It indicated that money in kind, the urban–rural income disparity and wage income in non-agricultural activities were important sources of the inequality.

The 1999 CASS survey, conducted in early 1996, covered 11 provinces and 60 cities, with 6,868 urban households and 21,533 individuals, and 7,998 rural households and 34,739 individuals (Griffin and Zhao 1993). It was designed to make comparisons with the previous survey and to search for the sources of rising inequality. The result shows that the Gini coefficients were 0.283 for urban households, 0.429 for rural households and 0.445 overall (Zhao, Li and Riskin 1999). Inequality had worsened since 1988, with an increase of 27 per cent for rural households, 23 per cent for urban households and 17 per cent overall. The research explained some reasons for rising urban inequality, for example, differences in asset income (subsidies on housing, food coupons, money in kind and savings) among urban households and the rapid development of non-state-owned enterprises. It also indicated that inequality in China has become worse than in many developing countries, including Bangladesh, Indonesia, Thailand and some Latin American countries. Regarding the poverty rates (poor people as a percentage of the total), the figures were 8 per cent (28 million people) for urban areas (60 cities) and 28.6 per cent (246 million people) for rural areas (Khan and Riskin 1999).

It is difficult to compare all items among the three surveys due to the differences in survey provinces (e.g. the absence of Sichuan in the 1988 survey) and questionnaires (e.g. the absence of questions on unemployment in 1988). Therefore, it is necessary to make some adjustments to the data and make them comparable to some extent. Here, we did a comparison on urban unemployment, inequality and poverty by choosing samples drawn from the same six provinces chosen for the 1999 survey (see Table 3.1).

Table 3.2 provides a summary of the comparison and it provides us with the following facts. The urban unemployment rate is rising. Urban unemployment was not a serious issue for decades in socialist China. However, as economic reform accelerated, especially reforms of state-owned enterprises (SOEs), unemployment increased as more and more workers were laid-off (*xiagang*). In the period 1995–1999, the unemployment rate in all provinces except Jiangsu rose from 9.5 to 11.6 per cent. There was a 130 per cent increase in Sichuan, a 50 per cent increase in Beijing and a 21 per cent increase in Liaoning. Obviously, these figures are much higher than the officially stated urban unemployment figures (3.1 per cent in 1999) and illustrate the seriousness of the unemployment problem. Urban income inequality has been worsening since 1988. The Gini coefficient rose from 0.185 in 1988 to 0.225 in 1995 and 0.256 in 1999. The percentage increase was 22 per cent for the period 1988–1995, 14 per cent for the period 1995–1999 and 38 per cent for the whole period 1988–1999. Among the six provinces, Beijing, Liaoning and Jiangsu had a large increase in inequality in the first period and Sichuan and Liaoning had a large increase in the second. However, both periods showed an increasing trend in inequality.

*Table 3.1* Data set description of the three surveys

| *Province* | *1988* | | *1995* | |
|---|---|---|---|---|
| | *Household* | *Individual* | *Household* | *Individual* |
| Beijing | 501 | 1,580 | 500 | 1,528 |
| Liaoning | 903 | 3,068 | | 400 |
| Jiangsu | 1,204 | 3,995 | 300 | 896 |
| Henan | 1,024 | 3,721 | 300 | 949 |
| Sichuan | — | — | 298 | 874 |
| Gansu | 600 | 2,232 | 300 | 961 |
| 6 Provinces | 4,232 | 14,596 | 2,098 | 2,453 |

| *Province* | *1999* | | | | | | | |
|---|---|---|---|---|---|---|---|---|
| | *Without unemployed* | | *With unemployed* | | *Migrant* | | *Total* | |
| | *Household* | *Individual* | *Household* | *Individual* | *Household* | *Individual* | *Household* | *Individual* |
| Beijing | 670 | 2,040 | 70 | 218 | 100 | 206 | 840 | 2,464 |
| Liaoning | 731 | 2,221 | 237 | 231 | 130 | 305 | 1,098 | 2,757 |
| Jiangsu | 729 | 1,384 | 79 | 117 | 130 | 162 | 938 | 1,663 |
| Henan | 800 | 2,436 | 100 | 284 | 159 | 362 | 1,059 | 3,082 |
| Sichuan | 900 | 2,685 | 99 | 315 | 170 | 349 | 1,169 | 3,349 |
| Gansu | 670 | 2,103 | 68 | 226 | 110 | 260 | 848 | 2,589 |
| 6 Provinces | 4,500 | 12,869 | 653 | 1,391 | 799 | 1,644 | 5,952 | 15,904 |

Source: The 1988, 1995 and 1999 CASS surveys.

Note: For comparability, we chose only 6 provinces from the 1988 and 1995 surveys. However, Sichuan was absent in the 1988 survey.

*Table 3.2* Inequality, poverty and unemployment by provinces, 1988, 1995 and 1999

| *Province* | *Urban unemployment rate (%)* | | | | *Inequality measured by Gini coefficient* | | | | | *Urban poverty rate (%)* | | | | |
|---|---|---|---|---|---|---|---|---|---|---|---|---|---|---|
| | *1988* | *1995* | *1999* | *Changes (1995–99)* | *1988* | *1995* | *1999* | *Changes (1988–95)* | *Changes (1995–99)* | *1988* | *1995* | *1999* | *Changes (1988–95)* | *Changes (1995–99)* |
| Beijing | — | 4.2 | 6.3 | 49.6 | 0.186 | 0.247 | 0.246 | 32.6 | –0.4 | 0.13 | 0.11 | 0.16 | –15.4 | 45.5 |
| Liaoning | — | 10.6 | 12.8 | 20.6 | 0.145 | 0.201 | 0.248 | 38.3 | 23.6 | 0.46 | 4.11 | 5.23 | 793.5 | 27.3 |
| Jiangsu | — | 11.8 | 7.5 | –36.5 | 0.162 | 0.219 | 0.243 | 35.1 | 11.2 | 0.43 | 0.25 | 0.59 | –41.9 | 136.0 |
| Henan | — | 15.1 | 15.3 | 1.5 | 0.194 | 0.243 | 0.260 | 25.3 | 6.8 | 7.29 | 7.50 | 9.11 | 2.9 | 21.5 |
| Sichuan | — | 6.3 | 14.4 | 128.2 | 0.211 | 0.207 | 0.280 | –1.8 | 35.5 | — | 2.80 | 7.26 | — | 159.3 |
| Gansu | — | 12.0 | 13.2 | 10.5 | 0.215 | 0.236 | 0.260 | 9.9 | 10.0 | 9.88 | 15.10 | 6.71 | 52.8 | –55.5 |
| 6 Provinces | — | 9.5 | 11.6 | 22.3 | 0.185 | 0.225 | 0.256 | 21.5 | 13.6 | 3.64 | 4.98 | 6.71 | 36.8 | 34.8 |

Sources: The 1988, 1995 and 1999 CASS surveys. The poverty rates for 1988 and 1995 are cited from Zhang and Wei (1999) and Zhao, and Riskin Li (1999: 416); the Gini coefficients for 1988 are cited from Griffin and Zhao (1993: 53).

Note: There were no unemployment data for all samples and poverty data for Sichuan in 1988 due to the absence of the related question and the exclusion of Sichuan province in the survey.

This means that urban income distribution has been worsening, and it could become worse in the future if the government takes no remedial action. Urban poverty has been increasing since 1988. For all six provinces, the urban poverty rates have increased from 3.6 per cent in 1988 to 5 per cent in 1995 and 5.7 per cent in 1999, an increase of 37 per cent in the first period and 15 per cent in the second. By provinces, Gansu, Sichuan and Henan are the serious cases. Particularly, Gansu suffered very high poverty rates of 9.9, 15.1 and 6.7 per cent in 1988, 1995 and 1999, respectively. The data show that Sichuan and Jiangsu experienced particularly rapid increases in poverty. It is also clear that the poverty problem is more serious in the western regions (Gansu, Sichuan) than in other regions.

## 3.2 An estimate of urban unemployment

### *3.2.1 Official unemployment statistics*

One of our purposes in this chapter is to examine the correlation among unemployment, poverty and income disparity, namely, whether unemployment is a cause of poverty or if poverty is a cause of increasing income inequality. However, we are aware that there are many problems in the official urban unemployment data. Consequently, we need to discuss these problems first, and then make an estimate of unemployment.

The official unemployment figures show that urban unemployment stood at a constant 3 per cent from 1995 to 1999. For a country with a huge population, the large size of surplus labour and the increasing number of laid-off workers, it is obvious that the figures were heavily underestimated and disguised the seriousness of urban unemployment in China. The main problems of the official data are: (1) it only covers the unemployed who are aged 16–45 years for women and 16–50 for men and who are officially registered in local labour administrations (*dengjishiye*); (2) laid-off workers and early retirees from the restructuring of SOEs and collectively owned enterprises (COEs), the main types of unemployment emerging in recent years, are not counted in official unemployment statistics; and (3) the figures are based neither on scientific statistics nor labour surveys but on the 'monthly or annual reports of labour' (*laodong yuebao, nianbao*) submitted by local government officers with a strong political consideration.[3] Hence, it is safe to say that the figures are unreliable.

To reveal the real urban unemployment situation, we first made an adjustment of the official data, and then estimated unemployment by using the population census data and our household surveys data.

### *3.2.2 Adjustment of official figures*

The largest component of unemployment missed in the official statistics is laid-off workers. Therefore, we need to adjust the official unemployment figures by adding the laid-off unemployment figures. For the adjustment, we defined urban unemployment as the officially registered unemployed and the laid-off (worker) unemployed (*xiagangshiye*). However, it is necessary to clarify here that not all laid-off workers are unemployed. The reason is that the so-called *xiagang* is a very special phenomenon in China and cannot be equated entirely to the concept of unemployment in Western countries. *Xiagang* refers to those who have been laid off while still nominally holding an employment relationship (or contract) with their enterprises. *Xiagang* differs from unemployment because *xiagang* workers can receive some subsidies or living expenses from their enterprises or government institutes (not unemployment insurance) and some of them can be re-employed (*zaijiuye*) with the help of the government under the system of the 'Re-employment Project' (*zaijiuye gongcheng*). However, some laid-off workers are not really 'unemployed' during the period of *xiagang* because they are actually self-employed running small businesses, or selling surplus factory products on the roadside. For that reason, only those laid-off workers who are not in the conditions mentioned above are fully unemployed.

Based on this consideration, we separated the number of fully unemployed from *xiagang* and calculated urban unemployment by adding these figures into officially registered unemployed. Column (a) in Table 3.3 is the adjusted figure of urban unemployment based on the data of *xiagang* and re-employed workers that have been published in the *China Labour Statistical Yearbook* since 1993. It shows that the number of laid-off workers increased rapidly from 3 million in 1993 to 14.54 million in 2000 while the laid-off unemployed increased from 1.79 million in 1993 to 10.92 million in 2000. According to the data, we calculated the adjusted unemployment rates and found that it rose from 3.2 per cent in 1993 to 4.4 per cent in 1999, and reached a high level of 6.8 per cent in 2000. Apparently, the adjusted figures are much higher than the official figures, approximately 2.2 times higher in 2000.

### *3.2.3 Estimate of urban unemployment*

It is inaccurate to obtain unemployment figures only by adding those laid-off unemployed into officially registered unemployment statistics because the above definition is still narrow. '*Daiye qingnian*' and '*zaotui*' are other components of the missing parts. '*Daiye qingnian*' is a well-known expression in China referring to those young school-leavers who are waiting for jobs at home or forced to wait for another chance of entering professional schools or colleges because of difficulties in finding jobs. However, '*zaotui*', or early retirees, is a common phenomenon at present that refers to some workers who retired involuntarily much earlier than the official retirement ages (60 years for men and 58 years for women). In fact, young job-waiters and early retirees are actually unemployed according to the unemployment definition of the International Labour Organization (ILO 2002) and should be counted in the unemployment statistics because they are willing to work or are seeking jobs, but there are no jobs available for them.[4]

Based on the above consideration, we will make two trials of estimates by using our surveys and the population censuses data.

*Table 3.3* Adjustment of urban registered unemployment (million, %)

| | *Officially registered unemployed* | | *Laid-off unemployed* | | | | | *Adjusted unemployed* | | *Urban labour force* | |
|---|---|---|---|---|---|---|---|---|---|---|---|
| | | | *Laid-off workers* | | *Re-employed* | | *Unemployed* | | | | |
| *Year* | *Number (a)* | *Rate (b)* | *Number (c)* | *Rate (d = c/(j–g))* | *Number (e)* | *Rate (f = e/c)* | *(g = c–e)* | *Number (h = a+g)* | *Rate (i = h/k)* | *Employed (j)* | *Labour force (k = h+j)* |
| 1993 | 4.20 | 2.60 | 3.00 | 1.66 | 1.21 | 40.3 | 1.79 | 5.99 | 3.2 | 182.62 | 188.61 |
| 1994 | 4.76 | 2.80 | 3.60 | 1.95 | 1.45 | 40.3 | 2.15 | 6.91 | 3.6 | 186.53 | 193.44 |
| 1995 | 5.20 | 2.90 | 5.64 | 3.02 | 2.27 | 40.2 | 3.37 | 8.57 | 4.3 | 190.4 | 198.97 |
| 1996 | 5.53 | 3.00 | 8.14 | 4.18 | 3.59 | 44.1 | 4.55 | 10.08 | 4.8 | 199.22 | 209.30 |
| 1997 | 5.70 | 3.10 | 12.74 | 6.32 | 6.40 | 50.2 | 6.34 | 12.04 | 5.5 | 207.81 | 219.85 |
| 1998 | 5.71 | 3.10 | 8.92 | 4.21 | 4.46 | 50.0 | 4.46 | 10.17 | 4.5 | 216.16 | 226.33 |
| 1999 | 5.75 | 3.10 | 9.37 | 4.27 | 4.69 | 50.0 | 4.69 | 10.44 | 4.4 | 224.12 | 234.56 |
| 2000 | 5.95 | 3.10 | 14.54 | 6.59 | 3.62 | 24.9 | 10.92 | 16.87 | 6.8 | 231.51 | 248.38 |

Source: (a), (b), (j), NBS (1996–2002), Mitsubishi Sogokenkyusho (2001: 380).

Notes:

(a) Laid-off worker data for 1996 and 1998 are calculated by the ratios of re-employed workers. See thhp//www.molss.gov.cn/tongji/gb1996.htm, and 1998.

(b) Labor force = employed + umemployed = employed + (registered unemployed + laid-off unemployed).

(c) The numbers of urban employed after 1990 are estimates made by the NBSC based on the data of the 2000 population census. Therefore, they differ from the figures published before 2001, which were estimated by the NBSC based on the 1990 population census data.

First, we make an estimate by using survey data of 1995 and 1999. Here, we define unemployment by classifying unemployment into four types:[5] (1) officially registered unemployed; (2) laid-off unemployed (laid-off workers who have not been re-employed, *xiagangshiye*); (3) young job-waiters; and (4) early retirees. Table 3.4 is the result and it demonstrates that the urban unemployment rate reached 9.5 per cent in 1995 and 11.6 per cent in 1999, three to four times higher than the officially stated figures. According to the above estimates, obviously the issue of urban unemployment in China is very serious and is becoming more so.

Second, we estimate urban unemployment by using the data of the population censuses from 1982, 1990 and 1995 (1 per cent sampling survey, treated as small census) and 2000. The purpose of doing this is to provide a time-series data of unemployment and compare it to our survey result.[6] However, there is a problem in using the data because of the incoherence of the definitions of urban unemployment. For example, there are three types of urban unemployment in the 1982 census: (a) city and town unemployed (*chengzhenshiye*), (b) persons waiting for job allocation, and (c) young job-waiters (see note 4). In the 1990 census, only (a) and (c) were defined as unemployed. In the 1995 sample survey, the new definition classified urban unemployment as (d) first job seeker, (e) job seeker after losing job, and (f) workers in an idling factory waiting for assignment. However, in the 2000 population census, the definition contains no (f) but only (d) and (e). We guess that these changes in definition are to illustrate the actual situation recently; for example, (b) reflects the situation of the labour market under the planned economy, in which most jobs were not hunted by job seekers but 'distributed' by government, (f) reflects the truth of *xiagang* and it is integrated into the definition of unemployment in the 2000 census. Although there is no unified definition, these are the most reliable figures we can obtain from the official statistical data.[7]

By using the population census data, we calculated the rate of urban unemployment as 4.2 per cent in 1982 and 1990, 7.7 per cent in 1995 and 11.5 per cent in 2000. Then, we use these figures as benchmarks and estimate urban unemployment rates by linking them with the adjusted unemployment data. Column (f) in Table 3.4 shows our estimates and they show that the real urban unemployment rates are two to three times higher than the officially stated figures and the adjusted official figures. Comparing our survey data to these estimates, we find that both figures are very similar. It might prove indirectly that our estimate is close to the accuracy of the current unemployment situation in China (see Figure 3.1).

### *3.2.4 Trend of urban unemployment*

Figure 3.1 illustrates the trend of urban unemployment. The real unemployment rate is 11.5 per cent calculated from the 2000 population census data and 11.6 per cent from the 1999 survey, which means that the numbers of urban unemployed are 22.2 million and 21.6 million,[8] five times as large as the official figures.[9] The urban unemployment rate declined in the early 1980s and rose slowly from 1986. After a slight descent in 1989, it rose rapidly after 1990 and reached two digits after 1997. This change can be explained as the consequences of the acceleration of

*Table 3.4* Estimates of China's urban unemployment rate (%)

| Year | Benchmark (census data) (a) | Officially registered unemployment (b) | Adjusted unemployment (c = a + laid-off unemployed) | Link ratio: Times (d = a/b) | Link ratio: Ratio (e = d/interval years) | Estimated unemployment (f = b*e) | Survey ratio (g) |
|---|---|---|---|---|---|---|---|
| 1980 | | 4.9 | | | | 2.8 | |
| 1981 | | 3.8 | | | | 2.9 | |
| *1982* | *4.2* | 3.2 | | 1.3 | 0.1647 | *3.0* | |
| 1983 | | 2.3 | | | 1.0495 | 2.4 | |
| 1984 | | 1.9 | | | 1.1659 | 2.2 | |
| 1985 | | 1.8 | | | 1.2824 | 2.3 | |
| 1986 | | 2.0 | | | 1.3989 | 2.8 | |
| 1987 | | 2.0 | | | 1.5154 | 3.0 | |
| 1988 | | 2.0 | | | 1.6318 | 3.3 | |
| 1989 | | 2.6 | | | 1.7483 | 4.5 | |
| *1990* | *4.2* | 2.5 | | 1.7 | 0.3398 | *4.2* | |
| 1991 | | 2.3 | | | 2.0387 | 4.7 | |
| 1992 | | 2.3 | | | 2.3785 | 5.5 | |
| 1993 | | 2.6 | 3.2 | | 2.7183 | 7.1 | |
| 1994 | | 2.8 | 3.6 | | 3.0581 | 8.6 | |

(Continued)

*Table 3.4* (Continued)

| *Year* | *Benchmark (census data)* | *Officially registered unemployment* | *Adjusted unemployment* | *Link ratio* | | *Estimated unemployment* | *Survey ratio* |
|---|---|---|---|---|---|---|---|
| | | | | *Times* | *Ratio* | | |
| | *(a)* | *(b)* | *(c = a + laid-off unemployed)* | *(d = a/b)* | *(e = d/interval years)* | *(f = b*e)* | *(g)* |
| *1995* | *7.7* | 2.9 | 4.3 | 2.7 | 0.5320 | *7.7* | *9.6** |
| 1996 | | 3.0 | 4.8 | | 2.4320 | 7.3 | |
| 1997 | | 3.1 | 5.5 | | 2.9640 | 9.2 | |
| 1998 | | 3.1 | 4.5 | | 3.4960 | 10.8 | |
| 1999 | | 3.1 | 4.4 | | 4.0280 | 12.5 | *11.6*** |
| *2000* | *11.5* | 3.1 | 6.8 | 3.7 | 4.3055 | *11.5* | |

Sources:
(a) Benchmarks are calculated based on the data of Tabulations of the 1982, 1990 and 2000 population censuses and the 1995 1% sampling survey. See Population Census Office of the State Council and the NBSC, *Tabulation of the 1982 Population Census in China*, pp.36–37, 468–469; *Tabulation of the 1990 Population Census in China*, pp.502–518; *Tabulation of the 1995 1% Population Sampling Survey in China* and NBS (1996–2002); *Tabulation of the 1990 Population Census in China*, pp.318–326; *Tabulation of the 2000 Population Census of China*, Vol. 2, pp.1241–1489.
(b) NBS (1996–2002).
* and ** are computed from the 1995 and 1999 CASS surveys.

Note:
(d) is the ratio of benchmark versus official figures.
(e) = (d/years of interval) + d (with an increasing trend).

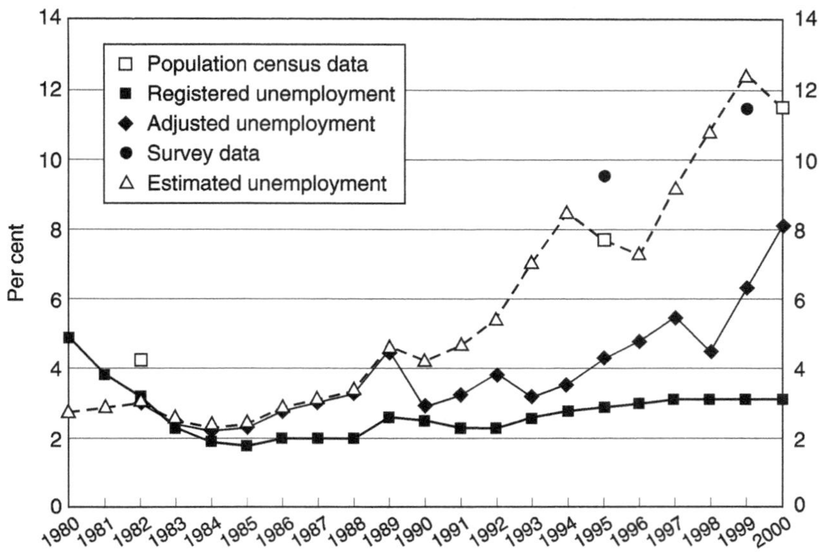


*Figure 3.1* Comparison of urban unemployment rates.

the market economy and the speedy reform of SOEs in the process of restructuring and productivity improvement.

### *3.2.5 Structure of urban unemployment*

Table 3.4 shows that urban unemployment is very serious in present-day China. Here, we will explore the main causes of the increase. In order to do so, we analyse the structure of urban unemployment and its regional distribution by using the panel data from the 1999 survey. Table 3.5 provides information on urban unemployment by types and provinces. On the structure of unemployment, we found that the laid-off unemployment rate is the highest in the four types of unemployment. Noticeably, the laid-off unemployment is the main part of urban unemployment and a major factor in the rising urban unemployment rate. This might be the most valuable and meaningful finding in our study.

Table 3.5 also demonstrates that unemployment rates differ among provinces. For example, in the western provinces of Henan, Sichuan and Gansu, the rates are 15.3, 14.4 and 13.2 per cent, respectively, certainly higher than in the eastern provinces of Jiangsu and Beijing, which are 7.5 and 6.3 per cent, respectively. Among provinces, Henan and Sichuan have the highest rates, reflecting their problem of large population and surplus labour.

## 3.3 Unemployment, migration and urban poverty

In this section, we will study urban poverty and analyse the factors causing it by verifying its relations with unemployment and with migration and poverty.

*Table 3.5* Types and rates of unemployment by province

| *Types* | *Sample/Rate* | *Officially registered unemployed* | *Young job-waiter* | *Laid-off unemployed* | *Earlier retired* | *Total unemployed* | *Total samples* |
|---|---|---|---|---|---|---|---|
| Liaoning | Sample | 11 | 74 | 67 | 38 | 190 | 1,487 |
| | Rate (%) | 0.7 | 5.0 | 4.5 | 2.6 | 12.8 | 100.0 |
| Jiangsu | Sample | 9 | 25 | 43 | 19 | 96 | 1,280 |
| | Rate (%) | 0.7 | 2.0 | 3.4 | 1.5 | 7.5 | 100.0 |
| Beijing | Sample | 20 | 9 | 17 | 33 | 79 | 1,252 |
| | Rate (%) | 1.6 | 0.7 | 1.4 | 2.6 | 6.3 | 100.0 |
| Henan | Sample | 14 | 25 | 106 | 13 | 158 | 1,031 |
| | Rate (%) | 1.4 | 2.4 | 10.3 | 1.3 | 15.3 | 100.0 |
| Sichuan | Sample | 25 | 30 | 99 | 27 | 181 | 1,254 |
| | Rate (%) | 2.0 | 2.4 | 7.9 | 2.2 | 14.4 | 100.0 |
| Gansu | Sample | 19 | 35 | 92 | 25 | 171 | 1,300 |
| | Rate (%) | 1.5 | 2.7 | 7.1 | 1.9 | 13.2 | 100.0 |
| Overall | Sample | 98 | 198 | 424 | 155 | 875 | 7,604 |
| | Rate (%) | 1.3 | 2.6 | 5.6 | 2.0 | 11.6 | 100.0 |

Source: The 1999 CASS survey.

Note: All samples are valid samples and individuals refer to ages 15–59 for men and 15–54 for women.

### *3.3.1 Poverty, poverty index and poverty line*

Poverty refers to a situation in which a person or family lacks the minimum standard of living. It is defined by a poverty line. The poverty line is the minimum expenditure on goods and services for a person or family. There are many poverty indexes such as income standard, consumption standard, nutritional standard, and so on. Here, we use income standard as the poverty index bearing in mind the strong preference for saving among the Chinese people. Because of the limitation of nutritional data in our survey, we will use the income index provided by the NBSC as our poverty line (2,152 yuan in 1999[10]). Meanwhile, we will set this standard as our poverty line for all the survey provinces and cities owing to the lack of price indexes for the sample cities in our survey.

### *3.3.2 Urban poverty rates*

To calculate urban poverty in a different way from previous studies, we classified the sample into three groups, urban households without unemployed, urban households with unemployed people, and migrant households.

Table 3.6 shows that the poverty rate for households with unemployed people was 19.9 per cent in 1999, nearly four times higher than that for households without unemployed (5.1 per cent). It is clear that the poverty problem is much more serious in households with unemployed people than in households without unemployed people.

*Table 3.6* Poverty rates by groups

| | *Frequency* | *Valid %* |
|---|---|---|
| *(1) Urban households without unemployed* | | |
| Non-poverty households | 11,448 | 94.9 |
| Poverty households | 612 | 5.1 |
| Subtotal | 12,060 | 100.0 |
| *(2) Urban households with unemployed* | | |
| Non-poverty households | 1,210 | 80.1 |
| Poverty households | 300 | 19.9 |
| Subtotal | 1,510 | 100.0 |
| *(3) Migrant households* | | |
| Non-poverty households | 1,553 | 87.1 |
| Poverty households | 230 | 12.9 |
| Subtotal | 1,783 | 100.0 |
| *(4) Urban mixed households* | | |
| Non-poverty households | 12,658 | 93.3 |
| Poverty households | 912 | 6.7 |
| Subtotal | 13,570 | 100.0 |
| *(5) All groups* | 15,353 | 7.4 |

Source: Valid samples from the 1999 CASS survey.

One of the features of this study is that we put the poverty issue of migrant households into the urban poverty study framework. As we know, with the reform of the urban labour market and the limited permission of migration of non-urban registered residents to the urban area in recent years,[11] more and more rural migrants have been rushing into the cities. Some of these migrants hold formal jobs, have a stable income and live with their families within the city for years and differ little from urban registered residents except for their rural resident status (*nongcun hukou*). In this case, urban registration has become less of a barrier for migrants to enter cities. Therefore, we should treat them not as being in the 'rural labour force or farmer' category but as urban residents, called 'the new urban migrants' (*chengshixinyimin*). For this reason, we try to analyse the urban poverty issue by taking migrants as a special group of urban residents. We calculate the poverty rate of migrant households and compare it to that of urban registered households. As a result, we observed that the poverty rate of migrant households is 14 per cent in 1999, higher than that of households without unemployed but lower than that of households with unemployed people. However, this rate might be low because migrant household samples in our survey were small and the definition is very narrow. It would be much higher if we had surveyed more migrant households, including those who lived in the city temporarily without stable income and/or a fixed dwelling.[12] Regarding the effect of poor migrant households on urban poverty, we found that the total urban poverty rate rose to 7.4 per cent, which is higher than that of all urban registered households (6.7 per cent) when we included migrant households.

We can conclude from the above analysis that: (1) urban poverty in China is a kind of 'structural poverty' and includes the general poverty of the urban registered households and the particular poverty of the urban households with unemployed people and migrant households, which means that we should be concerned not only about rates but also about the structure of urban poverty; (2) extreme urban poverty occurs mainly in households with unemployed people; therefore, we should pay great attention to this group; and (3) migrant poverty is a new problem and worth studying further. We think that these findings are important not only for theoretical studies but also for policy making for reducing poverty.

### *3.3.3 Unemployment and poverty*

It is true that poverty is connected with educational levels, family size, age, and so on, as is pointed out in the literature (Zhang and Wei 1999). However, considering the recent development in China, we should look for other factors affecting urban poverty. Unemployment is one of them. Table 3.7 shows that the poverty rate is 13.2 per cent for households with unemployed people and only 2.8 per cent for households without unemployed people. As the simulation indicated, unemployed members increase from one person to three persons and over, and the poverty rate rises from 10.5 per cent to 50.1 per cent. Observably, poverty is very sensitive to unemployment.

Households with unemployed people suffer from low income and fall easily into poverty. In a comparison of poverty rates by cities, the poverty rate of households with unemployed people is higher than that of households without unemployed, and the more members of a household that are unemployed, the higher the poverty rate (see Table 3.8). Regression analysis shows that there is a strong correlation between the unemployment rate and the poverty rate by city (coefficient of correlation = 0.854). Consequently, we can conclude from the above analysis that unemployment is a significant source of urban poverty.

### *3.3.4 Migrant and urban poverty*

To study poverty of migrant households and its effect on total urban poverty, we did a sensitivity analysis of migrants and poverty. Table 3.9 demonstrates that the poverty rate for all urban households rose from 5.3 to 5.5 and 5.6 per cent as the percentage of migrant households in all urban households increased from 2.6 to 5 and 6.7 per cent. The larger the share of migrant households, the higher the total poverty rate.

On the other hand, Table 3.9 shows that as the percentage of migrant households in all urban registered households increases from 2.6 to 6.7 per cent, the percentage of poor households in migrant households rises from 6.3 to 15.4 per cent, while the share of urban registered households falls from 93.7 to 84.6 per cent. The increasing speed of poverty for migrant households (14.4 per cent) is much higher than the decreasing speed of poverty for urban registered households

*Table 3.7* The relationship of unemployment and poverty

| *Types of household* | *Samples/Rates* | *Persons of non-poverty* | *Persons of poverty* | *Total* |
|---|---|---|---|---|
| Households without unemployed | Number of samples | 9,129 | 259 | 9,388 |
| | Rate of poverty | 97.2 | 2.8 | 100 |
| | Rate of poor person in households without unemployed | 79.7 | 42.3 | 78 |
| Households with unemployed | Number of samples | 2,319 | 353 | 2,672 |
| | Rate of poverty | 86.8 | 13.2 | 100 |
| | Rate of poor person in households with unemployed | 20.3 | 57.7 | 22 |
| Total | Number of samples | 11,448 | 612 | 12,060 |
| | Rate of poverty | 94.9 | 5.1 | 100.0 |
| | Rate of poor person in all households | 100.0 | 100.0 | 100.0 |

| *Numbers of unemployed in households* | *Rate of poverty* | *Number of samples* |
|---|---|---|
| None | 2.8 | 9,388 |
| One person | 10.5 | 2,242 |
| Two persons | 23.7 | 375 |
| Three persons and over | 50.9 | 55 |
| Total | 5.1 | 12,060 |

Source: The 1999 CASS survey.

(−9.7 per cent), although the change in percentage points is the same (9.1). This means that migrant households are more sensitive to poverty than urban registered households.

The surprising fact is that the poverty rate of migrant households reached 12.9 per cent in 1999, 2.5 times higher than that of urban registered households (5.1 per cent). It suggests that poor migrant households are the expanding urban poverty group and are changing the structure of urban poverty. We may be the first to point out this phenomenon, which future studies might want to take note of.

## 3.4 Unemployment, poverty and urban income inequality

In this section, we will analyse the income distribution of urban registered households, urban households with unemployed people, migrant households, and their effects on urban income distribution.

*Table 3.8* Comparison of the poverty ratios of households with unemployed and without unemployed

| *Province* | *City* | *Households without unemployed* | | *Households with unemployed* | | *Mixed households* | |
|---|---|---|---|---|---|---|---|
| | | *HC index* | *Frequency* | *HC index* | *Frequency* | *HC index* | *Frequency* |
| Liaoning | | 3.35 | 1,461 | 10.40 | 529 | 5.23 | 1,990 |
| | Shengyang | 1.79 | 1,059 | 9.30 | 312 | 3.50 | 1,371 |
| | Jinzhou | 7.46 | 402 | 11.98 | 217 | 9.05 | 619 |
| Jiangsu | | 0.26 | 1,558 | 2.41 | 291 | 0.59 | 1,849 |
| | Nanjing | 0.37 | 1,095 | 1.74 | 172 | 0.55 | 1,267 |
| | Xuzhou | 0.00 | 463 | 3.36 | 119 | 0.69 | 582 |
| Beijing | | 0.19 | 1,585 | 0.00 | 237 | 0.16 | 1,822 |
| | Beijing | 0.19 | 1,585 | 0.00 | 237 | 0.16 | 1,822 |
| Henan | | 4.27 | 1,640 | 24.61 | 512 | 9.11 | 2,152 |
| | Zhengzhou | 4.12 | 729 | 20.30 | 202 | 7.63 | 931 |
| | Kaifeng | 7.96 | 377 | 30.47 | 233 | 16.56 | 610 |
| | Pingdingshan | 1.87 | 534 | 18.18 | 77 | 3.93 | 611 |
| Sichuan | | 3.95 | 1,772 | 17.06 | 598 | 7.26 | 2,370 |
| | Chengdu | 2.32 | 947 | 6.41 | 234 | 3.13 | 1,181 |
| | Zigong | 6.40 | 375 | 29.46 | 241 | 15.42 | 616 |
| | Nanchong | 5.33 | 450 | 13.01 | 123 | 6.98 | 573 |
| Gangsu | | 4.59 | 1,372 | 12.48 | 505 | 6.71 | 1,877 |
| | Lianzhou | 2.14 | 887 | 12.43 | 370 | 5.17 | 1,257 |
| | Pingliang | 9.07 | 485 | 12.59 | 135 | 9.84 | 620 |

Source: The 1999 CASS survey.

### *3.4.1 Income distribution of urban households*

We divide the income distribution of all urban households into three groups: urban registered households, households with unemployed people, and migrant households. For the purpose of comparison, we calculate inequality indexes: the Gini coefficient, the Theil index and the coefficient of variation.

Table 3.10 indicates that the Gini coefficient was 0.3175 for urban registered households in 1999. Compared to the figure of 0.225 in 1995, there was a 40 per cent increase over the four-year period. The Gini coefficients were 0.2868, 0.2983 and 0.4498 for households without unemployed people, households with unemployed people and migrant households, respectively. Income distribution is slightly worse among households with unemployed people than among households without unemployed people. Both the Gini coefficient (0.4498) and the Theil index (0.7209) show that income inequality is greater among migrant households.

### *3.4.2 Effects of unemployment and poverty on urban income distribution*

Table 3.10 shows that the Gini coefficient for households with unemployed people is 0.2983, 4 per cent higher than for households without unemployed

*Table 3.9* Sensitivity analysis of poverty (%)

| | *Items* | *Case (1) 2.6% shares of migrant households* | | *Case (2) 5% shares of migrant households* | | *Case (3) 6.7% shares of migrant households* | |
|---|---|---|---|---|---|---|---|
| | | *Shares of samples* | *Poverty ratio* | *Shares of samples* | *Poverty ratio* | *Shares of samples* | *Poverty ratio* |
| 1 | Urban registered households | 97.4 | 5.1 | 95 | 5.1 | 93.3 | 5.1 |
| 2 | Households without unemployed | 75.8 | 2.8 | 74.0 | 2.8 | 72.6 | 2.8 |
| 3 | Households with unemployed | 21.6 | 13.2 | 21.0 | 13.2 | 20.7 | 13.2 |
| 4 | Migrant households | 2.6 | 12.9 | 5.0 | 12.9 | 6.7 | 12.9 |
| 5 | All households | 100 | 5.3 | 100 | 5.5 | 100 | 5.6 |
| Number distribution of poverty (ratio of poverty of each group to total poverty population): | | | | | | | |
| 1 | Urban registered households | | 93.7 | | 88.3 | | 84.6 |
| 2 | Households without unemployed | | 40.0 | | 37.7 | | 36.2 |
| 3 | Households with unemployed | | 53.7 | | 50.6 | | 48.5 |
| 4 | Migrant households | | 6.3 | | 11.7 | | 15.4 |
| 5 | All households | | 100.0 | | 100.0 | | 100.0 |

Source: The 1999 CASS survey.

Notes:
(a) 1=2+3, 5=1+4
(b) The shares of (1), (2) and (3) refer to the shares of the migrant households in all samples.

*Table 3.10* Comparison of some inequality indexes

| *Index/Group* | *Households without unemployed (1)* | *Households with unemployed (2)* | *All migrant households (3)* | *Urban registered households (4=1+2)* | *All urban households (5=1+2+6)* | *2.6% samples in urban households (6)* | *All urban households (7=1+2+8)* | *5% samples in urban households (8)* | *All urban households (9=1+2+10)* | *6.7% samples in urban households (10)* |
|---|---|---|---|---|---|---|---|---|---|---|
| Samples | 9,388 | 2,668 | 1,781 | 12,056 | 12,380 | 324 | 12,690 | 634 | 12,921 | 865 |
| Mean income | 7,013 | 4,423 | 6,832 | 6,440 | 6,433 | 6,155 | 6,433 | 6,291 | 6,484 | 7,094 |
| Coefficient of variation | 0.5872 | 0.6247 | 2.0147 | 0.6221 | 0.6357 | 1.0468 | 0.6481 | 1.0371 | 0.9354 | 2.5423 |
| Theil index($I_0$) | 0.3057 | 0.3420 | 0.7209 | 0.3577 | 0.3659 | 0.6581 | 0.3736 | 0.6701 | 0.3832 | 0.7706 |
| Gini coefficient | 0.2868 | 0.2983 | 0.4498 | 0.3049 | 0.3078 | 0.4083 | 0.3110 | 0.4171 | 0.3175 | 0.4672 |
| Ratio of sample | Household without unemployed | | | 0.7787 | 0.7583 | | 0.7398 | | 0.7266 | |
| | Household with unemployed | | | 0.2213 | 0.2155 | | 0.2102 | | 0.2065 | |
| | Migrant household | | | | 0.0262 | | 0.0500 | | 0.0669 | |
| Inequality of intra-group | | | | 0.3138 | 0.3228 | | 0.3316 | | 0.3443 | |
| Inequality of inter-group | | | | 0.0439 | 0.0431 | | 0.0421 | | 0.0389 | |
| Contribution of inequality of intra-group to total inequality | | | | 87.72 | 88.21 | | 88.74 | | 89.85 | |
| Contribution of inequality of inter-group to total inequality | | | | 12.28 | 11.79 | | 11.26 | | 10.15 | |

Source: The1999 CASS survey.

people (0.2868). However, the Theil index is 0.3420 for households with unemployed people, 12 per cent higher than for the households without unemployed people (0.3050). By both measures, unemployment had a negative effect on income distribution.

### *3.4.3 Effect of migrant households on urban income distribution*

We perceive from Table 3.10 that the Gini coefficient of migrant households is 0.4498, 48 per cent higher than that of urban registered households (0.3049), and the Theil index is 0.7209 for migrant households, twice as high as for urban registered households (0.3577). According to the above figures, we imply that the effect of migrant households on income distribution is much larger than that of urban registered households.[13]

To prove the above hypothesis, we conducted a simulation in Table 3.10. We found that as the percentage of migrants in the total increased, all inequality indexes become larger. The larger the share of migrants, the worse the income distribution became. The conclusion is that the income distribution of migrant households has a strong effect on overall urban income distribution.

### *3.4.4 Factors causing urban income inequality*

There are many factors causing urban income inequality. However, in this chapter, we try to explore some new sources in addition to such factors as education, age, status of job or position, and so on. As is revealed in the above analysis, we found that unemployment, poverty and migration are new factors affecting urban income inequality.

For further analysis of the main factors affecting income distribution, we conducted a decomposition analysis. At the bottom of Table 3.10, the contributions of the inequality of each group to total inequality are indicated. It shows that intra-group inequality (0.3138) is greater than inter-group inequality (0.0439). Meanwhile, the intra-group contribution is larger than the inter-group contribution (88:12) to total inequality. This means that urban income disparity comes mainly from intra-group inequality, namely, the unequal income distribution in each group.

## 3.5 Conclusion

The main findings and conclusions of the chapter can be summarized as follows. Urban unemployment is very serious and becoming a social and political problem in China. Based on the 1999 survey, we observed that the urban unemployment rate is as high as 11.5 per cent, nearly three times the officially stated figure. Meanwhile, we found that urban unemployment had an increasing trend in the 1990s. We also revealed that the rapid increase of laid-off unemployed from the restructuring of SOEs and COEs is the main cause of rising urban unemployment.

Urban poverty is not only a new phenomenon but also a serious problem in China. Our survey data show that the urban poverty rate for urban registered households was as high as 6.7 per cent in 1999, and there has been a rising trend since 1995. We also found that urban unemployment has a strong correlation with urban poverty, and it is a new cause of urban poverty.

Income distribution among urban households has worsened. By classifying households into subgroups, we found that income inequality is larger among households with unemployed people than among households without unemployed. Income inequality is highest within the migrant household group. Unemployment and poverty, especially the poverty of urban households with unemployed people and migrant households, are worsening urban income distribution and are becoming the main reasons for rising urban inequality. Especially, the increase of poor migrant households is widening urban inequality.

Most studies of urban income distribution in the past have focused on calculating inequality indexes and finding the components causing inequality. However, because urban unemployment and poverty have been increasing dramatically, greater concentration is needed on these two issues. Meanwhile, as more and more rural migrants come into urban areas, the migrant household's poverty and its influence on urban poverty and urban income distribution deserve attention. All these subjects should be the focus of future research into urban income distribution in China.

## Notes

This chapter is the revised version based on the original paper cited from *Asian Economic Journal*, Vol. 17, No. 4, 2003. We are grateful to the editorial board of *Asian Economic Journal* and Blackwell Publishing for granting us permission to reproduce it. We also thank Professor John Knight (University of Oxford), Professor Lina Song (University of Nottingham), Professor Li Shi (CASS), Professor Colin R. McKenzie (Keio University) and William A. McBean (Oita University) for their comments and great help.

1 See Wei and Gustafsson (1999) and Chapter 7 by Li Shi in this volume.
2 We define rural migrants as those who have a fixed address or house, have formal jobs and stable income, and have been living in the urban area for longer than 6 months. In this case, we take them to be new urban residents because they differ little from urban residents except for urban registration status.
3 According to the current bureaucratic system, economic growth and urban unemployment are the two important criteria for appreciating local government officers' political achievements during their terms. Therefore, some local government officers prefer to over-report the economic growth rate and under-report the unemployment rate intentionally in order to keep a good political record or get higher appreciation.
4 Some young persons are exceptional in that they are not willing to work or they want to wait for another chance of having higher education after failing the university entrance exam (*fudu, luobansheng*). However, these numbers are relatively small. It is difficult to judge whether they really want or are forced to have higher education (e.g. lacking good working opportunities).
5 It is very difficult to define unemployment following the ILO unemployment definition because of the lack of data and the complex current situation in China.
6 For details of the estimate, see Xue and Knight (2002). In addition, Xue and Minami (2002) made a time-series estimate of urban unemployment for 1949–1999 by using the data of urban unemployment and labour force from the population censuses of 1982, 1990 and 1995.

7 Although there are some criticisms of the population census data, they are much better than other official data and some informal survey data, considering the methodology, process, checking system and seriousness of the census.

8 Number of unemployed = labour force × 'unemployment rate (urban employed + urban unemployed) × unemployment rate. The figure of urban employed is the estimated number based on the 2000 population census data.

9 The official figure of unemployment (5.8 million) is not matched to the real figure. We know from officials of the NBSC that the rates and figures were not statistics but 'reported' by local governments and the relative functional government departments. Even they do not know how the figures were calculated. Obviously, the figure is not reliable.

10 The NBSC defines the poverty line by estimating the minimum calories for a person and then converting the calories into food expenditures, based on a large random sampling survey covering 17,000 urban households in 1998. The poverty line in 1999 is calculated by an adjustment of income and price index.

11 Some cities have carried out the so-called Blue Card Registration System (*lanyin-hukou*) and permitted limited migrants to live longer in urban areas. Meanwhile, some cities are experimenting to repeal the urban registration system (Xue 1999).

12 For an analysis of rural migrants and their lives in urban areas, see details in Xue (1999).

13 In the 1999 survey, there were cases of annual per capita income over 200,000 yuan in some rich households and less than 2,000 yuan in some poor households.

## References

Griffin, K. and Zhao, R. (eds) (1993) *The Distribution of Income in China*, London: Macmillan.

International Labour Organization (2002) *Yearbook of International Labour Statistics 2001*, Geneva: ILO.

Khan, A.R. and Riskin, C. (1998) 'Income inequality in China: composition, distribution and growth of households income, 1988 to 1995', *The China Quarterly*, 154: 221–53.

Khan, A.R. and Riskin C. (1999) 'Poverty analysis in the period of economic reform and development in China', in Zhao, Li and Riskin (eds) (1999).

Mitsubishi Sogo Kenkyusho (ed.) (2001) *Handbook of Chinese Information 2001*, Tokyo: Mitsubishi Sogokenkyusho.

National Bureau of Statistics (NBS) (1996–2002) *Zhongguo Tongji Nianjian* (China Statistical Yearbook), Beijing: China Statistics Press.

Population Census Office of the State Council and National Bureau of Statistics (1985) *Zhonguo 1982 Nian Renkou Pucha Ziliao* (The 1982 Population Census of China), Beijing: China Statistics Press.

Population Census Office of the State Council and National Bureau of Statistics (1993) *Zhonguo 1990 Nian Renkou Pucha Ziliao* (The 1990 Population Census of China), Beijing: China Statistics Press.

Population Census Office of the State Council and National Bureau of Statistics (1996) *1995 Nian Quanguo 1 per cent Renkou Chouyang Diaocha Ziliao* (The 1995 1 per cent Population Sampling Survey of China), Beijing: China Statistics Press.

Population Census Office of the State Council and National Bureau of Statistics (2002) *Zhonguo 2000 Nian Renkou Pucha Ziliao* (The 2000 Population Census of China), Beijing: China Statistics Press.

Wei, Z. and Gustafsson, B. (1999) 'Zhongguo zhuanxing shiqi de pinkun biandong fenxi' (An analysis of changes in poverty under the systemic transition in China), in Zhao, Li and Riskin (eds) (1999).

World Bank (1985) *China: Long-Term Issues and Options*, Baltimore: Johns Hopkins University Press.

Xue, J. (1999) 'Rural labour migration and labour market in urban China', *Economic Review of Oita University*, 51: 17–37.

Xue, J. and Minami, R. (2002) 'Estimate of population and labour force in China: 1949–99', *Zhongguo Renkou Keshue*, 2002(3): 1–16.

Xue, J. and Knight, J (2002) 'An estimation of China's urban unemployment', mimeo.

Zhao, R,. Li, S. and Riskin, C. (eds) (1999) *Zhongguo Shourufenpei Zaiyanjiu* (Re-examination of the Distribution of Household Income in China), Beijing: China Finance and Economics Publisher.

Zhang, W. and Wei, Z. (1999) 'Zhongguo chengzhen jumin de pinkun wenti' (Poverty issue of urban households in China), in Zhao, Li and Riskin (eds) (1999).

# 4 Economic restructuring and income inequality in urban China

*Xin Meng*

## 4.1 Introduction

Economic transition from a planned to a market-oriented economy is often associated with a widening of income inequality (see Gustafsson and Li 1997, 1998, 2001; Milanovic 1997; Brainerd 1998; Flemming and Micklewright 2000; Khan, Griffin and Riskin 1999; Yang 1999; among others). Such an increase, however, may be induced by different forces and may affect social stability in different ways. One type of increase in income inequality can be as a result of a reform-induced economic gain that is distributed more to high-income than to low-income groups. Another type can be as a result of economic restructuring. As a labour market liberalizes, the disparity in the rate of returns to low and high skills may enlarge. In addition, economic restructuring will reallocate labour from a previously distorted state sector to the market sector, inducing both large-scale unemployment and a sectoral shift in employment (Flemming and Micklewright 2000). Such a restructuring may reduce incomes at the lower end while increasing incomes at the higher end of the income distribution. In terms of generating social instability, the type of increase in income inequality that reduces incomes at the lower end of the distribution may be particularly worrisome.

In contrast to most Eastern European countries, economic restructuring in China took place gradually. Although it began in the late 1970s, little had changed in urban areas in terms of wage determination, job security and sectoral composition of employment until the late 1980s to the early 1990s (Meng 2000). This gradual approach may have affected the way in which the increase in income inequality in China differs from that in the Eastern European economies during the initial stages of economic reform. For example, according to Flemming and Micklewright (2000), the significant increase in income inequality in most Eastern European countries was accompanied by income increases at the top together with decreases at the bottom of the distribution, whereas Zhao and Li (1999) indicate that during the period 1988–1995, income for the top 3 per cent of households in urban China increased by 53 per cent and for the bottom 20 per cent it increased by 20 per cent. Thus, until the mid-1990s, although the income distribution widened, everybody was better off. As a result, the widening income distribution during this period generated limited social and political concerns.

Since the mid-1990s, however, economic restructuring in urban China has accelerated in the areas of state enterprise reform, social security reform and labour market reform. As a result, the state and collective employment share has reduced from 76 per cent of total urban employment in 1995 to 49 per cent in 1999 and unemployment has increased significantly. Although official unemployment figures have been kept very low, at around 3 per cent, several different estimates suggest that as many as 15 to 27 million state sector workers were laid off (*xiagang*) in 1999, which accounts for an additional 7 to 12 per cent of the urban labour force (Fan 2000; Appleton *et al.* 2001).

Questions naturally arise as to whether the acceleration of economic restructuring has changed the nature of the increase in income inequality in urban China and to what extent the increase in inequality after the mid-1990s is due to economic restructuring. Using three comparable urban household surveys, this chapter investigates these questions by comparing the change in income inequality between the periods 1988–1995 and 1995–1999 and identifying the different contributing factors to the changes in each period. Answers to these questions may add to our knowledge about the relationship between the process of economic transition and income distribution and help policy makers to formulate more appropriate policies to establish social stability.

Previous studies on changes in income inequality in China focused mainly on the period up to the mid-1990s (Knight and Song 1991; Khan, Griffin and Zhao 1992; Aaberge and Li 1997; Gustafsson and Li 1997, 1998, 2001; Knight and Li 1999; Yang 1999; Khan and Riskin 2000; Riskin, Zhao and Li 2001). Due to the lack of available data, there are, as yet, no published studies on recent developments. In early 2000, however, the Institute of Economics at the Chinese Academy of Social Sciences, with assistance from the China Statistical Bureau, conducted a new household income distribution survey, which collected information on household income and expenditure in 1999 in six provinces. This chapter utilizes this new survey together with two other comparable surveys conducted by the same Institute for the years 1988 and 1995.

In addition to studying the most recent developments in income inequality, this study adopts a new methodology. Most previous studies of income inequality in China adopt methodologies that allow only for a limited number of contributing factors (see, e.g., Aaberge and Li, 1997; Gustafsson and Li 1998, 2001). This study employs a regression-based decomposition approach developed by Fields (1998) that permits an assessment of a wider range of contributing factors.

The chapter is structured as follows. The next section provides background information on the process of economic reform in urban China, its relationship to income distribution, and data and summary statistics on income inequality. Section 4.3 describes methodology. Section 4.4 investigates the contributing factors to the level and the change in income inequality. Concluding remarks and policy implications are given in Section 4.5.

## 4.2 Background and data

China has experienced rapid economic growth since economic reforms began in the late 1970s. During the period 1978–1999, per capita real GDP increased by 8.3 per cent per year. Household income also increased considerably but varied from period to period. The annual increase in urban household real income was 5.6, 8.3 and 7.3 per cent for the periods 1982–1988, 1988–1995 and 1995–1999, respectively (China State Statistical Bureau 2000).

Income inequality also increased. The World Bank (1997) reports that the Gini coefficient for China as a whole increased from 28.2 per cent in 1981 to 38.8 per cent in 1995. This increase also varied across different periods of economic reform. Before the early 1990s, economic reform was mainly concentrated on product markets and little was changed in terms of the compressed wage structure, immobility of labour, and the domination of state sector employment (Meng 2000). Consequently, income distribution changed very slightly and was remarkably egalitarian during this period (Khan and Riskin 2001).

Factor market reform proceeded gradually from the early 1990s. By the mid-1990s, labour mobility across urban regions and between rural and urban areas increased (see, e.g., Meng 2000; West and Zhao 2000) and the rate of return to different levels of labour market skills widened (Knight and Song 1999). Accompanying this reform process, income inequality increased sharply (Khan, Griffin and Zhao 1992; Aaberge and Li 1997; Gustafsson and Li 1997, 1998, 2001; Knight and Li 1999; Yang 1999; Khan and Riskin 2001; Riskin, Zhao and Li 2001). Gustafsson and Li (2001) report that the Gini coefficients of household income for urban areas in ten provinces increased from 22.8 in 1988 to 27.6 in 1995. Using the same data, Khan and Riskin (2001) report a larger increase in the Gini coefficient from 23.3 to 33.2 for the same period.[1] Increase in regional dispersion is identified as one of the main contributors to the increase in income inequality in this period (see, e.g., Gustafsson and Li 2001; Khan and Riskin 2001).

Since 1995, urban economic reform has taken a sharp turn. Due to soft budget constraints and other property rights-related problems, the Chinese state sector has been performing badly. In 1995–1996, around 50 per cent of enterprises were making losses. To vitalize the Chinese economy, the policy of radical reform for the state enterprises was introduced in 1997 (Appleton *et al.* 2001). Many small and medium-sized loss-making state enterprises were bankrupted as a result of this policy and the survivors began to take efficiency measures seriously. These two forces led to large-scale retrenchments. Fan (2000) estimates an accumulation of 15 million state sector workers being laid off in 2000, whereas Appleton *et al.* (2001) estimate the number to be 27.7 million. The 1995 and 1999 CASS surveys reveal that the urban unemployment rate defined to include laid-off workers increased from 8 per cent to 17 per cent over this period.

Such significant economic restructuring, leading to large increases in unemployment, may widen the income distribution in a number of important ways. Initially, most of the unemployed who lose employment income may be pushed into the lower end of the income distribution and the income distribution may widen. As time passes, high unemployment is likely to have other effects. Wage levels among the unskilled who compete with the unemployed may fall, leading to a further widening of the income distribution generated by a widening wage distribution among those with jobs. In addition, the ability of the unemployed to re-enter the workforce under conditions similar to the previous income levels may vary considerably and may have long-term income distribution effects. For example, young, educated and energetic workers who are laid off may easily find better-paid jobs elsewhere in the economy or set up their own businesses, while laid-off workers who are older or less skilled may fall into long-term unemployment or accept jobs in the lower-paid informal sector.

This study uses 1988, 1995 and 1999 CASS surveys. The questionnaires were designed in a relatively consistent manner for the three years indicated and provide a good basis for a comparative study. The sample size for the three years is 8,992, 6,930 and 4,493 households, respectively. For 1988 the survey mainly covers ten provinces, including Beijing, Shanxi, Jiangsu, Liaoning, Anhui, Henan, Hubei, Guangdong, Yunnan and Gansu.[2] In 1995, Sichuan province is added to the previous ten provinces. The six provinces included in the 1999 survey are Beijing, Jiangsu, Liaoning, Henan, Sichuan and Gansu. Thus, only five provinces were surveyed in all three years. For consistency in an over-time comparison, this chapter only uses the data from these five provinces. Excluding missing values, the number of households included in this study is 3,700, 2,746 and 3,215 for the three survey years, respectively.[3] The issue of how representative are the five-province data naturally arises. Using the National Bureau of Statistics (NBS)'s Urban Household Survey Data, it is found that the inequality measures presented using five-province data are consistent with those using the data for urban economy as a whole for 1995 and 1999.[4] Thus, it is fair to say that the trend of change in inequality found in this study is sufficiently representative of the national trend.

The income variables used are 'real household disposable income' and 'real household per capita disposable income'. The surveys ask direct questions on income (including individuals' labour market earnings, government subsidies, income in kind, interest–dividends–rent, and public and private transfers) and income tax of each household member. Household disposable income in this study is defined as the sum of individual income from all sources and household members minus their income tax, plus household incomes that are not attributable to individuals, including from family enterprises and property. Real income is derived by deflating with an urban CPI (1988=100) provided by the NBS (NBS 2000). The summary statistics of the data are reported in Appendix 4.A.

According to the survey data, average real household per capita disposable income grew from 1,372 yuan in 1988 to 2,101 yuan in 1995, and further to 2,694 yuan in 1999. The average annual growth rate is 7.6 per cent for the period 1988–1995 and 6.4 per cent for the period 1995–1999. These growth rates are slightly lower than those reported earlier using the national statistical data.

Table 4.1 presents the measures of income inequality. It is clearly shown that income inequality increased during the period of interest, regardless of the

*Table 4.1* Various inequality measures of income, 1988, 1995 and 1999

| | *Real per capita HH income* | | | *Real HH income* | | |
|---|---|---|---|---|---|---|
| | *1988* | *1995* | *1999* | *1988* | *1995* | *1999* |
| Relative mean deviation | 0.149 | 0.194 | 0.222 | 0.148 | 0.184 | 0.221 |
| Coefficient of variation | 0.447 | 0.558 | 0.636 | 0.442 | 0.514 | 0.663 |
| Standard deviation of logs | 0.392 | 0.506 | 0.601 | 0.404 | 0.484 | 0.605 |
| Gini coefficient | 0.215 | 0.273 | 0.313 | 0.215 | 0.260 | 0.313 |
| Mehran measure | 0.300 | 0.380 | 0.429 | 0.302 | 0.364 | 0.428 |
| Piesch measure | 0.173 | 0.220 | 0.255 | 0.172 | 0.209 | 0.255 |
| Kakwani measure | 0.044 | 0.068 | 0.088 | 0.044 | 0.062 | 0.088 |
| Theil entropy measure | 0.082 | 0.126 | 0.166 | 0.082 | 0.114 | 0.170 |
| Theil mean log deviation | 0.079 | 0.126 | 0.171 | 0.081 | 0.115 | 0.173 |

inequality measure or income measure. Using the Gini coefficient as an example, our estimates of the Gini for per capita household disposable income increased from 21.5 per cent in 1988 to 27.3 per cent in 1995, and further increased to 31.3 in 1999. The observed Gini coefficients for 1988 and 1995 are very close to those calculated in Gustafsson and Li (2001), where from the same surveys using ten provinces' data they obtained the Gini coefficients for urban per capita income changing from 23.93 per cent in 1988 to 27.55 per cent in 1995.[5] According to the State Statistical Bureau, the Gini coefficients for the urban economy as a whole changed from 22.3 per cent in 1988 to 28.9 per cent in 1995, and further increased to 30.5 per cent in 1999. These data further confirm that the data set used in this study is valid in representing the change in inequality in urban China.

Figure 4.1 plots the Lorenz curves for the three survey years. The small dashed curve indicates income distribution in 1988, the dashed and dotted line indicates the 1995 situation, and the large dashed curve presents the 1999 situation. If one Lorenz curve lies everywhere above another, it is said to 'Lorenz dominate' the other curve and all inequality measures will show inequality to be lower for the higher curve. Figure 4.1 indicates that the 1988 Lorenz curve dominates that of 1995, which in turn dominates that of 1999. This again confirms that income inequality increased over the period.

To understand whether the increase in income inequality affected social welfare over the period studied, Figure 4.2 presents the generalized Lorenz curve for 1988, 1995 and 1999 (left-hand side) and the difference between the curves of 1988 and 1995 and the curves of 1995 and 1999 (right-hand side). The vertical axis represents the cumulative percentage of per capita household income multiplied by the mean. It shows the total resources being accessed by each percentile of the population. If one generalized Lorenz curve lies everywhere above another, it is said that the higher curve is preferable to the lower curve with regard to social welfare as every percentile of the population distribution has access to more resources.

Figure 4.2(A) illustrates the comparison between the 1988 and 1995 distributions. It is clear that although income inequality had increased by 1995, the income growth over the period more than compensated for the inequality increase, as social welfare in 1995 is everywhere greater than in 1988.

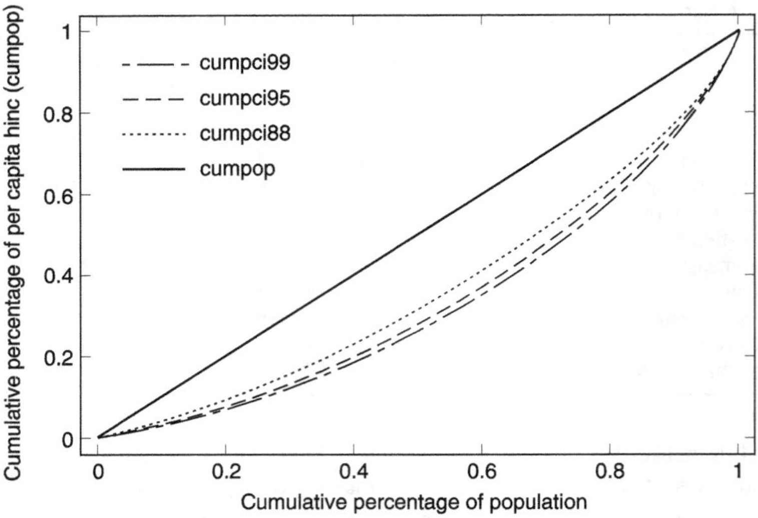


*Figure 4.1* Lorenz curves for real per capita household disposable income, 1988, 1995 and 1999.

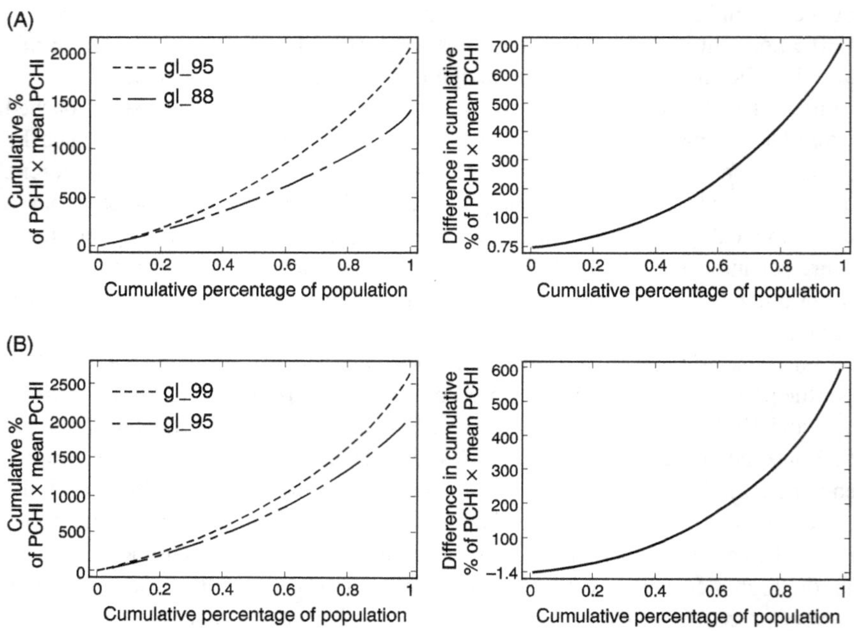


*Figure 4.2* Generalised Lorenz curve. (A) 1988 and 1995. (B) 1995 and 1999.

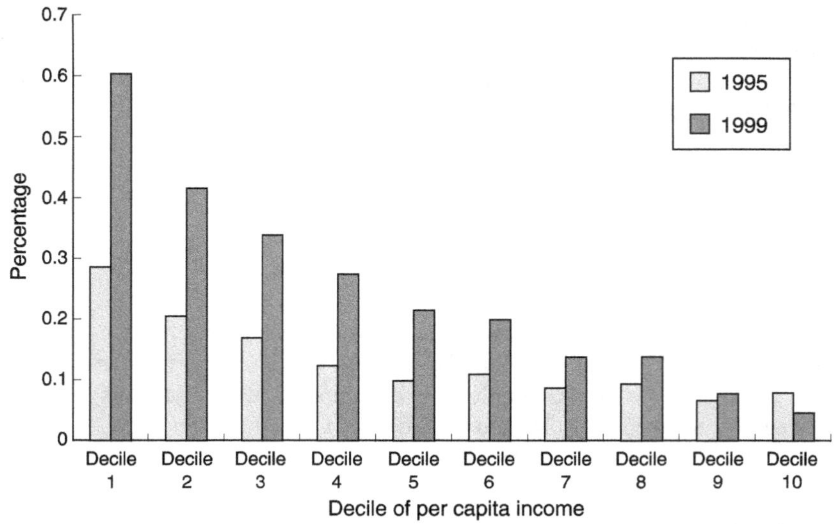


*Figure 4.3* Distribution of households with unemployed members across income deciles.

Figure 4.2(B) demonstrates the comparison between 1995 and 1999. The 1999 generalized Lorenz curve lies below that of 1995 at the bottom 5 per cent of the distribution (shown by the negative value of the vertical axis of the right-hand graph indicating the difference between the two years) and above the 1995 curve everywhere after the bottom 5 per cent of the distribution. This result suggests that the social welfare of the bottom end of the income group was worse in 1999 than in 1995, while each percentile above the fifth percentile was better off.

Why, then, did income at the lower end of the distribution fall while medium- and high-income families enjoyed significant income gains over the period 1995–1999? As economic restructuring may be an important cause, Figure 4.3 presents the distribution of households with unemployed members across different income deciles in 1995 and 1999.[6] It indicates that the number of households with unemployed members more than doubled for the lower two deciles while it hardly changed for the top two deciles.

If unemployment is an important cause of the reduction in income at the lower end of the distribution between 1995 and 1999, why is it that not all unemployed households fall into the lowest income group? Perhaps the reduction in household income from one member being unemployed can be offset by income earned by other employed members. Of course, households with more unemployed members are less likely to be able to compensate within the household and hence more likely to fall into the lower end of the distribution. Indeed, in 1999 around 50 per cent of the households with two or more unemployed members were located at the bottom decile of the income distribution, and about 30 per cent of these households were concentrated at the lowest 5 percentiles of the distribution. In 1995 only 25 per cent of households with more than one member unemployed were located in the bottom 10 percentiles of income distribution, indicating a better ability for households to compensate for unemployment in 1995 than in 1999.

To sum up, income inequality in urban China has increased. The change, however, may be due to different factors over different periods of economic reform and hence may have different effects on social and political stability.

## 4.3 Methodology

Decomposition of the contributing factors to income inequality has long been an important methodological issue in the income distribution literature (Cowell 2000). Most previous studies employ the decomposition methodology formally developed by Shorrocks (1984) and extended by Cowell and Jenkins (1995) and Jenkins (1995). These methods decompose certain inequality indices into between and within mutually exclusive population subgroups. Although this type of decomposition is widely used, it has some shortcomings. One is that the relative contributions of factors critically depend on the order in which the factors are introduced into the analysis (Fields 1998). In addition, the decompositions require a partition of the population and if the sample size is not large enough, there may not be a meaningful measure of within-group inequality for each cell. Given that most empirical studies have limited sample size, the number of contributing factors to income inequality, which can be controlled for, is limited.

Another set of decomposition methodologies has been developed by DiNardo, Fortin and Lemieux (1996) and modified by Cameron (2000).[7] These methods use simulation techniques to impose a structure of income-generating factors from the terminal year on the initial year to analyse the contributing factors to the change in income/wage inequality. Although these decompositions are useful for looking at changes in inequality, they suffer from similar shortcomings to Shorrocks (1982) and Cowell and Jenkins (1995).

Recently, regression-based decomposition approaches have been developed (Fields 1998; Morduch and Sicular 2002). Assuming an income-generating function $\ln Y_{it} = \Sigma_j \alpha_{jt} Z_{ijt}$, where $j$ is the number of explanatory variables, Fields (1998) shows that the contribution of an income-generating factor $Z_j$ to the total income inequality can be written as:

$$p_j (\ln Y) = s_j(\ln Y)/R^2(\ln Y) \tag{4.1}$$

where

$$s_j (\ln Y) = \text{cov}[a_j Z_j, \ln Y]/\sigma^2(\ln Y) = \frac{a_j^* \sigma(Z_j) * \text{cor}[Z_j, \ln Y]}{\sigma(\ln Y)} \tag{4.2}$$

The contribution of the income-generating factor $Z_j$ to the change in total income inequality measured by any inequality index $I(.)$ over time or between countries/groups can be written as:

$$\Pi_j(I(.)) = \frac{s_{j,2} * I_2 - s_{j,1} * I_1}{I_2 - I_1} \tag{4.3}$$

where the subscripts 1 and 2 refer to time, country or group.

Fields (1998) points to two important qualifying issues related to the methodology. First, unless there is Lorenz-dominance, it is impossible to determine whether inequality has increased or decreased over time as there always exists an inequality measure that registers an increase and another that registers a decrease in inequality (Sen 1973). Thus, with Lorenz-crossing it is impossible to specify which factor is responsible for the change in inequality over time. The fact that Figure 4.2 shows no Lorenz-crossing across the three data periods enables an unambiguous study of the factors contributing to the increase in income inequality. Second, the proportion of each factor contributing to the change in income inequality over time depends on the choice of inequality measure used.

Although simple, the Fields (1998) methodology is particularly powerful. It can identify the factors contributing to the level of income inequality and its change over time (or between countries/regions) without any limitation on the number of factors that can be included in the analysis. In addition, all factors can be controlled for at the same time, hence the results do not rely on the order in which the factors are introduced.[8]

To utilize Fields' (1998) decomposition approach, the income-generating function needs to be specified. Household income (or per capita household income, PCHI) is normally defined as a function of the earnings of household members, income from household business, and household demographic characteristics. In the case of urban China, only a limited number of households have a family business, hence income from this source is not important. Thus, household income can mainly be attributed to factors that affect the earnings of household members and demographic features of the household. The household income-generating function may be specified as follows:

$$\ln Y_i = \beta_j X_{ij} + \gamma_j R_{ij} + \delta HH_i + \lambda\ Region_i + \varepsilon_i \tag{4.4}$$

where $\ln Y_i$ is the logarithmic of household real PCHI for household $i$. $X_{ij}$ is a vector of human capital and other factors that affect the earnings of member $j$ in household $i$, including age and its squared term, years of schooling, and a dummy variable indicating whether or not the individual is a party member. $R_{ij}$ is a vector of factors indicating the effect of economic restructuring on the earnings of individual $j$ of household $i$. Variables included in this vector contain a dummy variable indicating whether or not the individual is working in a loss-making firm, whether or not the individual is unemployed, and the ownership of the enterprise in which the individual is employed. $HH_i$ is a vector of household demographic composition variables, including the gender of the household head, household composition, household size, and the proportion of household members who are in the labour force. Finally, $Region_i$ is the regional indicator of the household.

## 4.4 Identifying contributing factors to the change in income inequality

### *4.4.1 Determinants of income variation*

The income-generating model specified in equation (4.4) is estimated for the three cross-sectional data sets. Table 4.2 reports the results with the log of real per capita household disposable income as the dependent variable.[9]

Before discussing the results, some data and estimation issues need to be addressed. Due to a high multicollinearity between the age and years of schooling of husbands and wives, the average age and years of schooling of household members who are in the labour force are used. Another issue is that the concept of 'working in a loss-making firm' did not exist in 1988 and hence the variable representing it is not included in the 1988 estimation. In addition, unemployment is very low in 1988 and the variables measuring husbands, wives or the-second generation unemployment have to be excluded from the 1988 estimation.

Table 4.2 reveals interesting results, especially when compared across the three survey years. The discussion below follows the order of human capital-related factors, economic restructuring, household composition and regional effects.

The effect of education on real PCHI has increased over time. One more year of education increased real PCHI by 1.7 per cent in 1988, 3.5 per cent in 1995 and 4.3 per cent in 1999. The increase in the return to education reflects the effect of market-oriented economic reform in the urban labour market.

The effect of average age of household members who are in the labour force does not appear to have a consistent pattern. Evaluated at the mean age, the effect increased from 1988 to 1995 and then decreased from 1995 to 1999. The change in the patterns of age-income profile could be a result of different factors, such as the change in the shape of the age-earnings profile, family composition, and the macroeconomic conditions of the survey years.

Party members earn significantly higher earnings than non-party members,[10] and this effect has increased significantly over the period of the study. In 1988, a household where both husband and wife were party members received 10 per cent more per capita income than households without any party member. This ratio increased to 12 per cent in 1995 and 20 per cent in 1999. This is a significant change, especially from 1995 to 1999 with an increase in return of 8 percentage points. The effect of party membership could reflect either unobservable human capital of party members or their political power. It may be reasonable to believe that with decentralized labour market institutions, the rate of returns to productivity-related unobservable characteristics as captured by party membership has risen significantly. It may, however, also be possible that party members received more favourable treatment in 1999 than previously. At this stage it is impossible to disentangle the two effects.

The most important changes over the period of this study come about in the effect of variables representing economic restructuring. The effects on household income of unemployment and working in a loss-making firm have changed

*Table 4.2* Determinants of real per capita household disposable income, 1988, 1995 and 1999

| | *1988* | | *1995* | | *1999* | |
|---|---|---|---|---|---|---|
| | *Coeff.* | *t-ratio* | *Coeff.* | *t-ratio* | *Coeff.* | *t-ratio* |
| Constant | 7.6732 | 73.78 | 7.1949 | 42.26 | 7.9629 | 39.71 |
| Average age of HH labour | −0.0125 | −2.40 | 0.0333 | 4.34 | 0.0041 | 0.46 |
| (Average age of HH labour)$^2$ | 0.0002 | 3.14 | −0.0003 | −3.65 | 0.0000 | −0.15 |
| Average years of schooling of HH labour | 0.0174 | 8.62 | 0.0353 | 13.20 | 0.0429 | 12.17 |
| H party membership | 0.0611 | 5.98 | 0.0699 | 4.93 | 0.1064 | 6.61 |
| W party membership | 0.0423 | 3.00 | 0.0513 | 2.85 | 0.0914 | 4.59 |
| H being unemployed | | | −0.1523 | −4.84 | −0.2901 | −10.43 |
| W being unemployed | | | −0.0947 | −3.48 | −0.2396 | −10.48 |
| 2nd generation unemployed | | | −0.0990 | −2.62 | −0.1703 | −4.19 |
| H working in loss-making firm | | | −0.0928 | −5.26 | −0.1807 | −9.85 |
| W working in loss-making firm | | | −0.0599 | −3.41 | −0.0876 | −4.75 |
| H working in local SOEs | −0.0280 | −2.12 | −0.1015 | −5.91 | −0.0669 | −3.42 |
| H working in collectives | −0.0740 | −4.47 | −0.1708 | −6.73 | −0.1365 | −4.42 |
| H working in private sector | 0.0496 | 0.97 | −0.0630 | −1.25 | 0.0198 | 0.58 |
| H did not report sector | 0.0891 | 3.43 | 0.0582 | 1.13 | −0.2020 | −2.41 |
| W working in local SOEs | 0.0011 | 0.08 | −0.0302 | −1.55 | −0.0176 | −0.82 |
| W working in collectives | −0.0627 | −4.25 | −0.0855 | −3.77 | −0.1121 | −4.28 |
| W working in private sector | −0.0379 | −1.06 | −0.0867 | −1.74 | −0.0613 | −1.77 |
| W did not report sector | −0.0091 | −0.54 | −0.2049 | −6.36 | −0.2608 | −7.10 |
| Male as the household head | 0.0029 | 0.13 | −0.0419 | −2.79 | −0.0344 | −2.03 |
| % of children aged 0–5 | −0.4603 | −9.41 | −0.1977 | −2.24 | −0.3669 | −3.47 |
| % of children aged 6–10 | −0.3086 | −7.13 | −0.0007 | −0.01 | −0.1027 | −1.30 |
| % of children aged 11–16 | −0.3903 | −8.83 | −0.0534 | −0.90 | −0.2164 | −3.34 |
| % of elderly | 0.1167 | 2.02 | 0.2424 | 4.21 | 0.1805 | 2.85 |
| Household size | −0.2134 | −32.75 | −0.2720 | −21.34 | −0.1791 | −11.78 |
| Number of employed HH members | 0.1963 | 19.57 | 0.1879 | 12.38 | 0.1345 | 8.28 |
| Liaoning | −0.0506 | −2.84 | −0.3115 | −14.67 | −0.4913 | −20.70 |
| Jiangsu | −0.0232 | −1.31 | −0.0515 | −2.43 | −0.1647 | −6.86 |
| Henan | −0.2955 | −17.38 | −0.4626 | −20.92 | −0.5322 | −22.68 |
| Gansu | −0.1408 | −7.39 | −0.4842 | −19.54 | −0.5114 | −20.68 |
| No. of observations | 3,700 | | 2,746 | | 3,215 | |
| Adjusted $R^2$ | 0.46 | | 0.56 | | 0.52 | |
| $R^2$ | 0.46 | | 0.56 | | 0.52 | |

Note: The central state-owned enterprises sector and Beijing are used as the omitted category for the sector of employment and region, respectively.

considerably, though the change in the return to different sectors of employment have not been particularly significant.

In 1988, there were few unemployed individuals (only 0.5 per cent of the total labour force if not including early retired workers), and hence the variables indicating unemployment are excluded from the 1988 estimation.

Things have taken a significant turn by 1995 when economic restructuring in the urban state sector began to accelerate. Thus, I observe a significant effect of economic restructuring on real PCHI. A household with a husband unemployed has a 15.2 per cent lower PCHI than a household without the husband unemployed. The income reduction for households with wives or sons/daughters being unemployed is 9.5 and 9.9 per cent, respectively. In addition, working in loss-making firms also reduces income substantially. A household with both husband and wife working in a loss-making firm receives 15.3 per cent less income than otherwise, which in income terms is equivalent to the household head being laid off. Working in a loss-making firm was generally a first step towards becoming unemployed, and in 1995 most laid-off workers received similar pay to those working in a loss-making firm but not yet laid off.

By 1999, radical urban state sector reform had been in place for about four to five years and the effect on household income variation was even more severe than in 1995. Households with unemployed husbands, wives or sons/daughters receive 29, 24 and 17 per cent less income, respectively, than households where these members were employed. These ratios are between double to triple those observed in 1995. Such significant change may reflect the change in the general economic environment. In 1995, most laid-off workers were still being paid by their previous enterprises. By 1999, many of these enterprises were bankrupted and state sector laid-off workers were re-assigned to the re-employment centre and guaranteed a minimum living standard.

The loss of income for households with husbands working in loss-making firms also increased. In 1995, the per capita income of these households was about 9.3 per cent less than households without husbands working in a loss-making firm. By 1999, this ratio had increased to 18 per cent.

As indicated at the end of Section 4.2, the poorest 5 per cent of households had the highest proportion of households with more than one unemployed member. It is therefore worthwhile investigating in more detail how the incomes of these households have been affected by economic restructuring. Income reductions for households with various combinations of unemployed members and/or working in loss-making firms are presented in Table 4.3. It shows that the income reduction for households with two unemployed members increased from 22 per cent in 1995 to 47 per cent in 1999. Other things being equal, if a household had both husband and wife unemployed, its real PCHI was reduced by 25 per cent in 1995 and 53 per cent in 1999. If an additional member (son/daughter) was also unemployed, real PCHI was reduced by 35 per cent in 1995 and 70 per cent in 1999.

Table 4.3 also presents the proportion of households with a different number of unemployed individuals and the demographic composition of unemployment within households for 1995 and 1999. The majority of households with unemployed

*Table 4.3* Percentage of different types of households with unemployed members or members working in loss-making firms

| | *1995* | | *1999* | |
|---|---|---|---|---|
| | | *% of HH income reduction* | | *% of HH income reduction* |
| Total number of households | 2,746 | | 3,215 | |
| HH without unemployed member | 86.27 | | 75.55 | |
| HH with one member unemployed | 11.58 | 11.0% | 21.28 | 23.2% |
| HH with two members unemployed | 1.93 | 22.0% | 3.03 | 46.5% |
| HH with three members unemployed | 0.22 | 33.0% | 0.06 | 69.7% |
| HH with four members unemployed | 0.00 | | 0.03 | 96.5% |
| HH with H unemployed only | 0.81 | 15.2% | 3.98 | 29.0% |
| HH with W unemployed only | 4.83 | 9.5% | 13.15 | 24.0% |
| HH with S/D unemployed only | 2.39 | 9.9% | 3.43 | 17.0% |
| HH with H and W unemployed | 0.52 | 24.7% | 2.34 | 53.0% |
| HH with H and S/D unemployed | 0.10 | 25.1% | 0.33 | 46.0% |
| HH with W and S/D unemployed | 0.36 | 19.4% | 1.51 | 41.0% |
| HH with H and W and S/D unemployed | 0.05 | 34.6% | 0.27 | 70.0% |
| HH with H working in LMFs | 10.52 | 9.3% | 12.78 | 18.1% |
| HH with W working in LMFs | 11.54 | 6.0% | 16.52 | 8.8% |
| HH with H and W working in LMFs | 11.76 | 15.3% | 19.35 | 26.9% |
| Total HH with members working in LMFs | 33.83 | | 48.65 | |

Note: The real per capita HH income equation is also estimated with a variable indicating the number of household members being unemployed for 1995 and 1999 data. The estimated coefficients are −0.0895 and −0.2376 for 1995 and 1999, respectively. The income reduction for the first panel of this table is calculated according to these estimates.

members had only one unemployed member in all three survey years. In addition, the proportion of households with an unemployed wife is very high, especially in 1999 where it is about three times higher than the number of households with only the husband unemployed (13 per cent vs. 4 per cent). The proportion of households with two members unemployed increased from 1.9 per cent in 1995 to 3.0 per cent in 1999. Among them the proportion of households with both unemployed husband and wife increased from 0.52 to 2.34 per cent over the two survey years. Only a very limited number of households had more than two members unemployed, even in 1999. The group of households with more than one member unemployed deserves more government attention as they are least likely to be able to cushion the effect of economic restructuring within the households.

Table 4.3 also indicates that 'working in a loss-making firm' may be a more widespread phenomenon in comparison to being unemployed. In 1995, around 34 per cent of the total households has at least one member working in a loss-making firm. This ratio increased to almost 49 per cent in 1999. However, the income reduction from 'working in a loss-making firm' was not as severe as being unemployed in 1999.

The pattern of sector of employment does not have a consistent trend, although the superior position of the central state sector (the omitted category) over local state and private sectors seems to have eroded over time, especially when comparing 1995 with 1999.

There is a particularly interesting effect with regard to the household composition. For both 1995 and 1999, households headed by females had significantly higher income than those headed by males. Given that female-headed households accounted for 27 per cent of the total sample used in both years, the effect is non-trivial. This is an uncommon result in studies of the determinants of household income for other countries, although Cameron (2000) found a similar phenomenon in Indonesia. In the case of urban China, this could be because female-headed households are more likely to be less traditional and hence better educated with better jobs. Indeed, 36 per cent of wives in female-headed households are managerial or professionals in 1995, while in male-headed households only 26 per cent of wives belong to this category. These proportions for 1999 are 31 and 23 per cent, respectively.

Other household composition variables indicate that, relative to working-age adults, households with a higher proportion of young children had lower incomes, while households with more members older than 65 had higher incomes. Larger households had lower per capita incomes, and households with more labourers had higher incomes. These patterns are consistent over the three survey years. In addition, regional dummy variables are an important determinant of income variation in all three survey years.

### *4.4.2 Decomposition of contributing factors to the level of income inequality and its change over time*

This subsection quantifies the degree to which the variables included in the income-generating equation account for the level of income inequality and its change over time. In particular, the interest is to identify the relative importance of the impact of economic restructuring compared to the regional effect on income inequality over the three survey years.

Table 4.4 reports the decomposition of the level of inequality on real per capita household income for the three years. The variables included in the estimated equation (4.4) (Table 4.2) are grouped into five contributing factors: (1) 'economic restructuring', which includes the effect of household member (husband, wife and sons/daughters) being unemployed, working in a loss-making firm, and their sector of employment; (2) 'regional effect', which is captured by the regional dummy variables; (3) 'party membership', which includes the two dummy variables indicating

*Table 4.4* Decomposition of the level of per capita household income inequality

| | *1988* | | *1995* | | *1999* | |
|---|---|---|---|---|---|---|
| | $S_j$ | $P(S_j)$ | $S_j$ | $P(S_j)$ | $S_j$ | $P(S_j)$ |
| Restructuring | 1.19 | 2.59 | 9.17 | 16.28 | 18.93 | 36.17 |
| Of which: | | | | | | |
| unemployment | 0.00 | 0.00 | 2.01 | 3.57 | 8.06 | 15.39 |
| loss-making firm | 0.00 | 0.00 | 2.06 | 3.66 | 6.33 | 12.10 |
| sector of employment | 1.19 | 2.56 | 5.09 | 9.05 | 4.54 | 8.68 |
| Regional effect | 10.07 | 21.97 | 19.09 | 33.90 | 16.40 | 31.33 |
| Party | 1.52 | 3.32 | 2.08 | 3.70 | 3.59 | 6.86 |
| Human capital | 3.47 | 7.58 | 8.75 | 15.53 | 6.07 | 11.60 |
| Household composition | 29.57 | 64.54 | 17.21 | 30.56 | 7.35 | 14.04 |
| Total explained | 45.81 | | 56.31 | | 52.34 | |
| Residual | 54.19 | | 43.69 | | 47.66 | |

Note: The exercises of decomposition of inequality reported in this table and the change in inequality over time reported in Table 4.5 are also applied to the regression results obtained from the full sample estimations; the results, which are available upon request from the author, are consistent with what is reported here.

whether the husband or wife is a party member; (4) 'human capital' effect, which is measured by the average age and years of schooling of household members who are in the labour force; and (5) 'household composition', which covers the effect of the gender of the household head, the young and old dependency ratios, family size, and the number of labourers in the household.

Notice from Section 4.3 that Fields' (1998) approach can only decompose the amount of income inequality explained by the variables included in the income regression, that is, the proportion represented by $R^2$'s. The rest of the inequality is due to the residual effect. Fortunately, the income-generating equations estimated in this study have strong explanatory power. The adjusted $R^2$'s are 46, 56 and 52 per cent for the 1988, 1995 and 1999 data, respectively.

The first columns of each of the three years in Table 4. 4 indicate the proportion of the total inequality of the log per capita household income accounted for by each of the five factors and the residual term. The second column takes the total explained portion (the $R^2$'s) as 100 per cent and measures the contribution of each of the five contributing factors as a proportion of the total explained component.

The results indicate that the most important contributing factor to income inequality changed from 'household composition' in 1988 to 'regional effect' in 1995, and to 'economic restructuring effect' in 1999. In 1988 there is hardly any effect on income inequality from economic restructuring. In 1995, about 9 per cent of income inequality is due to this effect, of which sector of employment accounted for more than half. The effect of economic restructuring increased to 19 per cent of the level of income inequality in 1999, of which the effect of unemployment contributed more than 8 percentage points. This indicates that economic restructuring has played an increasingly significant role in the level of income inequality

*Table 4.5* Decomposition of the contributing factors to the change in the Gini coefficient, 1988–1995 and 1995–1999 (6 provinces data)

| | *1988* | *1995* | *1999* | *Change* | *Change* |
|---|---|---|---|---|---|
| | *Gini = 0.215* | *Gini = 0.273* | *Gini = 0.313* | *1988–1995* | *1995–1999* |
| | $S_j(lnY)$ | $S_j(lnY)$ | $S_j(lnY)$ | $\Pi_j(Gini)$ | $\Pi_j(Gini)$ |
| Restructuring | 0.25 | 2.51 | 5.92 | 38.25 | 87.51 |
| Of which: | | | | | |
| unemployment | 0.00 | 0.55 | 2.52 | 9.33 | 50.53 |
| loss-making firm | 0.00 | 0.57 | 1.98 | 9.59 | 36.31 |
| sector of employment | 0.25 | 1.40 | 1.42 | 19.34 | 0.67 |
| Regional effect | 2.16 | 5.23 | 5.13 | 51.99 | −2.54 |
| Human capital | 0.33 | 0.57 | 1.12 | 4.13 | 14.17 |
| Party | 0.75 | 2.40 | 1.90 | 27.98 | −12.72 |
| Household composition | 6.36 | 4.72 | 2.30 | −27.80 | −61.95 |
| Residual | 11.65 | 11.97 | 14.92 | 5.45 | 75.54 |
| Total | 21.50 | 27.30 | 31.30 | 100.00 | 100.00 |

over the period studied. Other effects that have gained some ground in 1999, relative to 1988 and 1995, are party membership and human capital effects, but these do not play as significant a role as the effect of economic restructuring.

The regional effect has always been significant, but it is more so in 1995 than in 1988 and 1999. This result is consistent with that found in Gustafsson and Li (2001) and Khan and Riskin (2001).[11]

The above analysis has identified the most important contributing factors to the level of income inequality in the three survey years. To what extent do these different factors contribute to the increase in income inequality over the periods? To quantify this, the decomposition approach specified in equation 4.3 is applied to the results presented in Tables 4.1 and 4.4

Table 4.5 summarizes the results for the change in the Gini coefficients between 1988 and 1995, and 1995 and 1999. [12] It shows that the 'regional effect' contributed 52.0 per cent of the increase in the Gini coefficient between 1988 and 1995, which is the most important contributing factor to the increase in the Gini coefficient in this period. Economic restructuring contributed around 38.3 per cent, of which unemployment accounted for 9.3 percentage points, while household members working in a loss-making firm and sector of employment contributed to 9.6 and 19.3 percentage points, respectively. Another important factor that contributed to the increase in income inequality between 1988 and 1995 is the human capital factor, which accounted for more than one-quarter of the increase in the Gini coefficient. This finding is consistent with other studies indicating that the effect of labour market reform increased the rate of return to human capital in the 1990s (see, e.g., Knight and Song 1999; Meng 2000).

During the period 1995–1999, the main contributing factor to the increase in the Gini coefficient is 'economic restructuring', which accounted for 87.5 per cent of the change, while the regional effect contributed to the decline of the Gini coefficient. Of the economic restructuring factor, unemployment contributed 50.5 per cent of the increase in the Gini coefficient, while working in a loss-making firm accounted for 36.3 per cent. The sector of employment has little effect on the increase in income inequality. Another important effect contributing to the increase in the Gini coefficient during this period was party membership. In both periods, household composition contributed to a decline in income inequality.

## 4.5 Conclusions

Urban income inequality in China has increased considerably over the period of economic transition from a planned to a market-oriented economy. This study has investigated this change over two important phases of the economic transition: the initial stage of acceleration of the state sector and urban labour market reforms (1988–1995) and the period of radical reform in the state sector and the urban labour market (1995–1999). An attempt is made to identify the difference in the type of income inequality and the causes of the increase in inequality over these different phases of the economic transition. The main findings may be summarized as follows.

First, although income inequality increased during each of the two periods, the nature of the increase is different. In the first period, everybody was made better off and the increase in inequality was due to the relatively stronger income growth at the top end of the distribution. In the second period, however, households at the lowest 5 percentile income distribution experienced an income reduction, while households at the top end of the distribution enjoyed significant income gains. Thus, the increase in inequality in the first period was compensated for by an unambiguous increase in social welfare at every level of income distribution, whereas this was not the case in the second period. Perhaps this is why social stability has become more of a concern since the late 1990s.

Second, while the increase in income inequality in the first period was mainly due to the increase in regional income variations, this effect was dominated by the impact of economic restructuring in the second period. The increase in the number of households with unemployed members and the significant increase in income reduction for households with unemployed members contributed more than 49 per cent of the increase in the Gini coefficient over the period 1995–1999. In addition, households with members working at a loss-making firm also contributed considerably to the increase in income inequality during this period.

An interesting issue, however, is that not all households with unemployed members fell into the low-income group. While around 40 per cent of such households had income at or below the 20th percentile, nearly 11 per cent of households with unemployed members received income above the 70th percentile. This difference may be closely related to the concentration of unemployed members within each household. Indeed, although only 3.7 per cent of households in 1999 had more than one unemployed member, on average these households earned more than 50 per cent less real PCHI than other households, *ceteris paribus*. The significant effect of unemployment concentration on income reduction, and hence on income inequality, suggests that, to a large extent, some of the unemployment effect may have been cushioned by within-household income transfers. Households whose members are unable to compensate each other are more likely to suffer from severe income reduction due to economic restructuring. Therefore, the households that deserve more government assistance may be those that have more than one member unemployed.

What remains unclear from the current study is whether those who fall into poverty because of economic restructuring will remain in that position for a long period. To examine this issue, the duration of unemployment and its impact on income distribution will have to be investigated.

Another equally important issue is related to the long-term trend of income inequality in urban China. Economic restructuring is a transitory phenomenon. Once it is completed, will income inequality reverse back to a more equal level? The answer to this question is probably no. The reason is twofold. First, the relatively equal distribution of income during the pre-reform era and at the beginning of the reform period is mainly the result of a compressed earnings structure. This structure has changed and is continuing to change towards a system where the earnings gap between skilled and unskilled workers is enlarged to reflect market demand for and supply of skilled and unskilled workers. This is indicated by the finding that over the period 1988–1999, human capital-related factors have been important contributors to the increase in income inequality.

Second, the current large-scale unemployment in urban China is likely to remain for some time because, in part, it is a reflection of the still inflexible urban labour market. There are jobs in urban China. Currently, at any point in time there are more than 50 million rural migrants working in urban China (West and Zhao 2000). The laid-off state sector workers, however, have been unwilling to take these jobs as they are low paid and have low status. As labour market reform proceeds further and the laid-off urban workers are more psychologically adjusted towards the new market environment, more and more urban unemployed will accept low-paying jobs. Once that happens, unemployment will decrease but income inequality may remain at the current level or even increase.

Two notes of caution should be borne in mind when interpreting the results from this study. The data used only include households with urban registration. Those migrant workers with rural household registration are excluded. Given that rural migrants on average earn much lower earnings and are not eligible for any government subsidies, an urban income inequality measure that takes into account rural migrant households may be larger than the estimates in this study and it should be more so for later years when migration becomes more widespread. In addition, our data cover five provinces. Although the general inequality trend obtained from this study is consistent with the national average, there may still be detailed differences.

## Notes

The author is grateful for the financial support from the International Centre for the Study of East Asian Development. This chapter was first published in *Review of Income and*

*Wealth*, Vol. 50, 2004. The author is grateful to Blackwell Publishing for permission to reproduce the paper.

1 The reason for this difference may be due to the different definition of income used in these studies. However, by reading the two papers it is not very clear exactly where the difference comes from.
2 Although there are four households being coded as located in Sichuan province in 1988 data, this is due to miscoding of the data as Sichuan province is not included in the 1988 survey.
3 The empirical works conducted later on in this chapter are not sensitive to the number of sample provinces included. For each calculation and estimation, the full sample, the sample of six provinces (five consistent provinces plus Sichuan) and five consistent provinces are used and the results obtained from these calculations and estimations are consistent. Although only results from the consistent five-province sample are reported, other results are available upon request from the author.
4 This will be discussed in detail later. The data are provided by the Urban Household Survey Team of the SSB.
5 Gustafsson and Li (2001) and Khan and Riskin (2001) used the same survey data from the 1988 and 1995 surveys. The disposable income used in their study, however, is adjusted for the housing subsidies received by households who were renting from the government and rental value of owner-occupied housing. The way they conducted such imputations is not discussed in detail in their works. To check the sensitivity of using our income measure rather than using a rental value adjusted income measure in inequality analysis, the simple explanation given in Gustafsson and Li (2001) is followed to carry out the imputation of the housing subsidy and the rental value of owner-occupied housing. These imputed values are then added to household income. It is found that adjusting for rental subsidy and rental value of owner-occupied housing has very little impact on the measure of income inequality. Some inequality indices using our income measure (original income) and that adjusting for rental subsidy and rental value of owner-occupied housing, together with the detailed imputation method, are reported in Appendix 4.B.
6 Unemployment in this study is defined as unemployed plus laid-off workers.
7 Bourguignon, Fournier and Gurgand (1998) independently developed a micro-simulation decomposition methodology, which is very similar to DiNardo *et al.* (1996) and Cameron (2000).
8 Morduch and Sicular (2002) pointed out some limitations of Fields' decomposition method.
9 Equation (4.4) is also estimated using the full sample for each year (10 for 1988, 11 for 1995 and 6 for 1999), the six-province sample (five consistent provinces plus Sichuan province), and using log real household income as the dependent variable, and the results are consistent. These results are available upon request from the author.
10 This is a common finding (see, e.g., Knight and Song 1999).
11 An issue arises as to whether using five-province data may misrepresent the general picture of the regional effect on inequality for the urban economy as a whole. Due to the lack of data for the 1999 survey, it is hard to answer this question. However, the 1988 and 1995 surveys include ten consistent provinces and the results for these two years do not change whether ten- or five-province data are used. The main contributor for income inequality in 1988 is always household composition and in 1995 it is regional effects. This consistency also applies to the analysis of contributing factor to the *change* in the Gini coefficients over time. Regardless which sample is used, the main contributing factor for the change over the period 1988–1995 is always the regional effect. If reducing provinces from our sample generated problems with regard to the finding of changing importance of regional inequality, then this would

have been true for the 1988–1995 changes as well. The fact that little difference between the two samples is found may indicate that the decomposition results are not sensitive to the number of provinces included.

12 As noticed in Fields (1998), the decomposition of the change in income inequality over time will differ across different inequality indexes. To ascertain that using different inequality indexes provides consistent qualitative results, two other inequality indices provided in Table 4.1 (standard deviation of logs and Theil entropy index) are decomposed as well. The results are consistent with what is observed here and are available upon request from the author.

## References

Aaberge, R. and Li, X. (1997) 'The trend in urban income inequality in two Chinese provinces, 1986–1990', *Review of Income and Wealth*, 43(3): 335–55.

Appleton, S., Knight, J., Song, L. and Xia, Q. (2001) 'Towards a competitive labour market? Urban workers, rural–urban migrants, redundancies and hardship in urban China', paper presented at American Economic Association Annual Conference, 2001, New Orleans, LA.

Bourguignon, F., Fournier, M. and Gurgand, M. (1998) 'Distribution, development and education in Taiwan, 1979–1994', unpublished manuscript.

Brainerd, E. (1998) 'Winners and losers in Russia's economic transition', *American Economic Review*, 88(5): 1094–1116.

Cameron, L. (2000) 'Poverty and inequality in Java: examining the impact of the changing age, educational and industrial structure' *Journal of Development Economics*, 62(1): 149–80.

China State Statistical Bureau (2000) *China Statistical Yearbook 2000*, Beijing: China Statistical Publishing House.

Cowell, F. (2000) 'Measurement of inequality', in Atkinson, A.B. and Bourguignon, F. (eds), *Handbooks of Income Distribution*, Vol. 1. Amsterdam: Elsevier.

Cowell, F. and Jenkins, S. (1995) 'How much inequality can we explain? A methodology and an application to the United States', *Economic Journal*, 105: 421–30.

DiNardo, J., Fortin, N.M. and Lemieux, T. (1996) 'Labour market institutions and the distribution of wages, 1973–1992: a semiparametric approach', *Econometrica* 64(5): 1001–44.

Fan, G. (2000) 'The dynamics of transition in China: change of ownership structure and sustainability of growth', paper presented at the International Conference on China Growth Sustainability in the 21st Century, Canberra, Australia.

Fields, G.S. (1998) 'Accounting for income inequality and its change', mimeo, Cornell University, Ithaca, NY.

Flemming, J. and Micklewright, J. (2000) 'Income distribution, economic systems and transition', in Atkinson, A.B. and Bourguignon, F. (eds), *Handbooks of Income Distribution*, Vol. 1. Amsterdam: Elsevier.

Gustafsson, B. and Li, S. (1997) 'Types of income and inequality in China at the end of the 1980s', *Review of Income and Wealth*, 43(2): 211–26.

Gustafsson, B. and Li, S. (1998) 'Inequality in China at the end of the 1980s: locational aspects and household characteristics', *Asian Economic Journal*, 12(1): 25–64.

Gustafsson, B. and Li, S. (2001) 'A more unequal China? Aspects of inequality in the distribution of equivalent income', in Riskin, C., Zhao, R. and Li, S. (eds), *China's Retreat from Equality: Income Distribution and Economic Transition*. Armonk, NY: M.E. Sharpe, pp. 44–83.

Jenkins, S. (1995) 'Accounting for inequality trends: decomposition analyses for the UK, 1971–86', *Economica*, 62: 29–63.

Khan, A.R. and Riskin, C. (2001) *Inequality and Poverty in China in the Age of Globalization*, Oxford: Oxford University Press.

Khan, A.R., Griffin, K. and Riskin, C. (1999) 'Income distribution in urban China during the period of economic reform and globalization', *American Economic Review*, 89(2): 296–300.

Khan, A.R., Griffin, K. and Zhao, Z. (1992) 'Household income and its distribution in China', *China Quarterly*, 132: 1086–1100.

Knight, J. and Li, S. (1999) 'Fiscal decentralization, redistribution and reform in China', *Oxford Development Studies*, 27(1): 5–32.

Knight, J. and Song, L. (1991) 'The determinants of urban income inequality in China', *Oxford Bulletin of Economics and Statistics*, 53: 123–54.

Knight, J. and Song, L. (1999) 'Zhongguo jingji zengzhang jingji gaige he shouru chaju de kuoda' (Economic growth, economic reform and increase in income inequality in China), in Zhao, R., Li, S. and Riskin, C. (eds), *Zhongguo Jumin Shouru Fenpei Zai Yanjiu* (Re-examination of Income Distribution of Chinese Households), Beijing: Publishing House of Chinese Finance and Economy.

Meng, X. (2000) *Labour Market Reform in China*, Cambridge: Cambridge University Press.

Milanovic, B. (1997) *Income, Inequality, and Poverty during the Transition from Planned to Market Economy*, Washington, DC: The World Bank.

Morduch, J. and Sicular, T (2002) 'Rethinking inequality decomposition, with evidence from rural China', *Economic Journal*, 112: 93–106.

National Bureau of Statistics (NBS) (2000) *China Statistical Yearbook 2000*, Beijing: China Statistics Press.

Riskin, C., Zhao, R. and Li, S. (2001) *China's Retreat from Equality: Income Distribution and Economic Transition*. Armonk, NY: M.E. Sharpe.

Sen, A.K. (1973) *On Economic Inequality*, Oxford: Oxford University Press.

Shorrocks, A. (1982) 'Inequality decomposition by factor components', *Econometrica*, 50(1): 193–211.

Shorrocks, A. (1984) 'Inequality decomposition by population subgroup', *Econometrica*, 52(6): 1369–85.

West, L.A. and Zhao, Y. (2000) *Rural Labour Flows in China*, Berkeley: Institute of East Asian Studies, University of California, Berkeley.

World Bank (1997) *Sharing Rising Incomes: Disparities in China*, Washington, DC: The World Bank.

Yang, D.T. (1999) 'Urban-biased policies and rising income inequality in China', *American Economic Review*, 89(2): 306–10.

Zhao, R. and Li, S. (1999) 'Zhongguo jumin shouru chaju de kuoda ji qi yuanyin' (The analysis of increase in household income inequality in China), in Zhao, R., Li, S. and Riskin, C. (eds), *Zhongguo Jumin Shouru Fenpei Zai Yanjiu* (Re-examination of Income Distribution of Chinese Households), Beijing: Publishing House of Chinese Finance and Economy.

## Appendix 4.A: Summary statistics of the data

| | *1988* | | *1995* | | *1999* | |
|---|---|---|---|---|---|---|
| | *Mean* | *SD* | *Mean* | *SD* | *Mean* | *SD* |
| Real PCHI | 1,372.08 | 585.99 | 2,101.22 | 1,187.85 | 2,694.00 | 1,700.16 |
| Log(Real PCHI) | 7.15 | 0.37 | 7.52 | 0.50 | 7.73 | 0.59 |
| Real HI | 4,723.24 | 1,958.54 | 6,428.41 | 3,273.15 | 8,134.93 | 5,363.45 |
| Log(RHI) | 8.39 | 0.36 | 8.66 | 0.47 | 8.84 | 0.59 |
| Av. age of HH labour | 37.70 | 7.88 | 42.02 | 8.84 | 42.44 | 8.35 |
| (Av. age of HH labour)$^2$ | 1,482.98 | 640.02 | 1,843.57 | 806.34 | 1,871.08 | 765.37 |
| Av. years of schooling of HH labour | 10.69 | 2.47 | 10.38 | 2.67 | 10.75 | 2.33 |
| H party membership | 0.39 | | 0.39 | | 0.41 | |
| W party membership | 0.14 | | 0.18 | | 0.19 | |
| H unemployed | 0.01 | | 0.05 | | 0.09 | |
| W unemployed | 0.05 | | 0.07 | | 0.15 | |
| 2nd generation unemployed | 0.01 | | 0.03 | | 0.04 | |
| H working in LMFs | | | 0.22 | | 0.32 | |
| W working in LMFs | | | 0.23 | | 0.36 | |
| H working in local SOEs | 0.42 | | 0.53 | | 0.43 | |
| H working in collectives | 0.14 | | 0.11 | | 0.08 | |
| H working in private sector | 0.01 | | 0.02 | | 0.07 | |
| H did not report sector | 0.04 | | 0.02 | | 0.01 | |
| W working in local SOEs | 0.30 | | 0.47 | | 0.41 | |
| W working in collectives | 0.25 | | 0.21 | | 0.17 | |
| W working in private sector | 0.02 | | 0.02 | | 0.07 | |
| W did not report sector | 0.14 | | 0.07 | | 0.06 | |
| Male as the HH head | 0.95 | | 0.73 | | 0.74 | |
| % of children aged 0–5 | 0.06 | 0.12 | 0.04 | 0.10 | 0.03 | 0.09 |
| % of children aged 6–10 | 0.08 | 0.14 | 0.06 | 0.12 | 0.05 | 0.11 |
| % of children aged 11–16 | 0.07 | 0.14 | 0.08 | 0.14 | 0.07 | 0.13 |
| % of elderly | 0.03 | 0.09 | 0.05 | 0.15 | 0.06 | 0.16 |
| Household size | 3.59 | 0.98 | 3.20 | 0.80 | 3.10 | 0.73 |
| No. of employed HH members | 2.15 | 0.70 | 2.25 | 0.68 | 2.18 | 0.68 |
| Liaoning | 0.23 | | 0.24 | | 0.21 | |
| Jiangsu | 0.27 | | 0.26 | | 0.20 | |
| Henan | 0.25 | | 0.20 | | 0.22 | |
| Gansu | 0.14 | | 0.14 | | 0.19 | |
| No. of observations | 3,700 | | 2,746 | | 3,215 | |

Note: Data exclude households with missing values.

## Appendix 4.B: Imputation of the rental subsidy and rental value of owner-occupied housing

Gustafsson and Li (2001) state that the way they impute the rental subsidy is to subtract the actual rent from the interviewees' self-estimated market rent of the housing they live in. The way they impute the rental value of owner-occupied housing is to assume that the rent is 8 per cent of the current market value of the house. Questions on the current market value of the house and the self-estimated market value of the rent are asked in the 1995 survey but not in the 1988 survey. It is not clear how Gustafsson and Li (2001) and Khan and Riskin (2001) imputed these values for the 1988 data.

Fortunately, the two questions from the 1995 survey are also asked in the 1999 survey, and hence, the rental subsidy and the rental value of owner-occupied housing for the 1995 and 1999 data can be imputed. However, when the data are studied carefully, a couple of issues arise. First, many households did not report their current housing value even though they own their house, and many households who rented from the government did not report their estimated market rental value. This situation is especially severe in the 1995 data (see Table 4.B.1). Second, because the market rental value is the households' own estimate, the data are very noisy. Large variations exist and there are noticeable outliers. It is not clear how Gustafsson and Li (2001) and Khan and Riskin (2001) handled these problems.

To fill in missing data, equations are estimated for current market value of owned houses and the market rental value of rented housing using explanatory variables of living area of the house, whether the house has a central heating system, how many rooms in the house (only available for the 1995 data) and provincial dummy variables. The current market value of owned houses and the market rental values of rented government housing for those who fail to report these data are then predicted using the estimated results.

To handle the second problem, the distributions of the household self-estimated market rental values are plotted and the extreme tails of the data are deleted from the estimation of the market rental equations. In the 1995 survey, 0.02 per cent of sample households were excluded and the estimated adjusted $R^2$ increased from 0.03 per cent to 0.38 per cent, whereas for the 1999 survey 0.04 per cent of the sample households were excluded and the adjusted $R^2$ increased from 0.02 to 0.43. The results of these estimations are reported in Table 4.B.2.

The inequality measures of the two income variables are reported in Table 4.B.3. They are: (1) original income variable used in the paper (original income), and (2) income including the imputed rental subsidy and imputed rental value of owner-occupied housing using predicted value to replace missing values and excluding outliers from the market rental value equation (adjusted income). The results show that adjusting for the rental values does not change the inequality levels and the trend.

*Table 4.B.1* Missing values for household self-estimated market rent, 1995 and 1999

| | *1995* | | *1999* | |
|---|---|---|---|---|
| | *Market housing value* | *Estimated market rental value* | *Market housing value* | *Estimated market rental value* |
| Total number of households | 2,896 | 3,935 | 2,862 | 1,278 |
| No. of households reported | 2,308 | 2,865 | 2,441 | 1,192 |
| Missing values | 588 | 1,070 | 421 | 86 |
| % of missing values | 0.20 | 0.27 | 0.15 | 0.07 |

*Table 4.B.2:* Estimated housing value and rental value equations for 1995 and 1999

| | *Current market value of housing* | | *Estimated market rental value of rented housing* | | | |
|---|---|---|---|---|---|---|
| | | | *Including outliers* | | *Excluding outliers* | |
| | *Coeff.* | *t-ratio* | *Coeff.* | *t-ratio* | *Coeff.* | *t-ratio* |
| *1995* | | | | | | |
| Constant | 22,671.92 | 3.82 | 522.67 | 4.59 | 498.33 | 34.29 |
| Living area (metres) | 397.48 | 11.09 | 4.80 | 4.36 | 1.36 | 9.83 |
| Central heating | 18,616.21 | 6.23 | 328.29 | 4.32 | 143.89 | 15.32 |
| No. of rooms | 1,171.21 | 1.91 | −4.58 | −0.35 | 0.16 | 0.11 |
| Regional dummies | Yes | | Yes | | Yes | |
| No. of observations | 2,487 | | 5,364 | | 5,208 | |
| Adjusted $R^2$ | 0.35 | | 0.03 | | 0.38 | |
| *1999* | | | | | | |
| Constant | 9,152.71 | 1.76 | −235.75 | −1.20 | −36.42 | −1.83 |
| Living area (metres) | 1,301.97 | 22.94 | 9.03 | 3.57 | 6.46 | 25.17 |
| Central heating | 9,346.06 | 2.52 | 279.64 | 1.89 | 183.63 | 12.28 |
| Regional dummies | Yes | | Yes | | Yes | |
| No. of observations | 2,765 | | 4,203 | | 4,187 | |
| Adjusted $R^2$ | 0.36 | | 0.02 | | 0.43 | |

*Table 4.B.3* Inequality measures of different income variables

| | *Per capita household real income* | | *Total household real income* | |
|---|---|---|---|---|
| | *Original income* | *Adjusted income* | *Original income* | *Adjusted income* |
| *1995* | | | | |
| Relative mean deviation | 0.194 | 0.196 | 0.184 | 0.182 |
| Coefficient of variation | 0.558 | 0.543 | 0.514 | 0.494 |
| Standard deviation of logs | 0.506 | 0.505 | 0.484 | 0.475 |
| Gini coefficient | 0.273 | 0.275 | 0.260 | 0.257 |
| *1999* | | | | |
| Relative mean deviation | 0.223 | 0.232 | 0.221 | 0.225 |
| Coefficient of variation | 0.631 | 0.640 | 0.654 | 0.636 |
| Standard deviation of logs | 0.603 | 0.607 | 0.606 | 0.595 |
| Gini coefficient | 0.313 | 0.324 | 0.313 | 0.316 |

# 5 Unemployment, consumption smoothing and precautionary saving in urban China

*Xin Meng*

## 5.1 Introduction

Economic shocks occur frequently, especially in the developing world, due to normal business cycles, financial shocks and economic restructuring. Facing such shocks, many individuals and households experience difficult periods of unexpected reduction in income, and perhaps even poverty. One mechanism used by governments in the developed world to offset the effect of adverse shocks is an income support scheme.[1] Putting aside the possible negative effects of redistribution measures on economic efficiency and any possible crowding-out effect on private precautionary savings (Engen and Gruber 2001), many developing countries have limited resources to provide such support. Thus, finding the most effective way to help the individuals and households that are affected adversely by economic shocks is an important policy issue.

The theoretical background for government-financed direct income support schemes assumes that individual households are limited in their ability to help themselves and that individuals are unable to save for their own uncertain future (Bauer and Paish 1952).[2] However, according to the permanent income hypothesis, individual households should be able to smooth their consumption by saving in normal times and dissaving during periods of adverse economic shocks. Many empirical studies find evidence to support the permanent income hypothesis in several developing economies (Bhalla 1979, 1980; Wolpin 1982; Paxson 1992). Furthermore, life-cycle models allowing for precautionary saving indicate that, if uncertainty over future income increases, current consumption falls and saving increases, especially in the developing world where liquidity constraints are significant (Carroll and Samwick 1994; Deaton 1997). If these theories are correct, governments from developing countries may be better off spending scarce resources in more effective ways, such as providing training to unemployed workers, incentives for self-employment, and direct income support only to the disabled, the elderly and the most severe cases of long-term unemployment. Therefore, whether individual households have precautionary saving motives and whether they are able to smooth consumption during difficult periods affect significantly the design of effective and efficient government income support policies.

This study focuses on the situation in urban China. In the last twenty years the Chinese economy experienced a significant transformation from a planned to a market-oriented economy. During the last decade or so, dramatic reforms in the state sector, the social welfare system and the labour market have brought more uncertainty to households. Urban unemployment has become one of the most important social and economic problems in China since the mid-1990s. Over the period from 1995 to 1999, around 15 million state sector workers have been made redundant (Fan 2000). In addition, the lack of formal credit markets indicates that urban households face significant liquidity constraints. The question naturally arises as to whether Chinese urban households are capable of smoothing their consumption in the face of a greater incidence of adverse shocks. In addition, the role of precautionary saving during this period of significant changes and dramatic increases in future uncertainty is an important topic.

Many authors have investigated the saving and consumption behavior of Chinese households (Qian 1988; Jefferson 1990; Qin 1991; Wang and Wen 1992; Ma 1993; Wang 1995; Jalan and Ravallion 1999, 2001; Kraay 2000; Aaberge and Zhu 2001). Most of these studies focus on explaining household saving behavior rather than the ability of households to smooth consumption with respect to unexpected shocks. In addition, the majority of the studies utilize aggregate data. Although Jalan and Ravallion (1999, 2001) and Kraay (2000) investigate the effect of income shocks on consumption and the impact of future income uncertainty on saving, Jalan and Ravallion (1999, 2001) is based primarily on rural household surveys while Kraay (2000) is based on aggregate provincial data. Moreover, Kraay (2000) uses data collected for the period before 1995, when the acceleration of urban economic reform had not been under way for a sufficient period to generate significant increases in future uncertainty for urban households. This fact may account for his results that neither the permanent income hypothesis nor precautionary saving motives explain urban household savings in China.

This chapter utilizes the 1999 CASS survey. The questions addressed in this chapter are how well urban households can smooth consumption and how well they can handle future income shocks, with a special focus on urban unemployment. The situation in urban China provides a unique opportunity to test the permanent income and precautionary saving hypotheses due to the sudden increase in adverse income shocks and the introduction of substantial income uncertainty.

The chapter is structured as follows. The next section describes briefly the background changes that have occurred in the Chinese economy with particular attention paid to the increase in unemployment and uncertainty faced by urban households. Section 5.3 provides the framework for the empirical analysis and discusses the data. Section 5.4 presents the empirical results, and conclusions with policy implications are given in Section 5.5.

## 5.2 Background

Per capita income in urban China has increased significantly since economic reforms began in 1978. From 1982 to 1998, per capita real income increased from 471 yuan to 1,461 yuan, a threefold increase and an average annual growth rate of about 7.3 per cent (NBS, various years). In addition, the social security system changed during the reform period. In the pre-reform era most welfare benefits, such as housing, medical care, pensions and children's schooling, were provided by the state-owned enterprises as an internal social security system. Every urban resident was guaranteed lifetime employment (Meng 2000). This security system has been gradually changing during the reform process, but the rate of change has accelerated since the early 1990s.

Starting from the late 1980s, almost all aspects of the old social security system have been gradually dismantled. Housing reform began with increases in official rents and proceeded to allow government housing occupants to buy their own house at a subsidized price. Finally, the housing market has opened so that, by the end of 1999, most urban households expected to be able to purchase their own housing. According to the 1999 CASS survey, among 4,474 households surveyed in 13 cities, 63 per cent owned their own house in 1999. Medical care changed from fully state-covered medical service to a two-tier system, in which the state covers a certain percentage of the costs and individuals pay the rest. According to the survey, among the 8,935 individuals who incurred medical expenses in 1999, less than 30 per cent of these expenses were paid by the state.

Pension reform divides old-age support into a mandatory basic system and a voluntary commercial system (Garnaut *et al.* 2001). A regional unified mandatory social pension fund, to which both firms and employees contribute, was established in some cities during the early 1990s. In the voluntary commercial system, a worker or a firm may buy retirement insurance voluntarily but regional variation is significant. More schools are charging fees and compulsory donations for primary and secondary education. Since the mid-1990s, tertiary education has also increasingly required financial contributions from parents.

Perhaps the most significant changes have occurred in the system of employment. Lifetime employment has been abolished for new labour market entrants, even in the state sector. As a replacement, new labour market entrants are employed mainly under fixed or continuous contracts (Meng 2000). More importantly, the employment share of the state sector is shrinking while the employment share of the other sector, which comprises private, foreign-owned and joint venture enterprises, is increasing significantly. Employment in the other sector is mainly under short-term contract or on a temporary basis. In 1998, the employment share of the other sector exceeded the employment share of the state sector (Meng 2003).

Accompanying these changes is the reform of state-owned enterprises. Due to soft budget constraints and other problems related to determining property rights, the Chinese state sector has been performing badly. In 1995 and 1996, around 50 per cent of the state-owned enterprises were making losses (East Asia Analytical Unit 1997). To invigorate the Chinese economy, a policy of drastic reform, in which many small and medium-sized loss-making state enterprises were bankrupted, was introduced. Those that survived began to take efficiency seriously. As a result of these two forces, around 15 million state sector workers have become redundant (Fan 2000). According to the 1995 CASS survey, also

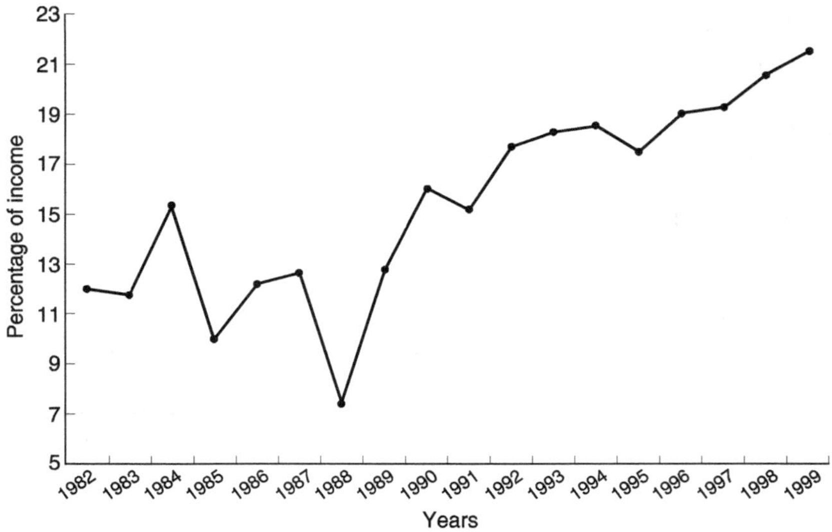


*Figure 5.1* Per capita saving rate, 1982–1998. Source: NBS (various years).

conducted by the Institute of Economics at the Chinese Academy of Social Sciences in 1996, and the 1999 CASS survey, the unemployment rate was 8.5 per cent in 1995 and had increased to 17.3 per cent by 1999. Thus, not only has lifetime employment been abolished for the young, but those who previously had expected lifetime employment, especially middle-aged and older employees, are facing a real possibility of being displaced. In summary, social security reforms implemented in urban China, together with a dramatic increase in unemployment in recent years, have changed urban household perceptions about their economic future.

Despite these growing uncertainties, the formal credit market in urban China has not been developing quickly and banks do not normally provide personal loans. Only since 1997 have some banks in some regions begun to provide housing loans and a limited number of other personal loans to individual households. This sudden increase in uncertainty of household income and the social safety net should have a significant impact on household consumption and saving behavior. Figure 5.1 shows the increase in the per capita saving rate for urban households since the late 1980s when the social security reform began. From 1995 to 1999, as layoffs in the state sector were increasing, average per capita income increased by 7.3 per cent per annum, while the average rate of per capita saving increased by 13.1 per cent per annum. In a survey of household saving motives from 1995 to 1997, Wu (1999) finds that the main motives for saving are buying houses, paying for children's education, health and old-age insurance, and preparing for unemployment.[3]

## 5.3 Model specification and data

According to the permanent income hypothesis, households smooth their consumption over a given time horizon. When realized income exceeds expected income, households save. When realized income is below expected income, households either borrow from banks, families or friends, or withdraw money from previous savings to finance current consumption. Thus, the consumption of household *i* is a linear function of its permanent income or expected income and transitory income, which is the difference between realized and expected income. Other variables related to household taste, such as household size and composition, also affect consumption (Friedman 1957; Bhalla 1980; Paxson 1992). Life-cycle models, which allow for precautionary saving, suggest that income uncertainty should also affect household consumption behaviour as long as households have precautionary saving motives (Carroll 1994; Carroll and Weil 1994; Deaton 1997). Following Paxson (1992), we specify the consumption function as follows:

$$C_i = \alpha + \beta Y_i^P + \gamma Y_i^T + \mu UC_i + \lambda X_i + \varepsilon_i \tag{5.1}$$

where

$C_i$ is household *i*'s consumption level;
$Y_i^P$ is the measure of permanent income for household *i*;
$Y_i^T$ is the measure of transitory income for household *i*;
$UC_i$ is income uncertainty facing household *i*; and
$X_i$ is a vector of household characteristics representing shift in tastes.

According to Friedman (1957), the marginal propensity to consume out of permanent income, $\beta$, should be equal to one and the marginal propensity to consume out of transitory income, $\gamma$, should be zero in the strict version of the permanent income hypothesis. However, empirical studies often find that this strict version does not fit the data, due to liquidity constraints (Zeldes 1989; Jappelli and Pagano 1994) or to an increase in the precautionary saving motive generated by increases in income uncertainty (Carroll 1994). Thus, a weaker version of the permanent income hypothesis, which suggests that $\beta > \gamma$, may be more appropriate (Bhalla 1980; Paxson 1992; Deaton 1997). Consumption theory also indicates that, if urban Chinese households are precautionary savers, the variable *UC* measuring income uncertainty should be negatively correlated with consumption.

Measuring permanent and transitory income is an important issue in the literature. When using a single cross-section of data, the normal procedure is to use at least one instrumental variable that is correlated with permanent income and orthogonal to consumption to identify permanent income. Such instruments have included assets and education, lagged income, and long-run averages of rainfall (Musgrove 1978, 1979; Bhalla 1979; Wolpin 1982; Deaton 1997). An alternative procedure is to find at least one instrument that can identify transitory income shocks. For example, Paxson (1992) uses regional rainfall to construct measures of a component of transitory income for Thai rice farmers and uses this instrument to facilitate the estimation of the propensity to save out of transitory income. Using panel data, Bhalla (1980) constructs two different permanent income measures; one is a weighted average of past incomes and the other is based on estimates of an earnings equation that accounts for unobservable personal characteristics.

The current study uses cross-sectional data to identify the effect of a transitory income shock, namely, employment displacement, on households' consumption behaviour. Although the methodology of Paxson (1992) would be ideal, displacement is not an exogenous shock and the determinants of displacement are highly collinear with the determinants of permanent income, so that this approach cannot be followed.[4] Another possible approach is to use predicted values of permanent income from cross-sectional estimates of household income based on human capital theory as a measure for permanent income (Wang 1995). However, Kraay (2000) argues that such methodology does not account for the rapid change in the economic environment in China. The permanent income measure most applicable is weighted average of past incomes used by Bhalla (1980) and specified as:

$$Y^P = \sum W_t Y_t \qquad t = -\infty, \ldots, 0 \tag{5.2}$$

where $W_t$ is the weights for time $t$ and $Y_t$ is the measured income in time $t$. The weight, $W_t$, is specified as follows:

$$W_t = \delta \frac{(1+\alpha)^{-t}}{(1+\delta)^{-t}}, \qquad t = -\infty, \ldots, -3, -2, -1, 0 \tag{5.3}$$

where $\alpha$ refers to the trend rate of growth in permanent income, $Y^P$, and $\delta$ refers to the weighting parameter, which is analogous to an adjustment coefficient relating actual to expected permanent income. If $Y^P$ is measured as a weighted average of past incomes, $\delta$ is a direct estimate of the discount rate (Bhalla 1980).

Although our data are cross-sectional, households were asked to report their last five years' income. However, the question is how to weight past incomes to obtain the best estimate of a household's permanent income. Bhalla's characterization does not take into account a change in future uncertainties because the normal definition of uncertainty only implies changes in the variance of expected income, whereas an increase in the probability of being unemployed involves not only changes in the variance of expected income but also changes in expected income itself. An increase in the probability of unemployment in China reduces income without any offsetting positive effect, and consequently reduces a household's expected income in addition to increasing uncertainty.

To take into account the change in expected income generated by the increased risk of unemployment, the permanent income measure is adjusted for the change in the average probability of being unemployed for each household. Thus, each year's income is adjusted by the estimated average household probability of being unemployed for that year. Following Bird (1995), the measure of permanent income can be written as:

$$Y^P = \sum W_t[(I - P_t)^* Y_t + P_t \overline{Y}^U_t] \qquad (5.4)$$

where $P_t$ is the average probability of individuals in household $i$ being displaced in time $t$, and $\overline{Y}^U_t$, is the average income of households that have unemployed members at time $t$.

The probability of each household labourer being unemployed or displaced is specified as:

$$Prob(UE_j = 1) = f(age_j, sage_j, edu_j, health_j, sector_j, sex_j, region_j) \qquad (5.5)$$

where *sage* is a squared term of age; *edu* is years of schooling; *health* indicates whether individual *j* was healthy in 1999; *sector* is individual *j*'s sector of employment, which is measured as the previous sector of employment if the individual is unemployed; and *region* refers to a group of regional dummy variables.[5] Equation (5.5) is estimated for all individuals from ages 16 to 65 who were in the labour force. The estimated results are used to predict the probability of being unemployed for each individual in the sample. The average of the unemployment probability for each household is calculated from the predicted probability for the individuals. Following other studies, transitory income is defined as the difference between realized and expected income.

Economic theory suggests that households with precautionary motives will consume less (more) when future income uncertainty is higher (lower). As we indicated, Chinese urban households have been subject to significant changes in social welfare arrangements. In addition, due to the lack of a formal credit market, high interest rates in the informal market, and a strong cultural bias against debt, Chinese households have historically been reluctant to borrow money. Each of these factors may contribute to a precautionary saving motive of urban Chinese households. We measure households' income uncertainty, *UC*, by two variables; one is the variance of past incomes and the other is the average predicted probability for the household's labourers of being unemployed or displaced in 1999.[6] The variables used to represent shift in household tastes include household size, the age and years of schooling of the household head, the proportion of individuals for each age and gender group in the household, and an indication of whether household *i* has experienced changes in household size in 1999.

Our main data source is the 1999 CASS surveys; however, to assist in estimating the probability of being unemployed in earlier years, data from the 1995 CASS suvey is also used. In the survey, information on household income and expenditure is recorded directly from a household income and expenditure diary.[7] Saving is derived from the income and expenditure data.

The calculation of the weight used to adjust permanent income, $W_t$, requires determination of $\delta$ and $\alpha$. Bhalla (1980) assumes a common income growth rate for all households, but we use a variable income growth trend to allow different types of households to have different expected income growth rates. For this purpose, the sample is divided into ten income deciles and, within each decile, the households are divided into three age groups based on the age of the household head, namely 20 to 40, 40 to 60, and above 60. The log-linear trends to the five years of recalled income data for each of the thirty groups of households are estimated and the average growth rate for each group obtained from these regressions for each group is then applied to the definition of permanent income. The parameter $\delta$, which should be the direct estimate of discount rate, is allowed to range from 10 to 90 per cent to test the sensitivity of the results, given that the discount rate for households is not observed.

To adjust permanent income, we trace the probability of being unemployed or displaced, $P_t$, for each of the four years by estimating equation (5.5) using both the 1995 and 1999 data sets. Predicted probabilities for both years for the sample households are obtained from the estimated results. We assume that the change in the probability of being unemployed takes an exponential form between the two years. The predicted probabilities for each household for the years from 1996 to 1998 are calculated according to the average annual growth rate of the probability for each household. The 1995 and 1999 CASS surveys have two questions on employment status. The first seeks information on the individual's current labour force status at the time the surveys were conducted, in 1996 and 2000, respectively. The second asks about the individual's employment and unemployment status in 1995 and 1999. Because both individual incomes and household consumption are given for 1995 and 1999, the second measure of employment status is used as the main indicator for unemployment. In addition to the two questions on employment status, the survey also interviewed 1,336 displaced workers, which is not the complete sample of displaced workers, and contains detailed information on their durations of unemployment. From this information, a rough measure of the stock of unemployment or displacement for each year from 1995 to 1999 can be derived.[8] To test the sensitivity of the unemployment adjustment to permanent income, we estimate equation (5.5) using this unemployment stock measure for each of these five years and obtain alternative predicted probability measures using results from these estimations.[9]

The 1999 CASS survey comprises 13,538 individuals from 4,494 households with an average household size of 3.01 people. Excluding missing values, the total number of households in the estimations ranges from 3,874 to 4,094, depending on the adjustment used for the permanent income measure. Among the sampled households, 24 per cent have unemployed or displaced members. An interesting phenomenon observed from the data is that, on average, the subsample of households with unemployed members has positive savings. Table 5.1 presents the average household real income, real expenditure and real savings in 1999 for the total sample and for the subsamples of households with and without unemployed members. Households with unemployed members have an average income about 66 per cent of that for households without unemployed members. The ratio of expenditure and saving between the two groups is 74 and 36 per cent, respectively. The average saving rates for the households with and without unemployed members are 12 and 22 per cent, respectively. Figure 5.2 presents the distribution of saving for these two subgroups by indicating household average saving by decile, arranged in ascending order. Apart from a vertical displacement,

*Table 5.1* Summary statistics of income, consumption and savings (in yuan)

| | *Total sample* | | *Households without unemployed member* | | *Households with unemployed member* | |
|---|---|---|---|---|---|---|
| | *Mean* | *CV* | *Mean* | *CV* | *Mean* | *CV* |
| Real income | 17,092.87 | 0.64 | 18,743.83 | 0.61 | 12,343.24 | 0.64 |
| Real total expenditure | 13,654.25 | 0.61 | 14,619.41 | 0.58 | 10,877.59 | 0.63 |
| Real saving | 3,438.62 | 2.63 | 4,124.42 | 2.33 | 1,465.65 | 4.73 |

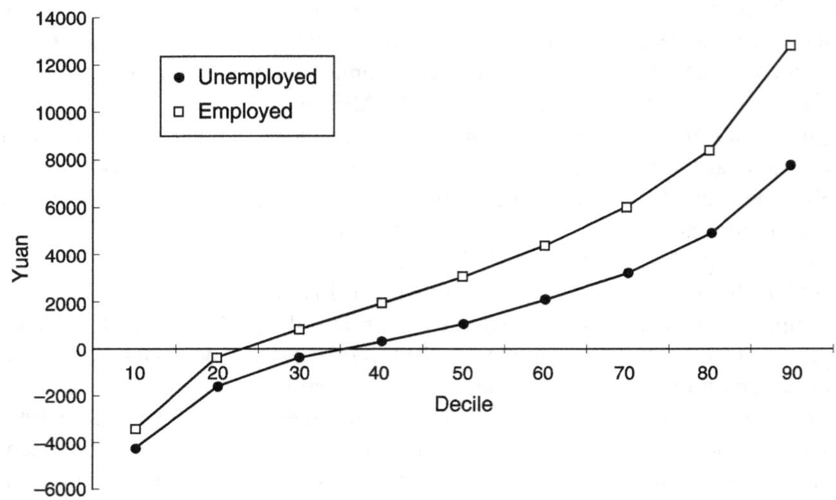


*Figure 5.2* Deciles of average savings for households with and without unemployed members.

the saving pattern is quite similar for the two groups. About 35 per cent of households with unemployed members dissave, while this ratio is about 23 per cent for the other group.

Average savings for households with unemployed members is positive, as Table 5.1 indicates, and about 65 per cent of these households has positive saving, as Figure 5.2 indicates. Hence, the unemployment shock to urban households, measured in terms of its impact on consumption and savings, is not as significant as might have been expected. Perhaps there are other income possibilities available to these households apart from formal employment that offset the unemployment shock, for example, employment in the informal sector and intra-family income transfers.[10] Although real total expenditure for households with unemployed members is about 33 per cent less than that of households without unemployed individuals, the expenditure patterns of these two groups are similar. Food consumption accounts for 42 per cent of total consumption for households without unemployment and 46 per cent for households with unemployed members. The proportion of educational expenditure is 12 and 10 per cent, respectively. The family size for households without unemployed individuals is slightly smaller than that of households with unemployed individuals. In addition, households with unemployed members have a slightly higher proportion of primary aged female members than other households, at 36 per cent compared to 33 per cent.

## 5.4 Empirical results

To examine the determinants of unemployment or displacement, the results from estimating equation (5.5) using the 1995, 1999 CASS surveys are reported in Table 5.2. The omitted category for the employment sector is the private sector, which is defined as a combination of the local private, foreign-owned, joint venture and self-employed sectors. Over this five-year period, unemployment increased from 8.5 to 17.3 per cent. Table 5.2 indicates that gender is not an important determinant of being unemployed or displaced in 1995, but that women are significantly more likely to be unemployed in 1999 and the result is significant. Moreover, older individuals have a much higher chance of becoming unemployed in 1999 than in 1995.[11] In addition, an individual's health condition has no effect on employment status in 1995 but it becomes a significant determinant in 1999.[12] Finally, the effect of the sector of employment on unemployment has changed. Individuals who were previously employed in the local state or collective sectors have less or no more chance of becoming unemployed than those employed in the private sector in 1995. By 1999, the chance of an employee who worked in the local state or collective sectors becoming redundant is much higher than it is for their counterparts in the private sector. Note that probability of unemployment is significantly less for those employed in the central state sector in both years.

These results coincide with expectations. Since 1995, more older women have been made redundant. In addition, because the drastic enterprise reforms occurred mostly in small and medium-sized enterprises and these enterprises are concentrated mostly in the local state and collective sectors, unemployment or displacement is more likely to occur in these sectors than in the private sector in the later years. This significant change in the determinants of unemployment or displacement will have an important impact on expected income of households. Hence, we must adjust permanent income measures for the predicted average probability of being unemployed or displaced.

To evaluate the impact of unemployment on household consumption, two adjustments are made to the normal empirical test of the permanent income hypothesis. First, permanent income is adjusted for the predicted probability of being unemployed or displaced. Second, the predicted probability of being unemployed or displaced is included in the consumption equation as an independent effect to capture whether households change their consumption behaviour over and above the adjustment to permanent income, because of the possibility of some members being displaced. In addition, we test to see if consumption behaviour differs between households with and without unemployed members. Separate consumption equations

*Table 5.2* Results from probit estimation of unemployment

| | *1995* | | *1999* | |
|---|---|---|---|---|
| | *Marginal effect* | *t-ratios* | *Marginal effect* | *t-ratios* |
| Age | −0.0022 | −9.49 | 0.0281 | 12.19 |
| $Age^2$ | | | −0.0004 | −14.09 |
| Years of schooling | −0.0121 | −13.5 | −0.0133 | −10.83 |
| Dummy for being healthy | −0.0071 | −0.26 | −0.0422 | −3.24 |
| Central state sector | −0.0537 | −6.37 | −0.0318 | −3.24 |
| Local state sector | −0.0392 | −4.34 | 0.0454 | 4.79 |
| Collective sector | 0.0118 | 1.19 | 0.1347 | 9.84 |
| Dummy for male | −0.0014 | −0.31 | −0.0231 | −3.89 |
| Regional dummies | Yes | | Yes | |
| No. of observations | 12,357 | | 9,379 | |
| Pseudo-$R^2$ | 0.073 | | 0.125 | |

Notes:

1 The results are marginal effects, which indicate how a unit change in the independent variable affects the change of the probability of being unemployed.

2 Both central state and local state sectors are state-owned.

are estimated for the two groups of households when a statistically significant difference in behavioural patterns is identified. The theoretical rationale is that households with unemployed members may face more serious liquidity or subsistence constraints and, hence, have different consumption patterns than households without unemployed members. In addition, because large-scale unemployment has only recently become recognized by Chinese urban households, households experiencing unemployment shocks may not have had enough time to adjust.

We test consumption smoothing separately for total consumption, food consumption and educational expenditure. Because education generates human capital, expenditure on education is an investment. In addition, households usually spend more on children's education than an adult's education so that the investment has a strong intergenerational effect. Hence, education can be viewed as a form of bequest. Because our main interest is whether households smooth their expenditure when facing transitory shocks, the distinction of whether educational expenditure is considered as consumption or investment is not important. Nevertheless, considering educational expenditure as an investment in human capital, which has an intergenerational effect, is important when policy implications are drawn.

We estimated equation (5.1) with controls for regional differences. $F$-tests for structural differences between households with and without unemployed members indicate that the two groups of households have significantly different behaviour patterns for total consumption and food consumption, but no statistically significant difference is observed for educational expenditure.[13] Nevertheless, the marginal propensity to spend on education out of permanent income is statistically different between the two groups. Thus, the results reported below for total consumption and food consumption include findings for the total sample as well as for the two subsamples of households with and without unemployed members separately. For educational expenditure, an interaction term between permanent income and a dummy variable for households with an unemployed member is included. To test the robustness of the results to the different ways of measuring permanent income, each consumption equation is estimated six times using different permanent and transitory income measures.

The predicted probability of unemployment is obtained in two ways, one according to the stock of unemployment in 1999 reported in the 1999 CASS data and the other according to the information on current employment status reported in the 1999 data. To test the sensitivity of the results to these differences, each of the six consumption regressions is also estimated twice for the different measures of predicted probabilities. The estimations using different permanent income measures and different measures of the predicted probability of being displaced produce similar results, which suggests that the results are robust. Selected results from the total consumption regression using permanent income adjusted for a variable growth rate, $\alpha$, a discount rate, $\delta$, as well as for the predicted probability of being displaced obtained from 1995 and 1999 data, are reported in Table 5.3.[14] The table consists of three panels with the results from the total sample in the top panel and the estimates for the subsamples of households with and without unemployed members in the middle and bottom panels, respectively.

To correct for heteroscedasticity, White's consistent estimator of the covariance matrix is used (Greene 1990). In addition, inconsistency of the variance–covariance matrix may also arise due to the use of the predicted regressor of average probability of being unemployed or displaced for the household labourers. However, the remedy provided by Pagan (1984) may not be appropriate because our predicted regressor is generated from a non-linear estimation. Furthermore, the consumption equations are estimated at the household level, whereas the probability of being unemployed is estimated at the individual level and then the average predicted probability for the household is calculated using these individual level probabilities. These factors make it difficult to correct for the inconsistent estimation of the variance–covariance matrix. To deal with this problem, all standard errors were bootstrapped and the results are consistent with those obtained using White's consistent estimates. Thus, all the reported $t$-statistics are calculated according to White's consistent estimator of the variance–covariance matrix.[15]

The coefficients on permanent and transitory incomes represent the marginal propensity to consume out of each type of income. The rows labelled as test of consumption smoothing indicate whether the marginal propensity to consume (MPC) out of permanent and transitory incomes are statistically significantly different from each other. Regarding total consumption, the MPC out of permanent income ranges from 50 to 52 per cent for the total sample. Although it is higher for households with unemployed members than for households without unemployment, the difference is not statistically significant. The MPC out of transitory income is statistically significantly different between households with and without unemployed members. For the former, almost 40 per cent of transitory income is spent; for the latter, the ratio is only around 30 per cent.[16] These differences

*Table 5.3* Selected results from total consumption regression

| | $\delta=0.1$ | | $\delta=0.9$ | |
|---|---|---|---|---|
| | *Coeff.* | *t-ratio* | *Coeff.* | *t-ratio* |
| *Total sample* | | | | |
| Permanent income ($\beta$) | 0.50 | 13.97 | 0.52 | 15.93 |
| Transitory income ($\gamma$) | 0.31 | 5.03 | 0.29 | 4.57 |
| Predicted probability of unemployment | −66.59 | −3.73 | −61.32 | −3.60 |
| Variance of last 4 years income*$10^5$ | −0.16 | −2.10 | −0.29 | −2.91 |
| Test on consumption smoothing: $\beta>\gamma$ | 0.18 | 3.41 | 0.22 | 3.62 |
| No. of observations | 4,094 | | 4,094 | |
| Adjusted $R^2$ | 0.40 | | 0.40 | |
| *Employed* | | | | |
| Permanent income ($\beta$) | 0.47 | 11.67 | 0.50 | 13.35 |
| Transitory income ($\gamma$) | 0.29 | 4.20 | 0.27 | 3.84 |
| Predicted probability of unemployment | −70.21 | −3.20 | −64.38 | −3.03 |
| Variance of last 4 years income*$10^5$ | −0.14 | −1.74 | −0.28 | −2.63 |
| Test on consumption smoothing: $\beta>\gamma$ | 0.18 | 2.97 | 0.23 | 3.36 |
| No. of observations | 3,038 | | 3,038 | |
| Adjusted $R^2$ | 0.38 | | 0.39 | |
| *Unemployed* | | | | |
| Permanent income ($\beta$) | 0.58 | 10.64 | 0.56 | 10.09 |
| Transitory income ($\gamma$) | 0.39 | 8.87 | 0.40 | 8.35 |
| Predicted probability of unemployment | −38.94 | −1.66 | −39.53 | −1.66 |
| Variance of last 4 years income*$10^5$ | −0.46 | −2.87 | −0.41 | −2.38 |
| Test on consumption smoothing: $\beta>\gamma$ | 0.19 | 2.69 | 0.16 | 2.11 |
| No. of observations | 1,056 | | 1,056 | |
| Adjusted $R^2$ | 0.36 | | 0.35 | |

Note: Other variables included in the regression are: age and years of schooling of the household head, household size, percentage of different age and gender group in the household, whether the household size changed in 1999, and a group of regional dummy variables.

indicate that households with unemployed members have a higher propensity to consume and, hence, a lower propensity to save.

The statistical test as to whether $\beta$ is significantly greater than $\gamma$ indicates that urban Chinese households are capable of smoothing their total consumption. For the total sample and for the subsamples of households with and without unemployment, the difference between $\beta$ and $\gamma$ is always statistically significant. This result that households with unemployed members spend less of their transitory income relative to permanent income when facing significant income shocks and that, on average, they have positive savings suggests that other sources of income and assets may be available to allow them to compensate partially for their income loss from unemployment. Considering the effect of uncertainty on household consumption and savings, for the total sample and the two subsamples, the variation of the last four years of household income has a negative and significant effect on total consumption. Hence, households with more income uncertainty are more likely to consume less and save more.

When the variable denoted household average predicted probability of being displaced is included in the total consumption regression, the coefficient is negative and statistically significant; this coefficient is larger for households without unemployed members. One percentage point increase in a household's predicted probability of being displaced reduces household consumption by from 64 to 70 yuan. Hence, households with no unemployed members are aware of their potential probability of being displaced and react accordingly in their consumption and saving behaviour. The average probability of being displaced for households without unemployed members is about 12 per cent, with a minimum of approximately zero and a maximum of around 46 per cent. Thus, on average, these households save about 768 to 840 yuan in anticipation of unemployment, which accounts for around 19 to 20 per cent of their average savings.

The predicted probability of being unemployed also has a negative and statistically significant effect on the consumption of households with unemployed members. There are two possible interpretations of this additional effect. First, because we use cross-sectional data, the variation in the predicted probability of being unemployed among households with unemployed members may capture the effect of the duration of unemployment. Individuals with a longer duration of being unemployed are more likely to be identified in any given time frame. Thus, the negative effect of the average predicted probability of being unemployed on consumption may suggest that households with a predicted longer duration of being unemployed are saving more. Second, the variable we use is the average predicted probability of being unemployed for all household labourers. Thus, the negative effect of this variable on total consumption may indicate awareness of the probability that more household members may become unemployed.

The above analysis is focused mainly on total consumption. For households facing transitory shocks, especially negative shocks, important policy implications should be drawn from a household's basic food consumption and educational expenditure smoothing. Food consumption smoothing is important because it is an indicator of economic well-being for poor households. In the absence of such smoothing, the government should provide immediate assistance to poor households so that they may sustain normal nutritional intake. Nutritional deficiency not only affects the productivity of the adults from these households but, more importantly, it has a significant impact on the future health of the children of the poor households. From an intergenerational perspective, educational expenditure smoothing may be even more important, because education affects human capital development. Over the period of the rapid economic growth in China, the importance of education in generating income has increased significantly. While the rate of return to an additional year of schooling was 3.8 per cent in 1988, it increased to 5.2 per cent in 1995 and 8.8 per cent in 1999, which is more than double the rate in 1988.[17] If poor households are unable to smooth educational expenditure, their children receive less or worse education than children from rich households. This difference in investment translates into even larger differences in future income. Thus, investment in education is related to intergenerational income mobility, and if poor households cannot smooth educational expenditure, the government should provide assistance.

*Table 5.4* Selected results from food consumption regression

| | δ=0.1 | | δ=0.9 | |
|---|---|---|---|---|
| | *Coeff.* | *t-ratio* | *Coeff.* | *t-ratio* |
| *Total sample* | | | | |
| Permanent income ($\beta$) | 0.13 | 13.50 | 0.13 | 14.42 |
| Transitory income ($\gamma$) | 0.07 | 5.03 | 0.07 | 4.72 |
| Predicted probability of unemployment | −21.25 | −4.24 | −20.21 | −4.12 |
| Variance of last 4 years income*$10^5$ | −0.02 | −0.80 | −0.05 | −1.70 |
| Test on consumption smoothing: $\beta > \gamma$ | 0.06 | 4.59 | 0.07 | 4.50 |
| No. of observations | 4,094 | | 4,094 | |
| Adjusted $R^2$ | 0.39 | | 0.39 | |
| *Employed* | | | | |
| Permanent income ($\beta$) | 0.12 | 11.09 | 0.13 | 11.81 |
| Transitory income ($\gamma$) | 0.06 | 4.22 | 0.06 | 3.97 |
| Predicted probability of unemployment | −20.13 | −3.31 | −19.00 | −3.17 |
| Variance of last 4 years income*$10^5$ | −0.01 | −0.45 | −0.04 | −1.45 |
| Test on consumption smoothing: $\beta > \gamma$ | 0.06 | 3.92 | 0.07 | 4.03 |
| No. of observations | 3,038 | | 3,038 | |
| Adjusted $R^2$ | 0.36 | | 0.36 | |
| *Unemployed* | | | | |
| Permanent income ($\beta$) | 0.18 | 9.82 | 0.17 | 9.88 |
| Transitory income ($\gamma$) | 0.10 | 6.02 | 0.10 | 5.80 |
| Predicted probability of unemployment | −14.64 | −1.81 | −14.77 | −1.83 |
| Variance of last 4 years income*$10^5$ | −0.10 | −1.45 | −0.08 | −1.18 |
| Test on consumption smoothing: $\beta > \gamma$ | 0.08 | 3.31 | 0.07 | 2.89 |
| No. of observations | 1,056 | | 1,056 | |
| Adjusted $R^2$ | 0.46 | | 0.46 | |

Note: Other variables included in the regression are the same as in Table 5.3.

Table 5.4 reports selected results for the food consumption regression. The marginal propensity to consume food out of permanent and transitory income for the total sample is 13 and 7 per cent, respectively. Although these ratios are higher for the subsample of households with unemployed members, these households seem able to smooth their food consumption effectively. The test shows that $\beta$ is statistically significantly different from $\gamma$, with *t*-ratios of 2.9 to 3.3 for the unemployed households. The variation of previous income has no significant impact on food consumption perhaps, because food is essential and there is little scope for reduction. Despite this insignificant result, households having a higher probability of being unemployed save out of their food consumption, indicating that past income uncertainty is not as strong an influence as the probability of being unemployed in the future. However, the rate of saving out of food consumption is much lower than the rate of saving out of total consumption. On average, every one percentage point increase in the predicted probability of unemployment reduces expenditure on food consumption by about 20 and 15 yuan for the subsamples of households without and with unemployed members, respectively. Thus, on average,

*Table 5.5* Selected results from educational expenditure regression

| | $\delta=0.1$ | | $\delta=0.9$ | |
|---|---|---|---|---|
| | *Coeff.* | *t-ratio* | *Coeff.* | *t-ratio* |
| *Total sample* | | | | |
| Permanent income ($\beta$) | 0.07 | 6.87 | 0.07 | 7.73 |
| Permanent income*dummy for unemployed | −0.02 | −2.80 | −0.02 | −2.84 |
| Transitory income ($\gamma$) | 0.05 | 3.68 | 0.05 | 3.33 |
| Predicted probability of unemployment | −11.56 | −2.33 | −11.02 | −2.25 |
| Variance of last 4 years income*$10^5$ | −0.05 | −2.15 | −0.06 | −2.31 |
| Test on consumption smoothing (employed): $\beta>\gamma$ | 0.02 | 1.29 | 0.02 | 1.51 |
| Test on consumption smoothing (unemployed): $\beta>\gamma$ | 0.00 | −0.14 | 0.00 | 0.26 |
| No. of observations | 4,094 | | 4,094 | |
| Adjusted $R^2$ | 0.17 | | 0.17 | |

Note: Other variables included in the regression are the same as in Table 5.3.

households in the two groups reduce food consumption by 240 and 270 yuan, which accounts for 4 and 5 per cent of the average food consumption for the two groups, respectively.

Turning to educational expenditure, the total sample average household expenditure on education is 1,545 yuan, while households without unemployed members spend 1,697 yuan and households with unemployed members spend 1,106 yuan on education. Total educational expenditure accounted for 11.6 and 10.2 per cent of total expenditure for the households without and with unemployed members, respectively. Table 5.5 reports selected results from the educational expenditure regression. Although an *F*-test indicates no structural difference between the two groups, the marginal propensity to consume out of permanent income is statistically significantly lower for households with unemployed members as the interactive term indicates.

The consumption-smoothing test indicates that, for both households with and without unemployed members, the difference between the marginal propensities to consume out of permanent and transitory income is statistically insignificant and the point estimate is close to zero. Thus, neither of the two groups of households is able to smooth educational expenditure. In addition, a significantly negative impact of income uncertainty on educational expenditure is observed. Both past income variation and the predicted probability of being displaced causes urban households to spend less on education.[18] On average, a household with the mean probability of being displaced, which is 14 per cent for the total sample, will reduce educational expenditure by 160 yuan, which accounts for around 10.5 per cent of the average educational expenditure in the total sample. For the sample of households with unemployed members, this reduction accounts for an even larger proportion of educational expenditure, at 15 per cent.

In summary, our results indicate that urban households in China have strong precautionary saving motives, especially with regard to the prospect of some members facing unemployment. Once displacement occurs, households consume more and save less, although saving is still positive for the majority of this group of households. Our results suggest that urban Chinese households have a reasonable ability to help themselves when facing temporary income shocks. On the other hand, they are unable to smooth their educational expenditure and households with high income uncertainty even reduce educational expenditure.

## 5.5 Conclusions and policy implications

The recent period in China involved great social and economic change so that households were faced with significant economic uncertainties. This chapter tests for the permanent income hypothesis and precautionary saving motives using 1999 data from urban China. We find that urban households, even those hit by a transitory unemployment shock, are able to smooth their total consumption and food consumption. However, the degree of consumption smoothing is higher for households without unemployed members. These results are consistent with the permanent income hypothesis, which implies that households should save more in normal times while spending some of their previous savings or saving less when temporary shocks occur. The fact that households with unemployed members can smooth their consumption and that, on average, they have positive savings, indicates that these households can compensate for income shocks from unemployment by withdrawing savings or by finding other sources of income.

We also find that Chinese urban households have a strong motive for precautionary saving. Not only does past income uncertainty increase a household's propensity to save, but the predicted probability of displacement has an even stronger effect on saving for households without unemployed members. This result indicates that, in a world of sudden uncertainties, households can insulate themselves from future income shocks. However, households in urban China are unable to smooth their educational expenditure. For households facing greater income uncertainty and a greater possibility of displacement, the reduction in educational expenditure is very high, especially for those with unemployed members. Unlike other consumption, educational expenditure is an investment in the future generation. Thus, the lack of educational expenditure smoothing is a source of concern because of its implications for intergenerational income mobility.

These findings have important policy implications. In general, Chinese urban households are rational consumers capable of protecting themselves from transitory income shocks. Given the possible negative effect of direct income support schemes, the scarce financial resources of the government, and the capability of households to save for their own uncertain future before a shock occurs and to smooth their consumption when the shock arrives, it is appropriate for the Chinese government to adopt an unemployment support system that relies heavily upon individual contributions. The government should devote its scarce resources to support the most needy, namely, the disabled and the elderly, rather than allocate substantial money to an income support scheme for all unemployed people. In addition, investment in the human capital of the next generation must be a primary concern of the Chinese government. The fact that urban households are unable to smooth educational expenditure and actually reduce such expenditure in response to future uncertainty is detrimental because poor families, with an increasing incidence of unemployment, are unable to finance adequately the education of their children. To prevent an intergenerational transmission of poverty that will lead increasingly to an inequitable distribution of income and wealth in China, the government should consider financing educational expenditure for poor families.

## Notes

I am grateful to Tom Crossley, Bob Gregory, Paul Miller, Adrian Pagan, two anonymous referees and the editor for helpful discussion and comments. Any opinion expressed is that of the author only. Financial support from the Ford Foundation and International Centre for the Study of East Asian Development, Japan, is highly appreciated. This chapter is reprinted from *Journal of Comparative Economics*, Vol. 31, Meng, Xin, 'Unemployment, consumption smoothing, and precautionary saving in urban China', 2003, with permission from Elsevier.

1 The various unemployment insurance schemes implemented in some developed countries have the benefit of pooling risks; however, these UI schemes often involve substantial income redistribution.
2 Another justification for a government-provided income support scheme for unemployed people is to allow them to conduct an appropriate job search while facing liquidity constraints (Topel 1983; Meyer 1990).
3 Using the terminology of Browning and Lusardi (1996), these motives may be summarized as the downpayment, bequest, life-cycle and precautionary motives.
4 Studies by Gruber (1997) and Browning and Crossley (2001) test the effect of unemployment insurance on the change in consumption. Their approaches require data on changes in consumption before and after unemployment; this information is not available in our data set.
5 The sector of employment is used as an instrument for unemployment because it is an important determinant of unemployment, but it does not affect household consumption behaviour.
6 In a normal situation, the predicted probability of being unemployed may not be a good measure of income uncertainty because the relationship between probability and uncertainty is non-linear, that is, uncertainty is at its peak when the probability of unemployment is 0.5. However, in urban China, the certainty situation involved a zero probability of being unemployed due to the labour market institutional setting until the mid-1990s. Hence, this past experience is the appropriate certainty measure for Chinese households so that anything which is above zero probability of being unemployed increases their future income uncertainty. An individual moving from a world of near-zero unemployment to a world in which the probability of unemployment is 70 per cent will save more for this future uncertainty than an individual moving to a world of 50 per cent unemployment probability. From this perspective, the predicted probability of being unemployed is a good indicator of future income uncertainty.
7 This survey requires each participating household to record income and expenditure information over a three-year period.

8 For this subsample of individuals, a question is asked as to how long they have been unemployed. From this question, the accumulated number of unemployed people in each year from 1995 to 1999 can be derived.

9 Summary statistics presented in Appendix 5.A show that different adjustments in $\delta$ and the predicted probability of being unemployed change the mean value and standard deviation of permanent income only slightly.

10 The average government income support for households with unemployed members accounts for only 5 per cent of the average household income for this group.

11 The quadratic term for age is not statistically significant for the 1995 data, so it is excluded from the regression.

12 The health variable is measured differently in the two data sets. In the 1999 survey, a direct question is asked about whether an individual is healthy, not healthy, disabled, or other. This question is not asked in the 1995 survey. However, information on sick leave and health expenditure is available in the 1995 survey. Therefore, a dummy variable is derived in which healthy is defined as having less than 30 days sick leave or less than 500 yuan in health expenditures. Unfortunately, sick leave information is unavailable in the 1999 data, which rules out the possibility of generating a consistent variable on health for the two data sets.

13 The $F$-statistics are 1.70 for total consumption and 1.99 for food consumption; both are greater than the critical value of 1.62 at the 2.5 per cent significance level. For educational expenditure, the $F$-value is 1.22, which is below the critical value even at the 10 per cent significance level.

14 Full results are available upon request from the author.

15 The bootstrapped results are available upon request from the author. The bootstrap replicated 1,000 times.

16 To conduct an $F$-test for structural difference, the pooled regression is estimated for the total sample with interaction terms between all the variables and the dummy variable for households with unemployed members. The $t$-statistics for each interaction term indicate whether the coefficient is statistically significantly different between the two groups of households. The $t$-ratios for the difference of the MPC out of permanent and transitory incomes between the two groups of households are 1.45 and 2.31, respectively.

17 Based on the author's own estimates from Urban Household Income Distribution Survey data for the years 1988, 1995 and 1999.

18 The estimated result for this variable is sensitive to the different adjustment used for calculating permanent income. In most cases, it is statistically significant at the 10 per cent significance level.

## References

Aaberge, R. and Zhu, Y. (2001) 'The pattern of household savings during a hyperinflation: the case of urban China in the late 1980s', *Review of Income and Wealth*, 47: 181–202.

Bauer, P. and Paish, F. (1952) 'The reduction of fluctuations in the incomes of primary producers', *Economic Journal*, 62: 750–80.

Bhalla, S.S. (1979) 'Measurement errors and the permanent income hypothesis: evidence from rural India', *American Economic Review*, 69: 295–307.

Bhalla, S.S. (1980) 'The measurement of permanent income and its application to saving behaviour', *Journal of Political Economy*, 88(4): 722–43.

Bird, E.J. (1995) 'An exploratory comparison of income risk in Germany and the United States', *Review of Income and Wealth*, 41: 405–26.

Browning, M. and Crossley, T. (2001) 'Unemployment insurance benefit levels and consumption changes', *Journal of Public Economics*, 80(1): 1–23.

Browning, M. and Lusardi, A. (1996) 'Household saving: micro theories and micro facts', *Journal of Economic Literature*, 34(4): 1797–1855.

Carroll, C.D. (1994) 'How does future income affect current consumption?', *Quarterly Journal of Economics,* 109(1): 111–47.

Carroll, C.D. and Samwick, A. (1998) 'How important is precautionary saving?' *Review of Economics and Statistics*, 80(3): 410–19.

Carroll, C.D. and Weil, D.N. (1994) 'Saving and growth: a reinterpretation' *Carnegie Rochester Conference Series on Public Policy*, 40: 133–92.

Deaton, A. (1997) *The Analysis of Household Surveys: A Microeconometric Approach to Development Policy*, Baltimore: Johns Hopkins University Press.

East Asia Analytical Unit, Department of Foreign Affairs and Trade, Australia (1997) *China Embraces the Market*, Canberra: EAAU.

Engen, E. and Gruber, J. (2001) 'Unemployment insurance and precautionary saving', *Journal of Monetary Economics,* 47(3): 545–79.

Fan, G. (2000) 'The dynamics of transition in China: change of ownership structure and sustainability of growth', paper presented at the International Conference on China Growth Sustainability in the 21st Century, Canberra, Australia.

Friedman, M. (1957) *The Theory of the Consumption Function*, Princeton: Princeton University Press.

Garnaut, R., Song, L., Wang, X. and Yao, Y. (2001) *Private Enterprise in China*, Canberra: Asia Pacific Press.

Greene, William H. (1990) *Econometric Analysis*, New York: Macmillan.

Gruber, J. (1997) 'The consumption smoothing benefits of unemployment insurance', *American Economic Review*, 87: 192–205.

Jalan, J. and Ravallion, M. (1999) 'Are the poor less well insured? Evidence on vulnerability to income risk in rural China', *Journal of Development Economics*, 58(1): 61–81.

Jalan, J. and Ravallion, M. (2001) 'Behavioral responses to risk in rural China', *Journal of Development Economics*, 66(1): 23–49.

Jappelli, T. and Pagano, M. (1994) 'Saving, growth, and liquidity constraints', *Quarterly Journal of Economics*, 109(1): 83–109.

Jefferson, G. (1990) 'The impact of economic structure on fertility, saving, and retirement behaviour of Chinese households', *Journal of Asian Economics*, 1(2): 205–23.

Kraay, A. (2000) 'Household saving in China', *World Bank Economic Review*, 14(3): 545–70.

Ma, G. (1993) 'Macroeconomic disequilibrium, structural changes and the household saving and money demand in China', *Journal of Development Economics*, 41: 115–36.

Meng, X. (2000) *Labour Market Reform in China*, Cambridge: Cambridge University Press.

Meng, X. (2003) 'Private sector development and labor market reform' in Garnaut, R. and Song, L. (eds), *China's Third Economic Transformation*, London: Routledge.

Meyer, B.D. (1990) 'Unemployment insurance and unemployment spells', *Econometrica*, 58: 757–82.

Musgrove, P. (1978) 'Determinants of urban household consumption in Latin America: a summary of evidence from the ECIEL surveys', *Economic Development and Cultural Change*, 26(3): 441–65.

Musgrove, P. (1979) 'Permanent household income and consumption in urban South America', *American Economic Review*, 69: 355–68.

National Bureau of Statistics (NBS) (various years) *China Statistical Yearbook*, Beijing: China Statistics Press.

Pagan, A. (1984) 'Econometric issues in the analysis of regressions with generated regressors', *International Economic Review*, 25(1): 221–47.

Paxson, C.H. (1992) 'Using weather variability to estimate the response of savings to transitory income in Thailand', *American Economic Review*, 82: 15–33.

Qian, Y. (1988) 'Urban and rural household saving in China', *IMF Staff Papers*, 35(4): 592–627.

Qin, D. (1991) 'Aggregate consumption and income in China: an econometric study', *Journal of Comparative Economics*, 15: 132–41.

Topel, R. (1983) 'On layoffs and unemployment insurance' *American Economic Review*, 73: 541–59.

Wang, Y. (1995) 'Permanent income and wealth accumulation: a cross-sectional study of Chinese urban and rural households', *Economic Development and Cultural Change*, 43(3): 522–50.

Wang, Z. and Wen, S.C. (1992) 'Effects of rationing on the consumption behaviour of Chinese urban households during 1981–1987', *Journal of Comparative Economics*, 16(1): 1–26.

Wolpin, K.I. (1982) 'A new test of the permanent income hypothesis: the impact of weather on the income and consumption of farm households in India', *International Economic Review*, 23: 583–94.

Wu, J. (1999) 'Saving, investment, and economic growth', unpublished manuscript, National Economic Research Institute, Beijing, China.

Zeldes, S.P. (1989) 'Consumption and liquidity constraints: an empirical investigation', *Journal of Political Economy*, 97(2): 305–46.

## Appendix 5.A: Summary statistics of household-level variables

| *Variable* | *Total sample* | | *Employed* | | *Unemployed* | |
|---|---|---|---|---|---|---|
| | *Mean* | *CV* | *Mean* | *CV* | *Mean* | *CV* |
| Real total expenditure | 13654.25 | 0.61 | 14619.41 | 0.58 | 10877.59 | 0.63 |
| Real food expenditure | 5817.21 | 0.48 | 6086.92 | 0.48 | 5041.28 | 0.47 |
| Real education expenditure | 1544.63 | 1.47 | 1697.10 | 1.44 | 1105.99 | 1.50 |
| Permanent income YP1 | 12408.69 | 0.57 | 13287.40 | 0.55 | 9880.71 | 0.58 |
| Permanent income YP2 | 11679.42 | 0.57 | 12531.94 | 0.55 | 9226.82 | 0.56 |
| Permanent income YP3 | 12181.02 | 0.57 | 13070.82 | 0.55 | 9613.38 | 0.57 |
| Permanent income YP4 | 12836.26 | 0.59 | 13852.49 | 0.57 | 9912.68 | 0.59 |
| Permanent income YP5 | 12051.55 | 0.59 | 13028.07 | 0.56 | 9242.20 | 0.57 |
| Permanent income YP6 | 12563.32 | 0.59 | 13584.21 | 0.57 | 9617.38 | 0.58 |
| Transitory income TP1=Y−YP1 | 4684.18 | 1.63 | 5456.42 | 1.48 | 2462.53 | 2.25 |
| Transitory income TP2=Y−YP2 | 5413.44 | 1.41 | 6211.88 | 1.30 | 3116.42 | 1.77 |
| Transitory income TP3=Y−YP3 | 5123.14 | 1.52 | 5887.55 | 1.40 | 2917.31 | 1.93 |
| Transitory income TP4=Y−YP4 | 4684.18 | 1.63 | 5456.42 | 1.48 | 2462.53 | 2.25 |
| Transitory income TP5=Y−YP5 | 5041.32 | 1.49 | 5715.76 | 1.40 | 3101.03 | 1.71 |
| Transitory income TP6=Y−YP6 | 4740.85 | 1.61 | 5374.17 | 1.52 | 2913.31 | 1.84 |
| Standard dev. of 95–98 real income | 2169.61 | 1.76 | 2260.67 | 1.81 | 1907.66 | 1.52 |
| Mean HH prob. unemp. in 1999 | 0.14 | 0.66 | 0.12 | 0.69 | 0.18 | 0.50 |
| Mean HH prob. unemp. in 1999 (stock) | 0.09 | 0.96 | 0.07 | 1.01 | 0.13 | 0.76 |
| Age of the household head | 46.64 | 0.23 | 47.38 | 0.23 | 44.51 | 0.23 |
| Years of education of the household head | 10.64 | 0.28 | 10.88 | 0.28 | 9.95 | 0.29 |
| Household size | 3.06 | 0.25 | 3.03 | 0.25 | 3.16 | 0.25 |
| % of children 0–5 | 0.03 | 3.15 | 0.03 | 3.26 | 0.03 | 2.88 |
| % of children 6–10 | 0.05 | 2.42 | 0.05 | 2.47 | 0.05 | 2.28 |
| % of children 11–15 | 0.07 | 1.99 | 0.07 | 2.03 | 0.07 | 1.88 |
| % of male 16–19 | 0.03 | 3.18 | 0.03 | 3.22 | 0.03 | 3.08 |
| % of female 16–19 | 0.03 | 2.95 | 0.03 | 3.07 | 0.04 | 2.68 |
| % of male ≥ 65 | 0.03 | 3.22 | 0.04 | 3.06 | 0.02 | 3.58 |
| % of female ≥ 65 | 0.02 | 3.59 | 0.02 | 3.60 | 0.02 | 3.48 |
| Dummy for change HH size in 1999: | | | | | | |
| city1 | 0.03 | | 0.03 | | 0.02 | |
| city2 | 0.06 | | 0.05 | | 0.08 | |
| city3 | 0.10 | | 0.11 | | 0.07 | |
| city4 | 0.05 | | 0.05 | | 0.06 | |
| city5 | 0.14 | | 0.15 | | 0.12 | |
| city6 | 0.07 | | 0.06 | | 0.08 | |
| city7 | 0.05 | | 0.04 | | 0.07 | |

(Continued)

*Appendix 5.A* (Continued)

| *Variable* | *Total sample* | | *Employed* | | *Unemployed* | |
|---|---|---|---|---|---|---|
| | *Mean* | *CV* | *Mean* | *CV* | *Mean* | *CV* |
| city8 | 0.05 | | 0.06 | | 0.04 | |
| city9 | 0.10 | | 0.10 | | 0.09 | |
| city10 | 0.05 | | 0.04 | | 0.08 | |
| city11 | 0.05 | | 0.05 | | 0.06 | |
| city12 | 0.10 | | 0.10 | | 0.11 | |
| city13 | 0.05 | | 0.05 | | 0.06 | |

Note:
YP1 = permanent income adjusted for $W_t$ with $\delta=0.1$.
YP2 = permanent income adjusted for $W_t$ with $\delta=0.9$.
YP3 = permanent income adjusted for $W_t$ and $P_t$ with $\delta=0.1$ and $P_t$ from 95–99 measure.
YP4 = permanent income adjusted for $W_t$ and $P_t$ with $\delta=0.9$ and $P_t$ from 95–99 measure.
YP5 = permanent income adjusted for $W_t$ and $P_t$ with $\delta=0.1$ and $P_t$ from stock measure.
YP6 = permanent income adjusted for $W_t$ and $P_t$ with $\delta=0.9$ and $P_t$ from stock measure.

# 6 The decline of in-kind wage payments in urban China

*Li Shi and Yaohui Zhao*

## 6.1 Introduction

A distinctive feature of the Chinese urban labour market is the practice of paying workers in kind in addition to base wages and bonuses. Commodities used for in-kind payments include a whole range of consumer products, from food items such as meat, rice, fruits and cooking oil, to hygienic products such as soap, toothpaste, shampoo, detergent, and so on. This practice was prevalent in the 1980s, but its importance has gradually declined.

Two questions immediately arise. First, how do we explain the prevalence of in-kind payments in the 1980s? Second, how do we explain the subsequent decline? These are the issues that this chapter intends to explore. Answers to the questions will shed light on the behaviour of state-owned enterprises (SOEs) during economic transition. Because SOEs have intrinsic incentives to overpay their workforce (Lin, Cai and Li 1996), the government tends to impose restrictions on the amount of wage payments. As the government reduces its oversight over the management of firms during economic transition, SOEs obtain a larger leeway in evading restrictions on wage bills. We argue that payments in kind represent one way that such evasions occur.

Using individual level data generated from household surveys in 1988, 1995 and 1999, we document and analyse changes in wage composition for workers in different sectors of the economy. We will show that substantial differences in wage structure exist between SOEs, urban collective enterprises (UCEs) and non-public enterprises (NPEs), and that although payments in kind have declined for all types of work units over the years, the pace of change varies. By exploring this variation, we are able to examine two alternative hypotheses about the functions of payments in kind. One is achieving economies of scale in purchasing consumer products, and the second is evading state controls on wage bills.

The chapter is organized as follows. Section 6.2 presents data on the magnitude of payments in kind and its decline using three household surveys in the 1980s and 1990s. Section 6.3 reviews the institutional background pertaining to wage setting and in-kind payments, and proposes testable hypotheses. Since most statistical tests are based on discerning behaviour of work units of different ownership, Section 6.4 makes a detour to describe patterns of payments in kind by ownership of work units. Section 6.5 presents empirical results from a tobit

*Table 6.1* Sample description: regional distribution of workers

| | *Three surveys* | *1988* | *1995* | *1999* |
|---|---|---|---|---|
| Beijing | 2,012 | 671 | 702 | 638 |
| Shanxi | 2,506 | 1,556 | 956 | 0 |
| Liaoning | 3,489 | 1,596 | 1,068 | 823 |
| Jiangsu | 3,669 | 1,866 | 1,050 | 751 |
| Anhui | 2,072 | 1,371 | 700 | 0 |
| Henan | 3,283 | 1,628 | 811 | 843 |
| Hubei | 2,758 | 1,667 | 1,092 | 0 |
| Guangdong | 2,466 | 1,672 | 792 | 0 |
| Sichuan | 2,262 | 0 | 1,303 | 959 |
| Yunnan | 2,651 | 1,612 | 1,039 | 0 |
| Gansu | 2,148 | 908 | 543 | 698 |
| Total | 29,333 | 14,565 | 10,056 | 4,712 |

Sources: The 1988, 1995 and 1999 CASS surveys.

regression model to analyse variations in payments in kind. Section 6.6 summarizes major findings and concludes the chapter.

## 6.2 Wage composition: some basic statistics

The data sets used in this chapter are the same as those described in Chapter 1. Each working member of the sample households answered questions about their employment and incomes. Major earning categories are: regular wage, bonus, subsidies, and payments in kind. Payments in kind are valued at going market prices. In the survey of 1988, individualized information on payments in kind was only available for household heads and their spouses; those for all other members were pooled. Therefore we chose a subset of workers composed of household heads and their spouses for our analysis. For reasons of consistency, we apply the same data selection method to the other two years as well. Provincial distribution of the selected worker sample is presented in Table 6.1.

The prevalence of in-kind payments in 1988 and the subsequent decline are obvious from Table 6.2. As is shown, 68.5 per cent of all workers received payments in kind in 1988. By 1995, the ratio of workers receiving payments in kind declined to 37.0 per cent. In 1999, the ratio further decreased to 10.5 per cent. Table 6.2 also presents the absolute size of payments in kind (in 1999 yuan) and their relative proportion to total earnings. Payments in kind were 128.5 yuan in 1988, representing 2.5 per cent of total earnings.[1] Although we do not have data for the years before 1988, anecdotal evidence indicates that in-kind payments were more significant. We also see that the magnitude of payments in kind declined significantly over the years, in both relative and absolute terms. The absolute value declined to 107.1 yuan in 1995, or 1.5 per cent of total earnings in 1995, and furthermore to merely 23.1 yuan in 1999, or 0.3 per cent of total earnings.

What explains the prevalence of payments in kind in 1988 and the subsequent decline? According to economic theory, workers generally prefer cash over

*Table 6.2* Data description: wage structure, 1988, 1995 and 1999

| *Year* | *Proportion of observations with PIK > 0* | *Mean of PIK (yuan)* | *PIK as % of earnings* | *Reference: total earnings (yuan)* |
|---|---|---|---|---|
| 1988 | 68.5 | 128.5 | 2.5 | 5,128.9 |
| 1995 | 37.0 | 107.1 | 1.5 | 7,285.3 |
| 1999 | 10.5 | 23.1 | 0.3 | 8,539.3 |

Data sources: The 1988, 1995 and 1999 CASS surveys.

Notes:
1 PIK = Payment in kind.
2 Mean of PIK in 1988 and 1995 is in 1999 prices.

in-kind payments because cash payments permit more freedom in consumption choice. However, there has been a rapid growth of non-wage benefits in the form of health insurance and pension programmes in such market economies as the European and American economies since the Second World War (Rice 1966; Lurie 1966; Long and Scott 1982; Woodbury 1983, etc.). Explanations include both market forces and institutional distortions. Among institutional factors, tax policy is seen as a major driving force behind the rise of non-wage benefits because favourable tax treatments of wage and non-wage benefits created powerful incentives for shifting payment to non-wage fringe benefits (Feldstein 1973; Cymrot 1980; Long and Scott 1982). Unionization is another factor that shifts emphasis towards non-wage benefits through better information sharing and collective bargaining (Mabry 1973; Freeman 1981). In addition, there are 'natural' market forces that favour group purchase of health insurance over individualized decision because of the problem known as 'adverse selection'.

None of the above factors is important in China. Personal income tax has remained an insignificant source of tax in China until very recently and minimum taxable income is much higher than average income in all three years in our data. Independent unions are non-existent and commercial health insurance was also very insignificant in our data period. Nonetheless, the analytical framework in these studies can be applied to study the determinants of payments in kind in the case of urban China. There are two possible sources of demand for wage payments in kind. First, market conditions create room for economies of scale from group purchasing; second, firms try to evade government control on wages. These two hypotheses and the related institutional background are examined in turn in Section 6.3.

## 6.3 Two alternative hypotheses

### *6.3.1 Marketization hypothesis*

In pre-reform China, most consumer goods were rationed. By the early 1990s, however, the market had distributed almost all consumer products. The market reform was undertaken by continuing to supply low-priced goods to ration coupon holders while making goods freely available on the market, often at higher prices. This dual-track approach is credited with providing incentives for the market segment to expand and eventually 'grow out of the plan' (Naughton 1994). The planned track was eventually phased out by replacing quota allocation with explicit cash subsidies to consumers.

In 1988, our first year of survey, planned allocation of consumer products was still prevalent, and the government maintained substantial monopoly power over retail and wholesale trade. As a result, many consumer products were not easily accessible in non-production areas and wide gaps between producer prices and consumer prices existed. This situation was exacerbated by local protectionism which inhibited the transfer of goods across provincial borders. Under this situation, it may be economical for a group of consumers to purchase consumer goods directly from producers.

The advantage of group purchase depends on the size of the work unit and the degree of market development. Since state units are usually larger than collective or private units, if imperfect marketization is responsible for payments in kind, we expect to see more payments in kind in state-owned units. Compared to 1988, consumer product markets were much more deregulated in 1995; thus, theory predicts a uniform reduction of payments in kind in 1995 compared with 1988 across all ownership types. Shortly after 1995, China experienced serious overcapacity in most consumer products, which further intensified competition. This is expected to further reduce payments in kind.

### *6.3.2 The hypothesis of evading government control of wages*

In the absence of a hard budget constraint, there is an inherent tendency for state-owned firms in socialist countries to overpay their workers, thus regulating wages has been a necessary task for the government (Lin, Cai and Li 1996). However, unless the government devotes great efforts, the game between the government regulators and the enterprises almost always favours the latter, because the latter enjoys a clear information advantage. Thus, the ideal regulation to control wages is to determine wages centrally without giving any discretionary power to the firms. As long as the firm has some discretion, it will exploit it to its advantage and defeat the wage regulation.

Such is the case with the former Soviet Union. 'One of the first steps of the Bolshevik government after it came to power was the regulation of wages' (Hewes 1922: 274). Wage scales were centrally established to determine wages for workers, but the regulators later introduced bonuses, hoping to induce more work efforts. As a result, 'It was reported in 1920 that the payment for labour was increasing at a far greater rate than the other types of business costs' (Hewes 1922: 275). The Yugoslav government experimented with giving workers the collective control of state firms in the 1950s. Subsequently, wage supplements in the form of bonuses grew rapidly, leading to the demise of the experiment and the reimposition of wage controls (Ward 1957). More recent experiments in Hungary and Poland with relaxing wage controls also met a similar fate. In both countries, direct central controls over the growth of enterprise wage bills were replaced with a complex system of taxes, but the new system failed to restrain wage growth (Wolf 1991).

China's experience had been strikingly similar to the examples mentioned above. Before financial disciplines were imposed on state firms, the government constantly struggled with ways to control excessive wages paid by state firms. Regulations became increasingly complex and ineffective. Luckily for China, temporary setbacks did not derail the enterprise wage reform and explorations continued in the general direction of more market reform. In the early 1990s, the government finally decided to impose hard budget constraints on its enterprises. We now provide a brief review of the roads that China has travelled thus far in regulating wages in state industries.

Chinese firms in the pre-reform era lacked autonomy in all major areas of business decision. Among the most strictly controlled areas was wage setting. Each employer's wage level was set by referring to wage calculation tables established by the central government. Variables that determined individual wage levels were position, seniority, education and skill level. Regional differences in costs of living were accounted for, whereas profitability of specific firms or the performance of specific workers was not. At the firm level, all profits were turned over to the government. The government, in turn, provided the firms with funds for investment. The regulation applied to all state and urban collective firms; there were very few private ones before the reform.

Recognizing the importance of incentives, more autonomy was granted to enterprises as the first step in enterprise reform. Starting from 1978, wage control was slightly relaxed to allow for the experimentation of reward systems. In 1979, firms were allowed to retain part of their profits and the retained profits were to be used for three purposes: investment, welfare of workers, and bonuses. It was further stipulated in 1980 that bonus payments must not exceed 2 months of salary (Li 1989).

In 1984, in a further relaxation of control, the government repealed the bonus ceiling and replaced it with a 'bonus tax'. According to the regulation, a bonus of up to 2.5 months of salary would be exempt from the tax. A bonus between 2.5 and 4 months of salary would be taxed at 30 per cent. The tax rate would be 100 per cent for a bonus between 4 and 6 months of salary, and 300 per cent for a bonus more than 6 months of salary (Li 1989).

Implicitly assumed under state regulation of bonuses was that base wages paid to workers continued to follow pre-reform formulae set by the central government. In a move intended to give firms fundamental control not only of bonuses but also of the whole wage package, a new experiment was initiated in January 1985 to cap total wage bills instead of specific components. A small number of large and medium-sized SOEs were chosen for the experiment. A firm undergoing such an experiment would have the total wage bill linked to its economic performance. According to the linkage formula, for each 1 per cent increase in an indicator of economic performance (tax and profits remittance being the most important measurement), the firm would increase its wage bill by 0.7 per cent or less. To restrict the growth rate of wages, a progressive tax on the growth of wage bills was imposed for experiment firms instead of the bonus tax, which continued to apply to firms not in the experiment (Li 1989). By the end of 1987, 38 per cent of workers in SOEs had been in firms experimenting with the system of linking the total wage bill with economic performance (Tang 1989).

Echoing the experience of East European economies, relaxed wage control under soft budget constraint led to a rapid increase in wage bills, which fuelled the inflation of 1988–1989. As part of the national retrenchment policy, the government tightened controls over wage bills in 1989. After the inflation was reined in, a new drive of enterprise reform was launched in 1992.

In the landmark 'Regulations on Transforming the Management Mechanisms of State-Owned Industrial Enterprises', state-owned enterprises were given more autonomy while having their budget constraint significantly hardened (State Council 1992). The regulation stipulated that the wage bill for all firms would be set according to their economic performance, and that within the justifiable size of the wage bill all firms would have the freedom to determine the composition of compensation. It further proposed 'two bellows' to be the basic principle for determining the size of wage bills: 'The growth of total wage bill must be below the growth of economic performance (measured by realized pre-tax profits); the growth of average wage must be below the growth of labour productivity (measured by net value of output)' (State Council 1992).

The hardening of budget constraint is reflected in the following harsh punishments to firms and their managers in case of loss-making due to poor management:

1 Within the first year of deficit, the total wage bill will be reduced; the management will be refused bonus; and in case of large deficits, wages to those responsible will be reduced.
2 If the deficit continues to rise in the second year, the total wage bill will be further reduced; no bonus for anyone; and the management may be dismissed.
3 Long-term money losers will be ordered to suspend operation. Moreover, mergers, takeovers or bankruptcy may be applied to firms unable to be resuscitated.

We now pause to reflect what difference a hard budget constraint makes in placing self-discipline over wage setting in state-owned enterprises. It is well known that state asset amounts to nobody's asset and the most fundamental problem with state-owned enterprises is the 'agency problem'. Without an outside owner, insider control becomes a serious problem, especially in socialist countries where ideology advocates the control of factories by workers. The objective of the insider-controlled firm is to maximize take-home payments, the same objective as a worker-managed firm (Bonin, Jones and Putterman 1993). However, worker-managed firms face hard budget constraints but state-owned enterprises often do not. When workers expect the government to cover financial shortfalls and provide funds for investment, they will have more incentives than in pure worker-managed firms to take more home and leave less for future development. Thus, the observation that state-owned enterprises have strong profit motives (Jefferson and Rawski 1994) and the fact that the state enterprises' wage payments are excessive (Woo *et al.* 1994) are mutually consistent. Note that the hard budget constraint only alleviates the problem of excessive payment up to the point where no financial loss takes place. The firm still tends to pay more than market wages to its workers and still tends to under-invest. Such firms are likely to be disadvantaged in market competition.

To summarize, under soft budget constraint, state-owned firms have incentives to pay workers above market wages. Under government control of base wages, the bonus is the channel for excessive payment. When bonuses are controlled as well, payments in kind are an alternative. Because payments in kind often come from the 'welfare funds' of a firm, they are usually under less scrutiny than wages or bonuses.

### *6.3.3 Discerning the two hypotheses*

To test the alternative hypotheses discussed above, we have the following propositions. If the evasion theory is correct, then we are expected to observe the following:

- H1 Firms in public ownership pay more in-kind wages than do non-public firms, and among public firms, state units pay more than do urban collective enterprises. This is because wages in privately owned firms are not subject to government controls and the government is more capable of monitoring urban collectives than SOEs.[2]
- H2 Payments in kind decline as the profitability of a firm decreases. This is because payments in kind are a way of grabbing a larger share of enterprise profits from the government. If there is no profit to share, then payments in kind cannot be financed.
- H3 Changing regulation from controlling bonus to the total wage bill between 1988 and 1995 is expected to reduce the magnitude of bonus payments for SOEs and urban collectives. The tightening of budget constraints for public enterprises between 1995 and 1999 is expected to induce a reduction in bonus payments and payments in kind.
- H4 Because government agencies are subject to stricter wage and bonus controls than are enterprises or non-government organizations,[3] it is expected that payments in kinds are higher for government officials.[4] Also, there has existed an unofficial regulation that the salary for managers of state-owned and urban collective enterprises must not exceed a certain multiple of workers' average wage;[5] thus, it is also expected that managers of state-owned and collective enterprises receive more payments in kind as alternative compensation.

If the marketization theory is true, then as market competition intensified over the years, we expect to see an across the board decline in payments in kind irrespective of ownership types.

## 6.4 Payments in kind by ownership of work units

As is shown above, to test our hypotheses, we need to study behavioural differences in work units under different ownership. There are three major categories of ownership among Chinese urban work units: state-owned, urban collectives, and non-public enterprises. State-owned enterprises are owned and directly controlled by either central or local governments. Urban collectives are usually owned by government below the levels of city or county. Regulations of urban collective enterprises usually mirror those of state-owned enterprises, but budget constraints are usually more binding because the government is less committed to support these firms. Because both SOEs and urban collectives are government owned, we call the rest non-public enterprises, which are a mix of enterprises owned by domestic private individuals, wholly or partially owned by foreign investors and, after 1992, those organized in the form of shareholding corporations whose shareholders may include the government and other state units. A major distinction between public and non-public enterprises is that the latter are subject to much less government regulation, and in the case of private and foreign-funded enterprises, firms are almost entirely free in setting wages.

Table 6.3 presents sample distribution across ownership of work units. As is shown, state-owned work units employed about 80 per cent of all sample workers, and the percentage showed no decline over the three survey years. Urban collectives employed 19.20 per cent of sample workers in 1988. The ratio declined to 10.25 per cent in 1999. The share of non-public employees grew from 3.63 per cent in 1988 to 8.11 per cent in 1999. The pattern of change is consistent with national statistics.

*Table 6.3* Distribution of the sample by ownership of work unit

| | *Three surveys* | *1988* | *1995* | *1999* |
|---|---|---|---|---|
| All | 29,333 | 14,565 | 10,056 | 4,712 |
| (%) | (100) | (100) | (100) | (100) |
| By ownership | | | | |
| State-owned | 24,382 | 11,493 | 8,142 | 3,847 |
| (%) | (80.05) | (78.90) | (80.97) | (81.64) |
| Urban collectives | 4,786 | 2,796 | 1,507 | 483 |
| (%) | (16.32) | (19.20) | (14.99) | (10.25) |
| Non-public | 1,065 | 276 | 407 | 382 |
| (%) | (3.63) | (1.89) | (4.05) | (8.11) |
| Private | 310 | 121 | 127 | 62 |
| (%) | (1.06) | (0.83) | (1.26) | (1.32) |
| FIEs | 24 | 7 | 7 | 10 |
| (%) | (0.08) | (0.05) | (0.07) | (0.21) |
| Other | 731 | 148 | 273 | 310 |
| (%) | (2.49) | (1.02) | (2.71) | (6.58) |

Data sources: The 1988, 1995 and 1999 CASS surveys.

Note: FIEs = foreign-invested enterprises.

*Table 6.4* Payments in kind (PIK) by ownership, 1988, 1995 and 1999

| | | *1988* | *1995* | *1999* |
|---|---|---|---|---|
| State-owned units | *N* | 11,477 | 8,142 | 3,833 |
| | Proportion of obs. with PIK > 0 | 70.14 | 38.95 | 9.34 |
| | PIK (yuan)* | 136.41 | 114.21 | 23.56 |
| | PIK as % of earnings | 2.58 | 1.51 | 0.23 |
| Urban collectives | *N* | 2,794 | 1,507 | 482 |
| | Proportion of obs. with PIK > 0 | 64.85 | 28.87 | 14.52 |
| | PIK (yuan)* | 102.60 | 75.28 | 13.05 |
| | PIK as % of earnings | 2.33 | 1.33 | 0.24 |
| Non-public enterprises | *N* | 273 | 407 | 381 |
| | Proportion of obs. with PIK > 0 | 35.53 | 22.11 | 9.71 |
| | PIK (yuan)* | 59.02 | 83.79 | 31.14 |
| | PIK as % of earnings | 1.10 | 1.14 | 0.39 |

Data sources: The 1988, 1995 and 1999 CASS surveys.

Note: *In 1999 yuan.

Table 6.4 presents payments in kind for state-owned units, urban collectives and non-public enterprises in the three years of survey. We can immediately notice two patterns. First, there exist significant differences in payments in kind across ownership types, with the state-owned units being the highest and non-public units the lowest. Second, the differences narrowed markedly between 1988 and 1999, which implies that the rate of reduction was not uniform across ownership types. The decline of payments in kind for state-owned and urban collectives was much more pronounced than for non-public firms.

In Table 6.5, we describe differences in in-kind payments across positions of the workers. The table confirms that government officials or managers of state or collective enterprises received more payments in kind than did other types of workers, but the magnitude of the difference was not large. This may imply that payments in kind were not the primary methods of alternative payments that officials or managers of public enterprises received.

## 6.5 Empirical results

Although the results provided in Tables 6.4 and 6.5 are consistent with some of our predictions, a multivariate regression model is necessary for a more comprehensive and encompassing analysis. Table 6.6 reports such a regression. The dependent variable is payment in kind (PIK), expressed as a dichotomous variable with positive payments in kind being one and zero otherwise.[6] Explanatory variables include year dummy (1988 being the reference), ownership dummy variables of the work unit (reference group being state ownership), job position of the worker (government official or manager of state or collective enterprise being the reference), and other control variables including industry and region dummy variables and the ratio of the bonus a worker received over his or her earnings, the latter to be used as a proxy for the profitability of the work unit.

*Table 6.5* Payments in kind (PIK) by position, 1988, 1995 and 1999

| | | *1988* | *1995* | *1999* |
|---|---|---|---|---|
| Government official or manager of state or collective firm | *N* | 1,113 | 1,318 | 654 |
| | Proportion of obs. with PIK > 0 | 74.39 | 44.08 | 9.48 |
| | PIK (yuan)* | 175.57 | 151.08 | 29.45 |
| | PIK as % of earnings | 2.90 | 1.70 | 0.27 |
| Professional or technician | *N* | 2,492 | 2,334 | 1,114 |
| | Proportion of obs. with PIK > 0 | 71.00 | 39.25 | 9.25 |
| | PIK (yuan)* | 127.97 | 110.68 | 23.24 |
| | PIK as % of earnings | 2.27 | 1.36 | 0.24 |
| Office clerk | *N* | 3,626 | 2,056 | 874 |
| | Proportion of obs. with PIK > 0 | 67.71 | 37.01 | 9.50 |
| | PIK (yuan)* | 147.55 | 113.00 | 18.69 |
| | PIK as % of earnings | 2.82 | 1.58 | 0.21 |
| Manual worker | *N* | 7,131 | 4,198 | 2,019 |
| | Proportion of obs. with PIK > 0 | 67.62 | 33.28 | 11.64 |
| | PIK (yuan)* | 112.69 | 88.34 | 20.39 |
| | PIK as % of earnings | 2.39 | 1.39 | 0.23 |
| Owner or manager of private firm | *N* | 182 | 150 | 35 |
| | Proportion of obs. with PIK > 0 | 46.70 | 27.33 | 27.71 |
| | PIK (yuan)* | 84.83 | 112.18 | 166.04 |
| | PIK as % of earnings | 1.44 | 1.58 | 2.42 |

Data sources: The 1988, 1995 and 1999 CASS surveys.

Note: *In 1999 yuan.

Model I of Table 6.6 presents an overall picture of the occurrence of payments in kind across different ownership types and changes over years. It shows that, after controlling for other things, the occurrence of earnings in kind was down by about 23.6 percentage points in 1995 compared with 1988; the incidence was further reduced by 36.4 percentage points between 1999 and 1995. These are quite substantial reductions because the occurrence of earnings in kind was 68.5 per cent in 1988 (Table 6.2). The reductions are consistent with our prediction of overall decline in the importance of payments in kind. Looking at different ownership types, we see that the occurrence of earnings in kind in urban collectives was 8.7 percentage points less than in state units, and that in non-public firms it was 18.3 percentage points less than in state units. We also find that more government officials or managers of public enterprises received more payments in kind than did other workers, confirming our prediction that in the presence of wage control, other forms of payments were used as compensation.

Model II provides a more detailed dissection of differences in payments in kind across years and ownership types. We can see that in 1988, the likelihood that workers in state-owned units received payments in kind was 7.3 percentage points higher than urban collectives, and 25.6 percentage points higher than non-public enterprises. Since state units and urban collectives were subject to similar regulation of wages and bonuses, their difference in payments in kind likely reflected different degrees of profitability. The large difference between public (state and

*Table 6.6* Logit model of in-kind payments (dependent variable: positive in-kind payment = 1, otherwise = 0)

| | *Model I* | | | *Model II* | | | *Definition of marginal effect* | *Variable mean* |
|---|---|---|---|---|---|---|---|---|
| | *Coefficient* | *Standard error* | *Marginal effect (%)* | *Coefficient* | *Standard error* | *Marginal effect* | | |
| Intercept | 0.496** | 0.210 | — | 0.621* | 0.220 | — | | — |
| Year95 | −0.969* | 0.199 | −23.61 | — | | — | 1995 vs. 1988 | 0.346 |
| Year99 | −3.476* | 0.067 | −60.05 | — | | — | 1999 vs. 1988 | 0.150 |
| UCE | −0.356* | 0.038 | −8.69 | — | | — | UCE vs. SOE | 0.163 |
| NPE | −0.790* | 0.095 | −18.30 | — | | — | NPE vs. SOE | 0.036 |
| UCE88 | — | | — | −0.321* | 0.048 | −7.30 | UCE88 vs. SOE88 | 0.163 |
| NPE88 | — | | — | −1.062* | 0.144 | −25.59 | NPE88 vs. SOE88 | 0.036 |
| SOE95 | — | | — | −1.088* | 0.210 | −26.21 | SOE95 vs. SOE88 | 0.280 |
| UCE95 | — | | — | −1.202* | 0.218 | −21.67 | UCE95 vs. UCE88 | 0.052 |
| NPE95 | — | | — | −0.708* | 0.240 | 8.81 | NPE95 vs. NPE99 | 0.014 |
| SOE99 | — | | — | −3.508* | 0.072 | −36.15 | SOE99 vs. SOE95 | 0.123 |
| UCE99 | — | | — | −3.424* | 0.225 | −32.91 | UCE99 vs. UCE95 | 0.015 |
| NPE99 | — | | — | −2.719* | 0.288 | −39.17 | NPE99 vs. NPE88 | 0.012 |
| Professional/technician | −0.170* | 0.053 | −4.24 | −0.171* | 0.053 | −4.27 | Reference: Govt official/manager of public firm | 0.203 |
| Office clerk | −0.312* | 0.051 | −7.78 | −0.312* | 0.051 | −7.78 | Same as above | 0.224 |
| Manual worker | −0.409* | 0.049 | −10.16 | −0.407* | 0.049 | −10.11 | Same as above | 0.454 |
| Private firm's owner/manager | −0.429* | 0.135 | −10.65 | −0.364* | 0.137 | −9.05 | Same as above | 0.013 |
| Bonus/earnings *100 | 0.015* | 0.002 | 3.71 | 0.015* | 0.002 | 3.69 | 10 percentage points above mean | 8.167 |
| Industry dummies | Yes | | | Yes | | | | |
| Province dummies | Yes | | | Yes | | | | |
| *N* | 29,059 | | | 29,059 | | | | |
| *N*=1 | 15,057 | | | 15,057 | | | | |
| Log-likelihood | 32,237.9 | | | 32,227.2 | | | | |

Data sources: The 1988, 1995 and 1999 CASS surveys.

Note: * and ** denote significance levels at 1% and 5% respectively.

collective) units and non-public firms was likely due to the tendency to evade wage controls in publicly owned sectors.

Between 1995 and 1988, workers from publicly owned (state and collective) units experienced a decline in payments in kind. For state units, the incidence of payments in kind decreased by 26.2 percentage points while in urban collectives the decline was 21.7 percentage points. However, in non-public firms, there was a slight increase (8.8 percentage points) in payments in kind. The latter fact contradicts the marketization story as it predicts uniform reduction in payments in kind. The most likely cause for the reduced payments in kind in state and urban collective units was reduced profitability in these firms due to the strong product market competition from private firms and rural enterprises.

Payments in kind experienced further decline between 1995 and 1999. As is shown in Model II, the likelihood that a state unit pays in-kind wages reduced by 36.2 percentage points; the reduction was 32.9 percentage points for urban collectives and 39.2 for non-public enterprises. Because the marketization reform for consumer goods was already completed by 1995, the decline was not likely due to improved individual access to consumer products. Instead, the likely explanation is over-capacity and deficit in many firms across ownership types. The money-losing firms were not only public firms but also private ones. When a firm loses money, the existing restriction on the total wage bill may cease to be binding. The firm may have no money to pay bonuses, let alone in-kind wages.

Both Models I and II demonstrate a positive correlation between bonus payment and in-kind payment. A 10 percentage points increase in the share of bonuses in total wages was associated with a 3.7 percentage points increase in the occurrence of payments in kind. If we interpret the bonus to earnings ratio as representing the 'wealth' of the work unit that a worker belonged to, this means that payments in kind were most fundamentally determined by the financial capability of the employer.

## 6.6. Summaries and conclusions

One of the most serious problems in Soviet-style economies was the lack of incentives due to excessive central control by the government. Consequently, the first step in reform usually started with granting autonomy to state-owned firms. However, enterprise reforms in many former socialist countries almost universally encountered a problem: autonomy of a state-owned firm and the cost-minimization principle often contradicted each other. Once given autonomy in wage setting, a firm tended to pay its workers excessively, often causing a reversal of reform programmes and turning back to central control.

Using payments in kind as an example, this chapter examines why and how firms engage in such 'irrational' behaviour. In-kind payments (payments made in terms of consumer goods) used to be an important aspect of urban life in China – 68 per cent of our sample workers received payments in kind in 1988. The ratio declined to only 10 per cent in 1999. In explaining the prevalence of in-kind payment

*Table 6.7* Bonuses as a proportion of earnings, 1988, 1995 and 1999

| *Year* | *Total earnings (yuan)* | *Mean of bonuses (yuan)* | *As % of earnings* |
|---|---|---|---|
| 1988 | 5,128.9 | 1,118.3 | 21.8 |
| 1995 | 7,285.3 | 1,106.7 | 15.2 |
| 1999 | 8,539.3 | 417.7 | 4.9 |

Data sources: The 1988, 1995 and 1999 CASS surveys.

in the 1980s and the subsequent decline in the 1990s, two hypotheses are put forward. One is the lack of access to consumer products by individuals. The second is associated with the government control of wages and the strategy of firms to evade such controls.

Data from three household surveys in 1988, 1995 and 1999 are consistent with the second hypotheses. Workers in government-owned state and collective units consistently received a higher proportion of their income in kind than non-government enterprises after controlling for other factors. Other things being equal, government officials and public enterprise managers received more payments in kind than other workers. Since public sector workers, especially government officials and managers, were subject to tighter wage control, the above facts are consistent with our theory that payments in kind were used to evade the control. Changes in payments in kind over the years suggest that decline in profitability in the 1990s might be responsible for the decline in in-kind payments. Of course, financial disciplines imposed on firms in the same period were a necessary condition for such a decline.

Our study implies that the Chinese firms had an upper hand in playing the principal/agent game with the government under soft financial discipline. Without a hard budget constraint, whenever the government permitted the firm to pay performance-related bonuses to stimulate work incentive, bonuses were paid out to everyone up to a precautionary ceiling placed by the government. In addition, payments in kind were used to further raise workers' total compensation.

Additional evidence is found when examining changes in bonuses. As Table 6.7 shows, as the government shifted from controlling the amount of bonus to total wage bills between 1988 and 1995, bonus payments decreased. As the shift was completed by 1999, total bonus payment in absolute value had already declined by nearly two-thirds. This implies that the original bonus was not used to stimulate more work effort.

The success of hard budget constraint in disciplining the wage behaviour of firms is demonstrated by the recent episode of wage rises for civil servants. In the summer of 1999, the government raised wages of civil servants by about 30 per cent. In the meantime, enterprises were told that they could follow suit if they wished. To our knowledge, very few firms did.

This is not to say that the wage policies of state-owned enterprises already conform to profit-maximizing principles. We made the point that these firms still have the tendency to overpay their workers and to under-invest.

## Notes

The chapter was first published in the *Journal of Chinese Economics and Business Studies*, Vol. 1, No.2, Li Shi and Yaohui Zhao, 'The decline of in-kind wage payments in urban China', 245–258, 2003. We are grateful to Taylor Francis for their permission to reproduce the paper.

1 All wages in this chapter are in 1999 prices.
2 SOEs are monitored by higher-level government agencies than urban collectives.
3 For example, it was stipulated in 1986 that bonuses paid to government officials in both central and local government could not exceed one month's salary. In contrast, the tax-exempt amount of bonus for enterprises and state-owned non-government organizations was four months' salary (Li 1989).
4 The funds may come from extra budgetary revenues of government agencies.
5 According to a conversation with Mr Wang Xueli of the Ministry of Labour and Social Security, the ceiling was set for 3 times the average salary of the firm in the late 1980s. It was changed to 4 times the average salary of the firm and 6 times the average salary of the local economy in the mid-1990s.
6 We use a dichotomous instead of a continuous variable for two reasons. First, values of payments in kind are difficult to estimate and thus the reported figures are unreliable, while information on whether or not an individual received payments in kind is relatively accurate. Second, nearly half of all observations do not receive any payments in kind.

## References

Bonin, J., Jones, D. and Putterman, L. (1993) 'Theoretical and empirical studies of producer cooperatives: will ever the twain meet?', *Journal of Economic Literature*, 31: 1290–1320.

Cymrot, D.J. (1980) 'Private pension saving: the effect of tax incentives on the rate of return', *Southern Economic Journal,* 47: 179–90.

Feldstein, M. (1973) 'The welfare loss of excessive health insurance', *Journal of Political Economy,* 81: 251–80.

Freeman, R. (1981) 'The effect of trade unionism on fringe benefits', *Industrial and Labor Relations Review,* 34: 489–509.

Hewes, A. (1922) 'Russian wage system under communism', *Journal of Political Economy,* 30: 274–8.

Jefferson, G.H. and Rawski, T. (1994) 'Enterprise reform in Chinese industry', *Journal of Economic Perspective,* 8: 47–70.

Li, J. (1989) 'Gongzi zhidu' (The reward system), in Editing Committee of the Almanac of Labour and Personnel (ed.), *Laodong Renshi Wenjian Huibian, 1949.10–1987* (Almanac of Labor and Personnel, 1949 10–1987), Beijing: Labour and Personnel Press.

Lin, J.Y., Cai, F. and Li, Z. (1996) *The China Miracle: Development Strategy and Economic Reform*, Hong Kong: The Chinese University Press.

Long, J.E. and Scott, F.A. (1982) 'The income tax and nonwage compensation', *Review of Economics and Statistics,* 64: 211–19.

Lurie, M. (1966) 'The growth of fringe benefits and the meaning of wage setting by wage comparisons', *Journal of Industrial Economics,* 15: 16–25.

Mabry, B. (1973) 'The economics of fringe benefits', *Industrial Relations,*12: 95–106.

Naughton, B. (1994) *Growing Out of the Plan: Chinese Economic Reform, 1978–1993*. New York: Cambridge University Press.

Rice, R.G. (1966) 'Skill, earnings, and the growth of wage supplements,' *American Economic Review,* 56: 583–93.

State Council (1992) 'Zhuanbian guoyou gongye qiye guanli jizhi de youguan guiding' (Regulations on transforming the management mechanisms of state-owned industrial enterprises), 23 July 1992, <http://www.molss.gov.cn/correlate/qmzhjzTL.htm>

Tang, C. (1989) 'Gongzi yu jingying xiaoyi guaigou: tansuo qiye gongzi gaige' (Linking wages with economic performance: exploring enterprise wage reform), in Editing Committee of the Almanac of Labour and Personnel (ed.), *Laodong Renshi Wenjian Huibian, 1949, 10–1987* (Almanac of Labour and Personnel, 1949, 10–1987), Beijing: Labour and Personnel Press.

Ward, B. (1957) 'Workers' management in Yugoslavia', *Journal of Political Economy,* 65: 373–86.

Wolf, T.A. (1991) 'The lessons of limited market-oriented reform', *Journal of Economic Perspective,* 5: 45–58.

Woo, W.T. *et al.* (1994) 'The efficiency and macroeconomic consequences of Chinese enterprise reform', *China Economic Review*, 4(2): 153–68.

Woodbury, S.A. (1983) 'Substitution between wage and nonwage benefits', *American Economic Review,* 73: 166–82.

# 7 Rising poverty and its causes in urban China

*Li Shi*

## 7.1 Introduction

Poverty has been perceived as a rural phenomenon in China. However, urban poverty has become a vital issue in China since 1995 as the restructuring of public-owned enterprises started to take place. Even official statistics confirm that the total number of unemployed workers plus *xiagang* (laid-off) workers reached 12 million in 1999 (NBS 2000). It has been attracting more attention from the central government as it is closely related to social instability.

Urban poverty is regarded as a new phenomenon in the late 1990s and as 'new poverty' (Knight 2000). It is believed to be more associated with rising unemployment and *xiagang* of urban workers. The government policy focusing on provision of financial assistance to the unemployed and *xiagang* workers seems not to be satisfactorily implemented within provinces and cities. Large numbers of *xiagang* workers could not get what they were entitled to from the local governments and enterprises (Institute of Labour Science 2000).

In these circumstances, it would be interesting to investigate the scale of poverty and the relationship between unemployment and poverty incidence in urban China. To examine these issues, poverty indices measuring both poverty rate and poverty intensity are calculated across sample cities and demographic groups and then the relationship between the probability of an individual falling into poverty and the status of being unemployed or laid off is analysed using a probit model. The results clearly show that poverty incidence may not be as high as shown in the urban areas of some developing countries, but it is higher than the officially published figures. Our results also show that there is a strong relationship between poverty and unemployment, and the majority of the urban poverty can be attributed to the increasing numbers of urban workers becoming *xiagang* and unemployed.

This chapter is organized as follows. The next section provides a literature review on poverty issues in urban China. Section 7.3 deals with appropriate poverty lines used in this chapter. Section 7.4 presents our results of analysis on poverty incidence and structure among groups with different household and individual characteristics. Section 7.5 focuses on analysing the causes of increasing poverty among urban households. Section 7.6 provides evaluation of the government policy for alleviating urban poverty, based on some simulation analysis. Conclusions and policy implications are drawn in the final section.

## 7.2 Literature review

Urban poverty had not been regarded by policy makers and scholars as a big problem in China until the mid-1990s. Therefore, few research references can be found in this area, in comparison with the voluminous literature on rural poverty. However, there are a few studies that should be mentioned, although it is hard to find a harmony among different estimates. Based on assumptions of subsistence consumption and grouped data of income distribution published by the National Bureau of Statistics (NBS), the World Bank produced time-series estimates of poverty in China for the period 1978–1990 (World Bank 1992). The estimates indicate very little poverty in urban China, less than 1 per cent during the 1980s. Khan (1998) estimated poverty incidence in urban China in 1988 and 1995, using the data sets from the two CASS surveys, and found poverty incidence for the two years of 6.7 per cent and 8.0 per cent if adjusted standard poverty lines were applied.

More interestingly, his estimation indicates that there would be a larger rise in poverty incidence between the two years if extreme poverty thresholds were applied. Using the same data for 1988 and applying a national relative poverty line equivalent to half the mean value of individual disposable income, Gustafsson and Li (1998) estimated poverty incidence to be less than 1 per cent in urban China, extremely low compared to that in rural China. Gustafsson and Wei (2000) updated the national relative poverty line for 1995 and estimated the urban poverty rate as being equivalent to 46 per cent of that in 1988.

A research team at NBS provided a different estimation on poverty incidence in urban China during the first half of the 1990s. According to their figures, poverty incidence varied between 4 and 6 per cent in the period 1991–1995 (Ren and Chen 1996). More recently, a project report supported by the Asian Development Bank made estimates of poverty incidences for 30 provinces in urban China in 1998. A general picture of urban poverty is that the poverty rate was 4.7 per cent in urban China in 1998 (Asian Development Bank 2001). The report also indicates that the urban poverty rate was highly sensitive to poverty lines. The poverty rate would jump to 20 per cent if the poverty line is raised by 50 per cent.

## 7.3 Specification of the poverty line

To measure poverty incidence and poverty intensity, a threshold or poverty line is required to identify poor households or individuals. As an absolute poverty line, it can be based either on income or on consumption, the former being called an income poverty line and the latter a consumption poverty line. When poverty is defined as lack of income to maintain a minimum standard of living, the living cost to maintain such a living standard should be specified in terms of money. A

*Table 7.1* Urban poverty lines for provinces, 1999

| *Province/City* | *NBS's food poverty line in 1998 (yuan)* | *Food price index in 1999* | *Food poverty line in 1999 (yuan)* | *Average poverty line in province (yuan)* |
|---|---|---|---|---|
| Beijing | 2,078 | 0.977 | 2,030 | 3,830 |
| Liaoning | 1,280 | 0.951 | 1,217 | 2,296 |
| Jiangsu | 1,512 | 0.950 | 1,436 | 2,709 |
| Henan | 1,072 | 0.946 | 1,014 | 1,913 |
| Xichuan | 1,289 | 0.957 | 1,234 | 2,328 |
| Gansu | 1,112 | 0.956 | 1,063 | 2,006 |

Source: Wang (2000).

Note: Provincial poverty lines are derived by food poverty lines × $(1+R_{nf})$, where $R_{nf}$ is ratio of non-food expenditure over food expenditure for the lowest quintile of households in urban China. The $R_{nf}$ is 0.887 in 1999.

conventional approach to specify the living cost for the poor is undertaken in two steps. Firstly, a food poverty line is defined after a basket of foods needed to satisfy minimum nutrition requirements and its costs are determined. Second, given the food poverty line, an income poverty line is consequently defined once a share of expenditure on food in total expenditure is fixed.

When defining a poverty line for our study, the work of NBS is recognized. Researchers at NBS estimated food poverty lines in 1998 for different provinces in urban China by using the data from the household survey in that year. The data cover 17,000 urban households, but exclude rural–urban migrants. The NBS's food poverty lines for the provinces included in our study are presented in Table 7.1.

It is crucial to estimate the share of non-food spending in total consumption expenditure for poor households in approaching a reliable poverty line. The poverty line depends on it, i.e. $PL = PL_f + PL_{nf} = PL_f\,(1 + R_{nf})$, where $PL$ is the total poverty line, $PL_f$ the food poverty line, $PL_{nf}$ the non-food poverty line and $R_{nf}$ the ratio of non-food expenditure to food expenditure. It is apparent that the poverty line would be higher if the share of non-food spending were assumed to be higher. NBS takes two-thirds as the ratio of non-food expenditure over food expenditure for the urban poor according to the average value of Engel coefficients in developing countries. This approach is, however, not justified in the Chinese circumstances. Looking at statistics of the consumption expenditure of the lowest 10 per cent of households in urban areas, the ratio of non-food expenditure over food expenditure was almost 90 per cent in 1999. Applying this ratio, we get a higher poverty line than did the NBS. Our provincial poverty lines are presented in Table 7.1.

The city poverty lines should differ from the provincial ones owing to differences in living costs among cities of varying size. Without accurate estimation of regional living costs, we have to make arbitrary adjustments for city poverty lines. Based on provincial poverty lines, the city poverty line is raised by 5 per cent for a capital city and is lowered by 5 per cent for other cities.[1] Table 7.2 shows adjusted poverty lines for the cities under study. Our estimation shows that the

*Table 7.2* Adjusted poverty lines for cities, 1999

| *Province/City* | *Poverty line adjusted for cities (yuan)* | *Monetary income per capita (yuan)* | *Poverty line as percentage of income per capita* |
|---|---|---|---|
| Beijing | 3,830 | 9,807 | 39 |
| Liaoning | | | |
| Shenyang | 2,410 | 5,483 | 44 |
| Jinzhou | 2,181 | 4,966 | 44 |
| Jiangsu | | | |
| Nanjing | 2,845 | 8,356 | 34 |
| Xuzhou | 2,574 | 6,734 | 38 |
| Henan | | | |
| Zhengzhou | 2,009 | 5,659 | 36 |
| Kaifeng | 1,817 | 4,145 | 44 |
| Pingdingshan | 2,009 | 5,865 | 34 |
| Sichuan | | | |
| Chengdu | 2,444 | 6,408 | 38 |
| Zigong | 2,212 | 4,727 | 47 |
| Nanchong | 2,212 | 5,395 | 41 |
| Gansu | | | |
| Lanzhou | 2,106 | 5,220 | 40 |
| Pingliang | 1,906 | 4,525 | 42 |

Source: The 1999 CASS survey.

Note: Poverty lines adjusted for cities are derived by using provincial poverty lines in Table 7.1 above to multiply by 1.05 for provincial capitals and 0.95 for other cities.

poverty lines vary across provinces and cities, both in terms of absolute value and as percentage of income per capita. Because of its high living cost, Beijing has the highest poverty line among the 13 selected cities. For instance, it is 90 per cent higher than that for Zhengzhou, and 110 per cent higher than that for Kaifeng. As a percentage of city income per capita, city poverty lines range from 34 per cent to 47 per cent. Moreover they are negatively correlated with income level, which means that richer cities have lower poverty lines as a proportion of per capita income.

## 7.4 Poverty incidence and poverty structure

To measure poverty, it is very important to search for a reliable poverty index. After a seminal paper of Sen (1976), there have been many suggestions about how to incorporate poverty intensity and inequality among poor people into aggregate poverty measures rather than merely counting the number of poor. In recent applied work, the most frequently used alternative is a family of indices suggested by Foster, Green and Thorbecke (1984):

$$FGT(\alpha) = \frac{1}{N}\sum_{i=1}^{q}\left[1 - \frac{y_i}{z_i}\right]^{\alpha} = \frac{1}{N}\sum_{i=1}^{q}\left[\frac{g}{z}\right]_i^{\alpha}$$

*Table 7.3* Poverty incidence estimates for cities, 1999

| *Province/City* | *Poverty incidence for provinces and cities (%): unweighted sample* | *Poverty incidence for provinces (%): weighted sample I* | *Poverty incidence for provinces (%): weighted sample II* | *Poverty incidence for provinces (%): weighted sample III* |
|---|---|---|---|---|
| Beijing | 3.02 | 3.02 | 3.02 | 3.02 |
| Liaoning | 7.04 | 6.55 | 6.49 | 8.21 |
| Shenyang | 6.05 | | | |
| Jinzhou | 9.21 | | | |
| Jiangsu | 2.38 | 2.29 | 2.21 | 3.67 |
| Nanjing | 1.18 | | | |
| Xuzhou | 4.98 | | | |
| Henan | 7.20 | 7.15 | 7.10 | 6.86 |
| Zhengzhou | 7.20 | | | |
| Kaifeng | 11.80 | | | |
| Pingdingshan | 2.26 | | | |
| Sichuan | 9.03 | 7.77 | 7.73 | 10.90 |
| Chengdu | 5.93 | | | |
| Zigong | 16.40 | | | |
| Nanchong | 7.50 | | | |
| Gansu | 5.38 | 5.30 | 5.34 | 5.41 |
| Lanzhou | 5.17 | | | |
| Pingliang | 5.81 | | | |
| All samples | 5.88 | 5.50 | 5.02 | 5.98 |

Notes: Weighted sample I is one obtained by weighing city sample within provinces; weighted sample II is one obtained by weighing city sample across provinces; weighted sample III is one obtained by weighing city sample by using population in cities with different size.

in which $Z_i$ is the poverty line; $y_i$ is the income of the *i*th person who has income below the poverty line; $g_i = z_i - y_i$ is the poverty gap of the *i*th person; and $\alpha$ is a parameter whose higher number gives increasing weights to large poverty gaps. When $\alpha = 0$, FGT becomes the head-count ratio; when $\alpha = 1$, FGT is the proportionate poverty gap; and when $\alpha = 2$, FGT is the squared proportionate poverty gap (or weighted poverty gap), which is more sensitive to income distribution among the poor.

Applying the formula above, we first computed poverty incidence for each city and province in our sample. Under some assumptions, we estimated poverty incidence for entire urban China as a whole in 1999. The results are presented in Table 7.3. It can be seen that the urban poverty is between 5 per cent and 6 per cent no matter whether the sample is weighted or not. With this poverty incidence, we can reckon that the urban poor number between 19.5 and 23.3 million in 1999. However, it should be noted that these figures exclude rural migrants, who may have a higher incidence of poverty.

Table 7.3 also shows a variation of poverty incidences across cities and across provinces. Jiangsu and Beijing have a lower incidence of urban poverty than do other provinces, while Sichuan and Henan have respectively a 54 per cent and 22 per cent higher incidence of urban poverty than the average level in the urban areas. Two cities out of the 13 have extremely high poverty incidence, Kaifeng in Henan Province and Zigong in Sichuan Province, as shown in Table 7.3.

*Table 7.4* Poverty indices in urban China by city, 1999

| *Province/City* | *Absolute value* | | | *Proportion to average (as 100%)* | | |
|---|---|---|---|---|---|---|
| | *Head-count (%)* | *Poverty gap (×100)* | *Weighted poverty gap (×100)* | *Head-count (%)* | *Poverty gap (×100)* | *Weighted poverty gap(×100)* |
| Beijing | 3.02 | 0.65 | 0.23 | 51 | 46 | 43 |
| Liaoning | | | | | | |
| Shenyang | 6.05 | 1.23 | 0.48 | 103 | 87 | 89 |
| Jinzhou | 9.21 | 1.94 | 0.56 | 157 | 137 | 103 |
| Jiangsu | | | | | | |
| Nanjing | 1.18 | 0.26 | 0.10 | 20 | 19 | 18 |
| Xuzhou | 4.98 | 0.58 | 0.13 | 85 | 41 | 24 |
| Henan | | | | | | |
| Zhengzhou | 7.20 | 2.35 | 1.38 | 122 | 167 | 255 |
| Kaifeng | 11.80 | 3.80 | 1.83 | 201 | 270 | 339 |
| Pingdingshan | 2.26 | 0.57 | 0.27 | 38 | 41 | 50 |
| Sichuan | | | | | | |
| Chengdu | 5.93 | 1.43 | 0.70 | 101 | 102 | 129 |
| Zigong | 16.40 | 4.78 | 2.07 | 279 | 341 | 383 |
| Nanchong | 7.50 | 1.24 | 0.33 | 128 | 88 | 61 |
| Gansu | | | | | | |
| Lanzhou | 5.17 | 1.02 | 0.36 | 88 | 72 | 67 |
| Pingliang | 5.81 | 1.09 | 0.29 | 99 | 78 | 54 |
| All samples | 5.88 | 1.40 | 0.54 | 100 | 100 | 100 |

The indices of the poverty gap and weighted poverty gap were also computed for each province and city under study (Table 7.4). The poverty gap index measures average distance of income of the identified poor people from a defined poverty line and the weighted poverty gap measures inequality of income among the poor population. This implies that if a larger proportion of the poor population stay far below the poverty line and the income variance of the poor population is bigger in a city, its poverty gap index and weighted poverty gap index would show higher values as a percentage of the average level. For instance, in Table 7.4, Zhengzhou City has a poverty rate 122 per cent higher, but it has a poverty gap 167 per cent higher and a weighted poverty gap 255 per cent higher than the average level. There was a larger proportion of the poor population with income far below the poverty line in Zhengzhou City in 1999. The same interpretation can be applied to Kaifeng City in Henan Province, and Chengdu City and Zigong City in Sichuan Province. In contrast, the two cities Shenyang and especially Jinzhou in Liaoning Province have quite high poverty rates, but have a poverty gap index and weighted poverty gap index relatively decreasing, implying higher average income of the poor population in these cities. Whether variation in the indices across the final three columns of Table 7.4 is largely due to government supporting programmes to the poor will be investigated in Section 7.7.

*Table 7.5* Poverty incidence by gender and age group

| *Age group* | *Poverty incidence (%)* | | | *Proportion to average (as 100%)* | | |
|---|---|---|---|---|---|---|
| | *All samples* | *Male* | *Female* | *All samples* | *Male* | *Female* |
| Under 7 | 7.41 | 8.26 | 6.54 | 100 | 111 | 88 |
| 7–15 | 7.62 | 7.65 | 7.59 | 100 | 100 | 100 |
| 16–20 | 7.13 | 6.38 | 7.89 | 100 | 89 | 111 |
| 21–25 | 3.40 | 2.28 | 4.08 | 100 | 67 | 120 |
| 26–30 | 6.83 | 6.23 | 7.40 | 100 | 91 | 108 |
| 31–35 | 6.69 | 6.80 | 6.60 | 100 | 102 | 99 |
| 36–40 | 6.60 | 5.34 | 6.50 | 100 | 81 | 98 |
| 41–45 | 7.36 | 6.80 | 7.91 | 100 | 92 | 107 |
| 46–50 | 5.33 | 5.75 | 4.94 | 100 | 108 | 93 |
| 51–55 | 3.19 | 3.63 | 2.74 | 100 | 114 | 86 |
| 56–60 | 4.55 | 5.23 | 3.85 | 100 | 115 | 85 |
| 61–65 | 2.07 | 0.72 | 3.15 | 100 | 35 | 152 |
| 66–70 | 4.27 | 2.74 | 6.28 | 100 | 64 | 147 |
| 71 and over | 7.49 | 3.90 | 11.21 | 100 | 52 | 150 |
| All samples | 5.88 | 5.49 | 6.25 | 100 | 93 | 106 |

Does poverty incidence differ across age groups in urban China? Are females more likely to fall into poverty than males, as in other countries? To answer these questions, we divide all sampled individuals into 14 age groups by gender and computed incidence of poverty for each category. The results are presented in Table 7.5 and Figure 7.1. It can be observed that there is no significant gender difference in poverty incidence, although the poverty incidence for female individuals is 0.76 percentage points higher than for males. Moreover, Table 7.5 displays a moderate variation in poverty incidence among age groups. Urban poverty is more likely to occur in the young age groups and the oldest age group. It is worth noting that the age groups 21–25 and 51–55 have a distinctly low incidence of poverty. These two age groups are likely to be two generations in the same household. If the two generations are employed at the same time, the resulting dependency ratio will be low. This confirms our hypothesis that urban poverty is more related to unemployment. In contrast to other countries, retirees do not show a relatively low poverty incidence in urban China; we see this for the age groups over 60 in Table 7.5, except for those aged over 70 years. The oldest group has a higher incidence of poverty largely due to the remarkably high incidence among females in the group. Our data demonstrate that only 50 per cent of the females in this group are retirees, compared to 91 per cent of their male counterparts.

To illustrate how important employment status is to poverty incidence, poverty incidences are computed for individuals with different employment status. All individuals are classified into ten categories according to their status at the end of 1999. Each group is also divided into two subgroups, with good and bad health. Poverty incidence is accordingly computed for each subgroup, and the results are shown in Table 7.6. It is apparent that three groups of individuals have the highest

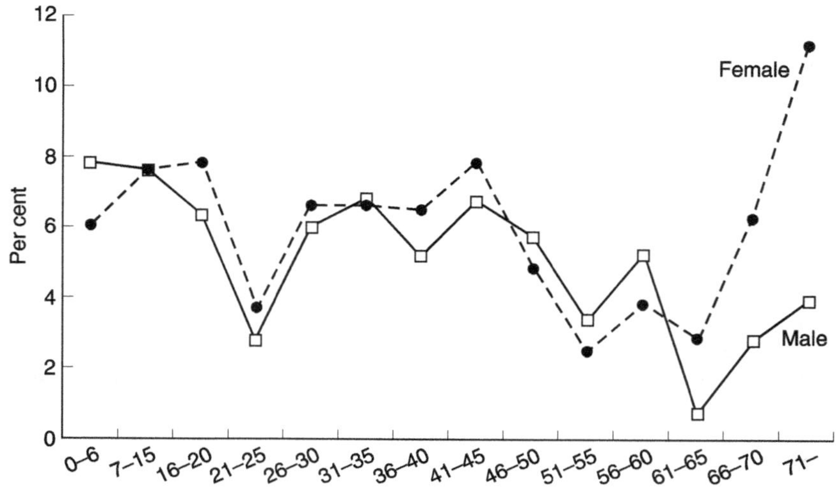


*Figure 7.1* Poverty incidence of age groups in urban China by gender, 1999.

incidences of poverty. They are *xiagang* (laid-off) workers, unemployed people and disabled persons, with poverty rates of 23 per cent, 21 and 26 per cent, respectively. Full-time homemakers and those never employed also have higher incidence of poverty. Furthermore, unhealthy persons are more likely to fall into poverty than healthy persons, the former having a poverty incidence 64 percentage points higher and the latter 5 percentage points lower than the entire sample. An individual with both unhealthy status and unemployment status would face a 50 per cent probability of falling into poverty, about 10 times higher than that for average people.

## 7.5 Analysing the effects of unemployment on poverty

This section attempts to explore why some households and individuals are more likely to fall into poverty than others, by concentrating on the effects of unemployment on poverty incidence. It is widely acknowledged that the causes underlying poverty vary from time to time and from location to location. However, they are more related to unemployment, illness, and even location. It would not be surprising that the unemployed and *xiagang* workers would experience a significant shortfall in their income after being in those statuses (Appleton *et al.* 2000).

To isolate the importance of those elements, we undertake an analysis using the probit model. The dependent variable is a binomial one, equal to 1 if an observation is in poverty and 0 if not in poverty. The independent variables include two categories, one for individual characteristics such as employment status (EMPi), health status (HEAi) and city location (CITYi), with control variables of age group (AGi), gender (SEX1 for male) and household size (NMHi). The category

*Table 7.6* Poverty incidence by health and employment status

| *Employment status* | *Poverty incidence (%)* | | | *Proportion to average (as 100%)* | | |
|---|---|---|---|---|---|---|
| | *All samples* | *Healthy* | *Not healthy* | *All samples* | *Healthy* | *Not healthy* |
| 1. Working or employed | 3.60 | 3.47 | 8.61 | 100 | 96 | 239 |
| 2. Retired | 3.33 | 3.06 | 4.30 | 100 | 92 | 129 |
| 3. Waiting for job assignment | 12.00 | 11.52 | 25.00 | 100 | 96 | 208 |
| 4. Laid off | 23.02 | 22.30 | 31.43 | 100 | 97 | 137 |
| 5. Unemployed | 20.87 | 18.69 | 50.00 | 100 | 90 | 240 |
| 6. Earlier retired | 5.42 | 4.14 | 14.29 | 100 | 76 | 264 |
| 7. Full-time homemaker | 17.86 | 16.75 | 21.82 | 100 | 94 | 122 |
| 8. Disabled, injured/chronic disease | 26.19 | — | 26.19 | 100 | — | 100 |
| 9. Full-time student | 7.06 | 7.10 | 0.00 | 100 | 101 | 0 |
| All samples | 5.88 | 5.56 | 9.64 | 100 | 95 | 164 |

Note: Category 'Other', mainly including pre-school children, is omitted from the table.

includes characteristics of household heads, in which employment status (H_EMPi), health status (H_HEAi) and city location (H_CITYi) of household heads are treated as explanatory variables and variables of age (H_Agi), gender (H_SEXi), education (H_EDUi), occupation (H_OCCi), ownership of work unit (OWNi), economic sector (H_SECi), type of work unit (H_TYPi) and party membership (H_PARi) are treated as control variables in the model. Finally, it should be noted that the estimation is corrected for clustering effects of households as the units of analysis are individuals rather than households.

Table 7.7 shows the results of the probit analysis based on the personal characteristics of individuals in the sample. Table 7.8 shows the results using information on the characteristics of household heads. The predicted probability of each variable, computed from the coefficients of explanatory variables and control variables, are presented. The results strongly indicate that status of employment for both individuals and household heads plays a very significant role in determining poverty. For instance, other things being equal, a youth waiting for job assignment would face twice the probability of an average person. For *xiagang* workers and unemployed persons, the probability would increase by nearly four times. When heads of household become *xiagang* workers, the members of their households would suffer from an even higher incidence of poverty, i.e. 34 per cent (Table 7.8). The results here are consistent with the findings in Appleton *et al.* (2000), which indicate that urban workers would suffer from income decreasing by 56 per cent if they were retrenched either as unemployed or *xiagang* workers.

To explore further the impact of unemployment on poverty incidence, we conducted the same analyses for two groups of individuals separately. The first group contains people who are fully employed and the second group consists only of people who are either unemployed or *xiagang*. The results are presented in Appendix 7.A. Among the *xiagang* workers and unemployed persons, poverty is more related explicitly and potentially with the following characteristics of household heads: age group of 26–35, 36–45, 65 years old and over; *xiagang* status, full-time homemakers; living in three cities Zhengzhou, Zigong and Nanchong; unhealthy status; low educational attainment; working in urban collective firms and informal sector; being unskilled workers; and being employed in loss-making enterprises.

The results also indicate that even among employees, some personal characteristics of household heads such as *xiagang* status, full-time homemaker, living in Jinzhou, Zigong and Nanchong, unhealthy status, low educational attainment, being employed in an urban collective enterprise and in a temporary or unskilled job, each contribute significantly to poverty incidence.

The second important element causing poverty is ill-health of individuals and household heads. Being unhealthy, an individual has a 74 per cent higher probability of falling into poverty than healthy people (Table 7.7). Having an unhealthy head, household members suffer a probability 135 per cent higher than people with healthy household heads (Table 7.8).

The third important element leading to higher incidence of poverty is location, as shown in Tables 7.7 and 7.8. Controlling for other variables, people living in Liaoning, Henan and Sichuan have a higher risk of becoming poor than those in other provinces. For instance, the predicted probability of people in Jinzhou, Kaifeng and Zigong falling into poverty is 9, 12 and 16 per cent respectively, compared to the average predicted probability of 5.8 per cent in urban China as a whole. Why does poverty incidence vary across locations? Even for two provinces with similar levels of poverty, does poverty have the same causes? To attempt to answer these questions, we ran probit models for Henan and Liaoning provinces separately using the same set of explanatory variables. The estimated results are presented in Appendix 7.B. They show analogous effects on poverty incidence of some characteristics of household heads such as *xiagang* status, low educational attainment, employment in the urban collective sector and as temporary workers, but also the dissimilar effects of some variables such as health status and party membership in the two provinces. The unhealthy status of household heads has potentially a large effect in Liaoning but not in Henan. In contrast, party membership of household heads is more important in interpreting variation of poverty incidence among individuals in Henan than in Liaoning. This might be associated with the more political concentration of decision making in Henan Province.

Finally, most economists would expect that women have a higher probability of falling into poverty in urban China. If not, they might nevertheless have different determinants of poverty than their male counterparts. Our results indicate that the predicted probability of becoming poor is 0.6–0.7 percentage points higher for women than for men when other variables are controlled, as shown in Table 7.7. To test for different causes of poverty for males and females, we estimate

*Table 7.7* Probit analysis and predicted probability of urban individuals falling into poverty in 1999 using individual own characteristics

| | *Name of variable* | *Mean value* | *Coefficient* | *Standard error* | *Predicted probability (%)* |
|---|---|---|---|---|---|
| Base probability | | | | | 5.79 |
| Male | sex1 | 0.496 | — | — | 5.40 |
| Female | sex2 | 0.504 | −0.0478 | 0.0302 | 6.17 |
| Age under 7 | ag1 | 0.036 | 0.2436 | 0.1909 | 7.12 |
| Age 7–15 | ag2 | 0.108 | 0.3832* | 0.1578 | 7.60 |
| Age 16–20 | ag3 | 0.077 | 0.3426* | 0.1449 | 7.08 |
| Age 21–25 | ag4 | 0.051 | — | — | 3.21 |
| Age 26–30 | ag5 | 0.063 | 0.3341* | 0.1600 | 6.40 |
| Age 31–35 | ag6 | 0.072 | 0.4861** | 0.1525 | 6.51 |
| Age 36–40 | ag7 | 0.112 | 0.4355** | 0.1505 | 5.95 |
| Age 41–45 | ag8 | 0.118 | 0.5532** | 0.1499 | 7.29 |
| Age 46–50 | ag9 | 0.110 | 0.4231** | 0.1426 | 5.41 |
| Age 51–55 | ag10 | 0.068 | 0.0694 | 0.1580 | 2.91 |
| Age 56–60 | ag11 | 0.053 | 0.2523 | 0.1664 | 4.66 |
| Age 61–65 | ag12 | 0.052 | −0.2098 | 0.2121 | 1.76 |
| Age 66–70 | ag13 | 0.043 | 0.1267 | 0.1992 | 4.26 |
| Age over 70 | ag14 | 0.038 | 0.1589 | 0.1955 | 7.77 |
| Working or employed | emp1 | 0.480 | — | — | 3.55 |
| Retired | emp2 | 0.187 | 0.1935 | 0.1011 | 3.31 |
| Waiting for job assigned | emp3 | 0.019 | 0.6925** | 0.1413 | 11.37 |
| Laid off (*xiagang*) | emp4 | 0.037 | 0.8988** | 0.0811 | 22.74 |
| Unemployed | emp5 | 0.010 | 1.0142** | 0.1437 | 21.39 |
| Earlier retired | emp6 | 0.014 | 0.2028 | 0.1907 | 5.68 |
| Full-time homemaker | emp7 | 0.021 | 1.0201** | 0.1188 | 17.71 |
| Disabled, injured | emp8 | 0.009 | 1.0202** | 0.1755 | 20.82 |
| Full-time student | emp9 | 0.177 | 0.3991** | 0.1452 | 7.05 |
| Others | emp10 | 0.047 | 0.4605** | 0.1604 | 7.08 |
| Beijing | city1 | 0.151 | — | — | 2.99 |
| Shenyang | city2 | 0.114 | 0.3326* | 0.1490 | 6.05 |
| Jinzhou | city3 | 0.051 | 0.4870** | 0.1718 | 9.36 |
| Nanjing | city4 | 0.105 | −0.3445 | 0.2016 | 1.19 |
| Xuzhou | city5 | 0.048 | 0.2353 | 0.2046 | 4.96 |
| Zhengzhou | city6 | 0.077 | 0.3551* | 0.1581 | 7.07 |
| Kaifeng | city7 | 0.051 | 0.6224** | 0.1646 | 11.96 |
| Pingdingshang | city8 | 0.051 | −0.5304 | 0.2909 | 1.82 |
| Chengdu | city9 | 0.098 | 0.2991* | 0.1527 | 5.86 |
| Zigong | city10 | 0.051 | 0.7993** | 0.1623 | 16.32 |
| Nanchong | city11 | 0.048 | 0.4291* | 0.1798 | 7.50 |
| Lanzhou | city12 | 0.104 | 0.1415 | 0.1591 | 5.20 |
| Pingliang | city13 | 0.051 | 0.2386 | 0.1934 | 5.97 |
| Healthy | hea1 | 0.922 | — | — | 5.47 |
| Unhealthy | hea2 | 0.078 | 0.2681** | 0.0800 | 9.53 |
| Number of HH members | nmh | 3.228 | 0.0892* | 0.0429 | |

*Table 7.7* (Continued)

| Name of variable | Mean value | Coefficient | Standard error | Predicted probability |
|---|---|---|---|---|
| nmh=1 | | | | 3.32 |
| nmh=2 | | | | 3.55 |
| nmh=3 | | | | 5.59 |
| nmh=4 | | | | 6.62 |
| nmh=5 | | | | 8.10 |
| constant | | −2.7586** | 0.2164 | |
| No. of obs. | | 12,060 | | |
| Wald chi$^2$ | | 496.0 | | |
| Pseudo-$R^2$ | | 0.123 | | |
| Log-likelihood | | −2,338.5 | | |

Notes:
1 Standard errors are adjusted for clustering of household members.
2 ** and * indicate the coefficient statistically significant at 1% and 5%.

probit models for the two gender groups. However, it is apparent that the estimation does not show substantial gender difference in the effects of characteristics of household heads in augmenting poverty incidence.

To sum up, our analysis indicates that urban poverty is more likely to occur for households or individuals with the following characteristics: being unemployed or *xiagang*; with unhealthy status or unable to work or as full-time homemakers; having low educational attainment; being employed in the urban collective sector or informal sector; and being unskilled workers. Among these characteristics, the most important one is unemployment or *xiagang* status.

## 7.6 Impact of government policy: evaluation

At least since 1998, the Chinese government has strengthened the implementation of anti-poverty policies by providing financial benefits to the urban poor, on the one hand, and by increasing employment opportunities for those households who are your due to being unemployed, on the other hand. In these circumstances, a question is naturally raised: How large an impact have government policies exerted on urban poverty? To estimate the impact, we conducted a simulation analysis. When unemployment benefits and other subsidies are deducted from household income, how large a reduction of poverty incidence is observed in the data?

Table 7.9 gives the simulated poverty incidences for the cities under study on the assumption of absence of government unemployment benefits and subsidies. The simulated results indicate that the impact of the government anti-poverty effort is strikingly modest. If governments had not provided the unemployment benefits and subsidies to urban households, poverty incidence would have increased by less than 10 per cent in 1999. This suggests that the implementation of the present anti-poverty policy reduced poverty by only less than 10 per cent. However, the anti-poverty policy was mainly focused on the poorest group, since the

*Table 7.8* Probit analysis and predicted probability of urban individuals falling into poverty in 1999 using characteristics of household heads

| | *Variable name* | *Coefficient* | *Standard error* | *Predicted probability (%)* |
|---|---|---|---|---|
| *Gender* | | — | — | |
| Male | h_sex1 | | | 6.17 |
| Female | h_sex2 | −0.4058** | 0.0548 | 5.34 |
| *Age group* | | | | |
| Age under 26 | h_ag1 | −0.1948 | 0.3988 | 3.01 |
| Age 26–35 | h_ag2 | — | — | 7.39 |
| Age 36–45 | h_ag3 | 0.0233 | 0.0720 | 7.45 |
| Age 46–55 | h_ag4 | −0.2543** | 0.0827 | 4.89 |
| Age 56–65 | h_ag5 | −0.1711 | 0.1176 | 3.53 |
| Age over 65 | h_ag6 | −0.1873 | 0.1414 | 5.62 |
| *Status of employment* | | | | |
| Working or employed | h_emp1 | — | — | 4.53 |
| Retired | h_emp2 | −0.3346** | 0.0961 | 3.73 |
| Waiting for job assignment | h_emp3 | ++ | ++ | 0 |
| Laid off (*xiagang*) | h_emp4 | 0.7846** | 0.0794 | 34.31 |
| Unemployed | h_emp5 | 0.2418 | 0.1843 | 16.38 |
| Early retirement | h_emp6 | −0.0692 | 0.1646 | 6.38 |
| Full-time homemaker | h_emp7 | 0.5680** | 0.2132 | 32.30 |
| Disabled, injured | h_emp8 | −0.2622 | 0.4140 | 37.37 |
| Full-time student | h_emp9 | ++ | ++ | 0 |
| Others | h_emp10 | 0.0963 | 0.1891 | 11.81 |
| *Location* | | | | |
| Beijing | h_city1 | — | — | 3.16 |
| Shenyang | h_city2 | 0.3751** | 0.0936 | 6.37 |
| Jinzhou | h_city3 | 0.2468* | 0.1122 | 9.43 |
| Nanjing | h_city4 | −0.4193** | 0.1348 | 1.25 |
| Xuzhou | h_city5 | −0.0336 | 0.1318 | 5.05 |
| Zhengzhou | h_city6 | 0.3759** | 0.1045 | 6.79 |
| Kaifeng | h_city7 | 0.4031** | 0.1089 | 11.91 |
| Pingdingshan | h_city8 | −0.1433 | 0.2813 | 2.94 |
| Chengdu | h_city9 | 0.2849** | 0.1013 | 5.94 |
| Zigong | h_city10 | 0.5456** | 0.1055 | 16.54 |
| Nanchong | h_city11 | 0.4096** | 0.1156 | 7.96 |
| Lanzhou | h_city12 | 0.0633 | 0.0983 | 5.18 |
| Pingliang | h_city13 | 0.3647** | 0.1228 | 6.23 |
| *Health status* | | | | |
| Healthy | h_hea1 | — | — | 5.26 |
| Unhealthy | h_hea2 | 0.4670** | 0.0709 | 12.35 |
| *Education* | | | | |
| College and above | h_edu1 | — | — | 0.48 |
| Professional school | h_edu2 | 0.1871 | 0.1986 | 1.44 |
| Middle-level prof. school | h_edu3 | 0.3548 | 0.2025 | 2.14 |
| Upper middle school | h_edu4 | 0.5445** | 0.1914 | 5.62 |
| Lower middle school | h_edu5 | 0.7912** | 0.1897 | 9.25 |
| Elementary school | h_edu6 | 10.1502** | 0.2050 | 12.20 |
| Below elementary school | h_edu7 | 0.9620** | 0.2368 | 15.24 |

*Table 7.8* (Continued)

| | *Variable name* | *Coefficient* | *Standard error* | *Predicted probability (%)* |
|---|---|---|---|---|
| *Party membership* | | | | |
| Party member | h_par1 | −0.1447* | 0.0629 | 2.36 |
| Non-party member | h_par2 | — | — | 8.06 |
| *Ownership* | | | | |
| Central/provincial SOE | h_own1 | — | — | 2.07 |
| Local SOE | h_own2 | 0.2454** | 0.0632 | 5.69 |
| Urban collective | h_own3 | 0.5669** | 0.0760 | 15.47 |
| Private firm and self-employed | h_own4 | 0.1543 | 0.1881 | 9.21 |
| Joint venture foreign-owned | h_own5 | 0.3845 | 0.2146 | 5.42 |
| Shareholder firm | h_own6 | 0.3534** | 0.1202 | 8.15 |
| Other ownership | h_own7 | 1.0150** | 0.2062 | 15.10 |
| *Job nature* | | | | |
| Permanent staff member | h_job1 | — | — | 4.20 |
| Long-term contract worker | h_job2 | 0.1583** | 0.0589 | 11.73 |
| Private or self-employed | h_job3 | 0.1440 | 0.2222 | 8.88 |
| Temporary worker or other | h_job4 | 0.2895** | 0.1068 | 16.04 |
| *Occupation* | | | | |
| Private owner or self-employed | h_occ1 | −0.3709 | 0.2573 | 3.87 |
| Professional | h_occ2 | — | — | 1.63 |
| Responsible person | h_occ3 | −0.0599 | 0.2035 | 0.97 |
| Department responsible person | h_occ4 | 0.2223 | 0.1149 | 2.61 |
| Clerical/office staff | h_occ5 | 0.0282 | 0.1074 | 2.78 |
| Skilled (grade 3 and below) | h_occ6 | 0.0795 | 0.1068 | 9.54 |
| Skilled (grade 4 and above) | h_occ7 | 0.1834 | 0.0955 | 8.54 |
| Unskilled worker | h_occ8 | 0.3324** | 0.0988 | 11.76 |
| Commercial and service worker | h_occ9 | 0.2467* | 0.1247 | 9.03 |
| Other occupation | h_occ10 | 0.3436* | 0.1675 | 20.21 |
| *Sector* | | | | |
| Agriculture | h_sec1 | −0.3038 | 0.2598 | 3.79 |
| Mineral | h_sec2 | 0.1810 | 0.1466 | 6.86 |
| Manufacturing | h_sec3 | — | — | 9.10 |
| Electricity, gas and water | h_sec4 | −0.3953* | 0.1618 | 1.78 |
| Construction | h_sec5 | 0.0900 | 0.0992 | 6.05 |
| Geological prospecting | h_sec6 | ++ | ++ | 0 |
| Transport and communication | h_sec7 | 0.2584** | 0.0859 | 3.59 |
| Commerce and food services | h_sec8 | −0.1525 | 0.0922 | 7.73 |
| Finance and insurance | h_sec9 | ++ | ++ | 0 |
| Real estate | h_sec10 | −0.2833 | 0.2761 | 3.98 |
| Social services | h_sec11 | −0.2559* | 0.1075 | 8.37 |
| Health and social welfare | h_sec12 | −10.074 | 0.3163 | 0.31 |
| Education, culture and arts | h_sec13 | −0.5224** | 0.1666 | 0.80 |

(Continued)

*Table 7.8* (Continued)

| | *Variable name* | *Coefficient* | *Standard error* | *Predicted probability (%)* |
|---|---|---|---|---|
| Scientific research | h_sec14 | −0.2165 | 0.1920 | 2.77 |
| Government/Party agents | h_sec15 | −0.9250** | 0.2047 | 0.41 |
| Other sector | h_sec16 | −0.4073** | 0.1349 | 5.28 |
| *Type of work unit* | | | | |
| Government agent institution | h_ins1 | — | — | 1.56 |
| Enterprise with high profit | h_ins2 | −0.3743* | 0.1550 | 1.96 |
| Enterprise with marginal profit | h_ins3 | −0.2871** | 0.0815 | 3.78 |
| Enterprise with loss | h_ins4 | 0.0322 | 0.0771 | 10.74 |
| Intercept | constant | −20.424** | 0.2191 | |
| | No. of obs. | 11,808 | | |
| | Wald chi$^2$ | 1,405.4 | | |
| | Pseudo $R^2$ | 0.266 | | |
| | Log-likelihood | −1,937.4 | | |

Notes:
1 Standard errors are adjusted for clustering of household members.
2 **and * indicate the coefficient statistically significant at 1% and 5%.
3 — denotes omitted variable and ++ no observations in this category.

poverty gap index and weighted poverty gap index decreased more substantially with the policy. For instance, the poverty gap index and weighted poverty gap index would increase by 28 and 54 per cent respectively without the implementation of the government financial support for poor households.

In Table 7.9, it is also clearly shown that the effects of the anti-poverty policy on reduction in poverty vary across provinces and cities. The poverty indices with and without the government financial support can be employed to evaluate the impact of the anti-poverty policy at the lower level of government. Our simulation analysis indicates that all levels of government provided financial support to poor households, but with notable variation. The general tendency is that the government in a richer province or city would be more willing to provide financial support to poor in terms of both coverage and quantity. Taking Nanjing as an example, the government support reduced poverty incidence by nearly 41 per cent, the poverty gap by 77 per cent and the weighted poverty gap by 190 per cent. In contrast, Kaifeng City in Henan Province displays another scenario: poverty incidence remained unchanged, the poverty gap decreased by only 8 per cent, and the weighted poverty gap decreased by less than 20 per cent. In this case, only a small amount of financial benefits was provided by the local government.

## 7.7 Conclusions and policy implications

As a new phenomenon, urban poverty in China has recently attracted more attention from academics and policy makers domestically. Although it is commonly

*Table 7.9* Simulated poverty indices in urban China by city, 1999

| *Province/City* | *Simulated poverty indices* | | | *Increase as a percentage of actual poverty index* | | |
|---|---|---|---|---|---|---|
| | *Head-count (%)* | *Poverty gap (×100)* | *Weighted poverty gap (×100)* | *Head-count (%)* | *Poverty gap (×100)* | *Weighted poverty gap (×100)* |
| Beijing | 3.51 | 0.90 | 0.46 | 116.2 | 138.5 | 200 |
| Liaoning | 7.54 | | | 107.1 | | |
| Shenyang | 6.42 | 1.36 | 0.56 | 106.1 | 110.6 | 116.7 |
| Jinzhou | 10.02 | 2.66 | 0.94 | 108.8 | 137.1 | 167.9 |
| Jiangsu | 3.03 | | | 127.3 | | |
| Nanjing | 1.66 | 0.46 | 0.29 | 140.7 | 176.9 | 290 |
| Xuzhou | 6.01 | 1.05 | 0.31 | 120.7 | 181.0 | 238.5 |
| Henan | 7.62 | | | 105.8 | | |
| Zhengzhou | 8.16 | 3.10 | 2.05 | 113.3 | 131.9 | 148.6 |
| Kaifeng | 11.8 | 4.11 | 2.18 | 100.0 | 108.2 | 119.1 |
| Pingdingshan | 2.62 | 1.19 | 0.92 | 115.9 | 208.8 | 340.7 |
| Sichuan | 10.21 | | | 113.1 | | |
| Chengdu | 6.69 | 1.76 | 0.87 | 112.8 | 123.1 | 124.3 |
| Zigong | 18.99 | 6.32 | 3.09 | 115.8 | 132.2 | 149.3 |
| Nanchong | 8.03 | 1.53 | 0.46 | 107.1 | 123.4 | 139.4 |
| Gansu | 5.38 | | | 100.0 | | |
| Lanzhou | 5.17 | 1.25 | 0.56 | 100.0 | 122.5 | 155.6 |
| Pingliang | 5.81 | 0.59 | 0.59 | 100.0 | 154.1 | 203.4 |
| All samples | 6.44 | 1.79 | 0.83 | 109.5 | 127.9 | 153.7 |

acknowledged that the expansion of poverty would be harmful to political and economic stability in the urban areas, few robust studies have been conducted on the relevant issues such as scale and intensity of poverty, the main causes of poverty, and the like. A contribution of this chapter is to provide estimates of poverty indices for provinces and cities and population groups in 1999, by using the data from a household survey in the selected urban areas. Our estimation demonstrates that urban poverty in China is not as severe as in most developing countries, but has a clear location dimension. Poverty is more likely to occur in the western cities than in the coastal cities. Poverty is also more likely to be found in the small cities than in the large cities.

Our analysis of the causes of poverty indicates the vital importance of unemployment or *xiagang* for poverty incidence in urban China. The estimation using the probit models provides consistent evidence that individuals being unemployed or *xiagang*, or with household heads being unemployed or *xiagang*, have a predicted probability of falling into poverty 3–6 times higher than the average people. In addition, unhealthy status of either individuals or household heads is another notable variable; low educational attainment and lack of skill also contribute. Poverty incidence varies across provinces and cities, partly due to unbalanced employment opportunities and partly due to dissimilar implementation of government anti-poverty programmes across locations. Even in the urban areas as a whole, the actual effect of the government policy aiming at alleviation of poverty is quite modest. Although the central government propose some policies, the success of their implementation is dubious.

Our simulation analysis demonstrates that promoting employment is a sound solution to alleviating poverty in urban China. For the households in chronic poverty, an effective solution perhaps requires provision of financial support for them.

## Notes

The data used in the paper come from the 1999 CASS survey. The author is very grateful for comments and language correction made by John Knight.

1 Pingdingshan City is treated as an exception because of higher income per capita and lower unemployment rate even compared to the capital city Zhengzhou.

## References

Appleton, S., Knight, J., Song, L. and Xia, Q. (2000) 'Towards a competitive labour market? Urban workers, rural–urban migrants, redundancies and hardship in urban China', *Paper for AEA Annual Conference 2000*, December 2000.

Asian Development Bank (2001) *Urban Poverty in PRC.* Project Report, prepared by a research group led by A. Hussain.

Foster, J., Greer, J. and Thorbecke, E. (1984) 'A class of decomposable poverty measures', *Econometrica*, 52: 761–6.

Gustafsson, B. and Li, S. (1998) 'The structure of Chinese poverty, 1988', *Developing Economies*, 36(4): 387–406.

Gustafsson, B. and Wei, Z. (2000) 'How and why has poverty in China changed? A study based on microdata for 1988 and 1995', *China Quarterly*, 164: 983–1006.

Institute of Labour Science (2000) 'Shenyang he wuhan xiagang zhigong zhuangkuang fenxi baogao' (Analytical report of situation of *xiagang* workers in Shenyang and Wuhan). *Yanjiu Luntan* (Research Forum), 19.

Khan, A.R. (1998) 'Growth and poverty in east and south-east Asia in the era of globalization', in Bhalla, A.S. (ed.), *Globalization, Growth and Marginali-zation.* New York: St. Martin's Press/London: Macmillan Press, pp. 125–48.

Knight, J. (2000) 'Trends in poverty, inequality and the achievement of international development targets in China', Paper prepared for the DFID China Programme Retreat, 29 June 2000.

NBS (2000) *China Statistical Yearbook 2000*, Beijing: China Statistics Press.

Ren, C. and Chen, X. (1996) 'Zhongguo chengzhen pinkun de guimo zhuangkuang he qushi' (Size, situation and trend of poverty in urban China), *Yanjiu Cankao* (Research Reference), No. 65.

Sen, A. (1976) 'Poverty: an ordinal approach to measurement', *Econometrica*, 44: 219–31.

Wang, Y. (2000) 'Measuring poverty in urban China', Research Report, NBS.

World Bank (1992) *Strategies for Reducing Poverty in China.* Washington, DC: World Bank.

## Appendix 7.A: Probit analysis of poverty incidence for unemployed and employed groups

| | *Variable name* | *Unemployed* | | *Employed* | |
|---|---|---|---|---|---|
| | | *Coefficient* | *Predicted probability (%)* | *Coefficient* | *Predicted probability (%)* |
| Base probability | | | 22.2 | | 3.7 |
| *Gender* | | | | | |
| Male | h_sex1 | — | 23.1 | — | 4.2 |
| Female | h_sex2 | −0.398* | 20.6 | −0.295** | 3.0 |
| *Age group* | | | | | |
| Age under 26 | h_ag1 | ++ | 0.0 | −0.026 | 2.4 |
| Age 26–35 | h_ag2 | — | 36.8 | — | 3.6 |
| Age 36–45 | h_ag3 | −0.229 | 28.9 | 0.142 | 4.9 |
| Age 46–55 | h_ag4 | −0.701** | 14.2 | −0.168 | 2.8 |
| Age 56–65 | h_ag5 | −0.658 | 9.0 | 0.096 | 2.8 |
| Age over 65 | h_ag6 | −0.018 | 29.3 | −0.168 | 2.1 |
| *Status of employment* | | | | | |
| Working or employed | h_emp1 | — | 15.3 | — | 3.6 |
| Retired | h_emp2 | 0.398 | 13.0 | −0.858** | 1.1 |
| Waiting for job assignment | h_emp3 | ++ | 0.0 | ++ | 0.0 |
| Laid off (*xiagang*) | h_emp4 | 0.490* | 40.1 | 0.553** | 22.9 |
| Unemployed | h_emp5 | 0.241 | 16.9 | 0.285 | 15.1 |
| Early retirement | h_emp6 | 0.122 | 16.0 | −0.298 | 2.3 |
| Full-time homemaker | h_emp7 | 1.199 | 49.9 | 0.409 | 28.2 |
| Disabled, injured | h_emp8 | ++ | 0.0 | ++ | 0.0 |
| Full-time student | h_emp9 | ++ | 0.0 | ++ | 0.0 |
| Others | h_emp10 | 0.256 | 32.4 | −0.297 | 4.0 |
| *Location* | | | | | |
| Beijing | h_city1 | — | 16.9 | — | 1.8 |
| Shenyang | h_city2 | 0.276 | 18.1 | 0.318 | 3.9 |
| Jinzhou | h_city3 | −0.164 | 19.0 | 0.391 | 8.3 |
| Nanjing | h_city4 | −0.432 | 6.1 | −0.484 | 0.7 |
| Xuzhou | h_city5 | −0.442 | 12.8 | 0.031 | 3.9 |
| Zhengzhou | h_city6 | 0.256 | 32.3 | 0.380 | 3.8 |
| Kaifeng | h_city7 | −0.110 | 22.9 | 0.466* | 7.0 |
| Pingdingshan | h_city8 | 0.140 | 18.6 | −0.072 | 2.3 |
| Chengdu | h_city9 | −0.120 | 17.5 | 0.125 | 2.2 |
| Zigong | h_city10 | 0.490 | 45.4 | 0.523* | 9.1 |
| Nanchong | h_city11 | 0.509 | 30.5 | 0.541* | 7.3 |
| Lanzhou | h_city12 | 0.089 | 18.1 | 0.144 | 3.4 |
| Pingliang | h_city13 | 0.083 | 16.8 | 0.579* | 5.1 |

(Continued)

*Appendix 7.A* (Continued)

| | *Variable name* | *Unemployed* | | *Employed* | |
|---|---|---|---|---|---|
| | | *Coefficient* | *Predicted probability (%)* | *Coefficient* | *Predicted probability (%)* |
| *Health status* | | | | | |
| Healthy | h_hea1 | — | 20.1 | — | 3.5 |
| Unhealthy | h_hea2 | 0.440 | 41.6 | 0.474** | 7.6 |
| *Education* | | | | | |
| College and above | h_edu1 | — | 9.3 | — | 0.7 |
| Professional school | h_edu2 | 0.363 | 13.8 | −0.229 | 0.8 |
| Middle-level prof. school | h_edu3 | 0.021 | 10.3 | −0.048 | 1.5 |
| Upper middle school | h_edu4 | 0.484 | 21.2 | 0.124 | 3.3 |
| Lower middle school | h_edu5 | 0.737 | 25.2 | 0.469 | 7.1 |
| Elementary school | h_edu6 | 1.070 | 29.2 | 0.723* | 7.8 |
| Below elementary school | h_edu7 | 0.239 | 26.9 | 0.405 | 6.8 |
| *Party membership* | | | | | |
| Party member | h_par1 | −0.079 | 12.5 | −0.030 | 1.9 |
| Non-party member | h_par2 | — | 25.3 | — | 4.9 |
| *Ownership* | | | | | |
| SOE at central/ provincial level | h_own1 | — | 10.5 | — | 1.3 |
| Local SOE | h_own2 | 0.265 | 19.6 | 0.313* | 3.9 |
| Urban collective | h_own3 | 0.743** | 36.3 | 0.544** | 9.4 |
| Private firm and self-employed | h_own4 | 0.581 | 24.0 | 0.379 | 8.4 |
| Joint venture/ foreign-owned | h_own5 | 1.074 | 32.8 | 0.356 | 3.1 |
| Shareholder firm | h_own6 | 0.584 | 28.0 | 0.353 | 5.1 |
| Other ownership | h_own7 | 1.443** | 45.2 | 0.662 | 6.6 |
| *Job nature* | | | | | |
| Permanent staff member | h_job1 | — | 17.6 | — | 2.7 |
| Long-term contract worker | h_job2 | 0.240 | 33.6 | 0.153 | 6.8 |
| Private or self-employed | h_job3 | ++ | 0.0 | 0.210 | 6.8 |
| Temporary worker or other | h_job4 | 0.098 | 31.2 | 0.403 | 11.5 |

*Appendix 7.A* (Continued)

| | *Variable name* | *Unemployed* | | *Employed* | |
|---|---|---|---|---|---|
| | | *Coefficient* | *Predicted probability (%)* | *Coefficient* | *Predicted probability (%)* |
| *Occupation* | | | | | |
| Private owner or self-employed | h_occ1 | 0.183 | 32.9 | −0.635 | 1.3 |
| Professional | h_occ2 | — | 14.7 | — | 0.9 |
| Responsible person | h_occ3 | −0.272 | 11.4 | 0.047 | 0.8 |
| Department responsible person | h_occ4 | −0.056 | 12.6 | 0.317 | 2.0 |
| Clerical/office staff | h_occ5 | −0.318 | 16.1 | 0.089 | 1.7 |
| Skilled (grade 3 and below) | h_occ6 | −0.434 | 27.8 | 0.214 | 6.0 |
| Skilled (grade 4 and above) | h_occ7 | −0.312 | 18.2 | 0.233 | 5.4 |
| Unskilled worker | h_occ8 | −0.121 | 31.9 | 0.576** | 9.3 |
| Commercial and service worker | h_occ9 | 0.331 | 24.6 | 0.214 | 5.4 |
| Other occupation | h_occ10 | −0.151 | 32.9 | 0.559 | 17.6 |
| *Sector* | | | | | |
| Agriculture | h_sec1 | −0.101 | 30.4 | −0.290 | 1.2 |
| Mineral | h_sec2 | 0.793 | 34.6 | 0.120 | 5.9 |
| Manufacturing | h_sec3 | — | 25.2 | — | 6.1 |
| Electricity, gas and water | h_sec4 | ++ | 0.0 | −0.129 | 2.1 |
| Construction | h_sec5 | 0.304 | 22.0 | −0.448 | 2.2 |
| Geological prospecting | h_sec6 | ++ | 0.0 | ++ | 0.0 |
| Transport and communication | h_sec7 | 0.181 | 17.4 | −0.405* | 1.7 |
| Commerce and food services | h_sec8 | 0.163 | 26.1 | −0.099 | 5.4 |
| Finance and insurance | h_sec9 | ++ | 0.0 | ++ | 0.0 |
| Real estate | h_sec10 | ++ | 0.0 | −0.200 | 3.7 |
| Social services | h_sec11 | −0.205 | 19.6 | −0.327 | 4.9 |
| Health and social welfare | h_sec12 | −0.329 | 7.6 | −0.839* | 0.3 |
| Education, culture and arts | h_sec13 | −0.760 | 3.3 | −0.391 | 0.8 |
| Scientific research | h_sec14 | −0.707 | 7.9 | −0.062 | 1.9 |
| Government/ Party agents | h_sec15 | ++ | 0.0 | −0.791 | 0.4 |
| Other sector | h_sec16 | −0.567 | 10.5 | −0.235 | 4.8 |

(Continued)

*Appendix 7.A* (Continued)

| | *Variable name* | *Unemployed* | | *Employed* | |
|---|---|---|---|---|---|
| | | *Coefficient* | *Predicted probability (%)* | *Coefficient* | *Predicted probability (%)* |
| *Type of work unit* | | | | | |
| Government agent institution | h_ins1 | — | 17.6 | — | 0.9 |
| Enterprise with high profit | h_ins2 | ++ | 0.0 | −0.403 | 1.3 |
| Enterprise with marginal profit | h_ins3 | −0.671** | 11.5 | −0.292 | 2.5 |
| Enterprise with loss | h_ins4 | −0.038 | 26.7 | 0.136 | 7.7 |
| Intercept | constant | −1.156 | | −2.537** | |
| | No. of obs. | 674 | | 5,666 | |
| | Wald chi² | 130.9 | | 321.8 | |
| | Pseudo $R^2$ | 0.248 | | 0.251 | |
| | Log likelihood | −267.8 | | −677.4 | |

Notes:
1 Standard errors are adjusted for clustering of household members.
2 **and * indicate the coefficient statistically significant at 1% and 5%.
3 — denotes omitted variable and ++ no observations in this category.

## Appendix 7.B: Probit models of poverty incidence for Henan and Liaoning

| | *Variable name* | *Liaoning* | | *Henan* | |
|---|---|---|---|---|---|
| | | *Coefficient* | *Predicted probability (%)* | *Coefficient* | *Predicted probability (%)* |
| Base probability | | | 8.5 | | 9.4 |
| *Gender* | | | | — | |
| Male | h_sex1 | — | 10.6 | −0.373 | 10.4 |
| Female | h_sex2 | −0.407 | 5.4 | | 7.6 |
| *Age group* | | | | | |
| Age under 26 | h_ag1 | ++ | 0.0 | ++ | 0.0 |
| Age 26–35 | h_ag2 | — | 6.0 | — | 8.9 |
| Age 36–45 | h_ag3 | 0.410 | 11.0 | 0.127 | 14.1 |
| Age 46–55 | h_ag4 | −0.210 | 7.8 | −0.259 | 7.9 |
| Age 56–65 | h_ag5 | −0.508 | 6.5 | −0.430 | 5.0 |
| Age over 65 | h_ag6 | −1.528* | 3.8 | −1.061* | 2.4 |

*Appendix 7.B* (Continued)

| | *Variable name* | *Liaoning* | | *Henan* | |
|---|---|---|---|---|---|
| | | *Coefficient* | *Predicted probability (%)* | *Coefficient* | *Predicted probability (%)* |
| *Status of employment* | | | | | |
| Working or employed | h_emp1 | — | 7.3 | — | 7.5 |
| Retired | h_emp2 | 0.481 | 6.8 | −0.335 | 4.9 |
| Waiting for job assignment | h_emp3 | ++ | 0.0 | ++ | 0.0 |
| Laid off (*xiagang*) | h_emp4 | 0.917* | 40.7 | 0.336 | 32.1 |
| Unemployed | h_emp5 | 1.848* | 75.6 | ++ | 0.0 |
| Early retirement | h_emp6 | 0.558 | 9.9 | ++ | 0.0 |
| Full-time homemaker | h_emp7 | 6.414** | 35.5 | ++ | 0.0 |
| Disabled, injured | h_emp8 | ++ | 0.0 | ++ | 0.0 |
| Full-time student | h_emp9 | ++ | 0.0 | ++ | 0.0 |
| Others | h_emp10 | ++ | 0.0 | 1.262 | 39.0 |
| *Location* | | | | | |
| Shenyang | h_city2 | — | 7.3 | | |
| Jinzhou | h_city3 | −0.106 | 11.1 | | |
| Zhengzhou | h_city6 | | | — | 9.6 |
| Kaifeng | h_city7 | | | −0.086 | 15.4 |
| Pingdingshan | h_city8 | | | −0.673* | 3.9 |
| *Health status* | | | | | |
| Healthy | h_hea1 | — | 7.7 | — | 9.8 |
| Unhealthy | h_hea2 | 0.437 | 16.1 | 0.368 | 5.1 |
| *Education* | | | | | |
| College and above | h_edu1 | — | 5.7 | — | 4.3 |
| Professional school | h_edu2 | 0.121 | 5.3 | −0.872 | 1.0 |
| Middle-level prof. school | h_edu3 | −0.327 | 3.2 | −0.570 | 1.5 |
| Upper middle school | h_edu4 | −0.449 | 5.6 | 0.392 | 14.2 |
| Lower middle school | h_edu5 | −0.099 | 12.5 | 0.345 | 13.0 |
| Elementary school | h_edu6 | 0.248 | 8.2 | 0.629 | 11.8 |
| Below elementary school | h_edu7 | ++ | 0.0 | 0.836 | 9.0 |
| *Party membership* | | | | | |
| Party member | h_par1 | — | 7.6 | — | 3.4 |
| Non-party member | h_par2 | 0.322 | 9.0 | −0.165 | 12.9 |

(Continued)

*Appendix 7.B* (Continued)

| | *Variable name* | *Liaoning* | | *Henan* | |
|---|---|---|---|---|---|
| | | *Coefficient* | *Predicted probability (%)* | *Coefficient* | *Predicted probability (%)* |
| *Ownership* | | | | | |
| SOE at central/ provincial level | h_own1 | — | 3.2 | — | 3.2 |
| Local SOE | h_own2 | 0.376 | 7.3 | 0.731** | 10.3 |
| Urban collective | h_own3 | 0.590 | 14.1 | 1.066** | 23.7 |
| Private firm and self-employed | h_own4 | −6.224* | 7.4 | ++ | 0.0 |
| Joint venture/ foreign-owned | h_own5 | 0.758 | 11.4 | ++ | 0.0 |
| Shareholder firm | h_own6 | ++ | 0.0 | 0.457 | 8.3 |
| Other ownership | h_own7 | 0.591** | 46.7 | 1.911* | 29.8 |
| *Job nature* | | | | | |
| Permanent staff member | h_job1 | — | 6.9 | — | 9.1 |
| Long-term contract worker | h_job2 | 0.213 | 10.8 | −0.239 | 10.6 |
| Private or self-employed | h_job3 | 7.452 | 21.9 | ++ | 0.0 |
| Temporary worker or other | h_job4 | 1.077** | 20.8 | −0.072 | 15.2 |
| *Occupation* | | | | | |
| Private owner or self-employed | h_occ1 | 0.744 | 10.2 | 0.445 | 37.5 |
| Professional | h_occ2 | — | 1.3 | — | 3.1 |
| Responsible person | h_occ3 | 1.051 | 6.7 | 0.114 | 5.8 |
| Department responsible person | h_occ4 | 0.763 | 4.9 | 0.244 | 4.6 |
| Clerical/office staff | h_occ5 | 0.900 | 7.2 | −0.058 | 6.5 |
| Skilled (grade 3 and below) | h_occ6 | 0.995 | 10.1 | −0.828 | 6.7 |
| Skilled (grade 4 and above) | h_occ7 | 1.142* | 11.0 | 0.136 | 13.3 |
| Unskilled worker | h_occ8 | 1.187* | 16.9 | 0.115 | 14.8 |
| Commercial and | | | | 0.235 | |
| service worker | h_occ9 | 1.279* | 8.1 | −0.316 | 15.8 |
| Other occupation | h_occ10 | −4.028 | 13.5 | | 10.8 |
| *Sector* | | | | | |
| Agriculture | h_sec1 | 0.628 | 13.0 | ++ | 0.0 |
| Mineral | h_sec2 | ++ | 0.0 | 0.246 | 4.8 |
| Manufacturing | h_sec3 | — | 12.9 | — | 13.5 |
| Electricity, gas and water | h_sec4 | −0.375 | 4.1 | ++ | 0.0 |

*Appendix 7.B* (Continued)

| | *Variable name* | *Liaoning* | | *Henan* | |
|---|---|---|---|---|---|
| | | *Coefficient* | *Predicted probability (%)* | *Coefficient* | *Predicted probability (%)* |
| Construction | h_sec5 | −0.628 | 4.7 | −0.599 | 2.5 |
| Geological prospecting | h_sec6 | ++ | 0.0 | ++ | 0.0 |
| Transport and communication | h_sec7 | −0.853 | 1.7 | −0.450 | 3.7 |
| Commerce and food services | h_sec8 | −0.725* | 5.7 | −0.472 | 13.3 |
| Finance and insurance | h_sec9 | ++ | 0.0 | ++ | 0.0 |
| Real estate | h_sec10 | ++ | 0.0 | ++ | 0.0 |
| Social services | h_sec11 | −0.461 | 9.3 | −1.037 | 5.3 |
| Health and social welfare | h_sec12 | ++ | 0.0 | −1.052 | 2.1 |
| Education, culture and arts | h_sec13 | ++ | 0.0 | ++ | 0.0 |
| Scientific research | h_sec14 | ++ | 0.0 | ++ | 0.0 |
| Government/Party agents | h_sec15 | ++ | 0.0 | ++ | 0.0 |
| Other sector | h_sec16 | −0.828 | 3.2 | −0.490 | 6.8 |
| *Type of work unit* | | | | | |
| Government agent institution | h_ins1 | — | 3.9 | — | 3.0 |
| Enterprise with high profit | h_ins2 | −0.460 | 1.7 | ++ | 0.0 |
| Enterprise with marginal profit | h_ins3 | −0.264** | 3.7 | −0.667 | 3.9 |
| Enterprise with loss | h_ins4 | 0.372 | 16.1 | 0.129 | 15.2 |
| Intercept | constant | −2.745** | | −1.480 | |
| | No. of obs. | 1,644 | | 1,499 | |
| | Wald chi$^2$ | 473.5 | | 102.0 | |
| | Pseudo-$R^2$ | 0.295 | | 0.306 | |
| | Log-likelihood | −337.8 | | −324.3 | |

Notes:

1 Standard errors are adjusted for clustering of household members.

2 **and * indicate the coefficient statistically significant at 1% and 5%.

3 — denotes omitted variable and ++ no observations in this category.

# 8 Can a subjective poverty line be applied to China?

## Assessing poverty among urban residents in 1999

*Björn Gustafsson, Li Shi and Hiroshi Sato*

### 8.1 Introduction

While rural poverty in China has historically been of great concern to inhabitants and policy makers alike, the problem of urban poverty is now cause for the same concern. The increased awareness of urban poverty is linked to several factors. One such factor is that during the reform period China experienced rapid economic growth which has given governments at various levels the means for combating poverty.

Other reasons for the increased awareness of the poverty problem in urban China stem from the current economic picture for various segments of the population. During the planned economy period, workers in urban China typically were tied to their work units on a lifelong basis, though this is no longer the case. Economic reforms in combination with decreased employment in the state-owned sector have led to workers becoming jobless; some are even unemployed without adequate compensation.

Official policy documents and statistics in China conceptualize and measure poverty in the rural and urban parts of China differently. Assessing the extent and profile of poverty in urban China is thus not without problems. In this chapter we attempt to increase the knowledge of urban poverty in China along several lines.

First, we address the difficult question of whether or not the present method of assessing urban poverty is reasonable when it comes to how large is proportion of the urban registered population that is regarded as poor. Our approach to defining poverty is to apply subjective poverty line methodology. This approach focuses on the respondent's perception of income adequacy as derived from the answers to one or more survey questions. The approach was first applied to industrialized countries and has more recently been applied to other countries. We are the first to apply this methodology to China using data referring to 1999 for twelve cities located in six provinces. This makes it possible for us to ascertain if the perception of poverty varies considerably by location.

However, this chapter aims to do more than contribute to the discussion of how to conceptualize and measure poverty. As a second task it seeks to assess the poverty profile for urban China in more detail than is found in official statistics and the recent (limited) literature on assessing urban poverty in China.[1]

The chapter is organized as follows. The subjective poverty line approach is reviewed in the next section while Section 8.3 discusses its application. The context and data are described in Section 8.4. In Section 8.5 we estimate response functions based on the methodology outlined in Section 8.2 and derive poverty lines. Those poverty lines are used to portray the face of urban poverty in China in Section 8.6. The chapter ends with a section summing up the conclusions of the analysis.

## 8.2 The subjective poverty line approach

The subjective poverty line approach puts the perception of income adequacy of the population in focus.[2] Different survey questions have been used to find the respondent's opinion on income adequacy. For example, in an early work, Kilpatrick (1973) analysed time-series data from the United States showing answers to the question 'What is the smallest amount of money a family of four (husband, wife and two children) needs each week to get along in this community?' Relating this measure of income adequacy to measures of average household income, a positive elasticity of less than one was found.[3]

While there are several ways of formulating questions for arriving at an assessment of income adequacy, the subjective poverty line approach requires the respondents to evaluate the situation of their own households, not a hypothetical household. The attractiveness of this approach is that it could be difficult for respondents to assess living costs for households having different attributes than their own.

The subjective poverty line approach was developed by economists in the Netherlands, and there is also similar work by social scientists in Belgium. Our ambition here is not to review all of the literature, but to describe the central idea of the approach and to discuss some issues of relevance to our study. Early applications of the subjective poverty line approach include studies comparing poverty lines and poverty in eight countries belonging to the European Community (e.g. van Praag *et al.* 1982; Hagenaars 1986) and studies from the United States (e.g. Colasanto *et al.* 1984; Danziger *et al.* 1984). More recently the approach has been spread and modified for the developing world, with Pradhan and Ravallion (2000) reporting results from Jamaica in 1993 and Nepal in 1995–1996.

Within this tradition, various questions to the respondents can be used. One frequently used question is the minimum income question (MIQ), which asks for the monetary amounts that people consider to be the minimum necessary for supporting their households. A poverty line can be derived from the responses to the minimum income question by the intersection method introduced by Goedhart *et al.* (1977). The thresholds are calculated as the income level where $Y_{min} = Y$ given the relationship

$$\log(Y_{\min}) = a_0 + a_1 \log(Y) \tag{8.1}$$

Here $Y_{\min}$ represents the reported minimum income response to the MIQ and $Y$ current household income (or consumption). The intersection where $Y_{\min} = Y$ (shown in Figure 8.1) rather than the mean or median of $Y$ is chosen as it is believed that only persons with actual incomes equal to their minimally necessary income have a realistic view of the minimum level.

The answer to the minimum income question can also depend on other attributes of the household. Family size is an obvious characteristic from which equivalence scales can be calculated from a fitted regression model. Other attributes that have entered the estimated model measure, for example, the location of the household, the education, as well as the age and labour force status of the household. In this case, equation (8.1) above is rewritten as

$$\log(Y_{\min}) = a_0 + a_1 \log(Y) + a_2 X_i \tag{8.2}$$

where $X_i$ are the variables representing other attributes resulting in significant impact on $\log(Y_{\min})$. After estimating the parameters such as $a_0$, $a_1$ and $a_2$ in equation (8.2), subjective poverty lines are accordingly derived by assuming $\log(Y_{\min}) = \log(Y)$, i.e.

$$\log \text{ SPL} = \log Y^*_{\min} = (a_0 + a_2 X_i)/(1 - a_1) \tag{8.3}$$

The subjective poverty line approach is an alternative to approaches that have been traditionally used for setting the poverty line. Instead of basing the poverty line on estimates of necessary consumption and prices for a basket of goods (an often lengthy process), it focuses on what people think is necessary. Thus, it offers a simplified procedure and needs little data. While consumption-based poverty lines are determined by experts, the subjective poverty line is the outcome of what people think. It can therefore be considered to be more democratic. Thus it is easy to understand that there is widespread interest in methodologies that build on people's own perceptions of income or consumption adequacy.

## 8.3 Applying the subjective poverty line approach

However, the subjective poverty line approach is not without methodological problems, and several have been illuminated in the literature (see, e.g., Kapteyn *et al.* 1988; Garner and de Vos 1995). The wording of the question posed to the respondents is important for the answers, as well as the income or consumption measure of the households that enter equation (8.1). It is vital for researchers to know how the respondents comprehend the question.[4]

The definitions of the two sides in equation (8.1) should be consistent. For example, evidence points towards not all incomes or all parts of consumption being considered when responding to the MIQ. The issue of phrasing the question on

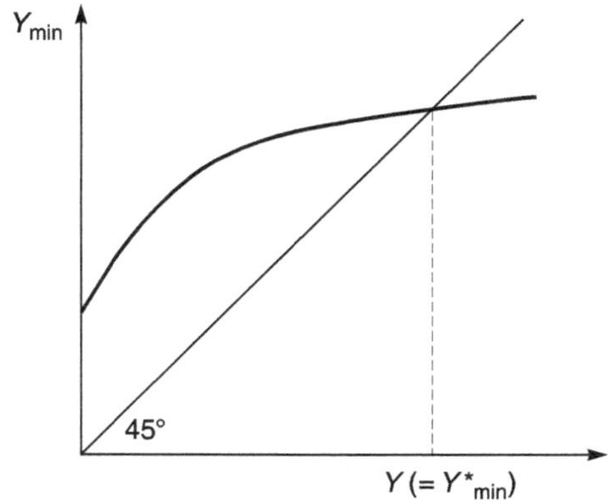


*Figure 8.1* The intersection method for determining a subjective poverty line.

adequacy is particularly relevant in subsistence economies as for many respondents the word 'income' is synonymous with money income.

When applying the subjective poverty line approach to defining poverty, there are also the usual methodological issues in deriving information from sample surveys: the sampling frame, the sample size and the issue of non-response.

While the approach of subjective poverty lines has been received with enthusiasm by some researchers, public statistical agencies and policy makers have not been converted. To our knowledge, no single country has adopted a statistical system for reporting poverty that is based on the subjective poverty line approach. The methodological issues might provide one reason for this lack of enthusiasm. Another reason could be that the subjective approach of defining a poverty line might be just too difficult to sell to policy makers and statistical authorities more persuaded by 'consumption-basket rhetoric'.

Let us return for a moment to the issue of which attributes should be included in a response function. What is the motivation for choosing variables in addition to the obvious ones of household income/consumption and household size? First there is the argument that costs can vary across households. There are costs for going to work, as well as possibilities for the non-employed to economize household expenditures by doing housework. Such reasoning makes one expect that labour market status affects the response to MIQ. There are also differences in consumer prices that can affect the response, for example due to regional differences.

A second group of reasons for persons in different households giving different answers to MIQ are variations in consumption needs. The age as well as the health status of the household members of the respondents are natural candidates. Young children need less food than adults, while non-healthy persons have medical expenditures that healthy persons do not. People living in a cold climate need more resources for heating than those living in a temperate climate.

Finally, there is the argument of aspiration and reference group. Often when people form their view of what is appropriate in various spheres of life by comparing with their peers and society in general, there are norms for what one deserves. Take, for example, an unemployed person. He or she might feel that the event of unemployment makes the household deserve fewer resources. The geographical area is often important for defining what a person's reference group is. The reference group is often people living at the same location, but could also be people in the same country, while the influence of circumstances among people in other countries could be fairly small.[5]

While estimating a response function for extracting the information from a data set is an issue of positive analysis, a normative element enters the picture when selecting which attributes to consider when defining a poverty line. To be more widely used, a poverty line needs to be politically accepted. For example, if the positive analysis shows that gender affects assessment of income adequacy, this need not lead to the poverty line being conditioned on gender. This example shows that a poverty line cannot be determined in a political vacuum.

Reference to political realities is also present when discussing whether or not poverty lines should vary across territories. One can make the point that the answer depends on the policy issue in question. At one extreme is the World Poverty line as derived by the World Bank. This can be useful for development aid policy as it can provide information regarding in which countries most poor persons are found, and where the highest proportions of persons are deemed to be poor. However, for many local policies this approach might not be useful. The World Poverty line might simply yield poverty rates either too low or too high to be relevant to the political process. Various countries have also adopted different poverty lines (sometimes official, sometimes not) and a statistically positive relation between average income and the purchasing power of such national poverty lines has been established (Ravallion *et al.* 1991; Chen and Ravallion 2001).

Policy making is also made at the sub-national level, thus a case can be made for establishing poverty lines at such a level. Therefore, following this line of reasoning, the motivation for different poverty lines within a country is the geographical area for policy making, not differences in costs.[6]

To sum up, until now the subjective poverty line approach has been applied to many countries, but not to China. We are interested in finding out which new insights into the methodology as well as into the situation in urban China can be obtained.

## 8.4 Context and data

Given the administrative and socio-economic situation in urban China today, we believe it is warranted not only to have a national urban poverty line, but also local urban poverty lines. This would to some degree correspond to the practice of the European Union, where its statistical agency Eurostat has for several years published poverty counts based not only on a poverty line common to the entire Union, but also derived from poverty lines defined for each member country.

The Chinese state has many layers. It is very much an open question at which layer a local poverty line should be defined. Actually, with the complex administrative structure of China, one can make a case for recommending that poverty lines be defined not only at the province level but also at the city level. In this chapter we derive, in addition to a national poverty line for urban China, poverty lines specific for each city using the subjective poverty line approach. Such city-specific poverty lines can be motivated by the fact that many policies directly related to people's well-being (employment, migration and social security) are made and implemented at the city level.[7]

The analysis reported in this study uses data collected for 1999 in twelve cities of various average incomes and population sizes. The cities are listed in Table 8.1. In addition to Beijing, the national capital, there are cities located in the five provinces of Liaoning, Jiangsu, Henan, Sichuan and Gansu. Chengdu, Lanzhou, Nanjing and Zhengzhou are provincial capitals. The city of Xuzhou has a population of more than one million inhabitants. The cities of Jinzhou, Kaifeng, Pingdingshan, Zigong and Nanchong have only around half a million inhabitants. The last city listed is Pingliang, a county town, which is small by Chinese standards.

Table 8.1 also shows a large variation in GDP per capita as well as in average wages across the cities. It is interesting to see that all cities experienced positive economic growth during the survey year. We also report registered unemployment rates, which are available for all cities with the exception of the smallest city. It should be understood that the registered unemployment rate captures only one part of the employment problem as many jobless persons are not included. Thus, the figures of 6 to 7 per cent reported for some of the cities (Jinzhou, Zigong and Nanchong) signal that joblessness in these cities is substantial. Beijing is at the other extreme with a very low rate of registered unemployment.

We used a sample of 3,370 households with urban household registrations (*hukou*) in the twelve cities for deriving the subjective poverty lines. The sample was selected by officials at the National Bureau of Statistics of China. The survey data contain detailed individual information on personal characteristics, consumption expenditures and various income components. Descriptive statistics for the sample are presented in Appendix 8.A. It shows, for example, that a majority of the households consisted of three persons.

The minimum income question in the data was worded in Mandarin as follows:

> *Anzhao ninjia de shiji qingkuang, nin quanjia zai 1999 nian mei yue weichi zuidi shenghuo shuiping de feiyong dayue duoshao yuan?*
>
> 'According to your actual situation, how much are your minimum household living expenses for a month in 1999?'

In the last column of Table 8.1, the city averages for the responses to the question are listed. A strikingly large variation is reported, as the numbers range from 3,446 yuan given by respondents living in Pingdingshan to 9,926 yuan for respondents

*Table 8.1* Population, GDP per capita, average wage and unemployment in 12 cities

| | *Urban population at year-end 1999 (million)* | *GDP per capita of urban population in 1999 (yuan)* | *Annual growth rate of GDP 1998–1999 (%)* | *Proportion of employment in secondary industry (%)* | *Annual average wage (yuan)* | *Rate of registered unemployment in 1999 (%)* | *Average of responses to the minimum income question (yuan)* |
|---|---|---|---|---|---|---|---|
| Beijing | 7.00 | 25,376 | 4.43 | 36.5 | 14,255 | 0.7 | 9,926 |
| Jinzhou | 0.67 | 10,049 | 8.7 | 53.2 | 7,187 | 6.1 | 5,272 |
| Nanjing | 2.47 | 27,051 | 11.1 | 49.3 | 12,624 | 2.9 | 7,959 |
| Xuzhou | 1.06 | 23,506 | 8.2 | 59.9 | 9,909 | 2.1 | 5,068 |
| Zhengzhou | 1.52 | 18,589 | 7.77 | 49.2 | 8,825 | 2.6 | 5,723 |
| Kaifeng | 0.57 | 8,900 | 8.93 | 55.5 | 5,805 | 3.5 | 4,959 |
| Pingdingshan | 0.64 | 13,474 | 4.33 | 70.6 | 7,639 | 4.7 | 3,446 |
| Chengdu | 2.21 | 27,280 | 10.93 | 50.0 | 9,592 | 4.8 | 5,939 |
| Zigong | 0.47 | 15,845 | 5.92 | 54.9 | 6,605 | 6.9 | 5,646 |
| Nanchong | 0.41 | 11,826 | 10.57 | 36.0 | 6,093 | 6.7 | 5,030 |
| Lanzhou | 1.45 | 14,549 | 4.93 | 55.6 | 8,359 | 2.8 | 5,120 |
| Pingliang | 0.13 | 11,262 | — | — | — | — | 5,247 |

Sources: *China Urban Statistical Yearbook*, 2000; *Gansu Statistical Yearbook*, 2000. City poverty line is derived from the survey data.

Notes:
1 Urban population is based on household registration status. Population of suburb areas is not included.
2 Pingliang's per capita GDP is on total population basis because Pingliang is a county-level city and detailed GDP statistics are not available.

living in Beijing. In the econometric analysis we relate the answers to this question to a variable measuring disposable income and other attributes.

It is important to note that our definition of disposable income is narrower than that which is usually used as we deduct the household's expenditures for healthcare as well as for education. Consistent with discussions in the literature, we found that respondents to the survey typically did not consider certain infrequent expenditures. The evidence is that when inspecting the data we found that some responses to the minimum income question were actually lower than the household's recorded expenditures on health and education for the same period.[8]

## 8.5 Results on response function and poverty lines

In Table 8.2 we present results from estimating three different specifications of the response function. In the first column, only household disposable income and household size are entered into the specification. In the second specification we add dummy variables for the various cities, while in the last column we also include variables measuring age of household members, the number of unemployed household members, as well as the number of unhealthy household members.

Turning to the results, they show as expected that the responses are positively affected by household income. The income coefficient differs somewhat by specification and is lower in the specifications in which city dummies are included. Also as expected, household size affects the response. These coefficients are not particularly high, which is in agreement with what is often found in previous studies using the same methodology.

A major finding in Table 8.2 is that the city dummies have very large coefficients. Coefficients for all variables that enter the third specification have reasonable signs and are estimated with high *t*-statistics, but they are not large. They indicate lower amounts for children (particularly the youngest) as well as the elderly compared with persons of other ages. Unemployed household members signify lower responses while unhealthy members signify higher responses. As discussed in the previous section, such variations can stem from various reasons: differences in costs, differences in needs, as well as perceptions of what is adequate.

Based on the three estimates reported in Table 8.2, we can compute subjective poverty lines. Table 8.3 shows subjective poverty lines for a household of three persons living in each of the twelve cities investigated based on estimates of specification II and III documented in Table 8.2. The table also provides information on the mean response to the MIQ by respondents living in a household of the same size in the different cities as well as the mean for the disposable household income. For example, the mean of the reported minimum income from respondents in Nanjing is 50 per cent of the mean of their income while the subjective poverty line according to specification II is as low as 36 per cent of the mean income.

Table 8.3 also shows that, for some cities, the different specifications of the response function result in rather similar thresholds.[9] For example, while for a family of three the national poverty line is 5,655 yuan, the city-specific poverty

*Table 8.2* Regression results for subjective poverty line in 1999

| | *Dependent variable: subjective perception of MIQ (in log term)* | | | | | |
|---|---|---|---|---|---|---|
| | *Model I* | | *Model II* | | *Model III* | |
| | *Coefficient* | *t-value* | *Coefficient* | *t-value* | *Coefficient* | *t-value* |
| Log of disposable household income | 0.3977 | 33.07 | 0.2849 | 23.88 | 0.2725 | 21.89 |
| 1-person household | −0.2239 | −3.47 | −0.2891 | −4.98 | −0.2985 | −5.15 |
| 3-person household | 0.0710 | 3.51 | 0.1083 | 5.94 | 0.1284 | 6.61 |
| 4-person household | 0.1431 | 5.25 | 0.2007 | 8.12 | 0.2332 | 9.12 |
| 5-person household | 0.2615 | 6.73 | 0.3240 | 9.22 | 0.3980 | 10.41 |
| Beijing | | | 0.1800 | 6.59 | 0.1698 | 6.21 |
| Jinzhou | | | −0.3213 | −8.83 | −0.3225 | −8.87 |
| Xuzhou | | | −0.3352 | −9.36 | −0.3383 | −9.45 |
| Zhengzhou | | | −0.2398 | −7.44 | −0.2373 | −7.37 |
| Kaifeng | | | −0.2952 | −7.8 | −0.2832 | −7.49 |
| Pingdingshan | | | −0.6186 | 17.22 | −0.6189 | −17.25 |
| Chengdu | | | −0.1330 | −4.48 | −0.1264 | −4.27 |
| Zigong | | | −0.2289 | −6.26 | −0.2291 | −6.25 |
| Nanchong | | | −0.3274 | −9.14 | −0.3280 | −9.18 |
| Lanzhou | | | −0.2400 | −8.01 | −0.2399 | −8.01 |
| Pingliang | | | −0.3407 | −9.38 | −0.3378 | −9.31 |
| Number of persons: | | | | | | |
| Aged 1–5 | | | | | −0.0811 | −3.23 |
| Aged 6–11 | | | | | −0.0369 | −2.16 |
| Aged 70 and over | | | | | −0.0437 | −2.48 |
| Unemployed or laid off | | | | | −0.0588 | −3.63 |
| Unhealthy | | | | | 0.0465 | 2.52 |
| Constant | 5.1335 | 44.81 | 6.3589 | 53.64 | 6.4831 | 52.22 |
| Adjusted $R^2$ | 0.288 | | 0.426 | | 0.431 | |
| *F*-value | 273.2 | | 157.3 | | 122.5 | |
| No. of observations | 3,370 | | 3,370 | | 3,370 | |

Note: Omitted variables are 2-person household and Nanjing.

line for Jinzhou derived from specification II in Table 8.2 is 5,405 yuan. However, the city-specific poverty lines for Chengdu and Nanjing (computed from specification II and III in Table 8.2) are higher than the national poverty line, and the poverty line for Beijing is much higher. The reverse is the case for Pingdingshan.

There is thus considerable variation in the city-specific poverty lines. In order to better understand what is behind the variation in city-specific poverty lines, we plot the thresholds against average household income as measured from the data in Figure 8.2 and against population size in Figure 8.3. Both show positive associations, and in both cases the city of Pingdingshan appears as an outlier. Pingdingshan is a coal-mining city, where the urban households still enjoy various subsidies, which might result in a low perception of income adequacy.[10]

In order to further investigate what is behind the variation in city poverty lines, we estimate regression models using different specifications. Having a data set of

*Table 8.3* Subjective poverty lines for households of three persons living in different cities and mean value of disposable income and answer to MIQ

| | *SPL derived from specification II* | *SPL derived from specification III* | *Mean value of answers to MIQ* | *Mean value of disposable household income* |
|---|---|---|---|---|
| The entire sample | 6,895 | 6,997 | 9,672 | 17,907 |
| Beijing | 10,900 | 11,079 | 15,387 | 26,866 |
| Jinzhou | 5,405 | 5,467 | 7,173 | 13,399 |
| Nanjing | 8,460 | 8,630 | 11,808 | 23,340 |
| Xuzhou | 5,307 | 5,401 | 7,859 | 18,900 |
| Zhengzhou | 6,058 | 6,131 | 9,511 | 15,025 |
| Kaifeng | 5,591 | 5,619 | 7,227 | 10,727 |
| Pingdingshan | 3,571 | 3,642 | 5,751 | 16,841 |
| Chengdu | 7,008 | 7,128 | 10,177 | 18,125 |
| Zigong | 6,143 | 6,185 | 7,458 | 12,833 |
| Nanchong | 5,347 | 5,410 | 7,187 | 13,884 |
| Lanzhou | 6,041 | 6,109 | 8,063 | 14,242 |
| Pingliang | 5,240 | 5,315 | 7,059 | 12,431 |

Note: Numbers in the second column are derived by predicting subjective poverty lines for each household based on their household characteristics and after this step averaging over all observations.

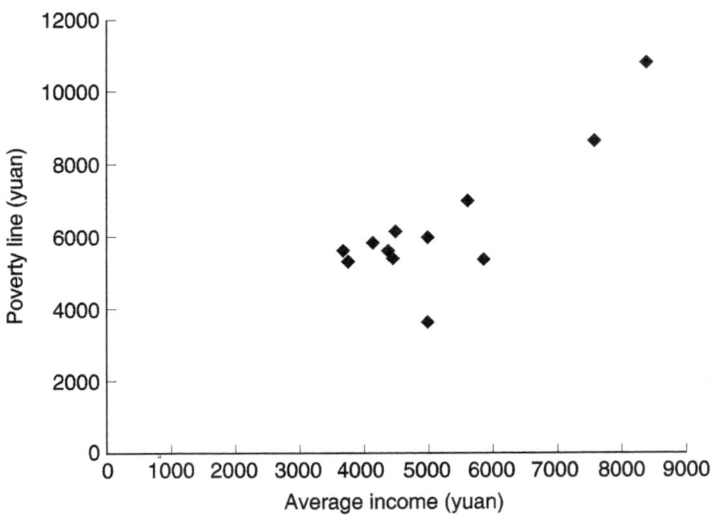


*Figure 8.2* The relation between city income per capita and the level of the subjective poverty lines (for a household of three persons) across cities.

12 observations, it is important not to read too much into the results from this exercise where these results are reported in Table 8.4. The dependent variable in the first set of regression models is the city-specific SPL of households with three members as reported in Table 8.3. The independent variables include the size of the city population and average income of the households. The second set of

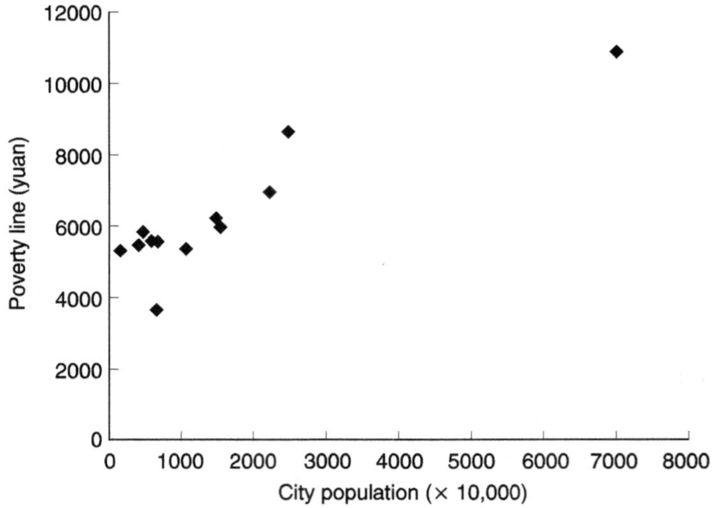


*Figure 8.3* The relation between population size and the level of the subjective poverty lines (for a household of three persons) across cities.

models contains the same variables but has taken them as log terms. The results indicate that the variable of city population is highly correlated with the city-specific SPL, but that the average income is not.

These findings lead to an immediate question: Why does city size in this analysis have such a strong influence on the perception of households of income adequacy? Our speculations run in the following direction. It is obvious that housing costs and transportation costs are higher in large cities, which might be one and perhaps also the main explanation.[11] We are also aware of some arguments in the literature of urban bias policy in developing countries: urban bias policy provides implications as well. It discriminates against development of rural areas and also puts a priority on construction and development in large cities while ignoring small and medium-sized cities. Moreover, more subsidies and welfare programmes combine with investments in urban areas than in rural areas, and in large cities than in smaller ones. This policy tends to raise the perception of income adequacy for households in large cities and their expectations of receiving subsidies from governments.

## 8.6 The extent and profile of poverty in the urban population, 1999

In this section we set the subjective poverty lines into motion in order to throw light on the extent and profile of poverty among urban residents in China in 1999. Starting with Table 8.5, we report poverty rates computed from each of the three subjective poverty lines documented in the previous section. In addition, poverty rates are reported that come from the data if the definition of the poverty line used for official statistics is applied to the data. The latter is based on estimated costs

*Table 8.4* Regression model explaining variation of SPL across cities

| | *Dependent variable: city-specific SPL* | | | | | |
|---|---|---|---|---|---|---|
| | *Coefficient* | *t-value* | *Coefficient* | *t-value* | *Coefficient* | *t-value* |
| Population size | 9.0450 | 6.82 | | | 9.0763 | 4.40 |
| Average household income per capita | | | 0.5933 | 2.82 | −0.0038 | −0.02 |
| Constant | 882 | 15.58 | 3378 | 3.03 | 4896 | 6.57 |
| Adjusted $R^2$ | 0.806 | | 0.387 | | 0.784 | |
| $F$-value | 46.56 | | 7.94 | | 20.95 | |
| Observations | 12 | | 12 | | 12 | |
| | *Dependent variable: logarithm of city-specific SPL* | | | | | |
| | *Coefficient* | *t-value* | *Coefficient* | *t-value* | *Coefficient* | *t-value* |
| Log of population size | 0.1952 | 3.43 | | | 0.2835 | 4.15 |
| Log of average household income per capita | | | 0.0281 | 0.73 | −0.0622 | −1.92 |
| Constant | 7.8207 | 29.46 | 8.4871 | 26.69 | 7.9118 | 32.92 |
| Adjusted $R^2$ | 0.540 | | 0.045 | | 0.602 | |
| $F$-value | 11.70 | | 0.53 | | 9.30 | |
| Observations | 12 | | 12 | | 12 | |

Notes: The dependent variable is city poverty lines for a household of three persons based on the estimates of Model II as reported in Table 8.3. Average household income per capita is derived from the survey.

for minimum nutrition intake in urban China and the food share among low-income households.[12] In addition, we report in Table 8.6 three poverty indices belonging to the FGT (Foster, Greer and Thorbecke 1984) family computed from the specification of the response function that includes the largest number of explanatory variables. Providing this information gives a more complete view of poverty than only counting the poor does.

One main conclusion from Table 8.5 is that the poverty rates derived from the subjective poverty line are similar to those obtained from the methodology used for producing official statistics. For example, while applying the official methodology, 5 per cent of the persons in the entire sample are considered poor; according to the subjective poverty lines the corresponding proportions are 6 or 7 per cent. As the two methods yield relatively similar poverty estimates, our estimates then become more trustworthy than if this had not been the case.[13]

Our second main conclusion is that there is considerable variation in poverty rates across the cities investigated. According to the information in Tables 8.5 and 8.6, Beijing, Nanjing and Pingdingshan emerge as having little poverty. At the other extreme, Jinzhou, Kaifeng, Zigong and Nanchong have more than average poverty. Common to the latter group of cities are relatively high registered unemployment rates and a population size of about half a million inhabitants.

*Table 8.5* Poverty rate based on different variants of the subjective poverty lines and on the official method by city, 1999

| | *Poverty rate derived from SPL based on the estimates of* | | | *Poverty rate using official methodology* |
|---|---|---|---|---|
| | *Model I* | *Model II* | *Model III* | |
| The entire sample | 6.12 | 7.15 | 7.05 | 4.6 |
| Beijing | 1.54 | 5.58 | 5.58 | 2.1 |
| Jinzhou | 9.41 | 8.91 | 9.41 | 8.9 |
| Nanjing | 0.63 | 2.73 | 2.31 | 0.9 |
| Xuzhou | 1.54 | 5.58 | 5.58 | 1.5 |
| Zhengzhou | 8.11 | 9.13 | 9.02 | 6.1 |
| Kaifeng | 11.73 | 11.73 | 12.29 | 10.3 |
| Pingdingshan | 4.80 | 2.98 | 2.98 | 1.3 |
| Chengdu | 4.55 | 6.91 | 6.74 | 4.4 |
| Zigong | 11.67 | 13.59 | 13.24 | 13.0 |
| Nanchong | 11.13 | 8.66 | 8.13 | 6.5 |
| Lanzhou | 6.69 | 8.28 | 8.28 | 3.7 |
| Pingliang | 13.30 | 9.45 | 8.79 | 3.1 |

Note: Numbers in the last column are from Knight and Li (2001).

*Table 8.6* Various indices of poverty in 1999 derived from the subjective poverty line, by city

| | *Proportion of sample (%)* | *Head-count* | *Poverty gap* | *Weighted poverty gap* |
|---|---|---|---|---|
| All samples | | 100 | 100 | 100 |
| Beijing | 17.5 | 79 | 77 | 75 |
| Jinzhou | 6.0 | 133 | 120 | 108 |
| Nanjing | 9.5 | 33 | 31 | 30 |
| Xuzhou | 5.6 | 79 | 106 | 133 |
| Zhengzhou | 8.7 | 128 | 109 | 82 |
| Kaifeng | 5.4 | 174 | 229 | 266 |
| Pingdingshan | 6.0 | 42 | 37 | 39 |
| Chengdu | 11.4 | 96 | 104 | 113 |
| Zigong | 5.7 | 188 | 204 | 231 |
| Nanchong | 5.6 | 115 | 126 | 131 |
| Lanzhou | 12.5 | 117 | 99 | 87 |
| Pingliang | 6.1 | 125 | 119 | 114 |

Note: When computing the indices we used the SPL estimates derived from specification III as reported in Table 8.2.

Our third conclusion based on Table 8.5 is that the variation in the poverty rates derived from city-specific poverty lines causes poverty rates to converge to some extent close to what is obtained by a national poverty line. For example, the poverty rates for the capital Beijing and the provincial capitals Nanjing and Chengdu, as well as for Xuzhou, move upwards and closer to the sample average, although they remain lower than the sample average.

*Table 8.7(a)* Various indices of poverty in 1999 derived from the subjective poverty line, by age group

| | *Proportion of sample (%)* | *Head-count* | *Poverty gap* | *Weighted poverty gap* |
|---|---|---|---|---|
| All samples | | 100 | 100 | 100 |
| Age under 6 | 3.1 | 74 | 63 | 50 |
| Age 6–11 | 6.1 | 86 | 72 | 58 |
| Age 12–18 | 10.5 | 143 | 148 | 155 |
| Age 19–23 | 4.5 | 118 | 134 | 138 |
| Age 24–30 | 9.5 | 68 | 67 | 62 |
| Age 31–40 | 18.9 | 94 | 83 | 71 |
| Age 41–50 | 22.3 | 120 | 123 | 126 |
| Age 51–60 | 11.9 | 62 | 76 | 87 |
| Age 61–70 | 9.5 | 82 | 77 | 84 |
| Age over 70 | 3.9 | 158 | 167 | 175 |

Note: When computing the indices we used the SPL estimates derived from specification III as reported in Table 8.2.

*Table 8.7(b)* Various indices of poverty in 1999 derived from the subjective poverty line, by population group

| | *Proportion of sample (%)* | *Head-count* | *Poverty gap* | *Weighted poverty gap* |
|---|---|---|---|---|
| All samples | | 100 | 100 | 100 |
| Work or employed | 48.1 | 66 | 36 | 56 |
| Retired elderly official | 1.6 | 35 | 31 | 54 |
| Retired worker | 16.7 | 77 | 88 | 91 |
| Unemployed youth | 1.7 | 162 | 172 | 201 |
| Laid off (*xiagang*) | 3.8 | 310 | 346 | 363 |
| Retired elderly | 1.3 | 149 | 169 | 195 |
| Unemployed | 1.0 | 281 | 351 | 178 |
| Homemaker | 2.2 | 259 | 215 | 275 |
| Student | 17.9 | 123 | 133 | 117 |
| Disabled adult | 0.8 | 321 | 314 | 443 |
| Other | 4.9 | 101 | 127 | 97 |

Note: When computing the indices we used the SPL estimates derived from specification III as reported in Table 8.2.

Now we investigate the poverty profile for urban residents in China. We address this issue by computing the three indices belonging to the FGT family for various subgroups of the population. The computation is based on one of the subjective poverty lines, and we have chosen the specification of the response function that incorporates the maximum number of explanatory variables. Table 8.7 reports results when splitting the sample by age and population group as well as health status of the individual.

We find a life-cycle pattern of poverty among urban residents. Children under 12 are less poverty-prone than the average urban inhabitant. There are several possible reasons for this. China has adopted a one-child policy and urban households

*Table 8.7(c)* Various indices of poverty in 1999 derived from the subjective poverty line, by health status of individuals

| | *Proportion of sample (%)* | *Head-count* | *Poverty gap* | *Weighted poverty gap* |
|---|---|---|---|---|
| All samples | | 100 | 100 | 100 |
| Healthy | 91.3 | 91 | 87 | 84 |
| Unhealthy | 7.4 | 181 | 215 | 251 |
| Disabled | 1.3 | 360 | 417 | 423 |

Note: When computing the indices we used the SPL estimates derived from specification III as reported in Table 8.2.

have responded by typically not having more than one child. A consequence of this is that Chinese mothers have typically only one interruption for childbirth in their working careers and the vast majority of them are employed. However, teenagers and to some extent young adults are more poverty-prone than the average inhabitant. While childhood in urban China does not indicate a high risk of poverty, the ages of transition from school to work and from school to higher studies do.[14]

People between the ages of 24 and 40 in urban China, many of them parents of young children, are less poverty-prone than the average inhabitant, while above-average poverty is found among persons aged 41 to 50. The latter might reflect two situations: these persons are more likely to be laid-off workers, and/or the family experiences financial problems stemming from their children's transition from school to employment or further studies. It is interesting to see that people who have passed the general retirement age (55 for women and 60 for men) by some years are slightly less poverty-prone than the average population, while the reverse is the case for people over 71.

Turning to the breakdown by population group and health status, several observations can be made. Laid-off workers still linked to their work units (*xiagang*) as well as the unemployed (including unemployed youth) are particularly poverty-prone. This is understandable as the system of unemployment compensation, although in existence, is far from being developed in urban China. We also report disabled adults being rather poverty-prone, as are homemakers. In the latter case, this might be caused to some extent by jobless females identifying themselves in the survey as being homemakers rather than as being unemployed. People self-reported as unhealthy are more poverty-prone than average. At the other extreme, we find people who are working or retired to be considerably less poverty-prone than the average urban inhabitant.

Turning to the breakdown by characteristics of household head as reported in Table 8.8, several conclusions can be drawn. The most important perhaps is that urban poverty in China is very strongly related to the educational level of the household head. It is most unlikely for persons living in households headed by someone with a college education to be poor. At the other end of the educational scale, people living in households headed by a person with lower middle school or less are more

*Table 8.8(a)* Various indices of poverty in 1999 derived from the subjective poverty line, by age of the household head

| | *Proportion of sample (%)* | *Head-count* | *Poverty gap* | *Weighted poverty gap* |
|---|---|---|---|---|
| All samples | | 100 | 100 | 100 |
| Age under 31 | 4.5 | 72 | 61 | 45 |
| Age 31–40 | 25.5 | 101 | 88 | 78 |
| Age 41–50 | 33.3 | 122 | 123 | 126 |
| Age 51–60 | 18.6 | 70 | 89 | 99 |
| Age 61–70 | 14.0 | 76 | 71 | 74 |
| Age over 70 | 4.3 | 169 | 174 | 181 |

Note: When computing the indices we used the SPL estimates derived from specification III as reported in Table 8.2.

*Table 8.8(b)* Various indices of poverty in 1999 derived from the subjective poverty line, by education of the household head

| | *Proportion of sample (%)* | *Head-count* | *Poverty gap* | *Weighted poverty gap* |
|---|---|---|---|---|
| All samples | | 100 | 100 | 100 |
| College (4–5 years) | 8.9 | 13 | 13 | 18 |
| College (2–3 years) | 17.4 | 42 | 36 | 38 |
| Professional school | 11.3 | 58 | 38 | 29 |
| Upper middle school | 21.1 | 97 | 99 | 101 |
| Lower middle school | 31.5 | 147 | 153 | 150 |
| Primary school | 7.5 | 160 | 169 | 180 |
| Illiterate and semi-literate | 2.3 | 268 | 266 | 269 |

Note: When computing the indices we used the SPL estimates derived from specification III as reported in Table 8.2.

*Table 8.8(c)* Various indices of poverty in 1999 derived from the subjective poverty line, by ownership of the household head's work unit

| | *Proportion of sample (%)* | *Head-count* | *Poverty gap* | *Weighted poverty gap* |
|---|---|---|---|---|
| All samples | | 100 | 100 | 100 |
| State-owned by central or provincial government | 40.1 | 47 | 44 | 43 |
| State-owned by local government | 41.8 | 106 | 103 | 102 |
| Urban collective | 9.2 | 228 | 256 | 268 |
| Others | 9.2 | 179 | 173 | 169 |

Note: When computing the indices we used the SPL estimates derived from specification III as reported in Table 8.2.

*Table 8.8(d)* Various indices of poverty in 1999 derived from the subjective poverty line, by occupation of the household head

| | *Proportion of sample (%)* | *Head-count* | *Poverty gap* | *Weighted poverty gap* |
|---|---|---|---|---|
| All samples | | 100 | 100 | 100 |
| Professional or technician | 20.3 | 51 | 39 | 38 |
| Manager or official | 16.4 | 39 | 49 | 59 |
| Clerical/office staff | 15.8 | 78 | 84 | 89 |
| Skilled worker | 16.6 | 120 | 115 | 106 |
| Unskilled worker | 20.1 | 161 | 132 | 108 |
| Commercial and service worker | 6.7 | 157 | 206 | 237 |
| Other occupation | 4.3 | 195 | 271 | 320 |

Note: When computing the indices we used the SPL estimates derived from specification III as reported in Table 8.2.

poverty-prone than the average urban resident. The small group of persons in households headed by an illiterate or semi-literate person is particularly poverty-prone.

We also report a strong relation between ownership of work unit (present, and in case of retirees, past) and poverty. As expected, a household head affiliated with a state-owned enterprise administered at the central or provincial level is less poverty-prone than average, while the converse would be true if he were affiliated with an urban collective work unit.

## 8.7 Conclusions

This is the first work to apply subjective poverty line methodology to China. The data were obtained from twelve cities and refer to 1999. In this chapter we have also used the poverty lines that were derived to throw light on urban poverty in China. The major conclusion of the analysis is that poverty counts based on the subjective poverty line approach are close to what is obtained when applying the methodology used when producing official estimates on poverty in urban China.

Another conclusion regarding poverty measurement is that the opinion of the general public can vary considerably across cities. Beijing is in a class of its own. People living there are of the opinion that the minimum income needed is much higher than in the other cities. The reason for the different opinions across cities can be given various interpretations. Differences in costs across cities is one obvious candidate. However, we think that the reference group argument should be given the most weight. Our finding that perceptions on income adequacy can vary greatly across cities speaks for applying not only a national urban poverty line for China but also local poverty lines that can be useful for evaluating policies at the sub-national level.

It is possible that the subjective poverty line approach can help explain a paradox often found in developing countries. It is not uncommon for governments to be more concerned about urban poverty, even though, as defined from national poverty lines, poverty is largest in rural areas. The government might be particularly concerned about poverty in large capital cities. This can appear to be a paradox and irrational. However, to remain in power, it is rational for governments to react not only to an actual situation, but to the person's perception of the situation. If the minimum income needed is perceived to be much higher in the capital than in other locations, and the government is more sensitive to the issue of poverty in the capital than elsewhere, it is then rational from the welfare function of the government to allocate considerable resources towards poverty alleviation in the capital. This is the more common scenario despite the fact that the same budget, if used elsewhere, could be used more efficiently to reduce the poverty problem (as evaluated from a national poverty line).

Turning to the second task of this chapter, we have clarified the poverty profile in urban China. There is considerable variation across cities as to the extent of poverty. The highest poverty rates as well as comparatively high rates of registered unemployment were found in cities of around half a million inhabitants. We think it is new, although not surprising, to have shown that poverty status in urban China greatly depends on the educational level of the household as well as the stage in the life-cycle. For example, while poverty rates among young children are relatively low, the rates are higher when the transition from education to work is made. Far from surprisingly, Chinese urban poverty is also clearly related to labour market status as well as health status. For example, being jobless means facing a high poverty risk, while being employed in a state-owned enterprise or being an old-age pensioner means a low poverty risk.

A final word. This is a study on poverty among registered inhabitants in urban China. We have not addressed the issue of poverty among rural migrants living in urban China. It is commonly understood that this group is large in size and has a lower living standard than the registered population. Further, the reader should not forget that poverty in rural China is in many respects a more pressing problem. Rural poverty affects more people and rural people survive on much lower incomes than their urban counterparts. It will be an important task to investigate what insight the subjective poverty line approach can provide if it is applied to rural–urban migrants as well as to rural China and its inhabitants.

## Notes

This chapter was originally published in *Journal of International Development*, Vol. 16, Björn Gustafsson, Li Shi and Hiroshi Sato, 'Can a subjective poverty line be applied to China? Assessing poverty among urban residents in 1999', 1089–1107, 2004, with permission from John Wiley & Sons Ltd. The original paper was written while Björn Gustafsson and Li Shi were visiting Hitotsubashi University in spring 2002. Björn Gustafson would like to acknowledge financial support from the Swedish Foundation for International Cooperation in Research and Higher Education as well as the Swedish Council for Working Life and Social Research. An earlier version of the paper was presented at the 27th International Conference of the International Association for Research in Income and Wealth, Djurhamn, Sweden, August 2002. We wish to thank our discussant Stephan Klasen and a referee of this journal for valuable comments. Hiroshi Sato is grateful for support from the Research Network Program, the Graduate School of Economics, Hitotsubashi University.

1 For a general discussion of the issue of emerging urban poverty in China, see for example Qian and Wong (2000). The design of the Urban Household Survey used for the official estimates is discussed by Gibson *et al.* (2003). Park and Wang (2001) discuss in detail how this information is used to obtain the official figures for poverty in urban China. Khan and Riksin (2001) portray urban poverty in 1988 and 1995 at the provincial level. Fang *et al.* (2002) analyse annual figures for urban poverty by three regions in 1992 and for each year from 1994 to 1998. We have not found any recent study showing the life-cycle pattern of poverty in urban China, or the relation between education and poverty.

2 Thus, the approach does not ask the respondents whether or not they consider themselves to be poor.

3 Another example is Dubnoff (1985), which reported a study in which respondents were presented with descriptions of stimulus families possessing various levels of income. The respondents were asked to judge the standard of living for each such family according to a scale where one of the end points was 'poor'. Analysing data obtained in Boston, in 1983, the author found, for example, that the income of the respondent affected the assessment of income adequacy.

4 For example, Garner and Short (2003) show for data collected in the United States in 1995 how different wording of the question generates different thresholds.

5 It is not surprising that in the early literature of international comparison, estimating subjective poverty lines for countries then belonging to the European Community (van Praag *et al.* 1982), large differences across countries were found. They were attributed not only to differences in costs but also to differences in aspirations. Perhaps more surprising is that a study for Nepal in 1995–1996 also showed large spatial differences in assessment of income adequacy (Pradhan and Ravallion 2000).

6 It is interesting to see that in a recent study of Australia, Canada and the United States, Rainwater *et al.* (2001) derive poverty lines for each state (of the United States) or province (Australia and Canada) from the median of disposable income in the state/province.

7 A similar approach to defining poverty lines for cities in China had earlier been taken by Wong (1995, 1997), who defined the poverty line at 50 per cent of the median income of the cities investigated (Guangzhou and Shanghai).

8 We feel it to be an important further task to investigate to what extent respondents in China respond differently depending on the wording of the question posed. From this follows that we do not claim that the poverty lines derived here represent 'the final truth' when it comes to applying the subjective poverty methodology to China.

9 We will use Nanjing as an example to illustrate how the subjective poverty lines are derived in Table 8.3. When computing the poverty line for a household of three persons living in Nanjing based on the estimates of Model II in Table 8.2, we follow the formula $SPL_{II} = \exp[(6.3589 + 0.1083 – 0.133)/ (1 - 0.285)]$. If the estimates of Model III are applied, the formula is $SPL_{III} = \exp[(6.4831 + 0.1284 - 0.1264)/(1 - 0.273)]$.

10 Some facts support our interpretation. Pingdingshan has an extremely high proportion of employment in secondary industry (see Table 8.1). Housing subsidies appear to be rather substantial, since the data show that inequality in the Gini coefficient for housing expenditure of households in this city (0.255) is considerably smaller compared to the average of twelve cities (0.429).

11 Unfortunately no official price index is available to make it possible to compare housing prices or other consumer prices across the cities under study.

12 For more details see, for example, Knight and Li (2001). Following the official methodology, we estimate those poverty rates from information on disposable income without corrections for the household's expenditures on health and education.

13 Khan and Riskin (2001) report urban poverty rates for 1988 and 1995 based on a survey covering 10 or 11 provinces using three different levels of the poverty rate. Our poverty rates for the 12 cities in 1999 are slightly lower than the 8 per cent they

obtained from their highest alternative poverty line for both years, and somewhat higher than their rates of 'deep poverty' of 3 and 4 per cent for the two years.

14 For example, nowadays many parents of teenagers in China have to pay school fees and other educational expenditures. Further, a considerable number of young adults in urban China have difficulty finding a first job and are maintained by their parents.

## References

Chen, S. and Ravallion, M. (2001) 'How did the world's poorest fare in the 1990s', *Review of Income and Wealth*, 47: 283–300.

Colasanto, D., Kapteyn, A. and van der Gaag, J. (1984) ' Two subjective definitions of poverty: results from the Wisconsin Basic Needs Study', *Journal of Human Resources*, 19: 127–38.

Danziger, S., van der Gaag, J., Smolensky, E. and Taussing, M. (1984) 'The direct measurement of welfare levels: how much does it take to make ends meet', *Review of Economics and Statistics*, 66: 500–5.

Dubnoff, S. (1985) 'How much income is enough? Measuring public judgments', *Public Opinion Quarterly*, 49: 285–99.

Fang, C., Zhang, X. and Fan, S. (2002) 'Emergence of urban poverty and inequality in China: evidence from household survey', *China Economic Review*, 13: 430–43.

Foster, J., Greer, J. and Thorbecke, E. (1984) 'A class of decomposable poverty measures', *Econometrica*, 52: 761–6.

Garner, T.I. and de Vos, K. (1995) 'Income sufficiency vs. poverty: results from the United States and the Netherlands', *Journal of Population Economics*, 8: 117–34.

Garner, T.I. and Short, K.S. (2003) 'Personal assessments of minimum income and expenses: what do they tell us about "minimum living" thresholds and equivalence scales?', in Bishop, J.A. and Amiel, Y. (eds), *Inequality, Welfare and Poverty: Theory and Measurement*, Vol. 9, pp. 191–243. Amsterdam: Elsevier.

Gibson, J., Huang, J. and Rozelle, S. (2003) 'Improving estimates of inequality and poverty from urban China's household income and expenditure survey', *Review of Income and Wealth*, 49: 53–68.

Goedhart, T., Halberstadt, K.A., Kapteyn, A. and van Praag, B. (1977) 'The poverty line: concepts and measurement', *Journal of Human Resources*, 12: 503–20.

Hagenaars, A.J.M. (1986) *The Perception of Poverty,* Amsterdam: North Holland.

Kapteyn, A., Kooreman, P. and Willemse, R. (1988) 'Some methodological issues in the implementation of subjective poverty definitions', *Journal of Human Resources*, 23: 222–42.

Khan, A.R. and Riskin, C. (2001) *Inequality and Poverty in China in the Age of Globalization*, Oxford: Oxford University Press.

Kilpatrick, R.W. (1973) 'The income elasticity of the poverty line', *Review of Economics and Statistics*, 55: 327–32.

Knight, J. and Li, S. (2001) 'Three poverties in urban China', Project Paper, Department of Economics, University of Oxford.

Park, A. and Wang, S. (2001) 'China's poverty statistics', *China Economic Review*, 12: 384–98.

Pradhan, M. and Ravallion, M. (2000) 'Measuring poverty using alternative perceptions of consumption adequacy', *Review of Economics and Statistics*, 82: 462–71.

Qian, Z. and Wong, T. (2000) 'The rising urban poverty: a dilemma of market reform in China', *Journal of Contemporary China*, 9(23): 113–25.

Rainwater, L., Smeeding, T. and Coder, J. (2001) 'Poverty across states, nations, and counties', in Vleminckz, K. and Smeeding, T. (eds), *Child Well-Being, Child Poverty and Child Policies in Modern Nations*, Bristol: The Policy Press.

Ravallion, M., Datt, G. and van de Wale, D. (1991) 'Quantifying absolute poverty in the developing world', *Review of Income and Wealth*, 37: 345–61.

van Praag, B.M.S., Hagenaars, A.J.M and van Weeren, H. (1982) 'Poverty in Europe', *Review of Income and Wealth*, 28: 345–59.

Wong, C.K. (1995) 'Measuring third world poverty by the international poverty line: the case of reform China', *Social Policy and Administration*, 29: 189–203.

Wong, C.K. (1997) 'How many poor people in Shanghai today? The question of poverty and poverty measures', *Issues and Studies*, 33: 32–49.

## Appendix 8.A: Mean and standard deviation of main variables used in the analysis of the MIQ

| | *Mean* | *SD* |
|---|---|---|
| Logarithm of MIQ | 9.0202 | 0.5268 |
| Logarithm of disposable household income | 9.5922 | 0.6535 |
| 1–person household | 0.0154 | 0.1233 |
| 2–person household | 0.1810 | 0.3851 |
| 3–person household | 0.6089 | 0.4881 |
| 4–person household | 0.1371 | 0.3440 |
| 5–person household | 0.0496 | 0.2171 |
| Beijing | 0.1712 | 0.3768 |
| Jinzhou | 0.0582 | 0.2341 |
| Nanjing | 0.1027 | 0.3036 |
| Xuzhou | 0.0582 | 0.2341 |
| Zhengzhou | 0.0855 | 0.2796 |
| Kaifeng | 0.0528 | 0.2237 |
| Pingdingshan | 0.0588 | 0.2352 |
| Chengdu | 0.1160 | 0.3203 |
| Zigong | 0.0576 | 0.2330 |
| Nanchong | 0.0605 | 0.2385 |
| Lanzhou | 0.1193 | 0.3242 |
| Pingliang | 0.0593 | 0.2363 |
| Number of children aged 1–5 | 0.0932 | 0.2928 |
| Number of children aged 6–11 | 0.2279 | 0.4252 |
| Number of elderly members 70 and over | 0.1445 | 0.4250 |
| Number of unemployed people | 0.1947 | 0.4598 |
| Number of unhealthy members | 0.1961 | 0.3971 |

# Part II

# The emerging labour market

# 9 From 'work-unit socialism' to hierarchical labour market in urban China

*Hiroshi Sato*

## 9.1 Introduction

This chapter examines the hierarchical structure of the Chinese urban labour market that is being formed through the collapse of 'work-unit socialism' and the massive flow of rural–urban migration, using the 1999 and 1988 CASS surveys. As mentioned in the introduction to this volume, the term 'work-unit socialism' refers to the work-unit-based system of income distribution, social security, social life and social control that had been the heart of Chinese socialism. (For the structure of 'work-unit socialism', see Womack 1991; Lü and Perry 1997; Yang and Zhou 1999; and Liu 2000.)

In addition to objective aspects of the labour market, such as wage level, determinants of wages and factors that relate to the probability of being retrenched, this chapter examines several labour market-related subjective aspects, such as people's perception of income determinants and people's expectations towards their next generation's educational attainments and occupational status. We examine subjective aspects because, in a period of systemic transition, certain gaps tend to develop between the objective aspects of socio-economic changes and the way people perceive them, and there is a possibility that these gaps may have a significant effect on the transition process.

In the following discussion, the term 'stratum' is used for convenience to refer to groups of urban workers (workers with urban household registration) and migrant workers (workers with rural household registration who migrated from rural areas). By doing so, however, we seek neither to argue that a fixed stratified structure is being formed in the urban society, nor to verify a social stratification based on specific theoretical assumptions. This chapter provides a cross-sectional view of the changing urban society captured in terms of employment and income.

This chapter is structured as follows. The first half of Section 9.2 outlines the process of urban labour market formation since the 1980s. Based on that outline, the second half of the section classifies urban workers and migrant workers into six strata, and sets out the profile of each stratum as well as disparities in wage income and social security among the strata. Section 9.3 clarifies the factors behind the hierarchical structure by analysing the determinants of wage income and employment stability. In Section 9.4, we examine how people perceive this hierarchical structure. Section 9.5 describes the labour market behaviour of the unemployed/*xiagang,* focusing on the relationship between job-search channels and economic outcomes of re-employment. (As explained in Chapter 1, *xiagang* is the Chinese variant of unemployment.) Section 9.5 also presents several alternative estimations of actual unemployment rates. Section 9.6 concludes.

## 9.2 From 'work-unit socialism' to hierarchical labour market

### *9.2.1 Outline of labour market formation*

Figure 9.1 shows a schematic diagram of the formation process of the urban labour market after the 1980s. This process began when the government permitted self-employment in the early 1980s–an emergency measure against the aggravated unemployment conditions in many urban areas, one of the after-effects of the Cultural Revolution. The process caused the urban society to have a concentric structure, in which the small private sector was relegated to the periphery around the public sector (periphery A and core A in Figure 9.1).

The private sector gradually expanded throughout the 1980s and the early 1990s, although it consisted of people who were alienated from work-unit socialism. The people populating the private sector were typically 'jobless youth' (*daiye qingnian*: new graduates who were unable to obtain jobs though the normal job allocation system), 'former sent-down youth' (*xiafang zhiqing*: members of the young generation who were sent from urban areas to rural areas during the Cultural Revolution, but who started to return to urban areas during the end of the 1970s), or 'jobless people' (*wuye renyuan*: people who were without employment for various reasons) (Li 1998). The fact that the urban labour market began to grow and develop from the periphery of the urban society, where the government had given up on employing the planned system, is representative of the characteristics of the incrementalist nature of marketization in China (Naughton 1999; Nakagane 2002).

During the 1990s, however, this simple concentric structure underwent dramatic changes. First, the number of cases where workers with sufficient careers in the public sector moved to the non-public sector or new graduates with high academic status went directly into the non-public sector increased noticeably during the 1990s (Li 1998). One reason for this development was that the non-public sector advanced in social status because of the growth of potent private enterprises, and the number of enterprises with foreign investment increased dramatically. The urban labour market is gradually changing its form from the concentric structure to an oval structure with two cores (core B in Figure 9.1) because of the growth and advancement in social status of the non-public sector. Second, the public enterprise reform also advanced, causing a discharge of the overemployment that used to be concealed within the public sector and creating a new public-peripheral stratum made up of unemployed/*xiagang* workers (periphery B in Figure 9.1). Third, the number of people who experienced job change increased even within

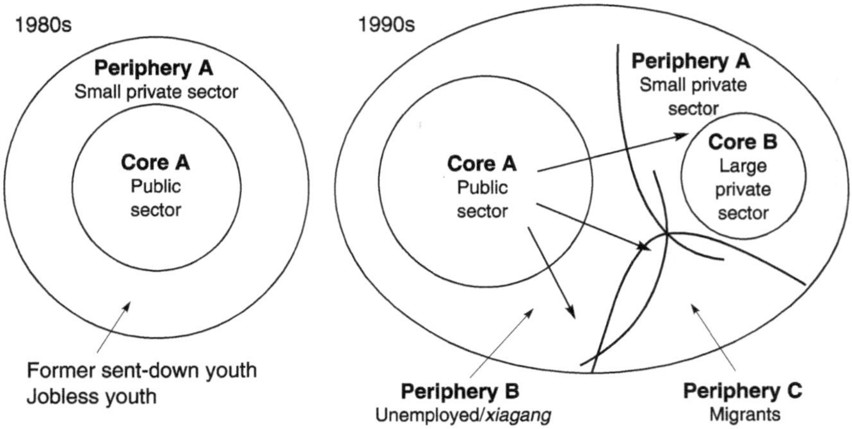


*Figure 9.1* Outline of the urban labour market formation.

the public sector. This includes not only ordinary conventional personnel changes, but also voluntary job changes by those looking for better opportunities. Fourth, due to the rapid increase in rural–urban migration, migrant workers with rural household registration have already occupied a part that, although positioned at the lowest stratum, is essential for the urban labour market (periphery C in Figure 9.1).

### *9.2.2 Hierarchical labour market*

Based on the discussion so far, this section attempts to classify urban workers and migrant workers into six strata as shown in Figure 9.2, according to two criteria. The vertical axis is the economic status measured by wage level and stability of employment, which is expected to be consistent with the occupational status perceived by people. The horizontal axis is the degree of penetration of the market mechanisms (in other words, the degree of breaking away from work-unit socialism) in job-related issues such as wage determination and job-search channels. In the case of urban workers, their positioning along the horizontal axis is expected to have a close relationship with the ownership and management style of the work units to which they belong; the public sector is positioned towards the left, while the non-public sector is positioned towards the right along the axis.

The six strata shown in Figure 9.2 are identified as follows. The first stratum is made up of urban workers who belong to state-owned work units at the central/provincial levels and who have no experience in voluntary or involuntary job turnover. These people have been working in stable employment environments within the superstructure of the urban labour market and constitute a stratum located inside the protective walls of work-unit socialism (hereafter referred to as

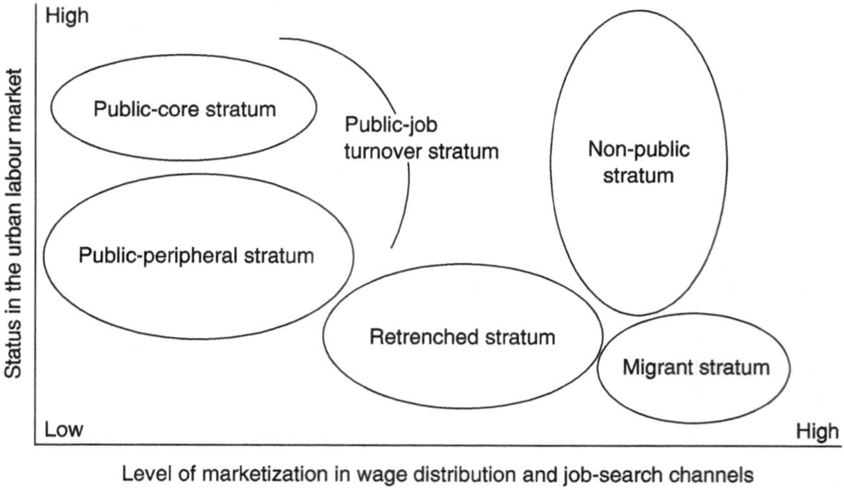


*Figure 9.2* Hierarchical structure of the emerging urban labour market.

the public-core stratum). The second stratum consists of urban workers belonging to the non-public sector (including private enterprises, foreign invested enterprises, and former state-owned enterprises converted to mixed ownership enterprises through ownership reform, with a major share of non-state capital). This stratum has withdrawn from work-unit socialism, and a part of it is developing into a new core stratum (core B in Figure 9.1, hereafter referred to as the non-public stratum). Note that the stratification does not discriminate between different scales of enterprises; employees from a wide range of enterprises, from small to large-scale, are included within this stratum. The third stratum consists of urban workers who have experienced job change within the public sector (hereafter referred to as the public-job turnover stratum). As mentioned earlier, job change here includes both purely voluntary job change and personnel changes between enterprises or organizations, because these two categories cannot be distinguished clearly for technical reasons relating to the survey. It does not, however, include workers who were asked to leave their job and then obtained jobs in the public sector again. The fourth stratum consists of employees of local-level (city, municipal or county), state-owned work units and urban collective-owned work units who experienced neither involuntary nor voluntary job turnover. These workers used to enjoy stable positions, but that stability is gradually becoming undermined. In a sense, they are positioned at the lowest rung of the work-unit socialist system (hereafter referred to as the public-peripheral stratum). The fifth stratum consists of workers who have experienced labour retrenchment (workers who were unemployed/*xiagang* at the time of the survey and workers who have experienced labour retrenchment in the past, hereafter referred to as the retrenched stratum). This stratum is generally alienated from work-unit socialism. Finally, the sixth stratum is composed of migrant workers with rural household registration (hereafter referred to as the migrant stratum). They are positioned at the periphery of urban society together with the public-peripheral stratum.

Table 9.1 summarizes the profiles of the six strata. The following points can be read from this table. First, the gender profile shows that the proportion of men is high in the migrant and public-job turnover strata, in contrast to a remarkably high proportion of women in the retrenched stratum. Second, regarding the age structure, the proportion of people up to 30 years of age is high in the non-public and migrant strata. Note that when looking at the age structure of only those who are of *xiagang* status among the people in the retrenched stratum, the proportion of the middle-aged generation is relatively high: 35 per cent are in their thirties, and 46 per cent are in their forties. That is to say, the retrenched stratum consists of two layers: unemployed youth, who are facing difficulties in entering the labour market after graduating, and middle-aged *xiagang* workers, who were expelled from the public sector because of intensified market competition and progress of the enterprise reforms. Third, there are clear disparities among the strata when looking at the educational level and political status. The educational level and the proportion of Communist party members are high in the public-core and public-job turnover strata. Fourth, regarding job-search channels, the overwhelming majority of the public sector found employment through administrative allocation. In contrast, the proportion of workers who obtained jobs through individual job-hunting activities reaches 42 per cent in the non-public stratum. (The proportion of workers who found employment through administrative allocation accounts for nearly half in the non-public stratum as well; this statistic is due to this stratum including former public-owned enterprises that went through ownership reforms.)

Table 9.2 summarizes the economic status of each stratum. First, the annual wage income of each stratum can be compared. For the public-core, public-job turnover, non-public and public-peripheral strata, the annual wage income is calculated here as the total sum of income each worker obtained from his or her work unit in 1999 (the total amount of salaries and various financial incentives/benefits; payments in kind are added by converting to monetary values). For re-employed workers in the retrenched stratum (those who found employment again after being retrenched), the annual wage income is calculated by converting the income obtained from his or her workplaces in the first month after re-employment into an annual income. For the migrant stratum, the annual income is obtained by converting the migrants' hourly wages to an annual income by multiplying them by the average number of annual working hours of urban workers (calculated based on Wang *et al.* 1999). Household samples that have both wage income and self-employment income are excluded if the latter exceeds the former.

This table clearly shows the order of income levels: workers in the public-job turnover stratum earn the most, followed by the public-core stratum, the non-public

*Table 9.1* Profiles of urban workers and migrant workers

| | *Urban workers by stratum* | | | | | | *Migrant workers* | | |
|---|---|---|---|---|---|---|---|---|---|
| | *Public-core* | *Non-public* | *Public-job turnover* | *Public-peripheral* | *Retrenched* | *Total* | *Employed* | *Self-employed* | *Total* |
| *Gender* | | | | | | | | | |
| Female | 41 | 45 | 41 | 46 | 56 | 46 | 34 | 42 | 39 |
| Male | 59 | 55 | 59 | 54 | 44 | 54 | 66 | 58 | 61 |
| | (1,461) | (427) | (845) | (2,065) | (1,076) | (5,874) | (344) | (678) | (1,022) |
| Age class | | | | | | | | | |
| 15–29 | 16 | 33 | 6 | 15 | 31 | 18 | 46 | 35 | 38 |
| 30–39 | 35 | 31 | 23 | 34 | 27 | 31 | 36 | 49 | 45 |
| 40–49 | 36 | 29 | 51 | 39 | 36 | 39 | 14 | 10 | 12 |
| 50–59 | 12 | 7 | 20 | 11 | 6 | 12 | 4 | 4 | 4 |
| ≥ 60 | 1 | 0 | 1 | 0 | 0 | 0 | 1 | 2 | 1 |
| | (1,461) | (427) | (845) | (2,066) | (1,076) | (5,875) | (344) | (680) | (1,024) |
| *Educational level* | | | | | | | | | |
| Primary school or less | 2 | 1 | 1 | 2 | 5 | 2 | 22 | 24 | 24 |
| Junior high school level | 20 | 21 | 22 | 31 | 42 | 28 | 45 | 57 | 53 |
| Senior high school level | 38 | 42 | 35 | 43 | 45 | 41 | 26 | 16 | 20 |
| Higher education | 41 | 36 | 42 | 25 | 8 | 29 | 8 | 2 | 4 |
| | (1,461) | (427) | (845) | (2,066) | (1,076) | (5,875) | (344) | (680) | (1,024) |
| Party member | 34 | 19 | 46 | 25 | 8 | 27 | 3 | 2 | 2 |
| | (1,461) | (427) | (845) | (2,066) | (1,076) | (5,875) | (344) | (680) | (1,024) |
| *Industrial sector* | | | | | | | | | |
| Manufacturing | 21 | 35 | 19 | 41 | 51 | 34 | 18 | 11 | 14 |
| Construction | 11 | 3 | 6 | 6 | 6 | 7 | 12 | 1 | 4 |
| Other secondary industries | 6 | 7 | 5 | 4 | 1 | 4 | — | — | — |

|  |  |  |  |  |  |  |  |  |  |
|---|---|---|---|---|---|---|---|---|---|
| Commerce and services | 22 | 37 | 25 | 29 | 32 | 28 | 51 | 80 | 70 |
| Government and non-business services | 36 | 9 | 43 | 15 | 4 | 22 | 13 | 1 | 5 |
| Other industries | 4 | 9 | 3 | 4 | 6 | 4 | 6 | 7 | 7 |
|  | (1,454) | (425) | (844) | (2,061) | (851) | (5,635) | (344) | (680) | (1,024) |
| *Job rank* |  |  |  |  |  |  |  |  |  |
| Ordinary jobs | 55 | 67 | 52 | 68 | 86 | 65 | 90 | — | — |
| Professional, skilled or managerial | 45 | 33 | 48 | 32 | 14 | 35 | 10 | — | — |
|  | (1,461) | (425) | (845) | (2,063) | (850) | (5,644) | (344) |  |  |
| *Job-search channel* |  |  |  |  |  |  |  |  |  |
| Administrative allocation | 87 | 51 | 78 | 84 | — | 81 | 5 | — | — |
| Social networks | 2 | 4 | 8 | 3 | — | 4 | 50 | — | — |
| Individual job-hunting activities | 9 | 42 | 10 | 12 | — | 13 | 44 | — | — |
| Others | 2 | 3 | 3 | 1 | — | 2 | 2 | — | — |
|  | (1,453) | (427) | (842) | (2,062) |  | (4,784) | (344) |  |  |

Source: The 1999 CASS survey.

Note: Working population was calculated as follows: Working population = (individuals over 15 years old) – (full-time students) – (those who are disabled) – (men who are retired and are over the standard retirement age of 60 years old) – (women who are retired and are over the standard retirement age of 55 years old). Public–core, public-job turnover, non-public and public-peripheral strata comprise people who were employed throughout 1999 (those whose main income source was self-employment income were excluded). People who had experiences of being unemployed/*xiagang* in 1999 or before (including those who had been re-employed in 1999 or before) were categorized into the retrenched stratum. Industrial sector and job rank of unemployed/*xiagang* workers are according to the former work units.

stratum, the public-peripheral stratum, the migrant stratum and, finally, re-employed workers in the retrenched stratum. What is noteworthy here is the very low level of income of the re-employed workers. Because the income level of the re-employed workers is calculated based on the wage of the first month after re-employment, it should not, strictly speaking, be directly compared with the income levels of the other strata. Nonetheless, it can be understood that the economic conditions of workers who have once been thrown outside work-unit socialism are extremely severe. Next, the inequality of wage distribution within each stratum is presented using Gini coefficients. For urban workers, the inequality within the stratum is highest in the non-public stratum, followed by the public-peripheral, public-job turnover and public-core strata, in that order. The inequality within the migrant stratum is the second highest after the non-public stratum. As a whole, it can thus be concluded that there is a positive correlation between wage inequality and the degree of penetration of the market mechanisms in the determination of employment and wages.[3]

Table 9.2 also shows that the disparities in social security among the strata are almost parallel with the disparities in wage income. The proportion of workers who join medical care programmes is 79 per cent in the public-core stratum, whereas it is only 56 per cent in the public-peripheral stratum. Most workers in the retrenched stratum are not covered under any medical care programmes.

Urban workers in the public-core stratum enjoy a high level of income and social security and low inequality within the stratum. These facts indicate that the vested interests of work-unit socialism are located within this stratum. It should be noted that the characteristics of income distribution in this stratum should not be regarded simply as a transitional phenomenon, because although the structure of income level and distribution may change in a short period of time due to market competition, the structure causing disparities in social security is considered to persist for a long period of time.

## 9.3 Comparison of labour market outcomes

### *9.3.1 Determinants of wage income*

To analyse the differences in wage determinants for each stratum, the wage income functions of urban workers not belonging to the retrenched stratum, workers belonging to the retrenched stratum, and workers belonging to the migrant stratum are compared in Tables 9.3 and 9.4.

Table 9.3 summarizes the wage income functions of urban workers (not including the retrenched stratum). The dependent variable is the log transformation of the annual wage income, defined as in Table 9.2. The explanatory variables used were personal attributes (educational level, party membership and gender), job-related and work-unit-related characteristics (years of employment, experience of voluntary job turnover, job rank, administrative rank and ownership statuses of work unit, and industrial sector), and city dummy variables.

*Table 9.2* Wage income, wage inequality and social security by stratum

| | *Urban workers* | | | | | | | | |
|---|---|---|---|---|---|---|---|---|---|
| | *Urban workers who have never retrenched* | | | | | *Retrenched stratum* | | | |
| | *Public-core stratum* | *Non-public stratum* | *Public-job turnover stratum* | *Public-peripheral stratum* | *Total* | | *Of which re-employed workers* | *Total of urban workers* | *Migrant stratum (employed)* |
| *All samples* | | | | | | | | | |
| Average annual wage income (yuan) | 10,389 | 9,789 | 11,199 | 7,993 | 9,447 | — | 5,259 | — | 5,511 |
| Gini coefficient of annual wage income | 0.302 | 0.347 | 0.311 | 0.315 | 0.322 | — | 0.274 | — | 0.332 |
| No. of observations | 1,461 | 427 | 845 | 2,066 | 4,799 | — | 346 | — | 344 |
| *≤ 39 years old* | | | | | | | | | |
| Average annual wage income (yuan) | 9,672 | 9,348 | 10,153 | 7,478 | 8,701 | — | 4,986 | — | 5,719 |
| Gini coefficient of annual wage income | 0.310 | 0.349 | 0.336 | 0.314 | 0.327 | — | 0.254 | — | 0.338 |
| No. of observations | 747 | 270 | 244 | 1,025 | 2,286 | — | 167 | — | 280 |
| *40–59 years old* | | | | | | | | | |
| Average annual wage income (yuan) | 11,109 | 10,605 | 11,657 | 8,491 | 11,018 | — | 5,514 | — | 4,630 |
| Gini coefficient of annual wage income | 0.289 | 0.335 | 0.299 | 0.312 | 0.313 | — | 0.288 | — | 0.290 |
| No. of observations | 705 | 156 | 596 | 1,039 | 2,496 | — | 179 | — | 61 |
| Those who receive medical insurance services by work unit/government (%) | 79 | 39 | 73 | 56 | — | 21 | — | 56 | 5 |
| Proportion of those who participate in social pension system (%) | 45 | 48 | 50 | 44 | — | 32 | — | 44 | 5 |

Source: The 1999 CASS survey.

Note: The annual wage income was calculated as the total sum of annual income received from the work unit in 1999 (wages, salaries, bonuses, various financial incentives/benefits and so on; payments in kind were added by converting to monetary values). Medical insurance service includes *dabing tongchou* (compulsory insurance for serious diseases).

*Table 9.3* Determinants of wage income of urban workers, 1999

| | *All* | | *Ordinary jobs* | | *Professional, skilled or managerial jobs* | |
|---|---|---|---|---|---|---|
| | *Coefficient* | *t* | *Coefficient* | *t* | *Coefficient* | *t* |
| Gender (male/female) | 0.103 | 6.49** | 0.123 | 5.83** | 0.065 | 2.73** |
| Years of employment | 0.040 | 12.25** | 0.045 | 10.26** | 0.027 | 5.48** |
| Years of employment (squared) | −0.001 | −8.57** | −0.001 | −6.75** | 0.000 | −3.97** |
| Years of education | 0.036 | 10.48** | 0.037 | 7.73** | 0.035 | 7.47** |
| Political status (party member/non-member) | 0.097 | 5.22** | 0.100 | 3.63** | 0.108 | 4.38** |
| Job rank (professional, skilled or managerial jobs/ordinary jobs) | 0.140 | 7.71** | | | | |
| Central/provincial-level work unit | 0.151 | 8.48** | 0.198 | 8.07** | 0.092 | 3.62** |
| Urban collective-owned work unit | −0.233 | −8.24** | −0.226 | −6.61** | −0.217 | −4.07** |
| State shareholding enterprises with major share of state capital | 0.018 | 0.37 | 0.007 | 0.11 | 0.067 | 0.90 |
| Private enterprises, mixed ownership enterprises with major share of non-state capital, and other non-public work units | 0.172 | 3.52** | 0.247 | 3.95** | 0.031 | 0.40 |
| Foreign joint venture and foreign invested enterprises | 0.308 | 5.80** | 0.353 | 5.23** | 0.229 | 2.65** |
| Other work units | 0.031 | 0.42 | 0.045 | 0.48 | 0.076 | 0.61 |
| Manufacturing | −0.224 | −10.74** | −0.218 | −8.24** | −0.251 | −7.27** |
| Construction | −0.230 | −6.93** | −0.231 | −5.36** | −0.254 | −4.91** |
| Other secondary industries | 0.254 | 6.76** | 0.236 | 4.82** | 0.289 | 4.95** |
| Governmental and non-business services | 0.063 | 2.79** | 0.079 | 2.37* | 0.040 | 1.31 |

| | | | | | | |
|---|---|---|---|---|---|---|
| Other industries | −0.162 | −3.99** | −0.180 | −3.49** | −0.135 | −2.05* |
| Having experiences of voluntary job turnover | 0.062 | 3.08** | 0.076 | 2.68** | 0.043 | 1.55 |
| Shenyang | −0.317 | −9.78** | −0.307 | −7.19** | −0.339 | −6.94** |
| Jinzhou | −0.386 | −8.93** | −0.308 | −5.76** | −0.606 | −7.91** |
| Xuzhou | −0.203 | −4.99** | −0.190 | −3.59** | −0.220 | −3.47** |
| Beijing | 0.097 | 3.19** | 0.081 | 1.98* | 0.112 | 2.49* |
| Zhengzhou | −0.330 | −8.90** | −0.344 | −6.62** | −0.328 | −6.37** |
| Kaifeng | −0.548 | −11.80** | −0.509 | −7.91** | −0.607 | −9.31** |
| Pingdingshan | −0.340 | −8.71** | −0.367 | −7.25** | −0.266 | −4.36** |
| Chengdu | −0.208 | −6.24** | −0.134 | −2.89** | −0.310 | −6.63** |
| Zigong | −0.300 | −6.78** | −0.336 | −5.48** | −0.259 | −4.17** |
| Nanchong | −0.240 | −5.43** | −0.196 | −3.27** | −0.292 | −4.59** |
| Lanzhou | −0.361 | −10.30** | −0.355 | −7.82** | −0.364 | −6.67** |
| Pingliang | −0.581 | −13.61** | −0.583 | −10.25** | −0.578 | −9.18** |
| Constant | 8.184 | 136.86** | 8.056 | 99.52** | 8.563 | 91.16** |
| Adjusted $R^2$ | 0.351 | | 0.299 | | 0.308 | |
| No. of observations | 4,685 | | 2,850 | | 1,835 | |

Source: The 1999 CASS survey.

Note: The dependent variable is the log transformation of total annual income received from the work unit in 1999. People who were over 15 years old, employed throughout 1999, and whose main income source was wage and salaries are included. Omitted dummy variables are junior high school level, local-level state-owned work unit, commerce and services, and Nanjing. ** denotes statistical significance at the 1% level, * at the 5% level.

*Table 9.4* Determinants of wage income of migrants, 1999

| | *Employed* | | *Self-employed* | |
|---|---|---|---|---|
| | *Coefficient* | *t* | *Coefficient* | *t* |
| Gender (male/female) | 0.029 | 0.48 | 0.007 | 0.09 |
| Years of employment | 0.042 | 1.86 | 0.059 | 2.21* |
| Years of employment (squared) | −0.001 | −0.43 | −0.003 | −1.73 |
| Years of education | 0.066 | 5.83** | 0.033 | 2.36* |
| Political status (party member/ non-member) | 0.279 | 1.62 | −0.092 | −0.34 |
| Job rank (professional, skilled or managerial jobs/ordinary jobs) | 0.142 | 1.38 | — | — |
| Central/provincial-level work unit | 0.221 | 1.87 | — | — |
| Urban collective-owned work unit | 0.191 | 1.77 | — | — |
| State shareholding enterprises with major share of state capital | 0.168 | 1.76 | — | — |
| Private enterprises, mixed ownership enterprises with major share of non-state capital, and other non-public work units | 0.016 | 0.09 | — | — |
| Foreign joint venture and foreign invested enterprises | 0.586 | 2.86** | — | — |
| Other work units | 0.102 | 0.80 | — | — |
| Manufacturing | 0.128 | 1.43 | 0.045 | 0.41 |
| Construction | 0.158 | 1.62 | 0.648 | 1.66 |
| Governmental and non-business services | −0.039 | −0.40 | 0.004 | 0.01 |
| Other industries | −0.001 | −0.01 | −0.262 | −1.83 |
| Household size (persons) | | | 0.144 | 3.79** |
| Shenyang | 0.194 | 1.72 | 0.615 | 3.45** |
| Jinzhou | 0.110 | 0.76 | 0.243 | 1.32 |
| Xuzhou | 0.105 | 0.47 | −0.249 | −1.52 |
| Beijing | 0.315 | 2.71** | 0.240 | 1.45 |
| Zhengzhou | −0.059 | −0.30 | −0.198 | −1.10 |
| Kaifeng | 0.264 | 1.60 | −0.060 | −0.33 |
| Pingdingshan | 0.057 | 0.30 | −0.142 | −0.84 |
| Chengdu | 0.166 | 1.26 | 0.479 | 2.38* |
| Zigong | −0.042 | −0.22 | −0.185 | −0.99 |
| Nanchong | −0.132 | −0.87 | 0.101 | 0.57 |
| Lanzhou | −0.134 | −1.00 | 0.078 | 0.39 |
| Pingliang | −0.020 | −0.12 | −0.457 | −2.50* |
| Constant | −0.217 | −1.23 | 8.515 | 40.95** |
| Adjusted $R^2$ | 0.315 | | 0.198 | |
| No. of observations | 297 | | 368 | |

Source: The 1999 CASS survey.

Note: The dependent variable is the log transformation of the wage income defined as in Table 9.2 for employed migrants, and the log transformation annual net revenues for self-employed migrants. One outlier (having more then 5,000 yuan monthly income) is omitted. Omitted dummy variables are junior high school level, local-level state-owned work unit, commerce and services, and Nanjing. **denotes statistical significance at the 1% level, * at the 5% level.

Based on this table, the following points can be made regarding the wage determinants of urban workers as a whole. First, with regard to personal attributes, both educational attainment and political status are significant wage determinants. Educational attainment has a positive effect on wages by about 3.6 per cent per year of education. Political status measured by party membership also has a positive wage premium of about 10 per cent. Thus, both meritocracy and political credentialism work in the determination of wages. Second, it is confirmed that job- and work-unit-related factors have significant effects on wages. As for the status of the work unit, compared with local-level work units, central/provincial-level work units and foreign invested enterprises have positive premiums of about 16 and 30 per cent, respectively, whereas urban collective-owned work units have a negative premium of about 23 per cent. The job rank, another indicator of meritocracy, is also significant. Those who are in professional, skilled or managerial positions earn about 14 per cent more than those who are in ordinary positions. Experience of voluntary job turnover increases one's wage by about 6.2 per cent. Dummy variables for the industrial sector reveal that, compared with the commerce and service industries, income is lower in the secondary industries, while it is higher in the administrative and non-business sector. Third, most of the city dummy variables are significant. This reflects the fact that the urban labour market is clearly segmented by regions and among cities in a particular region.

Table 9.4 shows the earning functions (wage income and self-employment income) of the migrant stratum. The dependent variable is the log transformation of the wage income defined as in Table 9.2. The income function of self-employed migrants is also presented in the table (in this case, the dependent variable is defined as the log transformation annual net revenues). First, educational level is a positive significant determinant of earnings in both employed and self-employed migrants. It should be noted that the employed migrant's coefficient value of years of education is larger than the urban worker's. Second, unlike in the case of urban workers, party membership is not a significant determinant of earnings, whereas studies of rural areas suggest that political status has a significant positive effect on income in rural areas (Walder 2001; Sato 2003). It is likely that the effects of any political status the peasants might have are lost once they leave their socio-political relations in rural areas. The third point that should be mentioned in comparison with the urban workers is that the city dummy variables are almost insignificant for both the employed and the self-employed migrants. This fact suggests that high labour mobility in the lowest layer of the urban labour market, into which the migrant stratum enters, brings about the relatively small regional disparity in earnings. Insignificant coefficients of industrial sectors can also be explained in a similar manner.

### *9.3.2 Education, political status and gender*

Next, the urban workers in the survey are classified into strata to compare the determinants of wage income. In doing so, the focus is placed on education, political status and gender as indicators that measure changes in the income determination mechanisms caused by marketization (degree of transformation of egalitarianism in work-unit socialism). The following hypotheses are proposed for each of the indicators.

First, the penetration of market mechanisms in the determination of employment and wages strengthens the positive correlation between educational attainment and wage income. This means that, when the public and non-public sectors are compared, educational level has larger positive effects on wage income in the non-public sector. Moreover, when the effect of educational level on wage income is observed longitudinally, it increases over time.

Second, contrary to the case of educational attainment, marketization weakens the positive correlation between political status and income. This means that the positive effects of political status on wage income are stronger in the public sector than in the non-public sector. Moreover, when the effect of political status on wage income is observed longitudinally, it will decrease over time.

Third, the gender wage gap will widen as market mechanisms penetrate further. This means that the effects of gender on wage income are more significant in the non-public sector than in the public sector, and that they tend to increase when observed over time.

To verify these hypotheses, wage income functions were estimated for each stratum, omitting the dummy variables related to administrative rank and ownership status of work units from the wage income functions in Table 9.3. Table 9.5 reports the coefficients for educational level and political status obtained as the result. From this table, the following points can be understood.

First, the effects of educational level are larger in the non-public stratum than in any stratum in the public sector, which indicates that the first hypothesis is valid. When observed by generation, however, the effects are not necessarily straightforward. Looking at the non-public stratum by generation, the coefficient for educational level is significant in the younger generation (up to 39 years of age), but it is no longer significant in the case of the middle-aged and old generations (40 years of age or more). On the other hand, in the case of all the public sector strata, the educational level is significant regardless of the generation, and its effect is larger for the younger generation. The differences among the generations in the non-public stratum can be explained by the unique structure of this stratum; that is, a large proportion of the middle-aged and old generation in the non-public stratum started small self-employed businesses as a result of being alienated from work-unit socialism. Thus, the correlation between educational level and income is considered weak in this case. The differences in the effects of educational level by generation in each of the public strata are consistent with this hypothesis. The younger generation here is the generation of workers that began to enter the labour market after the employment system reforms in the mid-1980s, that is, at the time of the transition from the lifetime employment system without labour contract (*gudinggong*) to the contract employment system (*hetonggong*). The fact that the effects of education are intensified in this generation reflects the significance of employment system reforms.

*Table 9.5* Effects of educational level and political status on wage income by stratum, 1999

| | *Total coefficient* | *Public-core coefficient* | *Non-public coefficient* | *Public-job turnover coefficient* | *Public-peripheral coefficient* |
|---|---|---|---|---|---|
| Years of education | 0.036** | 0.041** | 0.056** | 0.032** | 0.037** |
| Party membership | 0.097** | 0.081* | 0.071 | 0.107** | 0.117** |
| Gender (male/female) | 0.103** | 0.070* | 0.148** | 0.080* | 0.151** |
| *≤ 39 years old* | | | | | |
| Years of education | 0.037** | 0.036** | 0.063** | 0.067** | 0.032** |
| Party membership | 0.119** | 0.124* | 0.152 | 0.162 | 0.097 |
| *40–59 years old* | | | | | |
| Years of education | 0.031** | 0.039** | 0.026 | 0.021** | 0.037** |
| Party membership | 0.097** | 0.069 | 0.030 | 0.086* | 0.151** |

Source: The 1999 CASS survey.

Note: The dependent variable and explanatory variables are the same as in Table 9.3. (The dummy variables related to administrative rank and ownership status of work units are omitted.) ** denotes statistical significance at the 1% level, * at the 5% level.

Second, the effects of political status are also consistent with the second hypothesis. As far as wage inequality among urban workers is seen as a whole, the marketization surely has the effect of weakening the relation between political status and income.

Third, the gender wage gap is larger in the non-public sector than in the public sector, which supports the third hypothesis. Another interesting fact is that when the strata in the public sector are compared, relatively small disparities by gender are observed in the public-core stratum, as opposed to the largest disparities by gender observed in the public-peripheral stratum.

### 9.3.3 Longitudinal changes in income determinants

How have the correlations between income and education, political status and gender changed when viewed over time? The changes from 1988 to 1999 are examined here, using the 1988 and 1999 CASS surveys. Table 9.6 compares the wage income functions of 1999 with those of 1988. The change in wage inequality measured by the Gini coefficient is also reported. The estimation covers nine cities–Beijing, Shenyang, Jinzhou, Nanjing, Xuzhou, Zhengzhou, Kaifeng, Pingdingshan and Lanzhou–that were investigated in 1988 and 1999. Because the ratio of workers belonging to the non-public sector was small around 1988, the examination here is limited to the public sector only. The following points can be made from this table.

Wage income inequality measured by Gini coefficients was 0.200 in 1988 and 0.324 in 1999. It is obvious that the degree of inequality increased substantially during this period. By looking at the changes in the income determination mechanisms working in the background, the following facts come to the surface.

*Table 9.6* Changes of wage determinants in public sector, 1988 and 1999

| | *1988* | | *1999* | |
|---|---|---|---|---|
| | *Coefficient* | *t* | *Coefficient* | *t* |
| Gender (male/female) | 0.098 | 10.35** | 0.117 | 5.94** |
| Age | 0.066 | 22.46** | 0.080 | 10.15** |
| Age (squared) | −0.001 | −16.85** | −0.001 | −8.62** |
| Higher education | 0.020 | 1.30 | 0.249 | 8.29** |
| Senior high school level | −0.003 | −0.32 | 0.067 | 2.70** |
| Primary school or less | −0.129 | −6.59** | −0.295 | −3.43** |
| Political status (party member/non-member) | 0.065 | 5.40** | 0.082 | 3.50** |
| Job rank (professional, skilled or managerial jobs/ordinary jobs) | 0.073 | 5.45** | 0.135 | 5.84** |
| Central/provincial-level work unit | 0.073 | 6.13** | 0.133 | 6.36** |
| Urban collective-owned work unit | −0.087 | −6.67** | −0.244 | −7.40** |
| Manufacturing | −0.009 | −0.71 | −0.240 | −9.58** |
| Construction | 0.013 | 0.47 | −0.217 | −5.43** |
| Other secondary industries | 0.002 | 0.13 | 0.143 | 3.07** |
| Governmental and non-business services | −0.042 | −2.71** | 0.058 | 2.10* |
| Other industries | −0.328 | −5.59** | −0.203 | −3.85** |
| Beijing | 0.002 | 0.12 | 0.083 | 2.57* |
| Shenyang | −0.069 | −3.86** | −0.332 | −9.62** |
| Jinzhou | −0.148 | −7.65** | −0.401 | −8.89** |
| Xuzhou | −0.007 | −0.37 | −0.217 | −5.12** |
| Zhengzhou | −0.154 | −8.05** | −0.358 | −9.05** |
| Kaifeng | −0.268 | −11.27** | −0.568 | −11.89** |
| Pingdingshan | −0.270 | −10.98** | −0.366 | −9.07** |
| Lanzhou | −0.068 | −3.61** | −0.374 | −10.12** |
| Constant | 5.959 | 103.71** | 7.256 | 46.79** |
| Adjusted $R^2$ | 0.443 | | 0.350 | |
| No. of observations | 4,114 | | 3,299 | |
| Gini coefficient of wage income | 0.200 | | 0.324 | |

Source: The 1999 and 1988 CASS surveys.

Note: The dependent variable is the log transformation of total annual income received from work units in 1999 and 1988. People who were 16–69 years old and whose main income source was wage and salaries were included. Omitted dummy variables are junior high school level, local-level state-owned work unit, commerce and services, and Nanjing. ** denotes statistical significance at the 1% level, * at the 5% level.

First, it is clear that the correlation between educational attainments and labour market outcomes has become stronger, which supports the first hypothesis above. Using graduation from junior high schools as the standard of educational level, the educational level dummy variable was significant only for primary school or less and not significant for educational levels higher than that in 1988, whereas it was significant for all the educational levels in 1999. Compared with graduates from junior high schools, people with senior high school-level education (including secondary vocational schools) have a positive premium of about 7 per cent, and people with a higher education level than senior high school have a positive premium of about 25 per cent. Moreover, the disparity between graduates from junior high schools and primary schools has widened as well. The fact that the effects of educational level on income become stronger as marketization advances has already been pointed out by preceding studies that compared the 1988 and 1995 CASS surveys (Li and Li 1994; Lai 1999). Table 9.6 indicates that this tendency has intensified further.[1] Moreover, the fact that the disparities among job ranks became wider from 1988 to 1999 also suggests that the significance of human capital in income determination has increased.

Second, no tendency for the effect of political status to decrease over time can be found. Wage income premium for party members became slightly larger from 1988 to 1999. As mentioned above, when ownership sectors are compared, the progress of the marketization surely lowers the significance of political status, but when the public sector is observed over time, the significance of political status in fact seems to have increased slightly, or at least to have been maintained at the same level. This fact is also consistent with preceding studies. For example, Knight and Song (1999, 2001), using the 1988 and 1995 CASS surveys, indicated that the rate of contribution of party membership to the overall urban income inequality became slightly higher from 1988 to 1995. Bian and Logan (1996) also concluded that party membership and status of executive officers in work units consistently maintain significant positive effects on income, and that the effect of the latter gradually increases. The correlation between political status and economic status is far from straightforward in China, where marketization progresses under the single-party system.

Third, there was already a disparity of about 10 per cent between the genders in 1988, and this disparity was slightly increased by 1999. This also agrees with the third hypothesis.

Fourth, the wage income premium for the work units to which workers belong intensified throughout the 1990s. Both the positive premium of central/provincial-level work units and the negative premium of urban collective-owned work units relative to local-level work units were larger in 1999 than in 1988. In the public enterprise reforms of the 1990s, selective policies where 'large enterprises are seized but small enterprises are released' (*zhuadafangxiao*) were implemented; that is, the government maintained its influence on the ownership and management of large-scale enterprises, whereas the choices of ownership and management style for medium and small enterprises were boldly deregulated. Given this policy environment, it can be said that the economic disparities originating from the administrative ranks of work units inherited from the planned economy era have been maintained or intensified, although their forms have changed.

Fifth, the disparities among industrial sectors also increased from 1988 to 1999. It is worth noting with respect to the industrial sectors that the governmental and non-business service sector (administrative agencies, institutions providing education/research, medical/welfare and other public services) was a low-income sector in 1988, but had become a high-income sector by 1999. This can be explained partly by the fact that favourable policy environments for workers in this sector were in place throughout the 1990s, based on the consideration that the previous policy of placing low priority on the public service sector (especially education and scientific research) during the Mao era inhibited economic growth. Advancement of Chinese-style cooperation between industry and academia, and increased demands for professional education because of marketization and globalization, are also considered to have contributed to this change. Another more direct factor is that the salaries of civil servants have been substantially raised since 1999 as an anti-recessionary policy.

Sixth, regional wage income disparity among cities also widened throughout the 1990s. Low levels of income in the north-eastern cities (Shenyang and Jinzhou) and inland cities (Zhengzhou, Kaifeng, Pingdingshan and Lanzhou) are noticeable.

### *9.3.4 Determinants of becoming unemployed*

Here, a logit estimation is conducted to examine the determinants of the probability of becoming unemployed/*xiagang*. The dependent variable is either having (= 1) or not having (= 0) experienced unemployment/*xiagang*. Profiles of urban workers presented in Table 9.1 are used as explanatory variables. Outcomes of the estimation are shown in Table 9.7. Briefly, the outcomes confirm the above discussion about Table 9.1. First, it is confirmed that personal attributes (that is, educational level, political status and gender) are all significant explanatory variables; the probability of being unemployed/*xiagang* is higher for workers with low educational levels, non-party members and women. It should be noted that having poor health or belonging to an ethnic minority group also heightens the probability of unemployment/*xiagang*, although the level of significance is low. Second, the administrative rank and ownership status of the work units are also important factors that affect the probability of being unemployed/*xiagang*. The administrative rank of a work unit is negatively correlated with the probability of being unemployed/*xiagang*. Furthermore, it is worth noting that the probability of becoming unemployed or *xiagang* is considerably higher when working for enterprises that have converted ownership and management style because of state-owned enterprise reform. This reflects the fact that enterprise reform, in many cases, involves personnel cuts. Third, looking at the industrial sector, it is confirmed that the probability of becoming unemployed or *xiagang* is high in the manufacturing industry and low in the governmental and non-business sector. Fourth, many of the regional dummy variables are significant here as well, indicating a large regional segmentation of the labour market.

## 9.4 Subjective aspects of labour market hierarchy

### *9.4.1 Labour market outcomes*

The issue is now examined from a different angle: how people perceive the correlation between personal attributes and labour market outcomes. Table 9.8

*Table 9.7* Determinants of becoming unemployed/*xiagang* (publicly owned and mixed ownership work units)

| | *Odds ratio* | *z* |
|---|---|---|
| Gender (male/female) | 0.634 | −4.93** |
| 20–24 years old | 0.660 | −1.47 |
| 25–29 years old | 1.764 | 3.29** |
| 30–34 years old | 1.350 | 1.90 |
| 40–44 years old | 1.102 | 0.73 |
| 45–49 years old | 1.506 | 2.79** |
| 50–54 years old | 1.361 | 1.52 |
| 55–59 years old | 0.921 | −0.23 |
| Higher education | 0.390 | −5.27** |
| Senior high school level | 0.914 | −0.87 |
| Primary school or less | 1.742 | 2.29* |
| Political status (party member/non-member) | 0.505 | −4.88** |
| Health condition (good/poor) | 0.774 | −1.43 |
| Ethnic minority | 1.074 | 0.32 |
| Job rank (professional, skilled or managerial jobs/ordinary jobs) | 0.712 | −2.61** |
| Central/provincial-level state-owned work unit | 0.432 | −6.79** |
| Urban collective-owned work unit | 2.118 | 7.01** |
| State shareholding enterprises with major share of state capital | 51.753 | 3.75** |
| Mixed ownership enterprises with major share of non-state capital | 116.662 | 6.42** |
| Manufacturing | 1.663 | 4.98** |
| Construction | 1.344 | 1.64 |
| Other secondary industries | 0.096 | −3.95** |
| Governmental and non-business services | 0.172 | −7.10** |
| Other industries | 0.783 | −0.90 |
| Shenyang | 1.220 | 0.94 |
| Jinzhou | 4.696 | 7.32** |
| Xuzhou | 1.629 | 2.01* |
| Beijing | 1.734 | 2.71** |
| Zhengzhou | 2.307 | 3.61** |
| Kaifeng | 4.010 | 6.19** |
| Pingdingshan | 0.944 | −0.20 |
| Chengdu | 2.156 | 3.60** |
| Zigong | 4.230 | 6.34** |
| Nanchong | 2.966 | 4.62** |
| Lanzhou | 3.657 | 6.45** |
| Pingliang | 4.514 | 5.98** |
| Pseudo $R^2$ | 0.272 | |
| No. of observations | 5,180 | |

Source: The 1999 CASS survey.

Note: The dependent variable is having experience of unemployment/*xiagang* (=1) or not (=0). People who were over 60 years old were excluded. Omitted dummy variables are 35–39 years old, junior high school level, local-level state-owned work unit, commerce and services, and Nanjing.** denotes statistical significance at the 1% level, * at the 5% level.

*Table 9.8* Perception of income determinants of urban workers (%, numbers in parentheses are numbers of samples)

| | *Public-core stratum* | *Non-public stratum* | *Public-job turnover stratum* | *Public-peripheral stratum* | *Retrenched stratum* | *Total* |
|---|---|---|---|---|---|---|
| **Educational level** | | | | | | |
| Decrease | 3 | 2 | 3 | 4 | 5 | 4 |
| No change | 61 | 69 | 55 | 63 | 66 | 62 |
| Increase | 36 | 29 | 42 | 33 | 29 | 34 |
| | (663) | (184) | (466) | (1,356) | (398) | Pr = 0.003 |
| *≤39 years old* | | | | | | |
| Decrease | 3 | 1 | 2 | 3 | 3 | 3 |
| No change | 59 | 69 | 51 | 68 | 75 | 59 |
| Increase | 38 | 30 | 48 | 29 | 22 | 38 |
| | (284) | (90) | (122) | (418) | (159) | (284) |
| *40–59 years old* | | | | | | |
| Decrease | 3 | 3 | 4 | 4 | 6 | 4 |
| No change | 62 | 69 | 56 | 60 | 60 | 60 |
| Increase | 35 | 28 | 40 | 35 | 34 | 35 |
| | (372) | (93) | (337) | (915) | (239) | Pr = 0.291 |
| **Political status** | | | | | | |
| Decrease | 3 | 3 | 4 | 4 | 3 | 4 |
| No change | 77 | 83 | 70 | 78 | 78 | 77 |
| Increase | 19 | 15 | 26 | 18 | 19 | 20 |
| | (661) | (184) | (466) | (1,352) | (398) | Pr = 0.035 |
| *≤39 years old* | | | | | | |
| Decrease | 5 | 1 | 6 | 2 | 3 | 3 |
| No change | 72 | 81 | 61 | 77 | 80 | 75 |
| Increase | 24 | 18 | 33 | 20 | 18 | 22 |
| | (283) | (90) | (122) | (416) | (159) | Pr = 0.007 |
| *40–59 years old* | | | | | | |
| Decrease | 2 | 4 | 4 | 4 | 4 | 4 |
| No change | 81 | 84 | 73 | 78 | 77 | 78 |
| Increase | 16 | 12 | 23 | 18 | 20 | 18 |
| | (371) | (93) | (337) | (913) | (239) | Pr = 0.122 |

Source: The 1999 CASS survey.

summarizes responses to the question 'Do you think one's educational level (political status) tends to have a stronger effect on personal income?' The question was asked in general terms, but it is considered that the respondents answered the question from the point of view of themselves and their immediate surroundings. Given this assumption, the tendencies of the responses in each stratum and the wage income functions of each stratum are compared. In the middle-aged generation, no significant differences among the strata are recognized in the perception of the relationship between educational level and income. In the younger generation, however, significant differences among the strata appear, as the proportion of respondents who think that the effects of educational attainment became greater increases in the public-job turnover stratum. This result is consistent with the objective situations indicated by the wage income functions. As for political status, its effect on income was the weakest in the case of the non-public stratum according to the objective indicators, and the perception of the workers belonging to the non-public stratum was consistent with the objective situation, especially among the younger generation.

Next, we examined what factors people feel have an effect on being unemployed/*xiagang*. The respondents were asked to choose up to two items from the options 'relationship with superiors and colleagues', 'skills and experience', 'age', 'educational level', 'gender' and 'political status'. The results showed no significant differences among the strata on the whole. It is interesting to note that the factor chosen the most often was human relations at the work unit, regardless of which stratum the respondents belonged to (51 per cent selected this item in total). This result suggests that the employment adjustment in the process of enterprise reform is perceived to be conducted based on ambiguous standards, rather than ability and qualifications. It is also worthy of note that only a few respondents perceived that political status and gender are important factors in determining the probability of becoming unemployed or *xiagang* in any stratum. (The total proportions of respondents who selected these items are less than 1 per cent for the former and 6 per cent for the latter.) This result is considerably different from the result of the objective analysis. An issue to be examined in the future is whether this result suggests that there are gaps between the objective situations and people's perceptions or whether people take disparities due to gender and political status for granted.

### *9.4.2 Expectations for the next generation*

Based on the objective hierarchical structure examined so far, we now examine how people's perceptions correspond to it. It is possible to depict the subjective hierarchical structure perceived by urban workers by examining their long-term expectations through asking what they expect from the next generation. Table 9.9, which summarizes what people expect from their next generation's educational attainment and political status, shows the following points.

The expectations towards the next generation's education were investigated by asking the question 'Do you wish to put your children (or grandchildren) through college?' Although the expectations towards children's education are very high as a whole, there are relatively low expectations in the public-peripheral stratum and the retrenched stratum. It seems to reflect the low educational level of those who belong to these two strata. The economic instability that these two strata face also seems to affect expectations, although the question was asked independently of actual economic conditions. It is noteworthy that there are no significant differences among strata in the younger generation as the expectations in the public-peripheral stratum and the retrenched stratum become higher.

The expectations towards political status were investigated by asking the question 'Would you like your children (or grandchildren) to become party members?' Significant differences among the strata can be recognized for this question as

*Table 9.9* Urban workers' expectations towards the next generation's educational level and political status (%, numbers in parentheses are numbers of samples)

| | *Public-core stratum* | *Non-public stratum* | *Public-job turnover stratum* | *Public-peripheral stratum* | *Retrenched stratum* | *Total* |
|---|---|---|---|---|---|---|
| **To enter college** | | | | | | |
| Do not wish | 1 | 2 | 3 | 4 | 6 | 3 |
| Little wish | 8 | 12 | 8 | 11 | 12 | 10 |
| Wish | 10 | 12 | 6 | 13 | 9 | 11 |
| Strong wish | 80 | 75 | 84 | 72 | 72 | 76 |
| | (661) | (182) | (461) | (1,344) | (394) | Pr=0.000 |
| ***By generation*** | | | | | | |
| *≤39 years old* | | | | | | |
| Do not wish | 0 | 1 | 2 | 1 | 1 | 1 |
| Little wish | 6 | 10 | 7 | 8 | 11 | 8 |
| Wish | 10 | 11 | 6 | 9 | 6 | 9 |
| Strong wish | 84 | 77 | 85 | 81 | 81 | 82 |
| | (283) | (88) | (122) | (417) | (156) | Pr=0.714 |
| *40–59 years old* | | | | | | |
| Do not wish | 1 | 2 | 3 | 5 | 9 | 4 |
| Little wish | 10 | 13 | 8 | 12 | 13 | 11 |
| Wish | 11 | 11 | 6 | 15 | 11 | 12 |
| Strong wish | 77 | 74 | 83 | 69 | 66 | 73 |
| | (371) | (93) | (333) | (905) | (238) | Pr=0.000 |
| **To enter the Communist Party** | | | | | | |
| Do not wish | 15 | 13 | 15 | 14 | 22 | 16 |
| Little wish | 35 | 43 | 34 | 32 | 31 | 33 |
| Wish | 23 | 26 | 24 | 25 | 21 | 24 |
| Strong wish | 28 | 18 | 27 | 29 | 26 | 27 |
| | (657) | (182) | (460) | (1,342) | (394) | Pr=0.003 |
| ***By generation*** | | | | | | |
| *≤39 years old* | | | | | | |
| Do not wish | 13 | 15 | 17 | 15 | 22 | 16 |
| Little wish | 38 | 47 | 26 | 39 | 33 | 37 |
| Wish | 24 | 26 | 30 | 24 | 20 | 24 |
| Strong wish | 25 | 13 | 27 | 22 | 25 | 23 |
| | (281) | (88) | (121) | (414) | (156) | Pr=0.038 |
| *40–59 years old* | | | | | | |
| Do not wish | 17 | 12 | 15 | 14 | 22 | 16 |
| Little wish | 32 | 41 | 37 | 29 | 29 | 32 |
| Wish | 22 | 25 | 22 | 25 | 22 | 23 |
| Strong wish | 30 | 23 | 27 | 32 | 27 | 29 |
| | (369) | (93) | (333) | (906) | (238) | Pr=0.037 |

Source: The 1999 CASS survey.

well; not surprisingly, the number of positive responses is smaller in the non-public stratum. This is also consistent with the result of the objective observation on the relation between political status and wage income, and there are no differences in the results by generation in this stratum. When differences by generation in all the strata are examined, it is found that the proportion of positive responses is low in the younger generation in general; the proportion is particularly low in the public-peripheral stratum. This is also consistent with the objective fact that the correlation between political status and income is weakened among the younger generation of this stratum.

Next, the aspect of expectations towards the next generation's occupational status is examined. Table 9.10 shows the result of presenting examples of two occupational statuses representative of the public and non-public strata to the subjects (full-time employees of a state-owned work unit and owners of private business), and asking whether they would like their children (or grandchildren) to have these occupational statuses. Significant differences among the strata are observed for both statuses.

First, for full-time employees of a state-owned work unit, there were more positive responses in the public-peripheral and retrenched strata, whereas the tendency is reversed in the non-public stratum. This tendency is similar when the responses are examined for each generation. This can be interpreted in such a way that, in reality, state-owned work units are evaluated more highly in the strata that are alienated from work-unit socialism.

Second, for owners of private businesses, there were more positive responses in the non-public stratum, and this tendency is especially prominent among the younger generation. It can be concluded that the positive self-evaluation in the younger generation reflects the improved status of the non-public stratum in recent years.

So how do migrant workers perceive the objective hierarchical structure? Table 9.11 summarizes the expectations of migrants towards their children. It seems that there is not so much difference in their expectations towards educational levels and political status compared with each stratum of urban workers. On the other hand, an examination of the expectations towards the next generation's occupational status reveals that there were more positive answers for both full-time employees of a state-owned work unit and owners of private businesses, compared with urban workers. Migrants who have been kept alienated from urban society have a strong yearning for both state-owned work units, the symbol of work-unit socialism, and success as private business owners, representing the new occupational status brought on by marketization.

## 9.5 *Xiagang*, job search and re-employment

### *9.5.1 An estimation of the unemployment rate*

Generally, the unemployment rate is defined as the percentage of unemployed workers to the total labour force. Unemployed workers are those who are jobless, seeking a job and ready to work if they can find a job. The total labour force is the sum of the employed and unemployed workers. The unemployment statistics of the International Labour Organization (ILO), generally used for international comparison, are based on sample surveys that investigate the employment situation

*Table 9.10* Urban workers' expectations towards the next generation's occupational status (%, numbers in parentheses are numbers of samples)

| | *Public-core stratum* | *Non-public stratum* | *Public-job turnover stratum* | *Public-peripheral stratum* | *Retrenched stratum* | *Total* |
|---|---|---|---|---|---|---|
| **Full-time employee of a state-owned work unit** | | | | | | |
| Do not wish | 33 | 36 | 34 | 27 | 26 | 30 |
| Little wish | 28 | 38 | 29 | 25 | 25 | 27 |
| Wish | 19 | 14 | 19 | 23 | 21 | 21 |
| Strong wish | 20 | 11 | 18 | 26 | 27 | 23 |
| | (658) | (182) | (460) | (1,345) | (393) | Pr=0.000 |
| ***By generation*** | | | | | | |
| *≤39 years old* | | | | | | |
| Do not wish | 34 | 41 | 37 | 33 | 29 | 34 |
| Little wish | 31 | 38 | 31 | 24 | 26 | 28 |
| Wish | 19 | 13 | 16 | 23 | 17 | 19 |
| Strong wish | 16 | 9 | 16 | 20 | 27 | 19 |
| | (281) | (88) | (122) | (417) | (155) | Pr=0.006 |
| *40–59 years old* | | | | | | |
| Do not wish | 33 | 32 | 33 | 24 | 24 | 28 |
| Little wish | 25 | 40 | 28 | 25 | 24 | 26 |
| Wish | 20 | 15 | 20 | 22 | 24 | 21 |
| Strong wish | 22 | 13 | 19 | 29 | 27 | 25 |
| | (370) | (93) | (332) | (906) | (238) | Pr=0.000 |
| ***Owner of private business*** | | | | | | |
| Do not wish | 57 | 53 | 61 | 56 | 52 | 56 |
| Little wish | 27 | 29 | 23 | 24 | 28 | 25 |
| Wish | 10 | 8 | 8 | 13 | 12 | 11 |
| Strong wish | 6 | 9 | 7 | 7 | 7 | 7 |
| | (657) | (182) | (459) | (1,342) | (390) | Pr=0.057 |
| ***By generation*** | | | | | | |
| *≤39 years old* | | | | | | |
| Do not wish | 53 | 42 | 59 | 57 | 51 | 54 |
| Little wish | 31 | 38 | 23 | 23 | 32 | 28 |
| Wish | 10 | 8 | 11 | 15 | 11 | 12 |
| Strong wish | 6 | 13 | 7 | 5 | 5 | 6 |
| | (280) | (88) | (121) | (416) | (154) | Pr=0.017 |
| *40–59 years old* | | | | | | |
| Do not wish | 60 | 63 | 62 | 56 | 53 | 58 |
| Little wish | 25 | 22 | 23 | 24 | 25 | 24 |
| Wish | 10 | 9 | 8 | 12 | 13 | 11 |
| Strong wish | 5 | 6 | 7 | 8 | 9 | 7 |
| | (370) | (93) | (332) | (904) | (236) | Pr=0.307 |

Source: The 1999 CASS survey.

during a fixed period (e.g. one week at the end of a month). People who worked, even if only a little, during that period are regarded as employed.

The official unemployment statistics of China are not comparable with the ILO's unemployment statistics or other unemployment rate statistics conforming to the

*Table 9.11* Migrant workers' expectations towards the next generation (%, numbers in parentheses are numbers of samples)

| | *Self-employed* | *Employed* | *Total* |
|---|---|---|---|
| *To enter college* | | | |
| Do not wish | 4 | 6 | 4 |
| Little wish | 8 | 12 | 9 |
| Wish | 13 | 9 | 11 |
| Strong wish | 76 | 73 | 75 |
| | (455) | (260) | Pr=0.133 |
| *To enter the Communist Party* | | | |
| Do not wish | 17 | 21 | 19 |
| Little wish | 30 | 28 | 29 |
| Wish | 19 | 23 | 20 |
| Strong wish | 34 | 28 | 32 |
| | (454) | (258) | Pr=0.266 |
| *To be a full-time employee of a state-owned work unit* | | | |
| Do not wish | 22 | 19 | 21 |
| Little wish | 25 | 27 | 26 |
| Wish | 19 | 23 | 21 |
| Strong wish | 34 | 31 | 33 |
| | (452) | (258) | Pr=0.454 |
| *To own a private business* | | | |
| Do not wish | 38 | 26 | 34 |
| Little wish | 24 | 27 | 25 |
| Wish | 20 | 29 | 23 |
| Strong wish | 17 | 19 | 18 |
| | (450) | (256) | Pr=0.008 |

Source: The 1999 CASS survey.

ILO's, because they are based on unemployment registration. The official register-based figure of urban unemployment rate was 3.1 per cent in 1999 and 3.6 per cent in 2001 (National Bureau of statistics 2002). This figure underestimates the reality because not all jobless urban workers are registered as 'unemployed' and because those who are of *xiagang* status are excluded by definition. Therefore, we attempt to estimate the actual unemployment rate at close to the ILO's definition.

Specifically, the number of 'unemployed' is defined as follows based on the self-reported employment status, income status and other individual attributes (e.g. age, and educational attainment):

1 Narrowest definition: only workers in the *shiye* or *daiye* (people belonging to the younger generation who finished education but are unable to find fixed jobs) status are defined as unemployed.
2 Standard definition: workers in the *shiye* and *daiye* statuses and in the *xiagang* status are defined as unemployed.

3 Broad definition: adding the case of 'early retirement' (*zaotui, neitui*), that is, workers retired before reaching the standard full retirement age, full-time homemakers who have not reached the standard full retirement age, and people with unknown employment status who had no income throughout 1999 (excluding people who could not work because of sickness, injury or physical disabilities). Full-time homemakers before the standard full retirement age (where women account for a large percentage) are added because, in the Chinese context, where the labour participation rate has been very high throughout the planned economy era, at least some of the workers on early retirement and full-time homemakers can treated in the same way as unemployed/*xiagang* workers.

The total labour force is the total number of urban residents aged 15 years or older, excluding full-time students, retired (*lituixiu*) workers who are over the standard full retirement age, homemakers, and those who are unable to work (because of physical disabilities). Workers in the *shiye*, *daiye* and *xiagang* statuses are added in cases 1 and 2 by adding the number of occupied people 15 years of age or older (including people who were re-employed after being unemployed or *xiagang*) at the end of 1999 and workers in the *shiye*, *daiye* and *xiagang* statuses. Other relevant populations (early retirement, full-time homemakers before the standard retirement age, and those who are of unknown employment status) are added in case 3.

Table 9.12 shows the result of estimating the unemployment rate for each city. The total unemployment rate of the 13 cities is 5.7 per cent according to the narrowest definition and 10.6 per cent according to the standard definition, which are considerably higher levels than the registered unemployment rate of 3.8 per cent. The unemployment rate according to the standard definition is lowest in Beijing (5.1 per cent) and highest in Zigong (22 per cent). It should be noted that large differences in unemployment rates are found among cities within the same province, for example between Shenyang and Jinzhou in Liaoning Province, as well as among Zhengzhou, Kaifeng and Pingdingshan in Henan Province. This fact suggests the regional segmentation of the urban labour market.[2]

Figure 9.3 shows the relation between annual average GDP growth rates from 1995 to 1999 and unemployment rates according to the standard definition for all the cities except Pingliang. From this figure, it is possible to observe a negative correlation between growth rate and unemployment rate. It suggests that the public enterprise reform after the mid-1990s advanced to the stage where employment adjustments to economic fluctuation were unavoidable.

### *9.5.2 Job-search channels and their outcomes*

Most of the unemployed/*xiagang* workers are engaged in job hunting, aiming to obtain stable jobs again while maintaining sources of income through temporary employment and small self-employment activities (e.g. roadside stands and repair

*Table 9.12* Estimated unemployment rate by city

| | *Registered unemployment rate (%)* | *Narrowest definition) (%)* | *Xiagang (%)* | *Standard definition (%)* | *Broad definition (%)* |
|---|---|---|---|---|---|
| Shenyang | 1.5 | 8.4 | 3.2 | 11.7 | 15.4 |
| Jinzhou | 6.1 | 7.3 | 9.3 | 16.6 | 19.7 |
| Nanjing | 2.9 | 4.3 | 1.5 | 5.8 | 12.3 |
| Xuzhou | 2.1 | 4.6 | 3.7 | 8.4 | 14.9 |
| Beijing | 0.7 | 3.7 | 1.4 | 5.1 | 10.8 |
| Zhengzhou | 2.6 | 3.8 | 7.8 | 11.6 | 19.3 |
| Kaifeng | 3.5 | 6.7 | 9.7 | 16.4 | 20.9 |
| Pingdingshan | 4.7 | 7.1 | 0.8 | 7.9 | 13.5 |
| Chengdu | 4.8 | 3.4 | 6.0 | 9.4 | 14.9 |
| Zigong | 6.9 | 10.6 | 11.4 | 22.0 | 25.7 |
| Nanchong | 6.7 | 6.9 | 3.9 | 10.8 | 15.5 |
| Lanzhou | 2.8 | 6.5 | 7.3 | 13.8 | 17.7 |
| Pingliang | — | 4.6 | 4.3 | 8.9 | 16.5 |
| Average | 3.8 | 5.7 | 4.9 | 10.6 | 15.9 |

Source: The 1999 CASS survey (General Team of Socioeconomic Survey 2001: 45–52, 332, 346).

Note: Registered unemployment rate was calculated by the author according to the following definition: Registered unemployment rate = (number of registered urban unemployed in downtown and near suburbs) / (number of employees in work units in downtown and near suburbs + number of self-employed population in downtown and near suburbs + number of registered urban unemployed in downtown and near suburbs).

businesses). In this section, we examine what kinds of channels are available for job search and what types of people select which types of channels, as well as how the possibility of re-employment and wage after re-employment relate to these job-search channels. Here, the enlarged data set that includes 500 additional samples of households with unemployed/*xiagang* workers is used to obtain a sufficient number of samples to examine the internal structure of the retrenched stratum.

The job-search channels used by unemployed and *xiagang* workers can be classified into three types: formal channels, social networks and individual job-hunting activities. Formal channels include mediation by work units to which unemployed workers used to belong (e.g. vocational guidance by re-employment service centres) and public placement agencies run by labour departments of local governments and other public organizations. Job search through a social network means introduction to jobs by family, relatives, friends and other people. Individual job-hunting activities refers to workers looking for jobs by gathering information, visiting employers and applying to advertisements entirely on an individual basis without going through formal channels or social networks; it does not refer to running one's own business.

In the 1999 CASS survey, the unemployed/*xiagang* workers were asked to choose up to two items to which they attached importance regarding a job search.

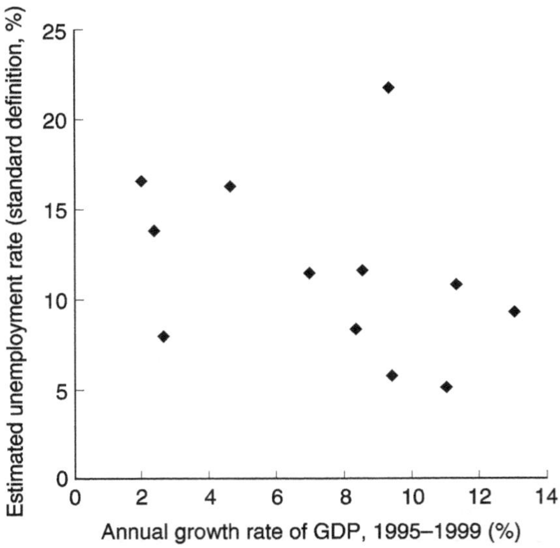


*Figure 9.3* Relationship between growth rate and unemployment rate. Source: The 1999 CASS survey.

The eight options (note that the responses regarding individual job-hunting activities are based on the subjective judgement of the subjects, which may make them difficult to distinguish strictly from the other two types of channels) were (1) mediation by the work unit to which the unemployed worker used to belong, (2) introduction by family or relatives, (3) introduction by friends, (4) mediation by placement agencies run by labour departments, (5) mediation by placement agencies run by public organizations other than labour departments, (6) searching for jobs by oneself, (7) application to advertisements (and/or taking open tests) and (8) preparing to run one's own business. Items are classified as follows: (1), (4) and (5) are formal channels, (2) and (3) are social networks, (6), (7) and (8) are individual job-hunting activities.

The distribution of each type of channel is as follows: formal channels, 22 per cent; individual job-hunting activities, 61 per cent; and social networks, 62 per cent. In general, dependence on formal channels is low compared with other channels. Moreover, the figure for mediation by the work units to which the workers used to belong is a little under 9 per cent, and most formal channels selected are public placement agencies run by labour departments or other organizations.[3]

Table 9.13 summarizes the relationship of personal attributes, work-unit attributes, regional characteristics and job-search channels. Workers who used to belong to work units with high administrative ranks (central/provincial-level, state-owned enterprises and state shareholding enterprises with a major share of state capital) tend to look for jobs exclusively through formal channels. This may mean that unemployed/*xiagang* workers have high expectations towards strong enterprises and organizations in their job search. When regional differences are examined, it is seen that the proportion of workers who rely solely on formal channels is high in Beijing. It is considered that this fact reflects the strength of the local government and enterprises. Dependence on formal channels is also high in Pingdingshan. This may be related to the fact that this city has characteristics unique to a town that grew up around enterprises specializing in coal-mining industries. On the other hand, no noticeable relations were recognized between personal attributes and job-search channels.[4]

Next, we investigated whether the choice of job-search channels has any effect on the possibility of re-employment. For this purpose, a logit analysis was attempted. The dependent variable was that either one has succeeded (= 1) or has not yet succeeded (= 0) in becoming re-employed. Four dummy variables that indicate the choice of job-search channels were used: three dummies for workers who are dependent on only one of the aforementioned three types of channels, as well as one dummy where workers are dependent on more than two types of channels. Other explanatory variables were personal attributes (gender, age, educational level, political status), unemployment duration (number of days elapsed after retrenchment), wage income before retrenchment, household structure (dependent population/population of working age), formal job training after retrenchment and city dummies.

The result is shown in Table 9.14. It was found that workers depending mainly on social networks have a higher probability of re-employment compared with workers who use various types of channels. On the other hand, workers depending mainly on formal mediations and those who have received job training, which is an important form of support provided in formal re-employment assistance, tend to have a higher probability of re-employment, but the level of significance is low. It looks as though informal social relations play greater roles in re-employment than formal assistance. Other noteworthy results include that gender is significant; women are placed at a more disadvantageous position than men, results similar to the determinants of the probability of becoming unemployed/*xiagang* discussed earlier. In contrast to gender, educational level and party membership do not influence the probability of re-employment. This may be because party members and workers with high educational levels are in higher demand for re-employment.

What kind of relation is found between job-search channels and wages after re-employment? Table 9.15 examines the wage determinants for re-employed workers. The dependent variable is the log transformation of the wage in the first month after re-employment. The following points in the results are worthy of note.

First, compared with the income determinants of urban workers in general, which were examined earlier, personal attributes clearly influence income in a different manner. The gender gap is considerably wider than among urban workers in general. Moreover, neither educational level nor political status is any longer a significant income determinant. This may be due to many of the work positions of re-employed workers being non-white-collar jobs. This fact suggests

*Table 9.13* Job-search channels of unemployed/*xiagang* workers (%, numbers in parentheses are numbers of samples)

| | *Depending on formal channel* | *Depending on individual job-hunting activities* | *Depending on social networks* | *Mixture of more than two channels* | *Total* |
|---|---|---|---|---|---|
| Total | 5 | 18 | 19 | 59 | (1,220) |
| *Gender* | | | | | |
| Female | 4 | 16 | 20 | 60 | (752) |
| Male | 5 | 20 | 18 | 57 | (468) |
| | | | | | Pr=0.245 |
| *Age* | | | | | |
| 15–19 years old | 50 | 0 | 0 | 50 | (2) |
| 20–24 years old | 3 | 31 | 7 | 59 | (29) |
| 25–29 years old | 3 | 14 | 25 | 58 | (145) |
| 30–34 years old | 3 | 13 | 16 | 67 | (181) |
| 40–44 years old | 6 | 18 | 20 | 56 | (254) |
| 45–49 years old | 4 | 17 | 17 | 62 | (282) |
| 50–54 years old | 5 | 20 | 18 | 56 | (240) |
| 55–59 years old | 4 | 19 | 21 | 56 | (73) |
| 60–64 years old | 8 | 38 | 31 | 23 | (14) |
| | | | | | Pr=0.039 |
| *Educational level* | | | | | |
| Primary school | 2 | 26 | 19 | 53 | (57) |
| Junior high school | 5 | 18 | 20 | 57 | (521) |
| Senior high school | 4 | 16 | 19 | 61 | (541) |
| Higher education | 5 | 21 | 12 | 62 | (101) |
| | | | | | Pr=0.353 |
| *Political status* | | | | | |
| Non-party member | 4 | 17 | 19 | 59 | (1,111) |
| Party member | 7 | 22 | 17 | 53 | (109) |
| | | | | | Pr=0.263 |
| *Administrative and ownership status of former work units* | | | | | |
| Central/provincial-level state-owned work unit | 9 | 11 | 15 | 65 | (156) |
| Local-level state-owned work unit | 5 | 20 | 20 | 55 | (578) |
| Urban collective-owned work unit | 2 | 16 | 20 | 61 | (366) |
| Private enterprises and mixed ownership enterprises with major share of non-state capital | 2 | 22 | 17 | 60 | (60) |
| State shareholding enterprises with major share of state capital | 12 | 8 | 12 | 69 | (26) |
| Foreign joint venture and foreign invested enterprises | 8 | 8 | 0 | 83 | (12) |
| Others | 14 | 21 | 14 | 50 | (14) |
| | | | | | Pr=0.007 |

*Table 9.13* (Continued)

| | *Depending on formal channel* | *Depending on individual job-hunting activities* | *Depending on social networks* | *Mixture of more than two channels* | *Total* |
|---|---|---|---|---|---|
| *City* | | | | | |
| Shenyang | 6 | 24 | 17 | 53 | (104) |
| Jinzhou | 5 | 27 | 19 | 50 | (108) |
| Nanjing | 4 | 22 | 21 | 53 | (95) |
| Xuzhou | 1 | 24 | 24 | 51 | (83) |
| Beijing | 10 | 11 | 21 | 58 | (151) |
| Zhengzhou | 2 | 18 | 15 | 66 | (61) |
| Kaifeng | 2 | 19 | 17 | 62 | (89) |
| Pingdingshan | 10 | 12 | 12 | 65 | (49) |
| Chengdu | 2 | 12 | 18 | 68 | (121) |
| Zigong | 2 | 11 | 30 | 57 | (61) |
| Nanchong | 2 | 13 | 30 | 54 | (82) |
| Lanzhou | 5 | 16 | 14 | 65 | (133) |
| Pingliang | 7 | 17 | 8 | 67 | (83) |
| | | | | | Pr=0.000 |

Source: The 1999 CASS survey (additional samples of unemployed/*xiagang* workers were included).

Note: Samples of which unemployment duration is more than eight years were excluded.

that waste of human capital occurs during the process of unemployment and re-employment.

Second, among the job-search channels, it is significant that those who depend mainly on social networks tend to earn less than others. It seems that social networks improve the probability of re-employment, but the jobs obtained in this manner tend to yield low wages.

Third, formal job training has no positive and significant influence on one's wage after re-employment. Although most (about 70 per cent) of the workers in the retrenched stratum who have received some kind of job training responded that training helps (or helped) in re-employment regardless of whether they succeeded in obtaining re-employment, this training did not lead to higher wages after re-employment. This fact indicates that there are limitations to the effectiveness of formal job-training systems.

Lastly, we examine how the workers in the retrenched stratum evaluate the re-employment assistance given to them by government and the work units to which they used to belong. On the whole, their evaluation is low, which reflects the actual conditions of the job-search activities and the conditions of re-employment. The percentage of workers who felt that the re-employment assistance provided by former work units was a help is only 6 per cent among those currently unemployed/*xiagang* and 12 per cent among those re-employed. The proportion of positive responses regarding assistance provided by the government is 9 per cent among workers who are currently unemployed/*xiagang*, and 12 per cent among

*Table 9.14* Job-search channels and probability of re-employment

| | *Odds ratio* | *z* |
|---|---|---|
| Gender (male/female) | 1.440 | 2.60** |
| 20–24 years old | 0.991 | −0.02 |
| 25–29 years old | 0.529 | −2.61** |
| 30–34 years old | 0.935 | −0.30 |
| 40–44 years old | 0.945 | −0.28 |
| 45–49 years old | 0.867 | −0.66 |
| 50–54 years old | 0.729 | −1.01 |
| 55–59 years old | 0.976 | −0.04 |
| Higher education | 1.109 | 0.40 |
| Senior high school level | 1.054 | 0.35 |
| Primary school or less | 1.730 | 1.73 |
| Political status (party member/non-member) | 1.310 | 1.11 |
| Number of days unemployed/*xiagang* | 0.933 | −7.16** |
| Number of days unemployed/*xiagang* (squared) | 1.001 | 4.68** |
| Wage before retrenchment (yuan) | 0.999 | −3.21** |
| Household structure (dependent population/population of working age) | 0.952 | −0.14 |
| Having experiences of formal job training | 1.503 | 1.87 |
| Depending on formal channel | 1.601 | 1.49 |
| Depending on individual job-hunting activities | 1.175 | 0.91 |
| Depending on social networks | 2.281 | 4.80** |
| Shenyang | 0.448 | −2.54* |
| Jinzhou | 1.326 | 0.89 |
| Xuzhou | 0.661 | −1.23 |
| Beijing | 0.373 | −3.35** |
| Zhengzhou | 0.286 | −3.23** |
| Kaifeng | 0.575 | −1.65 |
| Pingdingshan | 0.079 | −4.97** |
| Chengdu | 0.265 | −4.23** |
| Zigong | 0.212 | −4.00** |
| Nanchong | 0.270 | −3.78** |
| Lanzhou | 0.368 | −3.31** |
| Pingliang | 0.595 | −1.55 |
| Pseudo-$R^2$ | 0.136 | |
| No. of observation | 1,212 | |

Source: The 1999 CASS survey.

Note: The dependent variable is that one has succeeded (=1) or not yet succeeded (=0) in re-employment. Additional samples of unemployed/*xiagang* workers were included. Omitted dummy variables are 35–39 years old, junior high school level, combining more than two job search channels, and Nanjing. ** denotes statistical significance at the 1% level, * at the 5% level.

workers who were re-employed. That is, they evaluate the government higher than the former work units, an opinion supported by the fact that the government plays a greater role than former work units in the utilization of formal job-search channels. Furthermore, when workers who are currently unemployed/*xiagang* and workers who are re-employed are compared, the latter group's evaluation is higher, which also makes sense.

*Table 9.15* Determinants of wage after re-employment

| | *Coefficient* | *t* |
|---|---|---|
| Gender (male/female) | 0.274 | 6.04** |
| 20–24 years old | −0.077 | −0.55 |
| 25–29 years old | −0.017 | −0.19 |
| 30–34 years old | −0.168 | −2.21* |
| 40–44 years old | −0.062 | −0.94 |
| 45–49 years old | −0.020 | −0.27 |
| 50–54 years old | −0.160 | −1.54 |
| 55–59 years old | −0.043 | −0.23 |
| Higher education | 0.087 | 0.99 |
| Senior high school level | 0.085 | 1.65 |
| Primary school or less | 0.056 | 0.57 |
| Political status (party member/non-member) | −0.091 | −1.13 |
| Having experiences of formal job training | 0.022 | 0.30 |
| Depending on formal channel | −0.067 | −0.68 |
| Depending on individual job-hunting activities | −0.064 | −1.05 |
| Depending on social networks | −0.112 | −2.08* |
| Shenyang | 0.148 | 1.39 |
| Jinzhou | 0.116 | 1.29 |
| Xuzhou | 0.199 | 1.97 |
| Beijing | 0.223 | 2.36* |
| Zhengzhou | 0.051 | 0.36 |
| Kaifeng | −0.017 | −0.16 |
| Pingdingshan | −0.178 | −0.90 |
| Chengdu | 0.102 | 1.00 |
| Zigong | −0.215 | −1.51 |
| Nanchong | −0.031 | −0.29 |
| Lanzhou | 0.176 | 1.78 |
| Pingliang | −0.252 | −2.46* |
| Constant | 5.824 | 59.02** |
| Average wage in the first month after re-employment (yuan) | 430 | |
| Adjusted $R^2$ | 0.124 | |
| No. of observation | 424 | |

Source: The 1999 CASS survey.

Note: The dependent variable is the log transformation of the wage in the first month after re-employment. Additional samples of unemployed/*xiagang* workers were included. Omitted dummy variables are 35–39 years old, junior high school level, combining more than two job-search channels, and Nanjing. ** denotes statistical significance at the 1% level, * at the 5% level.

## 9.6 Conclusion

This chapter stratified people working in urban areas using two indicators – economic status and the degree of marketization in labour-market-related issues – to describe the hierarchical structure of the emerging urban labour market. Both objective and subjective aspects were discussed.

As for the objective aspects, it was suggested throughout this chapter that the formation of a labour market is not simple and straightforward, but a complicated series of processes involving different vectors. First, in the urban society as a whole, egalitarianism began disappearing along with the marketization of labour relations in the 1990s. When the six strata were compared, intra-stratum wage income inequality was larger among the strata in which the market mechanisms had penetrated further. The collapse of egalitarianism paralleled the breakdown of the Maoist legacy of 'anti-meritocracy'. Observing both situations by stratum, it was confirmed that the effect of educational attainment on wage income was strongest in the non-public stratum. It was also shown that the effect of educational attainment became stronger in 1999 compared with 1988. Second, unlike educational attainment, political status has a complicated relation to wage income, a fact that reflects the characteristics of systemic transition in China where marketization progresses under the single-party system. The analysis by stratum in 1999 indicated that political status had no significant effect on wage income in the non-public stratum. In the public strata, however, the positive premium of political status on wage income in 1999 became slightly greater or was at least maintained compared with that in 1988. In conjunction with this, it was found that political status had a highly significant effect in avoiding the risk of unemployment. Third, the significance of administrative rank of work units on income and stability of employment has not weakened. The socialist 'work unit' surely has been changing its characteristics, as do 'firms' in a market economy. However, it would not be appropriate to resolve the employment and income-related disparities among the work units of different administrative ranks simply by pointing to firm size or firm profitability. In the systemic transition under the single-party system, there still exists the strong government–industry complex at the local level, and selective policy arrangements are used according to the administrative ranks of the work units.

Concerning the subjective aspects, it was shown that people's perceptions of the hierarchical structure of the labour market were consistent with the objective structure. First, as for the urban workers' perception of income determinants (educational level and political status), differences among strata that were consistent with the objective evidence were found. When the expectations for the next generation were examined, lower expectations regarding becoming a party member were found among the younger urban workers and among those who belong to the non-public stratum, whereas the reverse was found in the expectation for higher educational attainment among the next generation. It was also found that those who were marginalized within the public sector tend to have a stronger yearning for stable employment in the public sector, whereas those in the non-public sector, especially among the younger generation, tend to have a positive evaluation of the non-public sector.

It was shown that formal assistance for unemployed/*xiagang* workers was weak and ineffective. Urban workers' expectations for formal re-employment assistance were very low. Most of the retrenched stratum was trying to gain re-employment by using informal job-search channels. Only a few workers relied mainly on formal job-search channels. Job search through social networks makes re-employment easier, but wages thus obtained tend to be lower. These results suggest that there are certain limitations to job-search activities based on informal information within a narrow range and that the role of public job mediation should be enhanced.

This chapter put 'settled' migrant workers into the analyses and compared them with urban workers. When wage levels were compared directly, the differences between the re-employed urban workers and migrant workers were not so large, and both of these strata formed the peripheral and low-income strata in the urban labour market. However, when the aspects of housing and social security were taken into account, there was still a large gap between them. When the migrant workers' expectations for the next generation were observed, two themes were found: strong yearnings for stable employment in the public sector, symbolic of the legacy of work-unit socialism, and a great desire for success as private business owners, symbolic of new economic opportunities opened by marketization.

## Notes

The author is grateful to the Ford Foundation, the Masayoshi Ohira Memorial Foundation, the Grant in Aid for Scientific Research (the Japan Society for the Promotion of Science) and the Graduate School of Economics, Hitotsubashi University, for their financial support.

1 Studies using other data sets show similar results; Bian and Logan (1996), for example, reached a similar conclusion in their study, in which wage income functions of individuals were measured for four different years (1978, 1983, 1988 and 1993) before and after the economic reforms using data from Tianjin.

2 Although it is not perfectly conclusive that the average unemployment rate of the survey area is representative of that of all urban areas in China, considering earlier studies we can say that the rate (about 10 per cent on average) is as adequate estimation (see Marukawa 2002).

3 A similar fact was found by the sample survey conducted by the China Federation of Trade Unions (*Zhonghua Quanguo Zonggonghui*) in 1999, which covered about 560 samples in 11 cities. About 36 per cent of the people found their new jobs through introduction by relatives and friends, 32 per cent were self-employed, 8 per cent found jobs through introduction by their former work units, 3 per cent found jobs through the labour department of local government, 10 per cent found jobs through the administrative units at the community level (*jiedao, jumin weiyuanhui*), 2 per cent found jobs through private job placement institutions, and 9 per cent found jobs through other channels (Zhonghua Quanguo Zonggonghui Zhengce Yanjiushi 2001).

4 As opposed to this, the above-mentioned survey of the China Federation of Trade Unions shows that people who are at a more disadvantageous position in the labour market in terms of personal attributes (female, non-party member, low educational level) tend to rely more on formal channels in job-search processes (Zhonghua Quanguo Zonggonghui Zhengce Yanjiushi 2001: 153–4). This result is not consistent with the discussion here. One possible interpretation is that the result is biased because the subjects of the survey were unemployed and *xiagang* workers who are traced by labour organizations (or the subjects were former employees of leading enterprises with labour organizations that are able to conduct follow-up checks of unemployed and *xiagang* workers). Whether this interpretation is enough to explain the inconsistency will be reserved for future study.

## References

Bian, Y. and Logan, J.R. (1996) 'Market transition and the persistence of power: the changing stratification system in urban China', *American Sociological Review,* 61: 739–58.

General Team of Urban Socioeconomic Survey, National Bureau of Statistics (Guojia Tongjiju Chengshi Shehui Jingji Diaocha Zongdui) (ed.) (2001) *Zhongguo Chengshi Tongji Nianjian* (Urban Statistical Yearbook of China) Beijing: China Statistics Press.

Knight, J. and Song, L. (1999) *The Rural–Urban Divide: Economic Disparities and Interactions in China*, Oxford: Oxford University Press.

Knight, J. and Song, L. (2001) 'Economic growth, economic reform, and rising inequality in China', in Riskin, C., Zhao, R. and Li, S. (eds), *China's Retreat from Equality: Income Distribution and Economic Transition*, Armonk, NY: M.E. Sharpe.

Lai, D. (1999) 'Jiaoyu, laodongli shichang yu shouru fenpei' (Education, labour market, and the household income distribution), in Zhao, R., Li, S. and Riskin, C. (eds), *Zhongguo Jumin Shourufenpei Zaiyanjiu* (Re-examination of the Household Income Distribution in China), Beijing: Public Finance and Economy Press (Zhongguo Caizheng Jingji Chubanshe).

Li, L. (1998) *Zhuanxing Shehuizhong de Siying Qiyezhu: Shehui Laiyuan ji Qiye Fazhan Yanjiu* (Private Entrepreneur in the Transitional Society), Beijing: People's University Press (Zhongguo Renmin Daxue Chubanshe).

Li, S. and Li, W. (1994) 'Zhongguo jiaoyu touzi de geren shouyilü de gusuan' (An estimation of the rate of individual return of investment on education in China), in Zhao, R. and Griffin, K. (eds), *Zhongguo Jumin Shouru Fenpei Yanjiu* (A Study on Household Income Distribution in China), Beijing: Social Sciences Press (Zhongguo Shehui Kexue Chubanshe).

Liu, J. (2000) *Danwei Zhongguo: Shehui Tiaokong Tixi Chonggou zhong de Geren Zuzhi yu Guojia* (China's Work Units), Tianjin: Tianjin People's Press (Tianjin Renmin Chubanshe).

Lü, X. and Perry, E.J. (eds) (1997) *Danwei: The Changing Chinese Workplace in Historical and Comparative Perspective*, Armonk, NY: M.E. Sharpe.

Marukawa, T. (2002) *Roudoushijou no Chikakuhendou* (Structural Change in the Labour Market) (in Japanese), Nagoya: University of Nagoya Press.

Nakagane, K. (2002) *Keizaihatten to Taiseiikou* (Economic Development and Transition in China) (in Japanese), Nagoya: University of Nagoya Press.

National Bureau of Statistics (ed.) (2002) *China Statistical Yearbook 2001,* Beijing: China Statitics Press.

Naughton, B. (1999) 'China's transition in economic perspective', in Goldman, M. and Macfarquhar, R. (eds), *The Paradox of China's Post-Mao Reforms*, Cambridge, MA: Harvard University Press.

Sato, H. (2003) *The Growth of Market Relations in Post-reform Rural China: A Micro-analysis of Peasants, Migrants and Peasant Entrepreneurs*, London: RoutledgeCurzon.

Walder, A.G. (2001) 'Rural cadres and the market economy in the Deng era: evidence from a national survey', in Wong, J. and Zheng, Y. (eds), *The Nanxun Legacy and China's Development in the Post-Deng Era*, Singapore: World Scientific.

Wang, Q., Zhang, W. and Jiang, H. (1999) *Chengshi Jumin de Shenghuo Shiijian Fenpei* (Time Allocation of Urban Residents), Beijing: Economic Science Press (Jingji Kexue Chubanshe).

Womack, B. (1991) 'Transfigured community: neo-traditionalism and work unit socialism in China', *The China Quarterly*, 126: 313–32.

Yang, D.T. and Zhou, H. (1999) 'Rural–urban disparity and sectoral labour allocation in China', *Journal of Development Studies,* 35: 105–33.

Zhonghua Quanguo Zonggonghui Zhengce Yanjiushi (Policy Research Office, All China Federation of Trade Unions) (ed.) (2001) *Zhongguo Feizhenggui Bumen yu Feizhenggui Jiuye Wenti* (Informal Sector and Informal Employment in China), Beijing: All China Federation of Trade Unions (Zhonghua Quanguo Zonggonghui).

# 10 Contrasting paradigms

## Segmentation and competitiveness in the formation of the Chinese labour market

*Simon Appleton, John Knight, Lina Song and Qingjie Xia*

### 10.1 Introduction

A labour market is in the process of formation and transition in urban China. Prior to the urban economic reforms since the mid-1980s, there was virtually no labour market. The great majority of urban workers were employed in state-owned enterprises (SOEs) and in urban collective enterprises; employment policies ensured that urban unemployment remained negligible; workers were allocated to work units, remaining with the same work unit throughout their working lives. Wages were institutionally determined according to a national system of grades and scales; seniority was important to pay, whereas education and skill were little rewarded (Knight and Song 1993: 221–39).

Labour market reform was initially limited and tardy but gained pace over the 1990s. The system of lifetime employment was ended for all workers recruited after 1984, although this made little difference until labour retrenchment became an important issue (Knight and Song 2003). It was only from the mid-1990s, however, that government seriously tackled the problem of SOE inefficiency, in particular overmanning; it introduced a radical programme of labour retrenchment. Rural–urban migration was increasingly permitted; the liberation of controls on movement to the cities created a great influx of migrants. These two dramatic changes – retrenchment and migration – shook the labour market and introduced potential competition among workers.

There are two entirely different perspectives on the consequences of these developments: one that they will create a more competitive labour market, the other that they will create a more segmented one. On the first view, the availability of migrants prepared to work at low wages provides potential competition for urban residents. Retrenchment creates an opportunity for firms to renegotiate old contracts, both formal and implicit, and may force urban residents to compete with migrants for work. On the alternative view, these developments simply create a three-tier labour market. Urban residents who keep their jobs may continue to be employed on preferential terms and retrenched urban workers may suffer prolonged unemployment or enter a secondary labour market. The retrenchment policy and the consequent rise in urban unemployment has led to tighter controls on migrants, aimed at restricting their numbers and in this way assisting the laid off.

Did the Chinese labour market become more competitive as a result of the labour market reforms? Competition should have narrowed the wage differences among equally productive workers. In an idealized setting of perfect competition, one would expect the 'law of one price' to hold. Earlier studies of the labour market in the mid-1990s, just prior to the redundancy policy, found clear evidence of segmentation. Knight and Song (1999a, 1999b), analysing a survey of workers in urban enterprises relating to 1995, found sharp segmentation between urban residents and rural migrants. This arose from the political and institutional arrangements that gave urban residents privileged access to secure employment at above market-clearing wages and that controlled the flow of peasants to the cities, allowing rural migrants to fill only the jobs that urban dwellers did not want. Production function analysis showed that the wage of urban residents exceeded their marginal product, implying the existence of surplus labour in the enterprises, whereas the wage of migrants fell short of their marginal product, reflecting government restrictions on their recruitment. Meng and Zhang (2001) also concluded that there was a two-tier labour market in urban China, with urban residents favoured over rural–urban migrants. However, analysing more recent data for 1999, Dong and Bowles (2002) found no significant differences among firms of different ownership category in the returns to human capital. This may be consistent with a degree of competition in the urban labour market across ownership categories.

To test this, this chapter compares wage functions across categories of labour rather than across categories of firm. Specifically, we compare wage structures across three groups of workers: non-retrenched urban workers, retrenched and re-employed workers, and rural–urban migrants. Are there wage differences among workers who share the same economic characteristics? Are rural–urban migrants still at a wage disadvantage by comparison with urban residents, i.e. is there an unexplained wage difference between these two groups? Do the wages of those urban residents who retained their jobs exceed the wages of those who were made redundant and had to find new jobs? Have the laid-off workers been forced into competition with migrants, or is there an unexplained wage difference between them?

Section 10.2 outlines the methods that will be used to compare the three tiers of the labour market, describes the data set available, and explains the econometric issues that arise. Section 10.3 tests for differences in the wage functions for the three groups of workers. Section 10.4 uses the wage functions to conduct simulations in order to compare wages across groups of workers, standardizing for differences in their observed characteristics. Section 10.5 uses the panel element in the data to examine changes in wages over time and to estimate the impact of re-employment on wages. Section 10.6 concludes.

## 10.2 Methods

### *10.2.1 Data*

The main data source for this chapter is the 1999 CASS survey. From the survey, we focused on three categories of worker:

1 *Non-retrenched urban workers*: residents with urban *hukous* who are both currently employed and have not been laid off since 1992.[1]
2 *Re-employed urban workers*: urban residents with urban *hukous* who had been retrenched since 1992 but were employed when the survey was conducted.
3 *Rural–urban migrants*: those working in the city without urban *hukous*.

Of the workers in our sample, 5,770 are non-retrenched urban workers, 433 are re-employed and 1,065 are rural-urban migrants. There are also 726 urban workers who have been retrenched since 1992 but were unemployed at the time of the survey. We use this fourth category of worker in controlling for the selectivity of retrenchment and re-employment. We use recall data on pre-retrenchment earnings to estimate historic wage functions for retrenched workers (the unemployed and re-employed).

Table 10.1 provides a description of the different groups. Non-retrenched urban workers are the most educated group, with an average of 11.4 years of education compared to 10.0 years for the re-employed workers and 8.2 years for the migrants. Re-employed workers tend to be older, averaging 23.5 years of potential work experience (years since completing full-time education) compared to 21.8 years for the non-retrenched workers and only 18.4 years for the migrants. Women account for a higher proportion of the unemployed (64 per cent) and re-employed (56 per cent) groups than of the non-retrenched urban workers (43 per cent) and migrant groups (41 per cent). Re-employed workers also include fewer Communist Party members (proportionately, a third as many as are in the non-retrenched group; even fewer migrants are party members). Re-employed urban workers are more likely to work in urban collectively owned enterprises and less likely to be employed in centrally controlled SOEs than non-retrenched workers. They are also more concentrated in lower-paid occupations, a greater proportion being industrial, commercial and service workers. Migrants are less dependent on SOEs for employment – over half report being self-employed (the 'urban individual' ownership classification).

### *10.2.2 Identifying three tiers of the urban labour market*

We investigate whether the labour market in urban China contains three tiers, corresponding to the institutional arrangements that three categories of worker face and their consequent openness to the forces of labour market competition. We hypothesize that the top tier comprises workers with urban *hukous* who have not been retrenched. Rural–urban migrants are commonly regarded as forming a

*Table 10.1* Descriptive statistics: means and percentages by type of worker

| | *(1) Non-retrenched urban worker* | *(2) Retrenched urban worker* | *(3) Of (2), still unemployed* | *(4) Of (2), re-employed* | *(5) Rural-urban migrant* |
|---|---|---|---|---|---|
| No. of observations | 5,770 | 1,159 | 726 | 433 | 1,065 |
| Wages (yuan per eight-hour period of work) | 33.49 | 17.24* | — | 25.17 | 24.84 |
| | (27.13) | (8.51) | | (20.43) | (55.84) |
| Median wage | 29.55 | 15.70 | | 19.32 | 16.00 |
| Log wage | 3.340 | 2.718 | | 3.009 | 2.824 |
| Male (%) | 56.8 | 38.7 | 35.5 | 43.9 | 59.2 |
| Potential work experience (in years) | 21.8 | 20.9 | 20.8 | 23.5 | 18.4 |
| | (9.83) | (8.55) | (8.70) | (8.29) | (9.37) |
| Education (in years) | 11.4 | 9.96 | 9.94 | 9.98 | 8.2 |
| | (2.7) | (2.2) | (2.29) | (2.2) | (2.81) |
| Ethnic minority (%) | 3.9 | 4.4 | 3.4 | 6.0 | 6.1 |
| Party membership (%) | 28.8 | 9.3 | 8.5 | 10.6 | 2.4 |
| Poor health (%) | 3.8 | 8.4 | 9.9 | 5.8 | 1.6 |
| *Ownership (%)* | | | | | |
| State-owned, central government | 36.8 | 12.1 | 13.8 | 12.0 | 4.3 |
| State-owned, local government | 40.9 | 47.8 | 46.1 | 44.1 | 6.0 |
| Urban collective | 9.9 | 31.1 | 31.1 | 27.0 | 6.2 |
| Urban private | 1.1 | 1.1 | 1.1 | 2.1 | 9.0 |
| Urban individual | 3.0 | 2.2 | 2.2 | 8.3 | 51.7 |
| Joint venture and foreign investment | 2.2 | 0.6 | 0.8 | 0.2 | 0.8 |
| Listed firms with majority state shares | 2.4 | 2.2 | 2.1 | 1.6 | 1.0 |
| Other shareholding | 1.8 | 0.8 | 0.8 | 1.4 | 1.9 |
| Rural private business or individual | 0.1 | 0.1 | 0.0 | 0.2 | 14.4 |
| Other | 1.3 | 1.2 | 1.2 | 2.3 | 4.0 |
| *Occupation (%)* | | | | | |
| Professional or technical | 23.2 | 9.5 | 10.1 | 9.7 | 3.8 |
| Administrative | 13.5 | 4.5 | 4.3 | 4.8 | 42.9 |
| Clerical | 18.4 | 8.5 | 8.1 | 10.6 | 4.3 |
| Industrial worker | 33.0 | 59.1 | 57.7 | 55.9 | 6.2 |
| Commercial staff | 5.1 | 9.2 | 10.6 | 9.0 | 8.3 |
| Service worker | 4.9 | 7.3 | 7.6 | 6.5 | 25.9 |
| Others | 1.5 | 1.6 | 1.4 | 2.1 | 8.4 |
| *City (%)* | | | | | |
| Beijing | 15.3 | 10.4 | 11.4 | 8.5 | 13.3 |
| Shenyang, Liaoning | 11.9 | 7.8 | 7.3 | 8.5 | 10.1 |
| Jinzhou, Liaoning | 4.8 | 10.2 | 5.1 | 18.7 | 7.4 |
| Nanjing, Jiangsu | 10.6 | 7.9 | 5.1 | 12.5 | 10.0 |
| Xuzhou, Jiangsu | 5.0 | 6.9 | 5.8 | 8.8 | 6.7 |

(Continued)

*Table 10.1* (Continued)

| | *(1) Non-retrenched urban worker* | *(2) Retrenched urban worker* | *(3) Of (2), still unemployed* | *(4) Of (2), re-employed* | *(5) Rural-urban migrant* |
|---|---|---|---|---|---|
| Zhengzhou, Henan | 7.3 | 5.3 | 6.3 | 3.5 | 4.0 |
| Kaifeng, Henan | 4.4 | 6.1 | 8.0 | 3.0 | 5.8 |
| Pingdingshan, Henan | 6.2 | 3.7 | 5.4 | 0.9 | 7.5 |
| Chengdu, Sichuan | 10.1 | 10.1 | 11.4 | 7.9 | 8.6 |
| Zigong, Sichuan | 4.6 | 7.1 | 9.5 | 3.0 | 6.8 |
| Nanchong, Sichuan | 5.1 | 6.6 | 6.6 | 6.5 | 6.9 |
| Lanzhou, Gansu | 9.5 | 11.0 | 11.8 | 9.7 | 6.2 |
| Pingliang, Gansu | 5.1 | 7.1 | 6.2 | 8.5 | 6.6 |

Source for this and all subsequent tables: The 1999 CASS Survey.

Notes:

1 * denotes wages in previous job, updated to allow for price inflation.

2 Standard deviations for continuous variables in parentheses.

3 Occupation and ownership sector for retrenched and for unemployed workers (columns 2 and 3) are those of their previous jobs (before retrenchment). For the re-employed, they are the characteristics of the new jobs (after re-employment).

lower tier. The segmentation between urban workers and migrants is partly the result of explicit government intervention. The government restricts access to certain occupations in the state sector to those with urban *hukous*. These occupations include those in the civil service, in banking, security and many other walks of life. Even in the private sector, the government discriminates against migrants, regulating the number of migrants who can be recruited or charging employers fees for employing migrants.

The institutional distinction between re-employed urban workers and non-retrenched urban workers is not as sharp as that between urban workers and migrants. Non-retrenched urban workers no longer have job security for life and risk losing their jobs in the future. However, it may be that they are still 'insiders' in the labour market, by virtue of having retained the posts they held prior to the retrenchment policy and of being employed on rather different wage contracts from the re-employed. Retrenchment may lower wages, even if re-employed workers do not operate in a different 'segment' of the labour market. There is an empirical literature on displaced workers in the US, the UK, Germany and elsewhere showing that displaced workers normally experience earnings losses after being retrenched and re-employed, and that these losses can last for many years (Gregory and Jukes 2002; Nickell, Jones and Quintini 2002). Many hypotheses for this phenomenon have been proposed (Fallick 1996). For example, individuals who are retrenched may have lost their firm-specific human capital by the time they are re-employed, they may also have lost some of their general labour market experience, and re-employment may have involved poorer matching of workers to jobs.[2]

It is not clear a priori what one should expect about the wages of migrants relative to those of re-employed urban workers. On the one hand, institutional factors favour the re-employed. They benefit from the labour market restrictions imposed on migrants that we noted above. Moreover, since 1997, the Chinese government has instructed local agencies to give priority to laid-off urban workers in allocating vacant jobs. On the other hand, migrants have not experienced the 'scarring' effect of retrenchment that has been much discussed in the empirical literature on OECD countries. Migrants may be more established in their current jobs, both because we focus on rural migrants who have established urban households – the more settled migrants – and because mass retrenchment of urban workers is a recent phenomenon.

Our first approach to investigating the existence of a three-tier labour market is to see whether wage structures differ across the three different groups of workers. In an idealized, perfectly competitive, labour market, wages should be identical for identical workers. For example, consider education. If the returns to education are high for one group but low for another, this suggests that the two groups are paid according to different wage structures and that at least one segment of the labour market is not competitive. However, equal returns to education alone do not ensure that wage differences are eliminated. Consider the wage function:

$$\ln W_{ji} = \beta_j' X_i + \varepsilon_{ji} \tag{10.1}$$

where $X$ is a vector of explanatory variables and $\beta_j$ the corresponding coefficients, which vary by group $j$ ($j = 1, 2, 3$: migrants, non-retrenched and re-employed urban workers). The first approach to investigating labour market segmentation, therefore, is to test whether the coefficients, $\beta_j$, in wage functions are similar across groups. This is conducted in Section 10.3, where we present the wage functions.

The information in the wage functions can be summarized by a more aggregative comparison: whether the wages of different groups of worker are the same when standardized for personal characteristics. If all workers face an identical set of coefficients, pay will be identical across comparable workers. However, we cannot expect perfection. Comparing standardized wages provides summary information about the extent to which differences in wage structure favour or disfavour particular groups of worker. This second investigation is conducted in Section 10.4.

Up to this point, we have relied on cross-sectional comparisons of wages. However, for urban residents (not migrants), we also have recall data on wages, making it possible to construct a short panel from 1995 to 1999. The panel data can show how wage structures have evolved during this period of labour market reform and mass redundancies in the state sector. We are interested in whether the returns to productive characteristics, such as education, have increased and whether the returns to characteristics less clearly related to productivity – such as membership of the Communist Party – have decreased. Such trends would be consistent with increased labour market competitiveness, although they are consistent with other explanations. Moreover, the panel data permit us to estimate the effect of retrenchment and subsequent re-employment on individual workers' earnings, controlling for the unobserved time-invariant characteristics of workers. One problem with cross-sectional comparisons is that it is possible that wages may appear to differ between different groups of workers because they differ in their unobserved personal characteristics (e.g. 'ability' or 'effort'). We test and reject this hypothesis using standard techniques to control for sample selectivity in cross-sectional data, but arguably estimates using panel data are a better means of overcoming this problem. The panel data estimates are presented in Section 10.5.

### *10.2.3 Econometric specification*

Our main focus is on the determinants of wages for the different categories of worker. We estimate semi-logarithmic functions for wages of the form given in equation (10.1) separately for each category. The dependent variable is the log of wage per eight-hour period of work.

One econometric issue in the estimation of separate wage functions for different subgroups of workers is possible sample selectivity bias. The subgroups might differ in characteristics that we do not observe in the surveys, and not controlling for these differences might bias our estimates of the effects of observed explanatory variables. We were able to test for possible sample selectivity among urban workers using Lee's (1983) two-stage method. In the first stage, we estimated a multinomial logit model for the probability of an urban resident being in one of three categories of workers: non-retrenched; retrenched and still unemployed in 1999; and retrenched and re-employed by 1999. In the second stage, we augmented the wage function with a sample selectivity correction, $\lambda_{ji}$, derived from the probability, $P_{ij}$, of a worker $i$ being in group $j$ predicted by the multinomial logit:

$$\lambda_{ji} = \varphi(h_{ij})/\Phi(h_{ij}) \text{ and } h_{ij} = \Phi^{-1}(P_{ij}) \qquad (10.2)$$

where $\varphi(.)$ and $\Phi(.)$ are the density and cumulative distribution functions respectively of the standard normal distribution.[3]

A key methodological issue in correcting for selectivity is identification: there needed to be variables in the multinomial logit that would not be included in wage functions. Among the identifying instruments we used were variables for the demographic composition of the household. A priori, these should primarily affect re-employment (via labour supply decisions) rather than wages. It is harder to conceive of variables that affect retrenchment and not wages directly. However, the government had undertaken to try to avoid dismissing both wage-earners in the same household. Consequently, one plausible instrument is a dummy variable for whether a SOE worker had a spouse who had been retrenched from a SOE. We would expect this dummy to have a negative effect on the probability of being retrenched. Having conceived of a number of instruments that appeared valid on a priori grounds, we then tested their validity empirically. Specifically, we tested whether they were collectively significant in the multinomial logit and whether they passed a test for over-identifying instruments (Deaton 1997: 112). We were able to find four instruments that passed both tests. Appendix 10.A reports the definitions of these variables, the statistics for the tests applied on them, and also the resulting estimates of the Lee (1983) selectivity correction terms.

The main conclusion of this work on selectivity corrections was that, despite having instruments for our selectivity corrections that were satisfactory on both a priori and empirical grounds, we could not reject the hypothesis that there was no selectivity bias in any of our wage functions. The coefficients on the selectivity corrections reported are all insignificant at the 10 per cent level. This implies that there are no significant correlations between the unobserved factors that determine wages and those that determine whether workers are retrenched or re-employed. Consequently, in what follows we rely on OLS estimates of the wage functions, since these are more precise. We should note in passing the unexpected signs of the estimated selectivity corrections. The negative sign on the selectivity correction for non-retrenched workers implies that there is a negative correlation between the unobserved factors that determine whether a worker is non-retrenched and those that determine wages. Conversely, the selectivity correction for the wage function for re-employed retrenched workers is positive.

One might expect that having unobserved characteristics that are unfavourable for wages – perhaps low 'ability' or employment in an unprofitable firm – might increase the risk of retrenchment, whereas our results, if anything, imply the opposite.[4] One need not read too much into these results, since they are not statistically significant. However, they do strengthen the conclusion that we subsequently reach, based on OLS results, that non-retrenched workers receive higher wages standardizing for their characteristics than do re-employed workers. If there is any selectivity bias, the signs on our selectivity corrections suggest that the bias will reinforce this conclusion rather than undermine it. Compared to re-employed retrenched workers, non-retrenched workers appear to have rather less favourable unobserved characteristics and hence such characteristics cannot explain the higher standardized wages they appear to receive.

## 10.3 Wage functions for different types of workers

We estimated wage functions separately for non-retrenched urban workers, re-employed urban workers and migrants. We also estimated a wage function for all retrenched workers (whether re-employed or not) based on their wages prior to retrenchment. As noted previously, two types of wage function are reported: a relatively parsimonious Mincerian specification (Mincer 1974) (Table 10.2) and a fuller specification including controls for ownership sector and occupation (results are not reported owing to space limitations). According to Breusch–Pagan tests, the wage functions exhibit heteroscedasticity, so we use White's heteroscedastic-consistent standard errors.

*Table 10.2* Mincerian wage functions (focus on human capital variables)

| | *Non-retrenched urban workers* | | *Re-employed urban workers* | | *Retrenched urban workers (historic earnings)* | | *Migrants* | |
|---|---|---|---|---|---|---|---|---|
| | *Coefficient* | *t-ratio* | *Coefficient* | *t-ratio* | *Coefficient* | *t-ratio* | *Coefficient* | *t-ratio* |
| Constant | 2.445 | 43.79*** | 2.452 | 9.07*** | 2.290 | 12.09*** | 2.244 | 15.34*** |
| Male | 0.149 | 10.45*** | 0.327 | 5.56***+++ | 0.073 | 2.30** | 0.232 | 5.52***+ |
| Education (in years) | 0.060 | 20.61*** | 0.017 | 1.20+++^^ | 0.031 | 3.62*** | 0.056 | 5.73*** |
| Experience (in years) | 0.036 | 11.67*** | 0.048 | 3.68*** | 0.014 | 1.41 | 0.027 | 3.48*** |
| Experience squared | −0.001 | −8.22*** | −0.001 | −3.21*** | 0.000 | 0.12 | −0.001 | −3.19*** |
| Ethnic minority | 0.056 | 1.59 | −0.116 | −1.11^ | −0.008 | −0.11 | 0.139 | 1.44 |
| Party membership | 0.147 | 9.61*** | −0.071 | −0.44 | 0.143 | 3.31*** | 0.182 | 0.93 |
| Poor health | −0.107 | −2.53** | −0.017 | −0.15 | −0.079 | −1.52 | −0.214 | −1.37 |
| Shenyang, Liaoning | −0.490 | −17.40*** | −0.253 | −1.61 | −0.125 | −1.61 | −0.103 | −1.16 |
| Jinzhou, Liaoning | −0.516 | −13.49*** | −0.489 | −4.26*** | −0.203 | −2.83*** | −0.250 | −2.76*** |
| Nanjing, Jiangsu | −0.192 | −7.23*** | −0.179 | −1.42 | 0.040 | 0.55 | −0.374 | −4.18*** |
| Xuzhou, Jiangsu | −0.369 | −11.08*** | −0.155 | −1.17 | −0.162 | −1.75* | −0.122 | −1.00 |
| Zhengzhou, Henan | −0.428 | −13.88*** | −0.418 | −2.34** | −0.105 | −1.24 | −0.525 | −4.46*** |
| Kaifeng, Henan | −0.719 | −19.89*** | −0.618 | −3.44*** | −0.268 | −3.64*** | −0.415 | −3.87*** |
| Pingdingshan, Henan | −0.465 | −14.90*** | −0.354 | −1.71* | −0.416 | −3.94*** | −0.581 | −6.59*** |
| Chengdu, Sichuan | −0.403 | −14.61*** | −0.162 | −1.27 | −0.126 | −1.63 | −0.156 | −1.68* |
| Zigong, Sichuan | −0.593 | −17.07*** | −0.702 | −4.24*** | −0.454 | −5.48*** | −0.513 | −5.37*** |

| | | | | | | | | |
|---|---|---|---|---|---|---|---|---|
| Nanchong, Sichuan | −0.570 | −15.95*** | −0.389 | −3.32*** | −0.460 | −5.61*** | −0.365 | −3.78*** |
| Lanzhou, Gansu | −0.434 | −14.82*** | −0.249 | −2.06** | −0.119 | −1.56 | −0.343 | −3.08*** |
| Pingliang, Gansu | −0.585 | −18.77*** | −0.584 | −4.05*** | −0.410 | −4.83*** | −0.783 | −9.79*** |
| No. of observations | | 5,770 | | 433 | | 1,158 | | 1,065 |
| Mean of dependent variable | | 3.340 | | 3.009 | | 2.721 | | 2.824 |
| Adjusted $R^2$ | | 0.269 | | 0.135 | | 0.157 | | 0.153 |
| Standard error of equation | | 0.508 | | 0.601 | | 0.504 | | 0.691 |

Notes:

1 Historic earnings are for the year of employment before the year of dismissal. Dummy variables for year of employment are included but not reported for brevity.

2 Default dummy variables are female, Han ethnicity, non-Party member, generally healthy, and Beijing.

3 For this and all subsequent tables: *** denotes statistics significance at the 1%, ** at the 5%, and * at the 10% level. t-ratios use White's heteroscedasticity-consistent standard errors.

4 Reports of Wald tests for differences in coefficients across types of workers: +++ denotes 1% significance level and + denotes 10% using non-retrenched urban workers to compare to re-employed and migrant workers; ^^ denotes 5% and ^ 10% significance level for using migrants to compare to re-employed urban workers.

We conducted Wald tests to explore whether any two wage functions can be pooled. In each case, pooling was rejected at the 5 per cent level. The three groups of worker do appear to be paid according to different standards. However, individual variables did often have similar coefficients in different wage functions. We tested whether two coefficients were significantly different using the Wald test:

$$(\beta_{1k} - \beta_{2k})^2/(\mathrm{Var}(\beta_{1k}) + \mathrm{Var}(\beta_{2k})) \sim \chi^2_{(1)} \quad (10.3)$$

where $\beta_{1k}$ and $\beta_{2k}$ are coefficients on the same explanatory variable $X_k$ estimated in different wage functions.

We begin by discussing the results of the Mincerian wage functions reported in Table 10.2. Since some of the personal characteristics – such as age, sex and education – may work via occupation and ownership variables, estimating wage functions without controlling for these intermediate variables provides a better estimate of the total effect of these characteristics.

It is particularly interesting to compare the coefficients on years of education in the wage functions for different categories of worker. These provide estimates of the returns to education. If workers in a particular group were confined to low-skill employment (where education did not affect productivity), one might expect the rates of return to education to be lower for that group. Interestingly, there are signs of this in the case of re-employed urban workers but not migrants. Education has almost exactly the same coefficient in the wage functions for migrants and non-retrenched workers: the Mincerian returns to education were 6 per cent for both (Table 10.2). Once controls for occupation and ownership sector are included in the wage functions, the returns to education for both types of worker fall to 3 per cent, implying that half the return to education comes via access to higher-paying occupations and/or sectors. By contrast, education is not a statistically significant determinant of the wages of re-employed urban workers. Interestingly, the historic wage functions suggest that the retrenched did receive a return to education in their previous jobs, although this was lower than that observed among the non-retrenched and migrants.[5] The lack of a return to education among re-employed workers may be due to a mismatch between the education of the re-employed and the occupations to which they are currently assigned.

Controlling for other factors, men are predicted to earn higher wages than women. However, the wage premium for men is significantly smaller (a 16 per cent premium) for non-retrenched urban workers than it is for the migrants (26 per cent) and the re-employed (39 per cent).[6] In this respect, the top tier of the labour market appears to be more 'gender-equitable' than the other tiers. It is also interesting that the pure gender gap in the historic wage function for retrenched workers prior to losing their jobs was smaller than is observed for any of the 1999 wage functions. It is sometimes argued that competitive forces may drive discriminatory behaviour out of the market. However, the Chinese experience suggests that sex discrimination may be greater among workers who are subject to less institutional protection and to greater managerial autonomy; they are also the workers who are exposed to greater competition.

Although the coefficients on experience and experience squared do not differ significantly from each other, their joint effect is very different for migrants and urban workers. To estimate the return to a year of experience, we evaluate it for a hypothetical worker with 20 years of potential experience, roughly the mean for the sample. For migrants an extra year of potential experience raises wages by 0.6 per cent; for urban workers (non-retrenched or re-employed) the corresponding effect is twice as large. This may reflect the fact that only a relatively small part of migrants' work experience will have been in urban areas; work experience in rural areas is likely to be less valuable.

Communist Party membership is a statistically significant determinant of wages only for the non-retrenched urban workers and historically for the retrenched prior to retrenchment. The re-employed appear to have lost a premium for party membership, consistent with their wages being determined more by the market, where political status is unimportant. We included a dummy variable for workers who reported being in poor health. Non-retrenched workers who report themselves to be in poor health tend to earn less than others, *ceteris paribus.*[7] Coming from a minority (non-Han) ethnic group has no significant effect in any Mincerian wage function.

We turn now to the results of the full wage functions, focusing on the comparison between the non-retrenched and re-employed urban workers.[8] The controls added for ownership sector generally matter more for the non-retrenched workers than for the migrants or the re-employed. Among the non-retrenched workers, there is a clear hierarchy of sectors in terms of the wages they offer. Enterprises with foreign investment are the highest paying, followed by centrally run SOEs and those listed on the stock market. Urban collectives and rural enterprises are the lowest paying. These patterns are generally not repeated for migrants and re-employed workers; indeed, few of the controls for ownership sector are statistically significant for these groups and those controls that are significant are often subject to small number problems. The most common ownership categories are centrally run SOEs, locally run SOEs (the default category) and urban collectives. Urban workers in centrally run SOEs appear to lose their wage premium when re-employed. The dummy for being in a centrally run SOE is statistically significant in the historic wage function for retrenched workers, but not in the current wage function for the re-employed. Migrant workers also do not receive a wage premium for working in centrally run SOEs. These results are consistent with centrally controlled SOEs hiring re-employed urban workers and migrants on more competitive terms than those given currently to the non-retrenched. The Wald tests reveal that few sectoral dummies have statistically significant differences in coefficients across categories of worker, the most reliable finding being that migrant workers, unlike urban residents, appear to be paid no less in urban collectives than in other types of enterprise.

Among the occupational categories, there is a clear three-way division for the non-retrenched. Administrative, technical and professional workers receive the highest wages, followed by clerical workers, with industrial, commercial and service occupations forming a relatively undifferentiated group. Clerical workers appear relatively hard hit by retrenchment. Among the non-retrenched, clerical workers are predicted to earn 7 per cent less than the default category of professional or technical worker, *ceteris paribus*. However, among the re-employed, they are predicted to earn 27 per cent less. The difference in these two effects is statistically significant at the 10 per cent level. The other occupational dummy showing statistically significant differences in coefficients across types of worker is that for service workers. Migrant workers in service occupations (a quarter of all migrants in our sample) receive lower wages relative to other occupations than do urban residents.

The generally negative and significant city dummy variables imply that workers in the default city, Beijing, receive a wage premium. However, the premium does vary across subgroups of worker. Pairwise Wald tests (not reported but available upon request) revealed that many of the city dummies have significantly different effects in the wage functions for the non-retrenched urban workers compared to other groups.

Overall, the comparison of wage functions suggests that workers in urban China are rewarded differently according to whether they are non-retrenched urban workers, retrenched and re-employed urban workers, or migrants. Urban workers in centrally controlled SOEs, Communist Party members, the educated and those in clerical occupations all receive wage premia if non-retrenched. Comparable wage premia do not exist among workers who were retrenched and take other jobs. In some ways, migrants appear to be an intermediate category – they are rewarded for their education and occupation, as are non-retrenched urban workers – but receive no premia for party membership or employment in a centrally run SOE.

## 10.4 Simulations from wage functions

Do the wage functions predict wages similar for workers of given characteristics, regardless of whether they are non-retrenched, re-employed or migrants? We have already noted that actual wages differ across the three groups (Table 10.1). Non-retrenched urban workers are the highest paid, with mean wages of 33 yuan per day. The comparison between migrants and re-employed workers is rather nuanced. Whereas they have the same (arithmetic) mean wages (25 yuan per day), median wages are higher for re-employed workers than for migrants (19 yuan per day compared to 16 yuan). This reflects higher variation in migrant wages. The mean log wage of re-employed workers – the dependent variable in our wage functions – is significantly higher than that for migrants, implying a significant difference in the geometric means. These differences imply that the typical (e.g. median) re-employed worker is likely to be better off than the typical migrant, but that some higher-paid migrants earn sufficiently large amounts to make mean wages the same across the two groups.

Differences in wages among categories of worker may be consistent with a competitive labour market if they can be explained by differences in the productive characteristics of the workers. To investigate this, we compare the predictions of our set of wage functions for given characteristics. In particular, we evaluate at the mean characteristics of each category. For example, we pose the counterfactual question: What is the predicted log wage of a worker with the mean characteristics of workers in group *i* if they are paid according to the wage function of group *j*? We also compute standard errors for our predictions, although these turn out to be rather large compared to the differences in the predictions of the various wage functions. Evaluating at mean characteristics is interesting since for any group *i*, the log wage predicted from its wage function at the mean of the explanatory variables is equal to its mean actual log wage. We can therefore investigate the extent to which differences in wage structure – as opposed to differences in characteristics – explain differences in mean log wages. Further, the difference in the predicted log wages can be interpreted as the percentage difference in predicted geometric mean wages.

When comparing migrants and urban workers, we focus mainly on the Mincerian wage functions (Table 10.2) that control for personal characteristics and location only. The Mincerian wage function may be more relevant in that it enables us to measure the full effects of discrimination, in jobs as well as in wages. The explanatory variables that distinguish the restricted and unrestricted wage functions – occupation and ownership sector – may standardize inappropriately. Migrants tend to be crowded into certain occupations, often self-employment, and retrenched workers are likely to find re-employment in disadvantageous ownership categories. Controlling for these variables may understate the full effects on wages of impediments to competition between groups of worker.

The simulations imply that workers of given characteristics are predicted to be paid considerably more if they were non-retrenched urban workers than if they were either migrants or re-employed workers (Table 10.3). Consider a non-retrenched urban worker with characteristics equal to the mean of such workers. They are predicted to be paid 25 per cent more than if they were re-employed workers. Likewise, a migrant with mean characteristics would be paid 24 per cent more if paid like a non-retrenched worker. The Mincerian wage functions predict similar differentials between non-retrenched and re-employed urban workers. Non-retrenched urban workers earn 28 per cent more than they would if paid like the re-employed; re-employed workers would earn 19 per cent more if paid like non-retrenched workers.

Do re-employed workers have to compete with migrants? Certainly, their pay is closer to that of migrants than it is to non-retrenched urban workers. The differentials between migrants and the re-employed are smaller than the differentials between either and non-retrenched workers. The re-employed are paid rather more than migrants. For example, a re-employed urban worker with mean characteristics is predicted to earn 7 per cent more than they would if paid like a migrant. A migrant of mean characteristics would earn 15 per cent more if paid like a re-employed worker. These results suggest that, even if the re-employed

*Table 10.3* Actual and simulated mean wages by type of worker

| | *If paid like non-retrenched workers* | *If paid like re-employed urban workers* | *If paid like migrants* |
|---|---|---|---|
| *(a) Predicted mean log wage from Mincerian wage functions (standard error in parentheses)* | | | |
| Non-retrenched urban workers | 3.340<br>(0.508) | 3.055<br>(0.603) | 3.072<br>(0.693) |
| Re-employed urban workers | 3.203<br>(0.508) | 3.009<br>(0.602) | 2.940<br>(0.692) |
| Migrants | 3.052<br>(0.508) | 2.974<br>(0.604) | 2.824<br>(0.691) |
| *(b) Predicted mean log wage from full wage functions (standard error in parentheses)* | | | |
| Non-retrenched urban workers | 3.340<br>(0.485) | 3.097<br>(0.593) | 3.042<br>(0.678) |
| Re-employed urban workers | 3.125<br>(0.485) | 3.010<br>(0.591) | 2.905<br>(0.676) |
| Migrants | 3.091<br>(0.485) | 3.105<br>(0.598) | 2.817<br>(0.672) |

Note: Wages are predicted using actual mean characteristics and the coefficients of the relevant wage function.

and migrants are not competing with each other on equal terms, they do seem to occupy segments of the labour market that are closer to each other than to that occupied by the non-retrenched.

The predictions of the full wage functions, shown in the lower part of Table 10.3, give qualitatively similar results to those of the Mincerian functions. For example, workers of given characteristics are predicted to have significantly higher wages if paid as non-retrenched workers than if paid as re-employed workers or migrants. However, the magnitude of the wage gap between the non-retrenched and the re-employed is considerably reduced if occupation and ownership sector are controlled for. For example, the actual gap between the mean log wages of the non-retrenched and the re-employed is 0.331. Part of this is due to differences in mean characteristics, so to abstract from that we can consider a re-employed worker with average characteristics. The gap between what such a worker earns and what they are predicted to earn if paid like the non-retrenched is 0.194 using the Mincerian wage function, falling to 0.123 using the full wage function. This implies that differences in occupation and in the ownership sector explain about a fifth of the wage gap between non-retrenched workers and the re-employed.[9]

In summary, the differences in wage structures estimated for our three groups of worker imply that non-retrenched workers have a distinct wage advantage over the other groups, even standardizing for their characteristics. Wage differentials between migrants and the re-employed are less sharp. These results suggest that retrenchment has led urban residents to lose most of the wage premium that might have derived from their urban *hukou* status.

## 10.5 Wages over time

As well as asking about current wages, the survey inquired about those in the previous four years. We can combine this information in order to create a five-year panel of wage information.[10] Although most of the explanatory variables (excluding experience) included in the cross-sectional wage functions are time-invariant, we can still use the panel to explore whether there are changes in the effects of these variables over time. For example, consider a model of the form:

$$\ln W_{it} = \beta'_{xt} X_i + \alpha_i + U_{it} \tag{10.4}$$

where $W$ is the wage, $X$ is a vector of time-invariant explanatory variables (such as education and sex), $\alpha_i$ are time-invariant unobserved characteristics of the individual, $\beta$ are time-varying coefficients, and $U$ is a random error term.

The above model can be estimated by five cross-sectional wage functions, one for each year. However, we estimate the model using a fixed effects estimator by re-writing it in terms of interactions between the explanatory variables and year dummies, $D_{it}$:

$$\ln W_{it} = \gamma_1 X_i + \sum_{t=2}^{5} \gamma_t D_{it} X_i + \alpha_i + U_{it} \tag{10.5}$$

The within-groups or fixed effects estimator is based on:

$$\ln W_{it} - \overline{\ln W_{it}} = \sum_{t=2}^{5} \gamma_t [D_{it} X_i - \overline{D_{it} X_i}] + [U_{it} - \overline{U_{it}}] \tag{10.6}$$

The fixed effects estimator will remove potential biases caused by correlations between the explanatory variables, $X_i$, and the time-invariant unobserved characteristics of the individual, $\alpha_i$.[11] However, this is at the cost of precluding an estimate of the overall effect of the explanatory variables ($\beta_t = \gamma_1 + \gamma_t$) at any one time. This cost is acceptable here, since our focus is not on the overall effect, but on the changes in the coefficients over time ($\beta_t - \beta_1 = \gamma_t$). Note that, for expositional purposes, equations (10.4) – (10.6) include only time-invariant explanatory variables; – in our actual models, we include a few time-varying ones, namely experience and a dummy for re-employment.

Table 10.4 reports the results of the fixed effects estimates, estimated separately for the non-retrenched and the retrenched.[12] We use a parsimonious Mincerian set of explanatory variables. As before, we classify workers as retrenched if they were retrenched at any time between 1992 and 1999/2000. Hence this classification is time-invariant. Such 'retrenched' workers are likely to have spent some of the period of the panel in their previous jobs prior to retrenchment, some of the time unemployed and possibly some of the time re-employed in new jobs.[13] To estimate the possible effects of re-employment on wages, we include a time-varying

*Table 10.4* Fixed effects estimates of changes in wage function coefficients, 1995–1999

| | *Non-retrenched* | | *Retrenched* | |
|---|---|---|---|---|
| | *Coefficient* | *t-ratio* | *Coefficient* | *t-ratio* |
| Male*99 | −0.003 | −0.26 | 0.113 | 1.52 |
| Male*98 | −0.008 | −0.65 | 0.037 | 0.94 |
| Male*97 | −0.005 | −0.45 | 0.035 | 0.91 |
| Male*96 | −0.005 | −0.38 | 0.021 | 0.56 |
| Experience*99 | −2.07E-02 | −7.48*** | 1.41E-02 | 0.69 |
| Experience*98 | −1.92E-02 | −7.19*** | −7.92E-03 | −0.75 |
| Experience*97 | −1.13E-02 | −4.34*** | −7.49E-04 | −0.08 |
| Experience*96 | −1.65E-03 | −0.65 | −8.78E-03 | −0.94 |
| Experience squared*99 | 3.60E-04 | 6.00*** | −4.43E-04 | −0.96 |
| Experience squared*98 | 3.76E-04 | 6.22*** | −2.83E-05 | −0.12 |
| Experience squared*97 | 2.33E-04 | 3.80*** | −1.46E-04 | −0.64 |
| Experience squared*96 | 4.32E-05 | 0.69 | 1.38E-04 | 0.61 |
| Education in years*99 | 0.012 | 4.61*** | −0.012 | −0.69 |
| Education in years*98 | 0.006 | 2.21** | −0.012 | −1.25 |
| Education in years*97 | 0.003 | 1.11 | −0.014 | −1.50 |
| Education in years*96 | 0.000 | 0.11 | −0.001 | −0.09 |
| Minority ethnicity*99 | 0.088 | 2.84*** | 0.020 | 0.11 |
| Minority ethnicity*98 | 0.047 | 1.50 | −0.032 | −0.32 |
| Minority ethnicity*97 | 0.043 | 1.38 | 0.024 | 0.25 |
| Minority ethnicity*96 | 0.028 | 0.88 | −0.002 | −0.03 |
| Party member*99 | 0.059 | 4.25*** | 0.122 | 0.94 |
| Party member*98 | 0.055 | 3.95*** | −0.001 | −0.02 |
| Party member*97 | 0.039 | 2.76*** | 0.066 | 1.01 |
| Party member*96 | 0.010 | 0.70 | −0.013 | −0.21 |
| Year dummy for 1999 | 0.370 | 7.84*** | 0.037 | 0.12 |
| Year dummy for 1998 | 0.283 | 6.20*** | 0.177 | 1.06 |
| Year dummy for 1997 | 0.129 | 2.91*** | 0.113 | 0.73 |
| Year dummy for 1996 | 0.000 | −0.00 | 0.055 | 0.37 |
| Dummy variable for re-employment (time-varying) | | | 0.842 | 2.93*** |
| *Interactions with a time-varying dummy variable for re-employment* | | | | |
| Male*re-employment | | | 0.169 | 2.62*** |
| Experience*re-employment | | | −3.35E-02 | −1.75* |
| Experience squared*re-employment | | | 5.79E-04 | 1.34 |
| School years*re-employment | | | −0.041 | −2.54*** |
| Minority* re-employment | | | 0.150 | 1.06 |
| CP member*re-employment | | | −0.319 | −2.83*** |
| Year dummy for 1999*re-employment | | | −0.131 | −1.19 |
| Year dummy for 1998*re-employment | | | 0.204 | 2.16** |
| Year dummy for 1997*re-employment | | | 0.066 | 0.70 |
| Year dummy for 1996*re-employment | | | −0.018 | −0.19 |
| Constant | 3.089 | 724.54*** | 2.710 | 206.89*** |
| No. of observations | 26,938 | | 4,639 | |
| $R^2$ across individuals | 0.1421 | | 0.0675 | |

Note: Variable *96, etc., denotes interaction between variable and a year dummy for 1996, etc.

dummy variable for being re-employed.[14] Since we have argued that the wage structure is different for the re-employed, we interact this dummy variable with variables for personal characteristics and also the year dummies.

Many variables interact significantly with the dummy variable for re-employment, so we cannot gauge the average impact of re-employment on wages by looking at the dummy variable in isolation. If we evaluate the combined effect of the dummy and its interactions at the mean personal characteristics of the re-employed, then the net effect is positive. This implies that re-employed workers, on average, do not have to work for lower wages than they would be paid if paid as retrenched workers were prior to being dismissed. For example, in 1995, re-employment is associated with an average increase in wages of 5 per cent over the counterfactual wage paid historically to the retrenched in their previous jobs. Re-employment does not seem to require that workers take cuts in wages below what they were paid historically, although, as we have seen, they are paid less than are workers who are not retrenched during the period.

However, the effect of re-employment on wages varies with numerous personal characteristics and is not positive for all types of worker. The interaction with the dummy variable for being male is positive, implying that men gain more (or lose less) than women from re-employment. The interactions with education and Communist Party membership are both negative, and can offset the overall positive impact of re-employment on wages. For example, consider a Communist Party member with other personal characteristics equal to the mean for the re-employed. The model predicts they would earn 21 per cent less when re-employed in a new job than they would have earned if they had remained in their old job. Similarly, a university graduate (16 years of education in total) with otherwise average characteristics is predicted to earn 18 per cent less when re-employed. The interactions with the dummy for re-employment and the quadratic for experience take a U-shape, but the turning point (29 years of experience) is relatively high. This implies that for most workers, the comparison between wages when re-employed and pre-retrenchment wages will be less favourable for the more experienced workers.

Our results suggest that re-employment has marked effects on the wages of retrenched workers. However, none of the interactions between personal characteristics and year dummies is statistically significant in the fixed effects wage function for the retrenched. These interactions were designed to identify any changes over time in the wage structure for retrenched workers' old jobs. By contrast, among non-retrenched workers, there are a number of statistically significant changes in the wage structure over time.

The year dummies in the wage function for the non-retrenched imply substantial wage increases over the period 1996–1999. For example, the year dummy for 1999 implies 45 per cent higher wages in that year compared to the base year of 1995 for a worker with default characteristics. Among retrenched workers, all the year dummies are statistically insignificant and, for 1998 and 1999, have much smaller coefficients than they do in the wage function for the non-retrenched. This implies that workers soon to be retrenched did not enjoy the wage rises experienced by the non-retrenched. This may be because the enterprises in which they worked were in financial difficulties and thus unable to fund wage increases. For re-employed workers, the picture is mixed. They appear to have experienced some rise in wages in 1998 at least, but the dummy variable for 1999 is negative and insignificant. This implies that in 1999, the re-employed – like the retrenched in their old jobs – were not enjoying significantly higher wages than in 1995.

The wage rise for the non-retrenched during a period of retrenchment and high unemployment suggests weakness of competition in the Chinese labour market. In a competitive labour market, one would expect a fall in the demand for labour to lead to a fall in real wages. Even if capital accumulation and technological change had increased the marginal product of labour, this should have raised employment rather than wages given an elastic labour supply. That real wages have risen is more consistent with a rent-sharing theory, whereby retrenchment of excess labour raises the surplus available to firms and some of this rise is shared with the remaining workers through higher pay.

Some non-retrenched workers have enjoyed larger increases in wages than others. The positive and statistically significant interactions between the year dummy for 1999 and a number of personal characteristics indicate that those characteristics are more highly rewarded in 1999 than they were in 1995. For example, the coefficients on the interaction terms between education and the year dummies rise with the year. The term for 1999 is statistically significant at the 1 per cent level and implies that the return to education is 1 percentage point higher in 1999 than in the default year of 1995. This change sounds modest, but it should be recalled that the selectivity-corrected Mincerian earnings function for 1999 found only a 4 per cent overall return to education, so returns to education may have increased by a third over the four years from 1995 to 1999. This finding of an increase in the return to education is consistent with a greater rewarding of productive worker characteristics and thus with the hypothesis of an increasingly competitive labour market. However, it could arise for other reasons such as a rise in the demand for educated labour relative to the supply, for instance on account of skill-biased technological change. In other words, the increase could represent a rise in the market equilibrium rate rather than a move from a wage-compressed disequilibrium towards the market equilibrium. Be that as it may, this rise in the returns to education was not observed among the retrenched workers, and re-employment is associated with a substantial fall in the returns to education.

The other productive worker characteristic in the model is potential experience, and here the findings are the reverse of those on education: returns appear to fall over time. The experience terms interacted with the dummy variable for 1999 imply a U-shaped curve, with a turning point at 29 years of experience. Most workers will be in the downward-sloping section of the U-shape. The panel data model implies that the wage differential between a worker with 20 years of potential experience and one with no experience would fall by 27 percentage points between 1995 and 1999. Potential experience is perhaps a less good measure of human capital than schooling. Prior to the reform of SOEs, seniority was a central aspect of China's administered wage system. For instance, Knight and Song (1993: 221–31) found in 1988 that the earnings of urban workers peaked only in their fifties, *ceteris paribus*. Given the extreme weakness of labour market forces at that time, it is unlikely that these payments reflected productivity benefits. Indeed, seniority was probably overpaid prior to reform.

A second corollary of the hypothesis of increasing competition is that non-productive characteristics would come to matter less. Here the evidence is mixed. There are statistically significant increases over time in the coefficient on being of minority (non-Han) ethnicity. From simple cross-sections (not reported), the coefficient changed from being negative (significant at the 10 per cent level) in 1995 to being insignificant in 1999. This could be interpreted as the removal of wage discrimination against non-Han Chinese, as might be expected in a competitive labour market. However, there are no statistically significant changes in the pure gender gap in wages. Moreover, the premium paid to Communist Party members rises by 6 percentage points from 1995 to 1999, a statistically significant increase. It appears that Party members who avoid retrenchment have done particularly well during the period of rising wages for urban workers in the second half of the 1990s.[15] This is in addition to the fact documented in a companion paper (Appleton *et al*, 2002) that Party members were less likely than non-members to be retrenched during this period.

## 10.6 Conclusions

China is in the process of developing a functioning urban labour market, i.e. one in which wages and workers are responsive to market forces. We were concerned to analyse how far the process had got in the fifteen years of urban economic reform up to the end of the century. We used the framework provided by two contrasting paradigms, the competitive labour market and the segmented labour market models. We did so not to dichotomize the Chinese case but to assess the extent and form of progress towards a functioning labour market.

The relatively privileged position of urban workers in China has been challenged in the 1990s, first by a great wave of migrants from rural areas and then by the programme of mass lay-offs within state-owned enterprises. Both developments might be expected to act as restraining forces on wages for urban workers and conceivably could usher in an era of labour market competition. What we have found, however, is more consistent with the creation of a 'three-tier' labour market. The highest-paid tier consists of those urban workers who were not made redundant during the 1990s. Even after standardizing for their personal characteristics (and occupations), this group are paid more than either migrants or urban workers who have been re-employed after being made redundant. The latter wage differential does not appear to reflect selectivity, as it might if the 'less able' workers were more likely to be sacked. Corrections for selectivity were found to be insignificant and, if anything, to exacerbate the estimated wage differential. It is less clear where the two lower tiers of the labour market – migrants and re-employed urban workers – stand in relation to each other. Their average wage rates are quite similar. However, they appear to be paid according to rather different wage structures, making it unlikely that they can be regarded as jointly forming a single 'secondary' labour market.

The wage structure for the 'primary' labour market, as indicated by the cross-sectional wage functions estimated for non-retrenched urban workers, is fairly conventional. Human capital – proxied by education, good health and experience – is rewarded and there are predictable occupational differentials. Some other wage differentials may be less justified by differences in underlying productivity but are nonetheless unsurprising. Men, Communist Party members and workers in centrally-owned SOEs all seem to earn wage premia. However, the cross-sectional wage structures for migrants and re-employed workers are often significantly different. Within both these tiers, there are no premia for Communist Party membership or for employment in central SOEs. One might be tempted to ascribe this to the effect of greater competition in eroding wage differentials not related to productivity. However, it should be noted that the 'pure gender gap' in wages is larger for migrants and re-employed workers: exposure to greater competition has not prevented the appearance of increased sex discrimination.

Where the migrants and re-employed workers do differ, however, is in wage differentials by education and occupation. For migrants, these differentials resemble those estimated for non-retrenched urban workers. However, for the re-employed, there appear to be no returns to education and few significant occupational differentials. The results for these re-employed workers suggest that the labour market they face is a fierce one that is not working well for them. The lack of rewards for productive characteristics implies that their employers still lack information on their productivity, or that the workers are forced by limited opportunities to accept low-grade jobs in which their productive characteristics have little value.

The estimates from the 1995–1999 panel data confirm the finding from the cross-sectional analysis that re-employment leads to the loss of wage premia for education and Communist Party membership, and an increase in the pure gender wage gap. However, except for a minority of workers for whom these premia were very important, re-employment seems not to require accepting a wage lower than that paid historically in one's previous employment. In absolute terms, urban workers are not 'scarred' by retrenchment but they have not enjoyed the substantial wage increases paid to non-retrenched workers. The scar is a relative one.

Which paradigm – competition or segmentation – does the labour market emerging in urban China come closest to? There are signs of emerging competitiveness in the rise in the return to human capital among non-retrenched urban workers and the fact that it is equally rewarded for migrants. However, despite the difficulty in interpreting residual differences, our evidence suggests that the urban labour market is segmented into three tiers, distinguished not only by the level but also by the structure of wages. These results bear out our hypothesis in that the three groups differ in the institutional arrangements that they face and thus in the extent to which they are open to market forces. The three tiers that we have identified may well prove to be a transitional phenomenon.

Although the scarring of retrenched workers may be long-lasting – as has been found elsewhere – some of the scars will no doubt heal as voluntary labour mobility increases, as re-employed workers and their jobs become better matched, and as relevant human capital is acquired. Similarly, the disadvantages experienced by urban-based rural migrants may wither as institutional discrimination based on *hukou* status diminishes, as the policy of easing restrictions on the acquisition of urban *hukous* (already announced) is implemented, and as migrants acquire more skills relevant to urban work. Moreover, the privileges enjoyed by non-retrenched urban employees can be expected to erode as product market competition stiffens and as the profit motive becomes more prevalent. In these ways, the current three tiers may become closer to each other. However, the paradigm of segmented rather than competitive markets may more closely match the varied experiences of different types of Chinese urban workers.

## Notes

The authors are grateful to the Department for International Development, United Kingdom, for their funding of the project (Escor grant R7526), to the CCK Foundation for a research grant (RG 019-U-01) and the Ford Foundation for their support of data collection. This chapter was first published in the *Journal of Chinese Economics and Business Studies*, Vol. 2, No. 3, pp. 185–205, September 2004. We are grateful to Taylor & Francis for their permission to reproduce the paper.

1 This year was chosen because it marked the appointment of a new Prime Minister and the beginning of significant moves to reform the SOE sector. Of the 1,364 workers in the survey who had ever been laid off, 96 per cent had been laid off in or after 1992. Twenty-five were laid off in 1992, compared to 9 in the year before and 55 in 1993. The ten-year SOE reform programme began officially in 1994, when 127 workers in our sample were laid off. 1998 saw the largest number of redundancies in our sample, with 305 workers losing their jobs.
2 These explanations do not reflect a lack of labour market competition. Hence, even if we find differences in the remuneration of the re-employed and the non-retrenched, we cannot necessarily conclude that this is evidence of weak competition. However, the scale of retrenchment in urban China in the 1990s still means that it is of interest to explore its impact, even if we cannot draw inferences from our results about competitiveness or segmentation.
3 We were not able to test for the selectivity of rural migrants, since we lack matching data on rural residents who did not migrate. There is also a wider issue of there possibly being unobserved differences between people with urban and rural *hukou*, but since residence registration is largely an accident of birth, this issue is not amenable to the standard econometric techniques for correcting for sample selectivity.
4 If the positive correlation does not arise by chance, it could arise because workers who, through good information or contacts, had attractive jobs lined up were allowed to opt for redundancy, or because the (continuing) threat of retrenchment raises personal effort and hence wages.
5 The lower return to education in the historic wage function may partly reflect a rise in returns to education over time. In addition, retrenched workers tended to be more concentrated in occupations where education is less rewarded. For example, over half of them were industrial workers compared to only a third of the non-retrenched. Including interaction terms between education and occupational dummies in the historic wage function for the non-retrenched revealed that industrial workers had significantly lower returns to their education than professional and technical workers.
6 We calculate the percentage effect of a dummy variable with coefficient $\beta$ to be $\exp(\beta)-1$.
7 Self-reported data on health are probably subject to systematic biases compared to objective clinical assessment. However, some reviews have found them to be as good a predictor of mortality as more objective measures (Idler 1991; Idler and Kasl 1991).
8 The results of this exercise are not reported because of space limitations. The authors are willing to provide the table on request.

9 Here we are essentially engaged in an exercise in decomposition following Oaxaca (1973). As is well known, there is a potential index number problem with such exercises. In this case, mean characteristics including occupation and sector, explain less of the wage gap between the non-retrenched and the re-employed if we evaluate using the wage structure of the re-employed.

10 With the recall data on wages, we take only observations where the worker was employed for the whole year. Years when workers were sacked or re-employed are dropped from the panel. This is for data reasons: the survey does not provide recall data on months worked and thus we cannot infer a reliable monthly wage rate. We thus have an unbalanced panel, where not all workers in the sample are included for all five years.

11 The fixed effects estimator eliminates bias from time-invariant unobserved factors that have a proportional effect on wages. Bias from factors that influence wages in other ways – for example, additively – will not be fully eliminated.

12 We do not correct for the selectivity of these two groups of workers because this can be viewed as giving rise to differences in the time-invariant unobserved characteristics of the individual, $\alpha_i$, which are eliminated by the fixed effects estimation.

13 Where workers are unemployed for a whole year, they have no wage and are thus not included in the panel analysis for that year (hence our panel for the retrenched workers is unbalanced).

14 Where a worker works in both their pre-retrenchment job and their re-employed job in the same year, we use the re-employed wage rate for that year.

15 There has been a change over time in the recruitment policy of the Communist Party, with recent attempts to welcome businessmen and other non-conventional recruits into its ranks. However, this cannot explain the panel data results because we treat Communist Party membership as a time-invariant variable (we observe it only for 1999 and assume that it is unchanged since 1995). In such a case, the entrepreneurial characteristics of recent recruits can be regarded as a fixed effect and thus controlled for in the panel estimates.

## References


Appleton, S., Knight, J., Song, L. and Xia, Q. (2002) 'Labor retrenchment in China: determinants and consequences', *China Economic Review,* 13(2–3): 252–75.

Deaton, A. (1997) *The Analysis of Household Surveys*, Baltimore: Johns Hopkins University Press.

Dong, X. and Bowles, P. (2002) 'Segmentation and discrimination in China's emerging industrial labor market', *China Economic Review*, 14(2–3): 170–96.

Fallick, B.C. (1996) 'A review of recent empirical literature on displaced workers', *Industrial and Labor Relations Review*, 50(1): 5–16.

Gregory, M. and Jukes, R. (2002) 'Unemployment and subsequent earnings: estimating scarring among British men 1984–94', *Economic Journal,* 111 607–25.

Idler, E.L. (1991) 'Self-assessed health and mortality: a review of studies', *International Review of Health Psychology*, 1: 33–54.

Idler, E.L. and Kasl, S. (1991) 'Health perception and survival: do global evaluations of health status really predict mortality?' *Journal of Gerontology*, 46(2): 55–65.

Knight, J. and Song, L. (1993) 'Why urban wages differ in China', in Griffin, K. and Zhao, R. (eds), *The Distribution of Income in China*, London: Macmillan.

Knight, J., Song L. and Jia, H. (1999a) 'Chinese rural migrants in urban enterprises: three perspectives', *Journal of Development Studies*, 35: 73–104.

Knight, J. and Song, L. (1999b) 'Employment constraints and sub-optimality in Chinese enterprises', *Oxford Economic Papers*, 51: 284–99.

Knight, J. and Song, L. (2003) 'Increasing urban wage inequality in China', *Economics of Transition*, 11(4): 597-619.

Lee, L.F. (1983) 'Notes and comments: generalized econometric models with selectivity', *Econometrica*, 51(1): 507–12.

Meng, X. and Zhang, J. (2001) 'The two-tier labour market in urban China: occupational segregation and wage differentials between urban residents and rural migrants', *Journal of Comparative Economics*, 29: 485–504.

Mincer, J. (1974) *Education, Employment and Earnings,* Chicago: University of Chicago Press.

Nickell, S., Jones, P. and Quintini, G. (2002) 'A picture of job insecurity facing British men', *Economic Journal*, 112: 1–27.

Oaxaca, R. (1973) 'Male-female wage differentials in urban labor markets', *International Economic Review*, 9: 693–709.

## Appendix 10.A: Detailed results on selectivity corrections for full wage functions

*Identifying instruments*

Number of children aged 7 to 14 years

Dummy for female sex interacted with number of children aged under 7 years

Dummy for female sex interacted with number of children aged 7 to 14 years

Dummy for worker who works or has worked in the state sector and is married to a worker who has been retrenched from the state sector

*Joint significance of instruments (critical value at 5% significance is 15.507)*

| | |
|---|---|
| Likelihood ratio test statistic for exclusion of instruments from multinomial logit | 24.365 |
| Over-identifying tests for instruments (critical value at 5% significance is 9.488): | |
| Non-retrenched wage function | 6.082 |
| Historic retrenched wage function | 7.697 |
| Re-employed wage function | 0.792 |
| Estimated coefficients on Lee (1983) selectivity corrections (*t*-ratios in parentheses): | |
| Non-retrenched wage function | −0.131(−1.31) |
| Historic retrenched wage function | −0.025 (−0.11) |
| Re-employed wage function | 0.593 (1.13) |

# 11 Job mobility of residents and migrants in urban China

*John Knight and Linda Yueh*

## 11.1 Introduction

During the period of central planning, China had an administered labour system. Urban labour was allocated bureaucratically and wages were determined institutionally, according to a centralized and egalitarian system of wage grades and scales (Knight and Song 1991, 1993, 1995). Labour mobility was not permitted, either across cities or across employers within a city, so that one's first job was often one's last. The relationship between a worker and his *danwei*, i.e., work unit, was close and pervasive; the enterprise provided lifetime employment within a mini-welfare state, which was denoted the 'iron rice bowl'. Hence, labour mobility or labour turnover in urban China was not studied.

With the reform of the state-owned enterprises (SOEs) in the late 1980s and 1990s, managers acquired some freedom to manage their employees; they had greater power to set wages and to decide recruitment and employment. More recently, managers were required by the government to reduce their surplus labour so that more than 25 million workers were made redundant from 1996 to 1999 (Appleton *et al.* 2002). At the same time, workers acquired more rights to move from one employer to another. However, voluntary mobility continued to be impeded by the employer-specific provision of social welfare services, such as pensions, medical care and housing, which were gradually being privatized.

A labour market in transition from a planned to a market-oriented system experiences increased mobility from a low level. Initially, involuntary mobility results from enterprises discarding surplus labour and producers adjusting to market demand and prices. As the transition progresses, the proportion of voluntary quits increases as individuals move to jobs that match better their productive characteristics and reflect expanding activities. Urban China is arguably in the first stage of this transition because labour mobility has risen recently from very low levels. In developed economies, mobility in labour markets is characterized by long-term employment relationships, most new jobs ending early, and the probability of a job ending declining with tenure (Farber 1999). The labour market in urban China may exhibit only the first of these characteristics.

The rate of job mobility is likely to be inversely related to the length of job tenure. Table 11.1 reports the length of tenure, i.e. job duration, in China and in

*Table 11.1* Average and median tenure for select countries

| *Country* | *Average tenure (years)* | *Median tenure (years)* | *Distribution of tenure (%)* | |
|---|---|---|---|---|
| | | | *Under 2 years* | *Over 20 years* |
| China (urban residents) | 19.9 | 19.0 | 5.6 | 45.5 |
| Poland | 17.5 | 17.0 | 5.7 | 43.9 |
| Japan | 11.3 | 8.3 | 23.6 | 21.4 |
| Germany | 9.7 | 10.7 | 25.5 | 17.0 |
| United Kingdom | 7.8 | 5.0 | 30.3 | 9.4 |
| United States | 7.4 | 4.2 | 34.5 | 9.0 |
| China (migrants) | 4.5 | 3.0 | 39.2 | 1.3 |

Sources: OECD (1997) and the 1999 CASS survey.

Notes:
1 The data relate to 1995, except for the US (1996) and China (1999).
2 The tenure of migrants in China is measured from the time of entry into the urban labour market.
3 For both urban residents and migrants, the data for China on the distribution of tenure include those with 2 years of tenure, which biases both figures slightly upwards.

various other countries, ranked by average length of tenure. Chinese urban residents are at the top of the list, having the longest average tenure at 19.9 years, while Chinese rural–urban migrants are at the bottom, having the shortest at 4.5 years. The figures for median tenure and for the distribution of tenure show almost identical patterns. Poland, the other transition economy for which data are available, is closest to Chinese urbanites, followed by Japan. The European countries occupy intermediate positions and the United States, with its flexible labour market, is closest to Chinese migrants. In this chapter, we investigate the reasons for the relatively long job tenure of urban residents and the relatively short tenure of migrants.

We use a household-based urban data set set to examine labour mobility for urban and rural workers. The data cover both urban residents having an urban *hukou*, i.e. registration certificate, and rural–urban migrants living in the city but having a rural *hukou*. The data set allows us to trace the employment history of each worker. We examine job tenure, job mobility, voluntary versus involuntary mobility, and the determinants of mobility over time.

Section 11.2 provides a conceptual and institutional framework for the analysis. Section 11.3 sketches a model that explains the differential mobility of urban and migrant workers. Section 11.4 describes the data and investigates empirically the extent, nature, causes and consequences of labour mobility among urban residents and rural–urban migrants. Section 11.5 concludes with policy implications.

## 11.2 Concepts and hypotheses

Concerning the unit of analysis, we distinguish labour turnover in which the employer is the unit and labour mobility in which the employee is the unit. Turnover is the number of quits per period as a percentage of the workers in a firm. Since our data are household-based, we focus on labour mobility, which can be measured as the number of quits per period by a worker. At various times, we use the tenure of workers, i.e. job duration, whether complete or incomplete, as an inverse measure of mobility between employers. A second distinction can be made between voluntary and involuntary mobility. In a competitive labour market with free choice, voluntary mobility occurs in response to changes in information, skills, tastes or wages. Under the system of labour allocation and lifetime jobs in China, a high degree of job mismatch was inevitable and was tempered only partially by intra-firm mobility. With greater labour market freedom, we expect to see increased voluntary mobility as a market response to the inefficient arbitrary job assignment of the past. The causes of involuntary mobility are related to the job or to the individual. The distinction between employee- and employer-induced quits is difficult to draw in practice. On the one hand, if workers recognize that their jobs are at risk, they have an incentive to search for another job and may quit before they are fired. On the other hand, workers intending to quit may volunteer for a retrenchment programme if it will provide benefits. For that reason, involuntary mobility may be understated or overstated.

The analysis of labour mobility is based on theories of firm-specific capital and theories of job matching so that mobility may be socially desirable or not. On the one hand, mobility results in the loss of firm-specific human capital. On the other hand, it can improve job matches and raise labour productivity by matching better individual skills and abilities or by movement to higher-productivity jobs as the economy changes. Do private economic agents left to pursue their own interests generate the optimal mobility rate for the economy, given its institutions and conventions? A worker's decision to quit depends on the associated private costs and benefits to him; similarly, a firm's decision to fire depends on its private costs and benefits. In either case, termination can impose costs and benefits on the other party or on third parties so that social and private net benefits may not coincide. In this situation, the degree of labour mobility will not be optimal, as Greenwald and Stiglitz (1988) and Hosios (1990) discuss. For example, a firm will not take into account the short-term or long-term income loss that it imposes on a fired worker, nor will a departing worker take into account the hiring and training costs that he imposes on his firm.

Labour mobility among employers depends partly on the degree of flux in the economy. In an entirely static economy, in equilibrium, zero mobility is optimal. However, in an economy subject to rapid structural transformation and growth, substantial job change is likely as some firms and sectors decline while others expand. As goods and factors are reallocated in response to developing product and factor markets, the inherent productivity of some jobs falls and that of others rises. Even standardizing for structural change, the individual productivity of workers in their jobs may be below the potential productivity of the jobs; such a shortfall offers workers and firms opportunities for improved matching. The mobility rate depends on the relative importance both of firm-specific skills and of the scope to improve idiosyncratic matching through job mobility. However, these factors depend on the nature of the labour market and its institutions. The boundary between firm-specific and general human capital is defined by marketability, which is determined not only by the intrinsic content of the skill but also by the conventions that sustain or inhibit a market. Similarly, the scope for matching by inter-firm mobility depends on the scope for matching within firms. Japan and the United States provide an interesting contrast, as Collier and Knight (1985), Hashimoto and Raisian (1985) and Mincer and Higuchi (1988) show. Hence, the rate of job mobility varies across countries or over time.

In the context of urban China, potentially highly beneficial job matching was prevented under the planning system. Even in the late 1990s, the provision of social services was often attached to the work unit; the process of reform and marketization was incomplete and ongoing because these arrangements continued to deter advantageous voluntary mobility. On the other hand, the draconian redundancy programme imposed on state-owned enterprises in the late 1990s created too much mobility. Many specific skills were lost to the economy and retrenched workers bore a heavy loss of income, both while unemployed and on re-employment (Appleton *et al.* 2002; Knight and Li 2002). However, the loss of production was minimal because the government had kept unemployment disguised in the enterprises rather than open. Nevertheless, the losses borne by redundant workers were not internalized fully in the decision processes that led to these retrenchments.

Under central planning, the migration of rural people to urban areas was strictly curbed, and even during the reform period, only the temporary migration of rural people is normally permitted (Knight and Song 1999). Rural *hukou*-holders are allowed into the residual jobs that urban *hukou*-holders do not want and the number of migrants that urban enterprises can employ is restricted (Knight, Song and Jia 1999). Generally, migrants are employed on short-term contracts. Regarding access to housing and to social services like education and healthcare, rural *hukou*-holders are discriminated against, so deterring them from settling in the cities. A pattern emerged in which migrants spend brief periods in urban employment, engaged on one or two short-term contracts, and then return to their rural homesteads. This pattern is changing only gradually as more migrants attempt to bring their families to the, still inhospitable, cities. In these circumstances, employers have little incentive to train their migrant workers. Therefore, labour mobility among rural–urban migrants may be too substantial to promote efficient human capital formation.

## 11.3 Towards a model of differential mobility

Before the policies concerning employment in the Chinese urban labour market were loosened, urban *hukou* workers were favored by placement in good jobs, i.e. permanent, secure 'iron rice bowls', while migrants were discriminated against and restricted to bad jobs, i.e. jobs that were temporary and had little job security and few non-wage benefits. To analyse differential mobility that reflects only these discriminatory arrangements, we begin with a segmentation model. If all urban and migrant workers are employed, and all vacancies are filled, good jobs are taken by urban workers and bad jobs are taken by migrants. Institutional arrangements ensure that jobs held by urbanites last longer than jobs held by migrants. The rate at which jobs turn over is the reciprocal of job duration. Hence, the rate at which vacancies occur for good jobs, and thus for urban workers, is less than the rate of vacancies for bad jobs, and thus for migrants. Therefore, in any period, the mobility rate of urban workers is less than that of migrants.

To include imperfect job matching in a labour market characterized by informational asymmetries and costly search for both individuals and firms, we analyse the determinants of differential mobility by considering not only the role of institutions but also the importance of search motivation and of firm-specific skill acquisition. The Chinese labour market resembles the search models in which there are good and bad jobs and different types of job-seekers. For example, Pissarides (1994) develops a model of equilibrium unemployment in which those in good jobs search for and accept only good jobs and those in bad jobs search for and accept both types of jobs. Occupants of good jobs stop searching when the returns to tenure offset the expected gains from search; similarly, occupants of bad jobs stop searching beyond a certain length of tenure. We adapt this model to the Chinese case by assuming that migrants are allocated initially to bad jobs and urban workers are in good jobs.

The total number of matches between firms and workers is given by the matching technology, $f = f(v, m + u)$, where $v$ is the number of vacancies, $m$ is the number of migrant job-seekers, and $u$ is the number of urban *hukou* job-seekers within a constant labour force. Initially, we make the following simplifying assumptions. First, there are two types of job-seekers, urban and migrant, and two types of jobs, good and bad, distinguished by their attractiveness to the worker. Second, the matching technology is the same for both types of jobs. Third, all urban job-seekers seek good but not bad jobs, whereas all migrants seek both types of jobs. Fourth, all matches sought by employers result in job offers. Fifth, urban job-seekers reject bad jobs.

The number of matches between good job vacancies and job-seekers is given by $f_g = f(v_g, m + u)$. For bad jobs, the number of matches is given by $f_b = f(v_b, m)$, which indicates that urban job-seekers do not cause congestion for migrants by taking bad jobs.

Assuming initially that the matching rate into good jobs ($r_g$) is the same for urban workers ($r_{u_g}$) and migrants ($r_{m_g}$), we have:

$$r_g = r_{u_g} = r_{m_g} = f_g/(u + m) \tag{11.1}$$

Moreover, the matching rate of migrants into bad jobs is:

$$r_{m_b} = f_b/m \tag{11.2}$$

whereas $r_{u_b}$ is zero. Hence, the overall matching rate of migrants ($r_m = r_{m_g} + r_{m_b}$) exceeds that of urban workers ($r_u = r_{u_g} = r_{m_g}$) and, in equilibrium, $r_u < r_m$. This result occurs because urban workers are allocated initially to good jobs and migrants are allocated initially to bad jobs. From equations (11.1) and (11.2), the difference between $r_u$ and $r_m$ depends on the extent to which $r_{m_b}$ exceeds $r_g$. The institutions that provide secure employment for urban workers and impose insecure short-term contracts on migrants lower $v_g$ and raise $v_b$. In turn, good job matches are reduced relative to bad matches so that $r_u$ falls relative to $r_m$.

The basic model can be modified to make it more applicable to China by changing all but the first assumption. We assume that matching technologies for good and bad jobs differ and that it is easier to find a match for a bad job because idiosyncratic skills are less important. If $f_g$ generates fewer matches than $f_b$, the initial inequality $r_u < r_m$ is accentuated. Moreover, the decision to search is assumed to be a function of the prospective wage relative to the current wage of an individual. Because urban workers are initially in good jobs, their incentive to search is reduced. By contrast, migrants have a strong incentive to search for good jobs because they are initially in bad jobs. The current wage depends on both the length of job tenure and the returns to tenure. If there are returns to tenure that result from firm-specific skill acquisition, some workers are deterred from job search by the prospect of losing this premium. Since $r_u < r_m$ implies longer tenure for urban workers, leading employers to invest more firm-specific skills in urban workers, a higher proportion of urban workers choose not to search, which reduces further $r_u$ relative to $r_m$. In addition, urban workers receive preferential treatment in hiring for good jobs so that not all potential matches for migrants result in job offers. This discrimination against migrants reduces their offer rate for good jobs, which lowers their mobility rate relative to that of urbanites. *Ceteris paribus,* this effect suggests that $r_{u_g} > r_{m_g}$, which weakens our prediction that $r_u < r_m$. Finally, if some urban workers have been laid off and remain unemployed, they may not reject all bad jobs. However, the basic result is maintained so long as $r_{u_b} < r_{m_b}$.

The matching rate for an individual worker is the number of matches in a particular period; for the economy, it is the number of matches in that period expressed as a proportion of the number of workers. These theoretical concepts correspond closely to the empirical measure of an annual mobility rate given by the number of job changes per year of employment experience averaged across workers. Having provided the basic hypothesis that the annual mobility rate of migrants exceeds that of urban residents, we test this empirically by contrasting the desire and ability of urban residents and migrants to move. In addition, we relate search behaviour, including latent mobility and actual mobility, to tenure and returns to tenure, as well as to actual and expected wage levels.

## 11.4 Empirical findings

### *11.4.1 The data*

The data set is the 1999 CASS survey; it pertains mainly to 1999 but contains much information on work histories. The total sample size is 4,000 urban households, 2,500 of which are urban *hukou* households drawn from the NBS urban household survey, and the remainder are from a representative sampling frame begun in 1999 that includes urban-residing households without an urban *hukou*. In addition, independent samples were drawn of 500 households from the NBS urban survey in which a member had experienced a lay-off, and of 800 migrant households. The survey covers six provinces and thirteen cities. The provinces are Beijing, which is chosen to represent the four cities that are independently administered municipal districts; Liaoning, which represents the north-east; Henan, which is in the interior; Gansu, which is in the north-west; Jiangsu, which is a coastal province; and Sichuan, which is in the south-west. In addition to Beijing, the capital of each province is taken as a city within the sampling frame; a total of three cities are chosen in Sichuan and Henan and two cities are considered in each of the other provinces.

The survey was not designed specifically to examine labour mobility. Although substantial, the information is not ideal but we have tried to make the best use of what is available. Normally, empirical analysis of labour turnover is conducted at an aggregative level. Therefore, aggregate variables that influence mobility, such as the growth of total employment, the growth of the labour force and structural change, are used. Since our analysis is conducted at the individual level, we cannot incorporate non-individual variables, except as proxies from available information in the survey, such as city dummies and ownership categories of employer.

### *11.4.2 Mobility within the labour market and its determinants*

We use the representative urban sample, which excludes the additional 500 households that were selected because a member had experienced unemployment in the previous five years. The most notable feature of this sample is a general lack of mobility. As many as 78 per cent of respondents had only one job and a further 16 per cent had two jobs. Thus, only 6 per cent had three or more jobs. No less than 74 per cent of current employees with 30 or more years of employment experience were still in their first jobs. For the select minority of workers who changed jobs, the average length of their completed tenure was 5.5 years. For the urban sample as a whole, the average length of first job tenure, including incomplete tenure, was 21.3 years. Considering only current job tenure, i.e. omitting completed jobs, the average length was 16.6 years. Allowing for future tenure in continuing jobs, the predicted duration of completed tenure for the sample as a whole would be extremely long.

The analysis of migrants is based on workers in a sample of rural–urban migrant households, i.e. households that establish residence in the survey cities but retain their rural *hukou*. Because they live in resident households, these migrants are unlikely to be representative of all rural–urban migrants. Migrants who leave their rural homesteads and come to the cities on their own to work temporarily, often living with other migrants at their workplaces or in dormitories, are likely to be under-represented in this sample. The mobility rate of this group is likely to be higher than that of migrants who establish urban roots. Regarding mobility, the migrants appear to be similar to the urban workers. As many as 77 per cent had only one job, another 10 per cent had two jobs, 7 per cent had three jobs, while only 6 per cent had more than three jobs. However, these similarities are misleading. For urban workers, the data consider the period since entry to the labour force, but for migrants, the data refer to the period from entry into the city labour market only. Thus, the average length of employment experience of urban workers is 22.8 years, whereas the average length of city employment experience of migrants is 5.9 years. This difference is due partly to migrants being younger, i.e. 28.6 years of age compared with 38.4 years, and partly to migrants not coming to the city immediately when they entered the labour force because most were engaged in rural household economic activities.

The average completed employment duration of migrants is 2.2 years; it is lowest for migrants in their twenties at 1.3 years and highest for those in their fifties at 4.1 years. The first job tenure, including incomplete spells, averages 5.0 years; the average length of the current job tenure is 4.5 years. Each of these tenure figures requires careful interpretation. First, briefly employed migrants are more likely to be unsuccessful and may have returned to the village. Second, predicting the length of incomplete spells is difficult because it may be misleading to double the length of the average current tenure from 4.5 to 9.0 years, as would be appropriate for a steady-state process. If migrants are more welcomed as urban residents, they will remain at their workplace longer than in the past. Nevertheless, even the figure of 4.5 years is high by comparison with the conventional wisdom about migrant employment tenure in China. Examining migrants and urban residents with comparable labour market experience at less than six years, migrants have a mobility rate of 0.1230, which is almost twice as high as that of urban residents at 0.0689. Even when the iron rice bowl no longer existed, entering urban residents had distinctly lower mobility rates than migrants with comparable amounts of urban employment experience.

Table 11.2 presents estimates of the determinants of mobility rates among urban residents aged 16 and over from tobit regressions. We define the overall mobility rate as the number of job changes over years of employment experience, the mean value of which is 0.019. The involuntary rate is computed from a question that asked respondents whether they had been laid off in the previous five years and, if so, how many times. Hence, we have the number of involuntary moves reported during the period 1995–1999. All other moves are assumed to be voluntary. Using that information, we derive a rate of voluntary mobility equal to 0.015 and a rate of involuntary mobility equal to 0.008. As Table 11.2 indicates, age up to 38 years, years of education, being self-employed, and locating one's current job through market avenues or referrals through one's social network all increase significantly the overall mobility rate. In addition, being a non-manual worker with more human capital, a home-owner who is less tied to the employer, and working currently in the preferred state and private sectors increase significantly the voluntary mobility rate.

The use of social networks in job search increases the mobility rate for urban residents, especially if it is voluntary. Having larger social networks and more

*Table 11.2* Urban resident sample: the determinants of mobility rates aged 16 and over, tobit estimates (dependent variable: mobility rates)

| | *Coefficient (t-statistic)* | | |
|---|---|---|---|
| | *Overall* | *Voluntary* | *Involuntary* |
| Intercept | –0.2385<br>(–3.120)*** | –0.4526<br>(–4.622)*** | –0.3239<br>(–2.226)** |
| *Personal characteristics* | | | |
| Gender | –0.0075<br>(–1.168) | –0.0011<br>(–0.136) | –0.0143<br>(–1.255) |
| Age | 0.0070<br>(3.524)*** | 0.0107<br>(4.403)*** | 0.0163<br>(3.415)*** |
| Age squared | –0.0001<br>(–3.659)*** | –0.0001<br>(–4.178)*** | –0.0002<br>(–4.053)*** |
| Years of education | 0.0037<br>(3.353)*** | 0.0045<br>(3.446)*** | –0.0021<br>(–0.966) |
| Married | –0.0232<br>(–0.981) | –0.0416<br>(–1.544) | 0.0053<br>(0.095) |
| *Occupation* | | | |
| Non-manual worker | 0.0125<br>(1.204) | 0.0355<br>(2.670)*** | –0.0513<br>(–3.217)*** |
| Production worker | –0.0036<br>(–0.335) | –0.0013<br>(–0.092) | –0.0199<br>(–1.300) |
| Self-employed | 0.0716<br>(2.780)*** | 0.1147<br>(3.472)*** | –0.0224<br>(–0.508) |
| *Ownership of employer* | | | |
| State | 0.0025<br>(0.269) | 0.0241<br>(1.866)* | –0.0589<br>(–4.383)*** |
| Private | 0.0195<br>(1.302) | 0.0423<br>(2.185)** | –0.0246<br>(–1.058) |
| *Household characteristics* | | | |
| Head of household | –0.0053<br>(–0.102) | 0.0193<br>(0.282) | –0.0337<br>(–0.429) |
| Number of people in household | –0.0031<br>(–0.775) | –0.0027<br>(–0.574) | –0.0004<br>(–0.053) |
| Home-owner | 0.0070<br>(1.114) | 0.0139<br>(1.814)* | –0.0118<br>(–1.095) |
| *Guanxi (social capital)* | | | |
| Communist Party member | 0.0069<br>(1.049) | 0.0092<br>(1.187) | –0.0264<br>(–2.006)** |
| Social network | 0.0013<br>(3.089)*** | 0.0020<br>(3.926)*** | –0.0010<br>(–1.095) |
| *Avenue of job search* | | | |
| Market forces | 0.0326<br>(3.514)*** | 0.0326<br>(2.877)*** | 0.0255<br>(1.597) |

*Table 11.2* (Continued)

| | Coefficient (t-statistic) | | |
|---|---|---|---|
| | *Overall* | *Voluntary* | *Involuntary* |
| Referral through social network | 0.0814<br>(5.576)*** | 0.1037<br>(5.865)*** | 0.0575<br>(2.367)** |
| Self-employment | 0.0409<br>(1.537) | 0.0530<br>(1.573) | 0.0038<br>(0.094) |
| *Cities* | Yes | Yes | Yes |
| Pseudo-$R^2$ | 0.2299 | 0.2228 | 0.2653 |
| $X^2$ (31) | 247.58*** | 265.34*** | 239.66*** |
| Mean of dependent variable | 0.0192 | 0.0149 | 0.0079 |
| No of observations | 3,437 | 3,216 | 3,454 |

Source of Tables 11.2–11.7: Household Survey of Urban *Hukou* Residents and Household Survey of Rural *Hukou* Migrants, the 1999 CASS survey.

Notes:

1 The omitted dummy variables are male gender, unmarried, unskilled worker, urban collective sector, not head of household, non-home-owner, not Communist Party member, obtained current job through state allocation, and Pingliang.

2 The symbols *** denote significance at the 1% level, ** at the 5% level and * at the 10% level, respectively.

3 Heteroscedasticity-consistent robust standard errors adjusted for clustering at the household level are computed.

4 As an avenue of job search, market forces refers to searching in newspapers, using job centres and employing methods that are not dependent on state allocation or on referral through one's own social network. The latter category includes hearing about job information and receiving a recommendation for a position.

connections improves employment prospects by learning about jobs, receiving referrals to jobs, and having the relationships facilitating job moves in an administered labour system. Those with more human and social capital have more opportunities, which may be reflected in greater mobility. Factors that reduce significantly the involuntary mobility rate are being a non-manual worker, working in the state sector and being a Communist Party member. Each of these characteristics provides relative protection against job loss. In addition, age increases the involuntary mobility rate so that older workers are more likely to be laid off.[1] Unfortunately, with one exception, no determinants of the migrant mobility rate or of the number of jobs held by migrants are both interesting and statistically significant. For migrants who have located their current job by a referral through a social network, mobility is reduced significantly.[2] In summary, the determinants of the mobility of urban workers can be well explained by predicted factors, but the mobility of migrants appears to depend on unobserved variables, for example, rural household characteristics, short-term contracts coming to an end, or luck.

### *11.4.3 The impact of economic reform on mobility rates*

Our objective is to determine the extent to which mobility rose as labour market reforms progressed. The Western literature suggests that job separations are highest in the first years of employment and decrease thereafter (see, e.g., Farber 1999), so that we must control for this effect. The data allow us to date the most recent job change of urban *hukou* residents and to analyse mobility in a disaggregated manner. Unfortunately, the rural *hukou* sample is not sufficiently large, or sufficiently dispersed in the relevant variables, to permit an equivalent analysis of migrants. For each entry cohort, Table 11.3 shows the percentage that has never changed jobs, the percentage that has done so more than once, and the percentage that has only one job change. For the last group, the period within which the single job change was made is reported.[3] Hence, we obtain a period-specific, first-job mobility rate by entry cohort.

The matrix in Table 11.3 can be read down the columns, which standardizes for the period in which separation occurred, across the rows, which standardizes for entry cohort, or along the diagonals, which standardizes for duration of tenure. Examining the columns, we observe the familiar tendency for mobility to decline with employment experience. In contrast to the Western pattern, the rows indicate that separation rates rise uniformly with time for post-1970 entrants. This result can be attributed to the increasing flexibility of the labour market over time, which is verified by the diagonals exhibiting an almost monotonic increase in mobility standardizing for the duration of employment. For example, whereas the 1965–69 entry cohort had a 1.4 per cent separation rate over the subsequent five-year period from 1970 to 1974, the 1990–1994 entry cohort had a 12.1 per cent separation rate in the corresponding five-year period from 1995 to 1999. To distinguish between voluntary and involuntary mobility, we rely on the worker's reported reason for leaving a job.[4] The voluntary mobility rate tends to be higher the more recent the cohort but also the more recent the period, whether or not we standardize for duration of employment. Involuntary separations were far higher from 1995 to 1999 than in any previous five-year period. The iron rice bowl became increasingly fragile over time and was effectively broken in the period from 1995 to 1999.

Those who had never changed jobs were asked whether they had ever wanted to do so. Their responses enable us to examine the latent demand for mobility using a logit analysis in Table 11.4. Importantly, 77 per cent of the urban sample never wanted to move, possibly because they did not view it as a feasible option. The urban workers who are more likely to want to move even though they have not yet done so are the self-employed, possibly because self-employment is not a preferred activity, unskilled workers, because they are possibly in unattractive jobs, and those who report larger social networks of contacts and acquaintances, possibly because the possession of a large social network raises expectations of mobility among those not yet mobile. State employees and party members, who may already be better positioned, and home-owners, the dissatisfied among whom may already have moved, are more likely to be content with their jobs. By predicting wages using the observable characteristics of urban workers, we find that

*Table 11.3* Job separations for urban residents: raw percentages (period of entry: one job change)

| | *Period of job separation* | | | | | | | | *Never changed* | *Multiple changes* |
|---|---|---|---|---|---|---|---|---|---|---|
| | *1960–64* | *1965–69* | *1970–74* | *1975–79* | *1980–84* | *1985–89* | *1990–94* | *1995–99* | | |
| 1960–1964 | 1.5 | 2.8 | 1.1 | 1.5 | 2.3 | 1.5 | 1.1 | 1.0 | 71.4 | 15.5 |
| (724) | (11) | (20) | (8) | (11) | (17) | (11) | (8) | (7) | (517) | (112) |
| 1965–1969 | — | 1.8 | 1.4 | 2.9 | 3.2 | 3.3 | 1.9 | 2.2 | 72.1 | 10.4 |
| (1,472) | | (26) | (21) | (42) | (47) | (49) | (28) | (32) | (1061) | (153) |
| 1970–1974 | — | — | 2.2 | 2.9 | 2.9 | 3.0 | 3.6 | 6.0 | 67.5 | 9.7 |
| (1,256) | | | (28) | (37) | (36) | (38) | (45) | (75) | (848) | (122) |
| 1975–1979 | — | — | — | 3.6 | 3.2 | 3.9 | 4.2 | 8.6 | 68.6 | 4.9 |
| (1,517) | | | | (54) | (48) | (59) | (64) | (130) | (1040) | (74) |
| 1980–1984 | — | — | — | — | 3.4 | 4.9 | 5.7 | 8.8 | 70.0 | 3.5 |
| (1,198) | | | | | (41) | (59) | (68) | (105) | (839) | (42) |
| 1985–1989 | — | — | — | — | — | 4.2 | 5.1 | 10.5 | 71.3 | 3.1 |
| (897) | | | | | | (38) | (46) | (94) | (640) | (28) |
| 1990–1994 | — | — | — | — | — | — | 5.4 | 12.1 | 72.8 | 4.2 |
| (626) | | | | | | | (34) | (76) | (456) | (26) |
| 1995–1999 | — | — | — | — | — | — | — | 7.7 | 82.1 | 6.8 |
| (532) | | | | | | | | (41) | (437) | (36) |

Notes:
1 The rows do not sum to 100 because we do not have information on the year of the separation for some people who changed job once.
2 The number of observations is in parentheses.
3 The matrix contains workers with only one job change.

*Table 11.4* Determinants of latent mobility for immobile individuals

| | *Coefficient (z-statistic)* | |
|---|---|---|
| | *Urban sample* | *Migrant sample* |
| Intercept | 0.8094<br>(0.704) | 0.1251<br>(0.097) |
| *Personal characteristics* | | |
| Gender | −0.1105<br>(−0.809) | −0.1191<br>(−0.432) |
| Years of education | 0.0292<br>(1.175) | 0.1144<br>(2.170)** |
| Years of tenure | −0.0068<br>(−0.232) | −0.0249<br>(−0.203) |
| Years of tenure squared | −0.0009<br>(−1.247) | 0.0016<br>(0.210) |
| Married | −0.4870<br>(−0.837) | −0.4124<br>(−0.388) |
| *Occupation* | | |
| Non-manual worker | −0.4028<br>(−2.081)** | −0.6736<br>(−1.327) |
| Production worker | −0.3541<br>(−1.726)* | −0.1470<br>(−0.236) |
| Self-employed | 2.6319<br>(3.318)*** | — |
| Other occupations | −0.3884<br>(−1.021) | −0.4383<br>(−1.291) |
| *Ownership of employer* | | |
| State | −0.5800<br>(−3.277)*** | −0.2310<br>(−0.493) |
| Private | −0.2300<br>(−0.762) | −0.7214<br>(−1.954)* |
| *Household characteristics* | | |
| Head of household | −0.6959<br>(−0.783) | 0.2361<br>(0.825) |
| Number of people in household | 0.1402<br>(1.461) | −0.0116<br>(−0.409) |
| Home-owner | −0.2628<br>(−2.105)** | −0.5455<br>(−1.030) |
| *Guanxi (social capital)* | | |
| Communist Party member | −0.2512<br>(−1.835)* | −0.5633<br>(−0.627) |
| Social network | 0.0191<br>(2.028)** | −0.0029<br>(−0.571) |
| *Wage residual (actual minus predicted wage)* | −0.2753<br>(−3.106)*** | −0.0213<br>(−0.113) |
| *Cities* | Yes | Yes |
| Wald $X^2$ (26) | — | 44.54*** |
| Wald $X^2$ (29) | 165.38*** | — |

*Table 11.4* (Continued)

| | *Coefficient (z-statistic)* | |
|---|---|---|
| | *Urban sample* | *Migrant sample* |
| Mean of dependent variable | 0.1983 | 0.3573 |
| No. of observations | 1,906 | 362 |

Notes:

1 The dependent variable equals one if the individual has never changed jobs but wants to and zero if the individual has never changed jobs and does not want to.

2 The omitted dummy variables are male gender, unmarried, unskilled worker, urban collective sector, not head of household, non-home-owner, not Communist Party member, and Pingliang. Social networks are defined as the number of people with whom a person regularly associates.

3 The symbols *** denote significance at the 1% level, ** at the 5% level and * at the 10% level, respectively.

4 Heteroscedasticity-consistent robust standard errors adjusted for clustering at the household level are computed.

5 The coefficients for domestic worker and for Jinzhou cannot be estimated for the migrant sample.

6 The predicted wage in this and the next table is estimated from an equation corresponding to Table 11.6, column (3), but excluding the mobility rate.

those non-movers whose actual wage exceeds their predicted wage are significantly less likely to be frustrated in their jobs, which suggests that the wage residual represents economic rent.

A high proportion, namely 72 per cent, of migrants who changed their job once did so voluntarily.[5] In addition, mobility is more likely to be voluntary for migrants than for urban workers. Table 11.4 reports a logit analysis of latent mobility among migrants. Of those who had never changed their job in the city and answered the question, 33 per cent wanted to change job and 67 per cent did not. Only two explanatory variables have significant coefficients. More education increases the desire to change jobs, probably because the job is ill-suited to the education, whereas working in the private sector reduces the desire to change jobs.

In Table 11.5, we explore latent mobility[6] by comparing those who have moved and those who have never moved but want to do so. The dependent variable in the logit analysis consists of 59 per cent of the urban sample and 23 per cent of the migrant sample, representing individuals who have changed jobs. For the urban sample, the chance of changing jobs declines, at an increasing rate, with length of tenure. This suggests that more recent recruits have fewer disincentives, or greater opportunities, to move. *Ceteris paribus,* non-manual workers and those classified as others are more likely to move than manual workers, both skilled and unskilled, indicating that the availability of opportunities is important. The other human and social capital variables, namely, education, Party membership and social network, have positive coefficients as expected, but they are not significant. Home ownership, which is likely to reduce the cost of changing employers, increases the chances of moving. An excess of the current actual wage over the predicted wage also promotes mobility, implying either that the movers gain rent from their moves or that unobserved productivity assists movement. Therefore,

*Table 11.5* Determinants of mobility for mobile and potentially mobile individuals

| | Coefficient (z-statistic) | |
|---|---|---|
| | *Urban sample* | *Migrant sample* |
| Intercept | −3.8672<br>(−2.424)** | −4.8539<br>(−4.511)*** |
| *Personal characteristics* | | |
| Gender | −0.1659<br>(−1.010) | 0.3634<br>(1.277) |
| Years of education | 0.0413<br>(1.265) | 0.0352<br>(0.685) |
| Years of tenure | −0.1321<br>(−3.730)*** | 0.4530<br>(5.213)*** |
| Years of tenure squared | −0.0024<br>(−2.491)** | −0.0132<br>(−3.349)*** |
| Married | 0.5098<br>(0.564) | −0.4223<br>(−0.780) |
| *Occupation* | | |
| Non-manual worker | 0.6090<br>(2.423)** | 0.2268<br>(0.535) |
| Production worker | 0.0691<br>(0.247) | −0.0213<br>(−0.043) |
| Self-employed | 0.9372<br>(1.212) | 0.7152<br>(0.491) |
| Other occupations | 1.0064<br>(2.387)** | 0.2366<br>(0.718) |
| *Ownership of employer* | | |
| State | 0.4440<br>(1.867)* | −0.2321<br>(−0.479) |
| Private | 0.4007<br>(1.156) | 0.9204<br>(2.712)*** |
| *Household characteristics* | | |
| Head of household | 0.2495<br>(0.199) | 0.2590<br>(0.886) |
| Number of people in household | −0.1189<br>(−0.922) | −0.0306<br>(−0.679) |
| Home-owner | 0.3131<br>(1.967)** | −0.2371<br>(−0.534) |
| *Guanxi (social capital)* | | |
| Communist Party member | 0.1911<br>(1.154) | −0.9270<br>(−0.674) |
| Social network | 0.0157<br>(1.335) | −0.0021<br>(−1.063) |
| *Wage residual (actual minus predicted wage)* | 0.7518<br>(5.271)*** | 0.0258<br>(0.163) |
| *Cities* | Yes | Yes |
| Wald $X^2(26)$ | — | 70.13*** |
| Wald $X^2(29)$ | 185.76*** | — |

*Table 11.5* (Continued)

| | *Coefficient (z-statistic)* | |
|---|---|---|
| | *Urban sample* | *Migrant sample* |
| Mean of dependent variable | 0.5949 | 0.2278 |
| No. of observations | 1,049 | 742 |

Notes:

1 The dependent variable equals one if the individual has changed jobs and zero if the individual has never changed jobs but wants to.

2 The omitted dummy variables are male gender, unmarried, unskilled worker, urban collective sector, not head of household, non-home-owner, not Communist Party member, and Pingliang. Social networks are defined as the number of people with whom a person regularly associates.

3 The symbols *** denote significance at the 1% level, ** at the 5% level and * at the 10% level, respectively.

4 Heteroscedasticity-consistent robust standard errors adjusted for clustering at the household level are computed.

5 The independent variables necessarily relate to the current position of those who changed jobs and must be interpreted accordingly. For example, occupation and ownership sector show the destinations of movers and the origins of non-movers. Moreover, years of employment experience and social network reflect the current position and not that at the time of the move.

whereas non-movers whose current wage exceeds their predicted wage are less keen to move, movement itself is associated with having a current wage above the predicted wage.

Only two variables are significant in a corresponding equation for migrants, also shown in Table 11.5. Unlike for urban residents, years of tenure increase the likelihood of changing jobs for migrants. Although the squared term is negative and significant, implying that migrants eventually become less mobile, the combined effect of tenure is positive over the relevant range. Most migrants would like to move and those with more labour market experience in urban areas have a greater likelihood of doing so. Current employment in the private sector is associated with success among the would-be mobile migrants in Table 11.5, whereas Table 11.4 indicates that immobile migrants are less likely to want to move if they work in the private sector. Hence, employment in the private sector appears to be the preferred choice for migrants.

### *11.4.4 The relationship between mobility and wages*

Table 11.6 reports coefficient estimates of the determinants of earned income for employed individuals in the urban and migrant samples in equations that include the mobility rates. For urban workers, seniority in the firm is rewarded. From column (5), ten years of tenure adds 22 per cent to earnings, whereas ten years of schooling adds 31 per cent.[7] The opposite sign of tenure squared indicates a non-linear relationship between tenure and wages, which is reflected in the estimates of returns to tenure. This result is consistent with urban workers acquiring substantial firm-specific skills, but it does not provide conclusive evidence. State

*Table 11.6* The determinants of earned income for employed individuals

| | Coefficient (t-statistic) | | | | | |
|---|---|---|---|---|---|---|
| | *Urban sample* | *Migrant sample* | *Urban sample* | *Migrant sample* | *Urban sample* | *Urban sample* |
| | *Uncorrected OLS (1)* | *Uncorrected OLS (2)* | *Selection-corrected MLE (3)* | *Selection-corrected MLE (4)* | *Uncorrected OLS (5)* | *Selection-corrected MLE (6)* |
| Intercept | 1.8717 | 2.7803 | 1.8920 | 2.6653 | 1.7839 | 1.8090 |
| | (25.418)*** | (15.617)*** | (25.820)*** | (11.336)*** | (25.588)*** | (26.060)*** |
| *Personal characteristics* | | | | | | |
| Gender | −0.1752 | −0.1394 | −0.1717 | −0.1869 | −0.1803 | −0.1750 |
| | (−10.627)*** | (−3.000)*** | (−10.451)*** | (−1.930)* | (−11.343)*** | (−10.893)*** |
| Years of education | 0.0311 | 0.0111 | 0.0304 | 0.0145 | 0.0311 | 0.0302 |
| | (8.445)*** | (0.672) | (8.321)*** | (1.200) | (8.440)*** | (8.225)*** |
| Years of tenure | 0.0256 | 0.0271 | 0.0252 | 0.0222 | 0.0285 | 0.0279 |
| | (6.671)*** | (2.173)** | (6.585)*** | (2.027)** | (7.202)*** | (7.016)*** |
| Years of tenure squared | −0.0006 | — | −0.0006 | — | −0.0007 | −0.0007 |
| | (−5.818)*** | | (−5.706)*** | | (−6.443)*** | (−6.163)*** |
| *Occupation* | | | | | | |
| Non-manual worker | 0.2548 | 0.4342 | 0.2518 | 0.4571 | 0.2617 | 0.2591 |
| | (8.295)*** | (2.576)** | (8.248)*** | (3.885)*** | (8.555)*** | (8.534)*** |
| Production worker | 0.0959 | 0.3050 | 0.0951 | 0.2929 | 0.0993 | 0.0987 |
| | (2.855)*** | (2.143)** | (2.844)*** | (1.894)* | (2.923)*** | (2.917)*** |
| Self-employed | 0.2842 | 0.1107 | 0.2969 | 0.1267 | 0.4465 | 0.4761 |
| | (1.985)** | (0.304) | (2.081)** | (0.221) | (3.214)*** | (3.442)*** |
| Other occupations | 0.0461 | 0.2134 | 0.0448 | 0.2184 | 0.0682 | 0.0685 |
| | (1.066) | (2.150)** | (1.041) | (2.514)*** | (1.582) | (1.592) |

| | | | | | | |
|---|---|---|---|---|---|---|
| *Ownership of employer* | | | | | | |
| State | 0.2559 | −0.2928 | 0.2511 | −0.2616 | 0.2741 | 0.2678 |
| | (8.913)*** | (−2.418)** | (8.798)*** | (−2.557)** | (9.455)*** | (9.270)*** |
| Private | 0.3170 | 0.0589 | 0.3120 | 0.0479 | 0.3183 | 0.3124 |
| | (7.225)*** | (0.527) | (7.145)*** | (0.569) | (7.035)*** | (6.924)*** |
| *Guanxi (social capital)* | | | | | | |
| Communist Party member | 0.1318 | −0.1970 | 0.1302 | −0.1635 | 0.1218 | 0.1207 |
| | (6.535)*** | (−0.444) | (6.491)*** | (−0.637) | (6.275)*** | (6.241)*** |
| Social network | 0.0068 | −0.0008 | 0.0068 | −0.0007 | 0.0063 | 0.0063 |
| | (4.873)*** | (−1.350) | (4.915)*** | (−1.243) | (4.692)*** | (4.759)*** |
| *Mobility rate* | | | | | | |
| Overall | 0.0219 | 0.3739 | 0.0217 | 0.3025 | — | — |
| | (0.358) | (4.017)*** | (0.353) | (1.838)* | | |
| Voluntary | — | — | — | — | 0.2655 | 0.2722 |
| | | | | | (1.023) | (1.046) |
| Involuntary | — | — | — | — | −0.3739 | −0.2637 |
| | | | | | (−0.353) | (−0.251) |
| *Cities* | Yes | Yes | Yes | Yes | Yes | Yes |
| Inverse Mills ratio | — | — | −0.0280 | 0.6757 | — | −0.0467 |
| | | | (−1.812)* | (0.562) | | (−1.818)* |

(Continued)

*Table 11.6* (Continued)

| | Coefficient (t-statistic) | | | | | |
|---|---|---|---|---|---|---|
| | *Urban sample* | *Migrant sample* | *Urban sample* | *Migrant sample* | *Urban sample* | *Urban sample* |
| | *Uncorrected OLS (1)* | *Uncorrected OLS (2)* | *Selection-corrected MLE (3)* | *Selection-corrected MLE (4)* | *Uncorrected OLS (5)* | *Selection-corrected MLE (6)* |
| $R^2$ | 0.2618 | 0.2336 | — | — | 0.2782 | — |
| $F(23, 334)$ | — | 20.34*** | — | — | — | — |
| $F(25, 2,877)$ | 59.83*** | — | — | — | — | — |
| $F(26, 2,775)$ | — | — | — | — | 57.29*** | — |
| Wald $X^2(25)$ | — | — | 1461.73*** | — | — | — |
| Wald $X^2(28)$ | — | — | — | — | — | 1418.76*** |
| Wald $X^2(47)$ | — | — | — | 539.01*** | — | — |
| Mean of dependent variable | 2.9499 | 0.8216 | 2.9499 | 0.8216 | 2.9499 | 2.9499 |
| No. of observations | 5,015 | 1,006 | 5,015 | 1,006 | 4,740 | 4,740 |

Notes:

1 The dependent variable for the urban sample is the log of daily earned income and it is the log of hourly wages for the migrant sample.

2 The omitted dummy variables are male gender, unskilled worker, urban collective sector, not Communist Party member, and Pingliang.

3 Sample selection bias may result because we do not observe wages for those who do not participate in the labour market. Our two-stage least-squares estimation with a valid exclusion restriction addresses this issue. The exclusion restriction for equations (2), (4) and (6) is a dummy variable that equals 1 if not in good health. Health is a valid exclusion restriction because it is a significant predictor of labour market participation but it is not correlated with wages. In China, with a high level of participation by both men and women, being healthy will determine the probability of employment.

4 The symbols *** denote significance at the 1% level, ** at the 5% level and * at the 10% level, respectively.

5 Heteroscedasticity-consistent robust standard errors adjusted for clustering at the household level are computed.

6 We have information on the reasons for the previous job change but not for other changes; thus, we cannot disaggregate the mobility rate into voluntary and involuntary rates for the migrant sample.

enterprises had no profit incentive to train their workers, so that if the coefficient reflects administratively based seniority scales rather than the reward for higher productivity, workers lacked an incentive to acquire skills. Nevertheless, the many urban workers having long tenure do receive a substantial earnings premium, for example, 32 per cent for those with the average current tenure of 16.6 years, which discourages them from engaging in job search.

The coefficient on the overall mobility rate for urban workers is slightly positive but insignificantly so. The voluntary mobility rate has a positive coefficient, as expected, but it is not significant. In contrast, the coefficient on the involuntary rate is negative, but it too is not significantly different from zero. The results for the selectivity-corrected estimates in columns (5) and (6) imply that the mobility rate resulting from a voluntary change of jobs every four years raises earnings by 7 per cent and lowers earnings by 7 per cent if the change is involuntary.[8] These estimates are qualitatively similar to those of Keith (1993), who finds that the overall mobility rate in the US is not significant whereas the voluntary rate has a positive impact on earnings, while the involuntary rate has a negative effect, and both are significant. In essence, workers quit voluntarily in expectation of better-paid jobs whereas those who are fired have difficulty finding equivalent jobs. However, we cannot reject the possibility that some unobserved characteristics, for instance, motivation, influence both earnings and mobility so that they could explain both the positive and the negative coefficients.

The earnings functions for migrants, also shown in Table 11.6, are estimated using both ordinary least squares (OLS) and two-stage least squares (2SLS) with correction for selectivity into employment. Since the two sets of results are similar, we discuss the latter. The coefficients confirm that private sector employment is the preferred state for migrants; they receive significantly higher pay in the private than in the state sector.[9] Migrants may look to the private sector because of an institutional distinction, namely, good jobs have been more tightly restricted to urban residents by the state than by the non-state sector. Interestingly, women are at a considerable disadvantage as they receive an hourly wage lower by 17 per cent. Neither education nor the proxies for possession of social capital are significant. However, one form of human capital is rewarded, namely, occupation, as non-manual jobs are the highest paid relative to unskilled workers. This result may indicate skill acquisition by moving either within or between firms. The coefficient on the mobility rate is positive and significant at 0.31. By comparison with migrants who remain in the same job, a move every four years results in an 8 per cent increase in earnings. Thus, mobility may improve job matches for migrants. Interestingly, the inverse Mills ratio is not significant for migrants as it is for urban residents, who are perhaps more able to choose to participate in the labour market.

The coefficient on tenure at 0.027 is positive and significant at the 5 per cent level in column (2). Hence, the earnings premium for migrants with the mean current length of tenure at 4.5 years is 13 per cent, which is much smaller than the premium for urban residents, so that migrants have less incentive to remain with their employer.[10] However, this coefficient may not represent the productivity

*Table 11.7* Transition matrix for urban residents: raw percentages

| *Previous sector* | *Current sector* | | | | |
|---|---|---|---|---|---|
| | *SOE* | *Urban collective* | *Self-employed* | *Private* | *Total* |
| SOE | 84<br>(555) | 3<br>(22) | 4<br>(27) | 9<br>(61) | 100<br>(665) |
| Urban collective | 41<br>(38) | 33<br>(31) | 14<br>(13) | 12<br>(11) | 100<br>(93) |
| Self-employed | 33<br>(4) | 8<br>(1) | 42<br>(5) | 17<br>(2) | 100<br>(12) |
| Private | 65<br>(28) | 5<br>(2) | 0<br>(0) | 30<br>(13) | 100<br>(43) |
| Total | 77<br>(625) | 7<br>(56) | 6<br>(45) | 11<br>(87) | 100<br>(813) |

Notes:
1 The matrix reports the percentage of job changes from one sector to another. The number of observations is in parentheses.
2 The information is available only for those urban residents who have changed jobs once.
3 SOE represents central, provincial and local state-owned enterprises.
4 Private includes partnerships, Chinese-foreign joint ventures, foreign companies, state shareholding companies, other shareholding companies, rural individual enterprises and other enterprises.

gain from longer tenure. On the one hand, it may indicate improved matching within the firm or a process of good workers selecting or being selected to stay on rather than skill formation. On the other hand, the actual return to tenure is likely to understate potential return because firms are discouraged from investing in migrants by the institutions favouring urban residents for the more skilled jobs. A vicious circle may arise in which short tenure discourages investment in skills and the lack of skills encourages short tenure because of lower earnings. Such a low-level equilibrium would be stable if an exogenous rise in tenure fails to induce sufficient investment in skills to raise tenure further.

A matrix of transition among ownership sectors can be estimated for the urban sample but not for the migrant sample. Table 11.7 presents a transition matrix for those urban workers who changed jobs once with four ownership sectors, namely, state, urban collective, self-employed and private, distinguished for both origin and destination. Voluntary and involuntary mobility are combined. Of those who moved from one employment to another, 84 per cent moved from one state sector job to another. Only 13 per cent of those leaving the state sector and 26 per cent of those leaving the urban collective sector entered the self-employed or private sectors. Whereas 73 per cent of the voluntary movers went to the state sector, only 33 per cent of the involuntary movers did so, indicating that the state sector is the preferred destination.[11] When urban workers who remain unemployed are added to the re-employed, 65 per cent came from the state sector, 31 per cent from urban collectives and 4 per cent from the self-employed or private sectors.[12] By contrast, among those currently employed, 77 per cent were employed in the state sector, 15 per cent in urban collectives and 8 per cent in the self-employed or private sectors. Hence, the propensity to move is highest from the urban collective sector in which wages are the lowest, as Table 11.6 indicates, and employment has declined.[13] This implication that the urban collective sector is disliked is consistent with the positive and significant coefficients for both state and private employment, with the collective sector being the omitted category, in the earnings functions for urban workers in Table 11.6.

## 11.5 Conclusion

In this chapter, we exploit an urban household survey covering both urban residents and rural migrants. Our simple model of the determinants of mobility in the Chinese case supports the basic hypothesis that the mobility rate of migrants exceeds that of urban workers. Before the urban reforms began in earnest, mobility among urban workers was negligible. Effectively, these workers had lifetime employment with their work unit so that any improvements in the matching of workers and jobs occurred only within the work unit. By contrast, mobility among rural–urban migrants was extremely high with migrants tending to leave their rural households temporarily for work on short-term contracts before returning home. Our evidence confirms that these patterns have not changed greatly. The vast majority of urban workers have had only one employer. A labour market is emerging gradually for urban workers, but many workers are not affected directly. We find that employment duration among migrants is now higher than conventional wisdom suggests. This result is due partly to our sample, which is drawn from rural migrants with urban households. As in other developing countries, migrants who establish urban roots are likely to be more rooted to their jobs.[14]

The mean mobility rate of migrants is almost six times that of urban workers, which confirms the basic hypothesis. Even considering only those who entered the labour market after the iron rice bowl had been smashed, the mean mobility rate of migrants is nearly double that of urban workers. These contrasting rates reflect the norms, rules, opportunities and restrictions on choice faced by the two groups. Their mobility rates are unlikely to be equalized if they continue to be treated differently. As the restrictions on the mobility of urbanites and the rules that impose mobility on migrants are lifted, the equilibrium degree of mobility in a unified market is likely to lie between the two current rates. Taking first urban *hukou* residents and standardizing for time period, we find that mobility is higher among young people, as in other countries. Standardizing for entry cohort, we find that mobility tended to rise over time as labour market reforms advanced. However, the state sector, rather than the growing non-state sector, remains the preferred destination. Among the immobile, the wish to move is related to proxies indicating that the current job is unattractive. Among would-be movers, success is related to proxies indicating the availability of opportunities to move. In particular, voluntary mobility is raised by the human and social capital variables; involuntary mobility is lowered by characteristics that have provided relative protection against job loss. Voluntary mobility increases and involuntary mobility decreases earnings, while a high earnings premium associated with tenure reduces the incentive to search.

Whenever possible, we posed the same questions for migrants. The great majority of their job changes have been voluntary. In contrast to urban workers, who show preference for the state sector, migrants appear to choose private sector employment. Employment in the private sector both deters further search and is the object of past successful search. In contrast to urban workers, longer tenure raises the chances that migrant search will be successful. The fact that education and tenure increase mobility suggests that human capital improves migrants' opportunities for advantageous job change. Mobility raises migrant earnings, reflecting improved inter-firm matching. Length of tenure also has a positive effect on migrant earnings, reflecting skill acquisition or improved intra-firm matching. However, in contrast to urban workers, the low average tenure of migrants blunts their incentive to stay with the firm.

Several policy issues underlie any evaluation of labour mobility. First, mobility involves a social cost because it destroys firm-specific human capital. Second, mobility, especially if involuntary, can create the hardship and social costs associated with unemployment. Third, mobility provides a social benefit in that it permits better matching of workers and their characteristics to jobs. Fourth, mobility should be high enough to create competitive market wages with their allocative social benefit. To judge whether the mobility rate is socially optimal, the private costs and benefits must be adjusted to include the social costs and benefits. In urban China, the private costs and benefits of both residents and migrants do not correspond to the social costs and benefits of mobility. For example, tying various non-marketed facilities, such as housing and pensions, to employment has imposed private costs on quitting that are not equal to social costs. The artificial restrictions under which rural–urban migrants work in the cities, i.e. the prohibition on or impediments to urban settlement, restricted access to skilled jobs and the system of short-term contracts, may have generated an excessively high migrant mobility rate. The voluntary mobility rate of urban workers and the mobility rate of migrants are converging, but they are still far apart. The maintained hypothesis in future research must be that the former are too low and the latter are too high.

## Notes

The chapter was first published in the *Journal of Comparative Economics*, Vol. 32, No. 4, 2004. We are grateful to Elsevier for their permission to reproduce the paper. The support of the Nuffield Foundation and the UK Department for International Development is gratefully acknowledged. We thank two referees and the editor for their helpful comments.

1 An alternative specification, which involves estimating a Poisson regression equation predicting the number of jobs held, produced the same set of significant coefficients, except that the negative coefficient on being married became significant.

2 A tobit regression for the mobility rate was estimated for the 1,256 migrants aged 16 and over but the results are not reported. Referral through one's social network was the only avenue of job search with a coefficient significantly different from the default category, state allocation.

3 We confine the analysis to those who changed job only once because we have information on the last job move only. The last job of those who had changed job more than once would have been the most recent. If these workers were included, the results of the table would be weighted and biased towards more recent periods. Fortunately, of those who changed jobs, more than two-thirds did so only once.

4 Question 155 in Questionnaire I of the Urban Household Survey asked: 'Why did you leave your previous job?' The following responses were taken to indicate voluntary separations: low income, lack of job security, unsatisfactory work conditions, insufficient benefits, and to start own business. The following responses were assumed to represent involuntary separations: contract expired, laid off by work unit, and became *xiagang*. A residual category of other was available as a response. The job separation of those who are currently unemployed is assumed to be involuntary because in current market conditions, employees are unlikely to quit voluntarily unless they have obtained another job.

5 Question 137 in the Rural–Urban Migrant Survey asked: 'What was the main reason for your leaving your previous job?' The following reasons were taken to indicate voluntary separations: low income, the job was not stable, working conditions were poor, benefits and social securities were not good, wanted to start your own business, and increased family burden. The following were assumed to indicate involuntary departure: contract expired, dismissed, and other.

6 This specification is identical to the determinants of mobility in Table 11.2 except that tenure can be used in this estimation. Age and its square are used instead of employment tenure in Table 11.4 because the dependent variable is a measure of mobility, which is correlated with tenure by definition. In contrast, Tables 11.5 and 11.6 can use a measure of tenure and its square in order to capture the effects of tenure on the propensity to move.

7 The relevant coefficients are multiplied by 10 or 100 to obtain the marginal values.

8 These findings might be stronger if we were able to distinguish better between voluntary and involuntary mobility.

9 A joint *F*-test on the coefficients for the state and the private sectors in Table 11.6 rejects the null hypothesis that they are equal for migrants.

10 The coefficient on tenure squared is positive but not significant so that it is dropped. Linearity is to be expected over the limited range of tenure in the sample.

11 In the interests of space, the information for voluntary and involuntary movers is not shown separately in Table 11.7.

12 In the interests of space, Table 11.7 shows only percentages of those who left one job and moved to another, and not the percentages of those who left one job and either moved to another or remained unemployed.

13 Official statistics record a fall by 52 per cent from 1990 to 1999.

14 Knight and Sabot (1982) analysed this process in the transition from migrant to proletarian among the urban labour force of Tanzania.

## References

Appleton, S., Knight, J., Song, L. and Xia, Q. (2002) 'Labor retrenchment in China: determinants and consequences', *China Economic Review*, 13: 252–75.

Collier, P. and Knight, J. (1985) 'Seniority payments, quit rates and internal labour markets in Britain and Japan', *Oxford Bulletin of Economics and Statistics*, 47: 19–32.

Farber, H.S. (1999) 'Mobility and stability: the dynamics of job change in labor markets', in Ashenfelter, O. and Card, D. (eds), *Handbook of Labor Economics*, Vol. 3B. Amsterdam: North-Holland, chap. 37.

Greenwald, B. and Stiglitz, J. (1988) 'Pareto inefficiency of market economies: search and efficiency wage models', *American Economic Review (Proceedings)*, 78: 351–5.

Hashimoto, M. and Raisian, J. (1985) 'Employment tenure and earnings profiles in Japan and the United States', *American Economic Review*, 75: 721–35.

Hosios, A.J. (1990) 'On the efficiency of matching and related models of search and unemployment', *Review of Economic Studies*, 57: 279–98.

Keith, K. (1993) 'Reputation, voluntary mobility and wages', *Review of Economics and Statistics*, 75: 559–63.

Knight, J. and Li, S. (2002) 'Unemployment duration and earnings of re-employed workers in urban China', unpublished.

Knight, J. and Sabot, R. (1982) 'From migrants to proletarians: employment experience, mobility and wages in Tanzania', *Oxford Bulletin of Economics and Statistics*, 44: 199–226.

Knight, J. and Song, L. (1991) 'The determinants of urban income inequality in China', *Oxford Bulletin of Economics and Statistics*, 53: 123–54.

Knight, J. and Song, L. (1993) 'Why urban wages differ in China', in Griffin, K. and Zhao, R. (eds), *The Distribution of Income in China*, London: Macmillan, pp. 216–84.

Knight, J. and Song, L. (1995) 'Towards a labour market in China', *Oxford Review of Economic Policy*, 11: 97–117.

Knight, J. and Song, L. (1999) *The Rural–Urban Divide: Economic Disparities and Interactions in China*, Oxford: Oxford University Press.

Knight, J., Song, L. and Jia, H. (1999) 'Chinese rural migrants in urban enterprises: three perspectives', *Journal of Development Studies*, 35: 73–104.

Mincer, J. and Higuchi, Y. (1988) 'Wage structures and labor turnover in the United States and Japan', *Journal of the Japanese and International Economies*, 2: 97–133.

Organization for Economic Co-operation and Development (OECD) (1997) *Employment Outlook*, Paris: OECD.

Pissarides, C.A. (1994) 'Search unemployment with on-the-job search', *Review of Economic Studies*, 61, 457–75.

# 12 How does firm profitability affect wages in urban China?

*John Knight and Li Shi*

## 12.1 Introduction

During China's period of central planning, state-owned enterprises (SOEs) were highly profitable: the state adopted a 'price-scissors' policy, keeping industrial prices high and agricultural prices low in order to finance industrialization. During the period of economic reform, increased market competition from various sources squeezed SOE profits generally. In response, the Chinese government initiated, and later accelerated, the reform of SOEs in urban areas. One of the principal elements in the reform is to accord more autonomy to enterprises in terms of prices, products, investment and operation, so allowing them greater freedom to cope with market competition. As a result, some enterprises have been successful in making profits and some have failed.

Management has also acquired greater powers to determine the wages of employees. The various pressures on managers may well have caused the wage level to be linked to the profitability of the enterprise. At the same time, governments have reduced subsidies to enterprises incurring losses, so making it difficult for loss-makers to pay even contracted wages. These changes can be expected to have strengthened the linkage between the wages of workers and the performance and profitability of their firms. The labour market is still in a rudimentary stage of development and job mobility among urban workers across regions and across work units within regions remains very low. This means that wage differences among firms are not ironed out by labour market competition: large and persistent wage segmentation across firms is possible.

Three questions arise. First, how does enterprise profitability affect the wages of workers? Second, how are profits shared among workers in profit-making enterprises (PMEs) and losses shared among workers in loss-making enterprises (LMEs)? Third, are there differences in wage distribution between the two types of enterprise? This chapter attempts to answer these questions using the data from two household surveys conducted in urban China, one in 1995 and the other in 1999.

This chapter is structured as follows. Section 12.2 offers a brief review of the relevant literature, and section 12.3 provides a theoretical framework. Section 12.4 describes the surveys and the basic statistics from the data sets. Sections 12.5 to

12.7 address the respective questions: How do profits affect the wage level? How are profits distributed among workers? How does profit-sharing affect wage inequalities? Section 12.8 concludes and reflects.

## 12.2 Literature review

There is a growing literature on the relationship between a firm's profitability and its workers' wage level. The work of Krueger and Summers (1987, 1988) – finding substantial, persistent and stable inter-industry wage differentials – with its suggestion of rent-sharing behaviour, was followed by a stream of publications on rent-sharing. Both Blanchflower *et al.* (1990), using cross-section data, and Nickell and Wadhwani (1990), using panel data, provided evidence of a positive relationship between wages and firm performance in the United Kingdom. Profits per worker were found to raise wages in Canada (Christophides and Oswald, 1992) and in the United States (Blanchflower *et al.* 1996). The relationship has also been found in some developing countries, for example, Teal (1996) for Ghana.

The empirical findings have attracted various causal explanations of the link between wages and performance or profits. The profit-sharing hypothesis and the efficiency wage hypothesis are the two main contending explanations. Nickell and Wadwhani (1990) note that, in the standard efficiency wage model, higher firm revenue has no effect on the efficiency wage, which requires simply that the effort-wage elasticity be unity, i.e. a rise in profits does not alter the efficiency wage. However, Krueger and Summers (1988) argue that rent-sharing cannot be separated from efficiency wages, for two reasons. First, if a firm generates rents, then a failure to share them with its employees may result in their withdrawal of cooperation. Second, in an efficiency wage environment, rent-sharing is less expensive for firms if an increase in wages above the optimum is partly offset by an efficiency gain. Thus, the possibility of rent-sharing may increase the efficiency wage and the possibility of efficiency wage gains may increase rent-sharing. Bewley (1999) provided an efficiency wage explanation for downward wage inflexibility: because they expect to be treated fairly, wage cuts reduce workers' morale and thus harm their employer. Just as the adverse effect of a wage cut is greater if it is perceived to be unjustified (Howitt 2002: 129), so the adverse effect of an employer's failure to share profits may increase with profits. Thus, the efficiency wage can be a positive function of (last period's) profits per worker (Layard *et al.* 1991: 161).

The potential endogeneity of the profits variable in the wage equation thus poses a problem for identifying the causal effect of profits on wages. The problem is generally solved in the literature by instrumenting the profits variable with one that is exogenous to wages but is well correlated with profits. In the absence of efficiency wage effects – given that an increase in the wage decreases profits, *ceteris paribus* – simultaneity bias reduces the estimated coefficient on profits; in the presence of efficiency wage effects, the direction of bias depends on the relative slopes of the two curves.[1]

In China, the association between enterprise performance and wages has been examined at the early stage of urban economic reform. In the 1980s, basic wages were strictly laid down but enterprises had some discretion in the payment of bonuses from their retained profits. Hay *et al.* (1994) estimated the determinants of wages in some 400 SOEs during the period 1984–1987, and found a significantly positive coefficient on the rate of profit on capital. Groves *et al.* (1994), using the same data set, found both that profit retention increased the bonus per employee and that (instrumented) bonus payments generally raised firm productivity. The interpretation placed on these results was that, as they acquired more autonomy during the 1980s, managers strengthened worker incentives, and that these efficiency wage payments were effective in improving enterprise efficiency. Hussain and Zhuang (1994) used a panel of some 500 SOEs for the period 1986–1991 to estimate the determinants of the bonus per employee. Profit per employee was treated as endogenous and instrumented in order to establish the causal effect of profit on bonus. Its coefficient was significantly positive for the group of profit-making enterprises.

By contrast, Zhuang and Xu (1996) used the same data set to explain the rate of profit on capital, with the bonus per employee treated as an endogenous explanatory variable and instrumented. Its significant positive coefficient was interpreted to show that enterprises pay efficiency wages in order to raise profits. Jefferson *et al.* (1999: 190–2), using a survey of 5,000 urban enterprises for the period 1988–1992 and two-stage least squares to correct for endogeneity, estimated an elasticity of bonus per worker to retained profits per worker of 0.19 and 0.24 for state-owned and collectively owned enterprises, respectively. However, since they also found that labour productivity was responsive to the bonus per worker – with an elasticity of 0.29 and 0.19, respectively – they argued that causation ran both ways. The evidence from all three surveys is thus consistent with there being two-way causation in the initial reform period, when managers lacked sticks and held only one carrot, in the form of the bonus.

In the early stages of Chinese SOE reform there was little managerial autonomy. Under the initial contract system, in the late 1980s and early 1990s, the contract was made between the enterprise as a whole – both workers and managers – and government. The enterprise was like a cooperative, and managers had little autonomy, for example over the level of employment or the dismissal of workers. It was therefore pointless to pay efficiency wages as a disciplinary device. However, relating wages to profits would have provided a group incentive to workers. Later, as the contract became one made between managers and government, managers acquired rather more autonomy. The environment now provided some incentive for worker effort, especially under the redundancy programme of the late 1990s. Nevertheless, it remained plausible that workers would expect to share SOE profits and would lose some motivation if this did not happen, i.e. the efficiency wage may well have remained a positive function of enterprise profitability.

## 12.3 Theoretical discussion

The theoretical framework for modelling the effect of profits on wages normally involves a bargaining game in which the firm maximizes profits and workers value the wage and employment. The bargained wage increases with the firm's ability to pay, and varies also with the strength of the union and with outside factors such as unemployment (e.g., Nickell and Wadhwani 1990). This approach does not fit the Chinese case well because managers need not maximize profits (given a history of soft budgets) and may instead promote the interests of their workers.

It is therefore appropriate to start with a model of the cooperative enterprise (Ward 1958). The theory of the cooperative, or collective, firm is based on the assumption that income per worker is maximized. Income per worker ($p$) comprises the competitive wage (fixed at $w$) plus enterprise surplus per worker ($s$). Given the production function $Y = Y(K, L)$, $Y_L > 0$, $Y_{LL} < 0$, where $Y$ is output, $K$ capital and $L$ labour, the cooperative firm maximizes

$$\begin{aligned}\pi &= w + s \\ &= w + \frac{Y - rK - wL}{L} \\ &= \frac{Y - rK}{L}\end{aligned} \qquad (12.1)$$

where $rK$ is a fixed capital charge on the firm, with given capital and constant rate of interest ($r$).

The maximization condition is

$$\begin{aligned}\pi_L &= \frac{Y_L}{L} - \frac{Y - rK}{L^2} \\ &= \frac{1}{L}\left(Y_L - \frac{Y - rK}{L}\right) = 0 \\ \text{i.e.} \quad Y_L &= \frac{Y - rK}{L}\end{aligned} \qquad (12.2)$$

If there were no capital charge, the marginal product of labour would be set equal to the average product, i.e. output per worker would be maximized. With a positive capital charge, because additional employment reduces the capital charge per worker, a higher level of employment is chosen. Employment will be lower under cooperative than under capitalist management provided that $(Y - rK)/L > w$, a condition that is likely to be satisfied. Collective firms have an incentive to restrict employment in the interests of their worker members.

This prediction of the cooperative model contrasts with the experience of state-owned enterprises (SOEs) and urban collective enterprises (UCEs) in China. The state is a crucial player in the game: enterprises are subordinated to party and government and the employment decision cannot be attributed to intra-firm bargaining. It has been official policy to ensure that all urban-registered workers are employed. The authorities have preferred unemployment to be disguised within the enterprise rather than open on the streets. Until the programme of redundancies was imposed on SOEs – becoming important only in the late 1990s – it was generally acknowledged that SOEs and UCEs contained surplus labour.

A third theoretical approach is provided by the efficiency wage model, adapted to make the efficiency wage a function of profitability. We start with the standard model, the unit of analysis being the firm. Each worker produces $y$ (= $Y/L$) units of output according to effort, with effort dependent on the firm's relative wage:

$$y = y(\pi, w) \tag{12.3}$$

where $\pi$ is the firm's chosen income per worker (the efficiency wage) and $w$ is the wage which would be paid in the absence of efficiency wage behaviour, assumed to be what a worker could get elsewhere. Profit maximization requires that the firm minimizes the wage cost per unit of output $\pi/y$. This implies a choice of $\pi$ such that

$$\frac{\partial w}{w} = \frac{\partial y}{y} \tag{12.4}$$

Output per head and the relative wage are related by

$$y = (\pi - w)^{\lambda} \tag{12.5}$$

where $\lambda$ represents the elasticity of output per worker in response to the relative wage. Combining (12.3), (12.4) and (12.5) yields

$$\frac{\pi - w}{\pi} = \lambda \tag{12.6}$$

The higher the elasticity, the higher the firm's chosen wage mark-up.

Departing from the standard model, we introduce the assumption that the efficiency wage is responsive to the profit per worker of the firm in the absence of efficiency wage setting, denoted by $s$. Workers expect to be paid more when the firm is profitable, and apply less effort if they are not paid more:

$$y = (\pi - w)^{\lambda s} \tag{12.7}$$

It follows that

$$\frac{\pi - w}{\pi} = \lambda s \tag{12.8}$$

Thus, the wage mark-up depends positively on the firm's profitability.[2]

Consider an application of our theoretical framework to the Chinese case. Assume that income per worker ($\pi$) is made up of the starting wage at the beginning of the reform ($w$) and a fraction ($\alpha$) of the firm's surplus per worker ($s$):

$$\pi = w + \alpha s \tag{12.9}$$

In an enterprise making a profit, $\alpha s > 0$, so $\pi > w$, i.e. employees of the enterprise share the profit. In one making a loss, $\alpha s < 0$, so $\pi < w$, implying that its employees share the loss. Differences in income per worker depend on the level of profits and losses per worker and on the profit-sharing rate. The value of $\alpha$ may differ according to whether a profit or loss is made.

With profits $\phi$, the profit function of the enterprise can be written as

$$\phi = Y(K, L) - rK - wL \tag{12.10}$$

Combining equations (12.9) and (12.10), we have

$$\pi = w + \frac{\alpha}{L}[Y(K, L) - rK - wL] \tag{12.11}$$

Many Chinese enterprises have contained surplus labour. Assume that this concession takes the form of $L_s = \beta L_o$, where $L_s$ is the number of surplus workers (employment beyond zero marginal product of labour), $\beta \geq 0$ is a policy variable imposed by government, and $L_o$ is the amount of labour employed when its marginal product is zero. Equation (12.11) can be rewritten as

$$\pi = w(1 - \alpha) + \frac{\alpha}{L_o(1 + \beta)}[Y(K, L_o) - rK] \tag{12.12}$$

Differentiating equation (12.12), we see that $\partial\pi/\partial\beta < 0$, i.e. an increase in $\beta$ implies that more workers have to share the profit available for distribution. It also means that laying off surplus labour raises the income of each worker who remains. Given this mechanism, it is understandable that the enterprises with redundant workers may not experience resistance from the majority of their workers in implementing a redundancy policy, at least once it is known, or can be predicted, who will be laid off. The majority can expect benefits from this policy, at the expense of the minority being laid off.

## 12.4 Data description

The data used in this chapter are from two urban household surveys, the 1995 CASS survey and the 1999 CASS survey. There are slightly different questions regarding the profitability of the work unit in the 1995 and 1999 surveys. In the former, the question is: 'Was your enterprise making a loss in 1995?' We can thus group workers into LMEs and PMEs. In the 1999 survey, the question offers three answers, i.e. '(1) making a loss (or at the edge of bankruptcy); (2) making marginal profit; (3) making high profit'. We can thus group workers either into two, as we do for the 1995 sample, or into three according to their answers.

One could argue that a worker's perception of profitability may be a misleading guide to the actual financial state of the firm. This argument is not valid because of the special nature of Chinese state-owned enterprises, whose employees account for nearly 80 per cent of the sample. On the one hand, SOE managers have no incentive to block information on profitability from their workers, and on the other hand, they are required by governments to provide open financial information to their workers. It is laid down that 'Managers must provide a financial report to the annual conference of workers' representatives in the enterprise'.[3]

Table 12.1 provides the notation and descriptive statistics of the main variables, and Table 12.2 presents basic survey information on two groups of workers, those in PMEs and those in LMEs. Whereas 30 per cent of workers reported working in LMEs in 1995, the figure reached 38 per cent in 1999. The average annual wage was 5,076 yuan for workers in LMEs and 6,453 yuan for workers in PMEs in 1995, the latter being 27 per cent higher than the former. Over the four years, the average LME wage increased by only 15 per cent, and the average PME wage by 41 per cent. In 1999 the average wage was 56 per cent higher in PMEs than in LMEs. Table 12.2 shows almost no difference between the two groups of workers in terms of gender composition, educational attainment and years of work experience. Indeed, in 1995 there is no substantial, or statistically significant, difference in any variable other than wages. In 1999, however, the PMEs have lower proportions of lower middle and primary school graduates and of manufacturing workers.

## 12.5 How do profits affect the wage level?

In order to standardize the wage difference between the two groups of workers, we estimate wage functions in which PME and LME are treated as dummy variables (LME being the omitted category). There are two specifications for the 1999 wage function. In the first, two dummies regarding profitability are introduced to make a comparison with the 1995 wage function, and in the second, three dummies are introduced to examine the effect of the size of profits.

Although we explained in the previous section why workers are unlikely to misunderstand the profitability of their enterprises, we cannot rule out the possibility that workers will judge profitability by their own wages, or that efficiency wage setting will raise profits. Accordingly, we need to test for the possible endogeneity of the dummy variables, PME and LME. The Hausman specification test is used here. The instruments chosen are whether father is a party member and whether he is in a professional or managerial occupation. The results show that the residual term is not statistically significant, and thus cannot reject the null hypothesis that the profit variables are exogenous in the wage functions.[4]

Table 12.3 shows the estimated wage functions for 1995 and 1999. The dependent variable is the logarithm of monthly wages (expressed annually). The control variables include gender, work experience (years), educational attainment, ownership of work unit, occupation, party membership, employment sector and province. The results from the 1995 wage function show that the workers in PMEs on average earned wages 21 per cent more than those in LMEs,[5] *ceteris paribus*. The difference is striking. However, it is even more striking in 1999, being as large as 41 per cent. Furthermore, when profitability is specified as three dummies, we see a notable difference between workers in enterprises with marginal profit (with wages 37 per cent higher than in LMEs) and those in enterprises with high profit (with wages 78 per cent higher than in LMEs). The average standardized wage of the latter is thus 30 per cent higher than that of the former.

*Table 12.1* Descriptive statistics and notation of the main variables

| *Name of variable* | *Notation* | *1995* | | *1999* | |
|---|---|---|---|---|---|
| | | *Mean* | *SD* | *Mean* | *SD* |
| Firm making loss* | *ent1* | 0.307 | 0.461 | 0.384 | 0.486 |
| Firm making profits | *ent2* | 0.693 | 0.461 | 0.616 | 0.486 |
| *of which*: | | | | | |
| Firm making marginal profits | *ent3* | | | 0.527 | 0.499 |
| Firm making large profits | *ent4* | | | 0.089 | 0.284 |
| Male | *sex1* | 0.531 | 0.499 | 0.548 | 0.498 |
| Female* | *sex2* | 0.469 | 0.499 | 0.452 | 0.498 |
| Years of work experience | *we* | 19.76 | 9.414 | 20.139 | 8.742 |
| Work experience squared | $we^2$ | 479.06 | 379.65 | 481.97 | 349.59 |
| 4-year college education | *ed1* | 0.039 | 0.194 | 0.053 | 0.224 |
| 2–3-year college education | *ed2* | 0.116 | 0.320 | 0.175 | 0.380 |
| Professional school education | *ed3* | 0.143 | 0.351 | 0.138 | 0.345 |
| Upper middle school education* | *ed4* | 0.272 | 0.445 | 0.289 | 0.453 |
| Lower middle school education | *ed5* | 0.367 | 0.482 | 0.324 | 0.468 |
| Primary school education or less | *ed6* | 0.062 | 0.242 | 0.021 | 0.143 |
| State-owned enterprise | *own1* | 0.779 | 0.415 | 0.774 | 0.419 |
| Urban collective enterprise* | *own2* | 0.190 | 0.392 | 0.139 | 0.346 |
| Private enterprise or other | *own3* | 0.014 | 0.119 | 0.086 | 0.281 |
| Professional or technician | *occ1* | 0.179 | 0.383 | 0.195 | 0.396 |
| Enterprise manager | *occ2* | 0.025 | 0.155 | 0.018 | 0.133 |
| Division head | *occ3* | 0.063 | 0.243 | 0.078 | 0.269 |
| Clerk | *occ4* | 0.166 | 0.372 | 0.141 | 0.348 |
| Skilled | *occ5* | 0.287 | 0.453 | 0.315 | 0.465 |
| Unskilled* | *occ6* | 0.211 | 0.408 | 0.236 | 0.425 |
| Other | *occ7* | 0.046 | 0.209 | 0.011 | 0.105 |
| Party member | *par1* | 0.199 | 0.399 | 0.258 | 0.438 |
| Non-party member* | *par2* | 0.801 | 0.399 | 0.741 | 0.438 |
| Agricultural sector | *sec1* | 0.024 | 0.154 | 0.051 | 0.219 |
| Manufacturing* | *sec2* | 0.574 | 0.494 | 0.459 | 0.498 |
| Construction | *sec3* | 0.041 | 0.198 | 0.063 | 0.242 |
| Transportation/communication | *sec4* | 0.059 | 0.235 | 0.122 | 0.327 |
| Wholesale/retail and food services | *sec5* | 0.178 | 0.383 | 0.109 | 0.312 |
| Real estate/social services | *sec6* | 0.029 | 0.168 | 0.108 | 0.311 |
| Health, education/culture and public services | *sec7* | 0.031 | 0.174 | 0.035 | 0.183 |
| Finance and insurance | *sec8* | 0.011 | 0.105 | 0.015 | 0.121 |
| Government/party/social organization | *sec9* | 0.012 | 0.109 | 0.007 | 0.086 |
| Other sectors | *sec10* | 0.040 | 0.195 | 0.032 | 0.177 |
| Beijing | *prov1* | 0.073 | 0.260 | 0.135 | 0.342 |
| Liaoning* | *prov2* | 0.121 | 0.326 | 0.200 | 0.400 |
| Jiangsu | *prov3* | 0.123 | 0.328 | 0.172 | 0.377 |
| Henan | *prov4* | 0.080 | 0.271 | 0.183 | 0.387 |
| Sichuan | *prov5* | 0.135 | 0.342 | 0.182 | 0.386 |
| Gansu | *prov6* | 0.044 | 0.206 | 0.128 | 0.334 |

Note: * denotes the default dummy category in the wage function analysis.

Table 12.2 Basic data on workers in PMEs and LMEs in 1995 and 1999

| | 1995 | | | 1999 | | |
|---|---|---|---|---|---|---|
| | (1) Workers in PMEs | (2 Workers in LMEs | (3) t-value for (1)–(2) | (4) Workers in PMEs | (5) Workers in LMEs | (6) t-value for (4)–(5) |
| AW | 6,452.9 | 5,076.4 | 14.7*** | 9121.8 | 5861.8 | 20.0*** |
| *in which*: | | | | | | |
| BW | 3,838.7 | 3,330.5 | 8.8*** | 8067.3 | 4991.0 | 22.1*** |
| BS | 1,205.2 | 589.2 | 12.6*** | 447.7 | 133.4 | 8.7* |
| SB | 971.3 | 765.5 | 8.1*** | 191.0 | 139.9 | 2.4 |
| OY | 437.7 | 391.2 | 2.0** | 415.8 | 597.5 | −4.0*** |
| lnAW | 8.600 | 8.402 | 11.3*** | 9.053 | 8.603 | 21.2*** |
| *sex1* | 0.535 | 0.522 | 0.95 | 0.549 | 0.548 | 0.07 |
| *sex2* | 0.465 | 0.478 | −0.95 | 0.451 | 20.817 | −0.03 |
| *we* | 19.563 | 20.205 | −2.58** | 19.716 | 0.038 | 3.61*** |
| *ed1* | 0.042 | 0.031 | 2.17** | 0.062 | 0.140 | 3.06*** |
| *ed2* | 0.117 | 0.113 | 0.40 | 0.196 | 0.128 | 4.21*** |
| *ed3* | 0.145 | 0.139 | 0.61 | 0.145 | 0.287 | 1.44* |
| *ed4* | 0.269 | 0.279 | −0.89 | 0.290 | 0.377 | 0.19 |
| *ed5* | 0.365 | 0.372 | −0.50 | 0.291 | 0.030 | −5.24*** |
| *ed6* | 0.061 | 0.065 | −0.50 | 0.015 | 0.758 | −2.91*** |
| *own1* | 0.794 | 0.746 | 4.40*** | 0.783 | 0.179 | 1.69* |
| *own2* | 0.174 | 0.227 | −5.21*** | 0.114 | 0.161 | −5.41*** |
| *own3* | 0.018 | 0.006 | 3.72*** | 0.102 | 0.170 | 4.21*** |
| *occ1* | 0.181 | 0.173 | 0.86 | 0.210 | 0.017 | 1.44* |
| *occ2* | 0.025 | 0.025 | −0.02 | 0.019 | 0.065 | 0.57 |
| *occ3* | 0.065 | 0.058 | 1.09 | 0.086 | 0.122 | 2.26** |
| *occ4* | 0.159 | 0.180 | −2.05** | 0.152 | 0.382 | 2.45** |
| *occ5* | 0.283 | 0.298 | −1.27 | 0.299 | 0.268 | −2.68** |
| *occ6* | 0.220 | 0.189 | 2.96*** | 0.217 | 0.008 | −3.44*** |
| *occ7* | 0.044 | 0.051 | −1.25 | 0.013 | 0.245 | 1.32 |
| *par1* | 0.195 | 0.207 | −1.14 | 0.266 | 0.754 | 1.39* |
| *par2* | 0.805 | 0.793 | 1.14 | 0.734 | 0.072 | −1.34 |
| *sec1* | 0.028 | 0.017 | 2.62** | 0.037 | 0.568 | −4.53*** |
| *sec2* | 0.559 | 0.608 | −3.75*** | 0.390 | 0.047 | −10.36*** |
| *sec3* | 0.041 | 0.041 | 0.04 | 0.072 | 0.068 | 3.08*** |
| *sec4* | 0.060 | 0.055 | 0.87 | 0.155 | 0.105 | 7.76*** |
| *sec5* | 0.177 | 0.182 | −0.56 | 0.111 | 0.062 | 0.57 |
| *sec6* | 0.034 | 0.018 | 3.67*** | 0.137 | 0.032 | 6.94*** |
| *sec7* | 0.036 | 0.02 | 3.48*** | 0.036 | 0.008 | 0.66 |
| *sec8* | 0.012 | 0.009 | 1.33 | 0.019 | 0.004 | 2.58** |
| *sec9* | 0.013 | 0.011 | 0.52 | 0.010 | 0.035 | 2.02** |
| *sec10* | 0.040 | 0.039 | 0.16 | 0.031 | 0.089 | −0.59 |
| *prov1* | 0.085 | 0.045 | 5.86*** | 0.163 | 0.170 | 6.23*** |
| *prov2* | 0.130 | 0.102 | 3.25*** | 0.219 | 0.157 | 3.51*** |
| *prov3* | 0.116 | 0.139 | −2.69** | 0.181 | 0.200 | 1.83* |
| *prov4* | 0.081 | 0.076 | 0.68 | 0.173 | 0.224 | −2.02** |
| *prov5* | 0.110 | 0.192 | −9.11*** | 0.155 | 0.159 | −5.15*** |

(Continued)

*Table 12.2* (Continued)

| | *1995* | | | *1999* | | |
|---|---|---|---|---|---|---|
| | *(1) Workers in PMEs* | *(2 Workers in LMEs* | *(3) t-value for (1)–(2)* | *(4) Workers in PMEs* | *(5) Workers in LMEs* | *(6) t-value for (4)–(5)* |
| *prov6* | 0.040 | 0.055 | −2.69** | 0.108 | 0.090 | −4.35*** |
| *prov7* | 0.084 | 0.068 | 2.28** | | | |
| *prov8* | 0.072 | 0.084 | −1.66* | | | |
| *prov9* | 0.108 | 0.094 | 1.74 | | | |
| *prov10* | 0.077 | 0.070 | 1.08 | | | |
| *prov11* | 0.097 | 0.076 | 2.73** | | | |

Notes:

1 AW = Average annual wage; BW = basic wage; BS = bonuses; SB = subsidies; OY = other income.

2 Wages are all expressed in 1995 prices and are based on reported monthly earnings. No correction was made for hours worked (data on hours being absent from the 1999 data set), but these tend to be standard in Chinese enterprises.

3 ***, ** and * denote statistical significance at the 1%, 5% and 10% level, respectively.

In order to explore the mechanisms by which profits affect wages, we estimated the equations of Table 12.3 for different province pairs and for different components of pay (Table 12.4). We combined Beijing and Jiangsu to represent provinces in which economic reform had gone far, and we took Henan and Gansu to be provinces in which reform had lagged.[6] Our hypothesis was that wages are more sensitive to profits in the more reformed parts of the Chinese economy. However, there is no substantial or significant difference between the two pairs.

It is clear that in 1995 the profit-sensitive component of pay was not the basic wage but 'other income', especially the bonus (Table 12.4). Employers had more control over the bonus than over the basic wage. However, we find a different pattern for 1999. The basic wage was then highly sensitive to profit-making (the coefficient of PME), and more so than was 'other income'. This is partly because employers had greater discretion than before over the basic wage, and partly because some LMEs were unable to pay even their contracted basic wages. Consistent with this latter interpretation, the difference in basic wages between loss-making firms and those making marginal profits was greater than the difference between marginally and highly profitable firms. There was wider disparity in 'other income' between high and marginal profit-making than between the latter and loss-making. This suggests that a rise in profits encourages profitable firms to increase the most discretionary form of remuneration – the bonus – rather than basic pay.

It is arguable that our use of the (annualized) monthly wage as the dependent variable instead of the hourly wage might exaggerate the difference in pay between profit-making and loss-making enterprises. For instance, it is plausible that longer hours are worked in more profitable firms. It is not possible either to

*Table 12.3* Estimates of wage functions, 1995 and 1999 (dependent variable: logarithm of annual wages)

| *Independent variable* | *1995* | | *1999* | | | |
|---|---|---|---|---|---|---|
| | | | *Specification I* | | *Specification II* | |
| | *Estimate* | *t-value* | *Estimate* | *t-value* | *Estimate* | *t-value* |
| Intercept | 7.407 | 179.05*** | 7.370 | 134.74*** | 7.351 | 135.51*** |
| *ent2* | 0.187 | 12.33*** | 0.345 | 18.16*** | | |
| *ent3* | | | | | 0.316 | 16.45*** |
| *ent4* | 0.202 | | | | 0.576 | 16.79*** |
| *sex1* | 0.135 | 9.27*** | 0.117 | 6.25*** | 0.115 | 6.19*** |
| *we* | 0.058 | 21.29*** | 0.047 | 12.19*** | 0.049 | 12.81*** |
| $we^2$ | −0.001 | −16.25*** | −0.001 | −8.46*** | −0.001 | −8.90*** |
| *ed1* | 0.202 | 3.60*** | 0.314 | 6.91*** | 0.297 | 6.57*** |
| *ed2* | 0.081 | 3.13*** | 0.147 | 4.98*** | 0.147 | 5.02*** |
| *ed3* | 0.029 | 1.22 | 0.069 | 2.29** | 0.069 | 2.34** |
| *ed5* | −0.066 | −3.64*** | −0.049 | −2.09** | −0.046 | −1.97** |
| *ed6* | −0.210 | −6.55*** | −0.161 | −2.54** | −0.164 | −2.60*** |
| *own1* | 0.149 | 8.37*** | 0.214 | 8.03*** | 0.206 | 7.80*** |
| *own3* | 0.300 | 4.97*** | 0.331 | 8.41*** | 0.305 | 7.79*** |
| *occ1* | 0.147 | 5.81*** | 0.214 | 6.92*** | 0.206 | 6.72*** |
| *occ2* | 0.167 | 3.37*** | 0.121 | 1.68* | 0.125 | 1.75** |
| *occ3* | 0.164 | 4.80*** | 0.150 | 3.63*** | 0.136 | 3.32*** |
| *occ4* | 0.027 | 1.15 | 0.128 | 4.04*** | 0.127 | 4.04*** |
| *occ5* | 0.073 | 3.70*** | 0.107 | 4.26*** | 0.105 | 4.20*** |
| *occ7* | 0.000 | −0.01 | 0.050 | 0.57 | 0.061 | 0.70 |
| *par1* | 0.067 | 3.44*** | 0.080 | 3.40*** | 0.080 | 3.46*** |
| *sec1* | 0.016 | 0.35 | 0.097 | 2.32* | 0.101 | 2.43** |
| *sec3* | −0.032 | −0.90 | −0.002 | −0.04 | 0.004 | 0.11 |
| *sec4* | 0.035 | 1.18 | 0.245 | 8.40*** | 0.222 | 7.65*** |
| *sec5* | −0.052 | −2.64** | 0.068 | 2.17** | 0.062 | 2.02** |
| *sec6* | −0.029 | −0.69 | 0.246 | 8.06*** | 0.228 | 7.53*** |
| *sec7* | −0.018 | −0.43 | 0.122 | 2.43** | 0.103 | 2.08** |
| *sec8* | 0.223 | 3.38*** | 0.361 | 4.83*** | 0.350 | 4.73*** |
| *sec9* | −0.064 | −1.02 | 0.058 | 0.56 | 0.010 | 0.09 |
| *sec10* | −0.330 | −9.15*** | −0.028 | −0.54 | −0.037 | −0.71 |
| Adjusted $R^2$ | 0.290 | | 0.361 | | 0.373 | |
| *F*-value | 75.60 | | 62.20 | | 63.40 | |
| Mean of dep. variable | 8.539 | | 8.881 | | 8.881 | |
| No. of observations | 6,748 | | 3,466 | | 3,466 | |

Notes:

1 Wage equations include province dummies, which are not shown in the table.

2 Wages are in 1995 prices.

3 ***, ** and * denote statistical significance at the 1%, 5% and 10% level, respectively.

4 The omitted dummy variable categories are enterprise making a loss, female, upper middle school, urban collective sector, unskilled, non-party member, manufacturing and Liaoning Province.

*Table 12.4* Coefficients on the profit variables in wage functions for subgroups, 1995 and 1999 (dependent variable: logarithm of annual wages)

| | *1995* | *1999* | | |
|---|---|---|---|---|
| | | *Specification I* | *Specification II* | |
| | *ent 2* | *ent 2* | *ent 3* | *ent 4* |
| Beijing and Jiangsu | 0.127*** | 0.345*** | 0.327*** | 0.512*** |
| Henan and Gansu | 0.113*** | 0.327*** | 0 .289*** | 0.598*** |
| Basic wage (BW) | 0.080*** | 0.745*** | 0.714*** | 0.984*** |
| Other income | 0.384*** | 0.384*** | 0.316*** | 0.917*** |
| *of which:* | | | | |
| Bonuses (BS) | 1.010*** | 0.737*** | 0.658*** | 1.350*** |
| Subsidy (SB) | 0.307*** | 0.267*** | 0.287*** | 0.113 |
| Other (OY) | 0.311*** | −0.134 | −0.166 | 0.117 |

Notes:

1 The equation specification is the same as for Table 12.3 except that in rows 1 and 2 the province dummy variables are excluded.

2 The omitted category is *ent1* (LMEs), columns 1 and 2 show the coefficients on *ent2* (PMEs), and columns 3 and 4 the coefficients on the dummies for firms making marginal profits and firms making large profits respectively.

3 *** denotes statistical significance at the 1% level.

standardize for hours worked or to predict wage per hour in the wage equations owing to the lack of data on hours in 1999. However, the information is available for 1995, and this is used as a check. In fact, workers in PMEs were employed for 2,200 hours on average in that year, and those in LMEs for 2,199 hours – only one hour less. The introduction of hours worked into the wage equation produced a positive and significant coefficient on hours, as expected. However, the coefficient on *ent2* (the premium on employment in a profitable enterprise) was barely altered, being 0.186 ($t = 11.67$) compared with 0.187 ($t = 12.33$) in Table 12.3. Similarly, when wage per hour was made the dependent variable, the coefficient was 0.190 ($t = 11.39$). Our results are robust.

## 12.6 How are profits distributed among workers?

To explore how profits were allocated to workers, we introduced interaction terms between the profitability variable and the other explanatory variables. Among all the interaction terms attempted, only two sets (interaction with work experience, *ent2.we*, and its squared term, *ent2.we*$^2$, and with ownership, *ent2.own*$_i$) have significant coefficients in the 1995 function. From Table 12.5 it can be observed that the introduction of the interaction terms dramatically changes the coefficient of the profit variable in 1995. The coefficient becomes negative and insignificant, which implies that the interaction terms are crucial. The interaction coefficients indicate that profits in PMEs were distributed to reward work experience in 1995. Since years of employment experience are the same as years of tenure for the

*Table 12.5* Estimates of wage functions with interaction terms for 1995 and 1999 (dependent variable: logarithm of annual wages)

| *Independent variable* | *1995* | | *1999* | | | |
|---|---|---|---|---|---|---|
| | | | *Specification I* | | *Specification II* | |
| | *Estimate* | *t-value* | *Estimate* | *t-value* | *Estimate* | *t-value* |
| Intercept | 7.577 | 123.87*** | 7.403 | 92.13*** | 7.402 | 92.95*** |
| *ent2* | −0.049 | −0.77 | 0.423 | 4.66*** | | |
| *ent3* | | | | | 0.382 | 4.09*** |
| *ent4* | | | | | 0.511 | 2.99*** |
| *sex1* | 0.135 | 9.26*** | 0.115 | 6.16*** | 0.114 | 6.16*** |
| *we* | 0.043 | 8.32*** | 0.054 | 8.42*** | 0.054 | 8.46*** |
| *we*$^2$ | −0.001 | −6.00*** | −0.001 | −6.12*** | −0.001 | −6.13*** |
| *ed1* | 0.147 | 3.72*** | 0.312 | 6.85*** | 0.295 | 6.52*** |
| *ed2* | 0.082 | 3.18*** | 0.149 | 5.03*** | 0.148 | 5.05*** |
| *ed3* | 0.031 | 1.33 | 0.069 | 2.31** | 0.068 | 2.29** |
| *ed5* | −0.063 | −3.50*** | −0.050 | −2.11** | −0.047 | −2.01** |
| *ed6* | −0.211 | −6.57*** | −0.164 | −2.58** | −0.169 | −2.67*** |
| *own1* | 0.107 | 3.66*** | 0.189 | 4.98*** | 0.188 | 4.99*** |
| *own3* | 0.075 | 0.47 | 0.239 | 3.53*** | 0.239 | 3.55*** |
| *occ1* | 0.146 | 5.76*** | 0.211 | 6.82*** | 0.206 | 6.72*** |
| *occ2* | 0.163 | 3.30*** | 0.120 | 1.68* | 0.124 | 1.74* |
| *occ3* | 0.162 | 4.75*** | 0.151 | 3.66*** | 0.137 | 3.34*** |
| *occ4* | 0.025 | 1.09 | 0.126 | 4.00*** | 0.124 | 3.97*** |
| *occ5* | 0.072 | 3.66*** | 0.105 | 4.19*** | 0.103 | 4.13*** |
| *occ7* | −0.003 | −0.07 | 0.046 | 0.53 | 0.062 | 0.71 |
| *par1* | 0.068 | 3.46*** | 0.079 | 3.37*** | 0.079 | 3.39*** |
| *sec1* | 0.013 | 0.29 | 0.097 | 2.31** | 0.100 | 2.40** |
| *sec3* | −0.032 | −0.92 | −0.001 | −0.02 | 0.004 | 0.10 |
| *sec4* | 0.037 | 1.24 | 0.244 | 8.36*** | 0.225 | 7.69*** |
| *sec5* | −0.051 | −2.58** | 0.061 | 1.94** | 0.057 | 1.82* |
| *sec6* | −0.028 | −0.68 | 0.241 | 7.89*** | 0.228 | 7.51*** |
| *sec7* | −0.014 | −0.35 | 0.119 | 2.38** | 0.102 | 2.05** |
| *sec8* | 0.226 | 3.42*** | 0.353 | 4.72*** | 0.343 | 4.63*** |
| *sec9* | −0.060 | −0.95 | 0.055 | 0.53 | 0.018 | 0.17 |
| *sec10* | −0.328 | −9.09*** | −0.034 | −0.64 | −0.043 | −0.83 |
| *ent2.we* | 0.021 | 3.56*** | −0.010 | −1.27 | | |
| *ent2.we*$^2$ | 0.000 | −3.38*** | 0.000 | 0.85 | | |
| *ent2.own1* | 0.062 | 1.73* | 0.050 | 0.97 | | |
| *ent2.own3* | 0.280 | 1.63* | 0.141 | 1.70* | | |
| *ent3.we* | | | | | −0.008 | −0.95 |
| *ent3.we*$^2$ | | | | | 0.000 | 0.64 |
| *ent3.own1* | | | | | 0.037 | 0.72 |
| *ent3.own3* | | | | | 0.057 | 0.68 |
| *ent4.we* | | | | | 0.002 | 0.17 |
| *ent4.we*$^2$ | | | | | 0.000 | −0.33 |
| *ent4.own1* | | | | | 0.052 | 0.38 |
| *ent4.own3* | | | | | 0.291 | 1.82* |

(Continued)

*Table 12.5* (Continued)

| *Independent variable* | *1995* | | *1999* | | | |
|---|---|---|---|---|---|---|
| | | | *Specification I* | | *Specification II* | |
| | *Estimate* | *t-value* | *Estimate* | *t-value* | *Estimate* | *t-value* |
| Adjusted $R^2$ | 0.296 | | 0.362 | | 0.373 | |
| *F*-value | 68.7 | | 55.5 | | 51.3 | |
| Mean of dep. variable | 8.539 | | 8.881 | | 8.881 | |
| No. of observations | 6,748 | | 3,466 | | 3,466 | |

Notes:
1 Wage equations include provincial dummies, which are not shown in the table.
2 Wages are in 1995 prices.
3 ***, **, and * denote statistical significance at the 1%, 5% and 10% level respectively.
4 The omitted dummy variable categories are enterprise making loss, female, upper middle school, urban collective sector, unskilled, non-party member, manufacturing, Liaoning Province and interaction terms *ent2.own2* and *ent4.own2*.

great majority of workers, it seems that tenure, i.e. length of service in the firm, was the major criterion for profit-sharing. The other interaction terms suggest that, for workers in SOEs and private enterprises, the profitability of the enterprise made a greater difference (6 per cent and 32 per cent more respectively) than for workers in the omitted ownership category, urban collective enterprises. Although these coefficients are significant only at the 10 per cent level, they hint that profit-sharing was more important in SOEs and private enterprises than in collectives.

Looking at the coefficients of the interaction terms in the 1999 wage function, we find a different pattern. None of the coefficients is statistically significant, neither in specification I nor in specification II. Seniority was no longer important to profit distribution in 1999, nor was ownership. As a result, the coefficients of the profitability variables alone remain very similar to those in Table 12.3: they are highly significant and large in size. The effect of profits on wages is uncorrelated with any of the other determinants of wages. These results suggest that the profits being shared by the PMEs were more equally distributed among their employees in 1999 than in 1995. This argument will be explored further and verified in the next section.

## 12.7 Does profit-sharing affect wage inequalities?

In urban China an employee shares either the profits or the losses of their enterprise. This is the main finding of Section 12.5. A consequential question arises. Are profits or losses shared equally among employees of the enterprise? We conduct two exercises. First, we decompose the difference between the two groups of worker in average wages in both years, and also in average wage growth over the four-year period, in order to identify the main components of these differences. Second, we simulate the wages of standardized workers with particular characteristics, in order to examine how wages differed for various types of worker according to profitability and over time.

The decomposition approach requires the estimation of wage functions for the two groups separately. This can involve a selectivity problem, implying that the coefficients in the wage equations are biased. To test for selectivity bias, we used the Heckman selection model. The channel of finding the job (*jobc* = 1 if job was assigned by government, and *jobc* = 0 if job was obtained through other channels) was chosen as the exclusion restriction variable. This exclusion restriction variable was valid in 1995, being significant in the selection model but not in the wage functions. A probit equation was estimated to predict whether a worker is employed in a profit-making or a loss-making firm. The inverse Mills ratio ($\lambda$) so obtained was then included in the wage functions. However, the estimation did not yield statistically significant coefficients on the $\lambda$ terms. This implies that selectivity was not a problem. When the same exclusion restriction variable was applied to the 1999 estimation, its coefficient was not significant in the selection model. Other variables were experimented with as exclusion restriction variables, but none proved to be valid.[7]

We investigated the possibility of sample selection bias in further ways. First, we restricted the sample to workers who had been employed in their enterprises for more than five years in the 1995 survey and for more than ten years in the 1999 survey. Before the 1990s, jobs were mainly assigned through official channels and there was little freedom for workers to find jobs by themselves. The wage functions showed that the coefficient of the profitability variable was slightly reduced, from 0.345 to 0.327 in the 1999 equation (Specification I), but slightly increased, from 0.187 to 0.205, in the 1995 equation. Our second test was to examine the extent of mobility in the urban labour market. Only 18.5 per cent of the workers in the 1999 survey have changed their jobs since first entering employment, and this proportion does not differ significantly between workers in PMEs and LMEs (19.1 per cent versus 17.3 per cent). Mobility is likely to be even lower in 1995 but there is no equivalent question in the 1995 survey. The extreme immobility of workers helps to explain why sample selectivity appears not to be a problem, i.e. the sorting of workers into profitable and non-profitable firms by unobserved 'ability' is negligible.

The decomposition results are presented in Tables 12.6 and 12.7, which are based on the estimates of the wage functions without selectivity correction (Appendixes 12.A and 12.B).[8] Table 12.6 decomposes the wage difference between the two groups of workers. In both years, the major part of this difference comes from the differences in coefficients between the two wage functions (89 per cent in 1995 and 81 per cent in 1999). In the 1995 decomposition, the difference due to coefficients can be further attributed largely to the work experience variable,

*Table 12.6* Decomposition of the wage difference between PMEs and LMEs

| | *Percentage of the total difference that is due to differences in* | | | |
|---|---|---|---|---|
| | *1995* | | *1999* | |
| | *Means* | *Coefficients* | *Means* | *Coefficients* |
| Total | 10.6 | 89.4 | 18.6 | 81.4 |
| *in which:* | | | | |
| Gender | 0.8 | 4.7 | 0.1 | −3.1 |
| Seniority | −5.9 | 84.9 | −6.3 | −26.1 |
| Education | 2.4 | 4.3 | 5.2 | 1.0 |
| Ownership | 2.7 | 23.5 | 2.9 | 20.1 |
| Occupation | 1.6 | 33.6 | 2.3 | 0.0 |
| Party membership | −0.3 | 0.3 | 0.5 | −1.6 |
| Economic sector | 0.2 | −10.8 | 7.8 | 1.2 |
| Province | 9.1 | −37.2 | 6.1 | −15.5 |
| Intercept | 0 | −13.8 | 0 | 105.4 |

Note: Being based on estimated equations in Appendixes 12.A and 12.B, in which the dependent variable is the logarithm of earnings, it is the difference in the means of log earnings that is decomposed in Tables 12.6 and 12.7.

which explains 85 per cent of the total difference. This suggests that the shared profits were distributed among workers according to their experience or seniority. That distribution pattern disappears in the 1999 decomposition analysis. The results indicate that work experience was rewarded even less in PMEs than in LMEs. Moreover, occupation (the second most important variable in 1995) made no contribution in 1999. Thus, the difference in mean wages can be entirely attributed to the difference in intercept terms. The intercept has been chosen (in the omission of dummy categories) to represent typical low-paid unskilled labour.[9] A further decomposition of the 1999 earnings differences between break-even and loss-making firms and between break-even and high-profit firms (not shown) indicates that it is particularly the workers with low-earning characteristics who share losses and who also share profits: each intercept accounts for more than the wage difference to be explained.

Table 12.7 decomposes the growth in average wages between 1995 and 1999. As shown in Table 12.2, wages grew much faster in PMEs than in LMEs over that period. The results show how the increased wages were distributed among workers of different characteristics. It is again the difference in coefficients that explains the great majority of the wage growth (86 per cent in PMEs and 87 per cent in LMEs). However, the two groups differ in the relative importance of their explanatory variables. First, the change in the intercept term is important in explaining the wage growth of PMEs: nearly two-thirds of the difference is attributable to the intercept terms. By contrast, the intercept term accounts for –90 per cent of the wage growth of LMEs. Second, the work experience variable is much less important for workers in PMEs than for those in LMEs. The reward for experience or seniority declines over the period for the former group but increases for

*Table 12.7* Decomposition of the wage increase between 1995 and 1999

| | *Percentage of the total difference that is due to differences in* | | | |
|---|---|---|---|---|
| | *PMEs* | | *LMEs* | |
| | *Means* | *Coefficients* | *Means* | *Coefficients* |
| Total | 13.8 | 86.2 | 12.8 | 87.2 |
| *in which:* | | | | |
| Gender | 0.4 | −4.9 | 1.4 | 1.0 |
| Seniority | 3.7 | −44.7 | 8.7 | 49.2 |
| Education | 4.3 | 10.7 | 3.9 | 20.4 |
| Ownership | 6.8 | 8.8 | 0.9 | 10.4 |
| Occupation | 1.2 | 2.3 | 1.2 | 35.3 |
| Party membership | 0.9 | 0.9 | 0.9 | 5.0 |
| Economic sector | 0.4 | 26.9 | 5.1 | 21.4 |
| Province | −3.7 | 20.9 | −9.2 | 34.7 |
| Intercept | 0 | 65.2 | 0 | −90.2 |

Note: Wages are in 1995 yuan.

the latter group. Third, the human capital variables, education and occupation, make a larger contribution in LMEs (56 per cent) than in PMEs (13 per cent).

The omitted dummy categories include female, low educational level, unskilled, urban collective, and manufacturing sector. The large and positive contribution made by the intercepts in PMEs indicates that relatively unskilled and poorly paid workers experienced a huge wage increase. By contrast, the large and negative contribution of the intercepts in LMEs indicates a sharp fall in the wages of workers with such characteristics. The relatively unskilled thus experienced very different fortunes according to the profitability of their employer. As a result of profit-sharing by those enterprises with profits to share, their poorly paid employees were able to improve both their absolute and their relative position over the four-year period.

Using the estimated wage function for workers in PMEs and LMEs in 1995 and 1999, we compute the predicted wages for particular groups of workers (Table 12.8), holding all other variables constant at their mean values. Comparing the predicted wages across groups, we can discover how the effects of profitability differ among groups. From this we calculate the relative predicted wages for the groups. Two clear patterns emerge from Table 12.9. First, while the wage difference between the workers in PMEs and LMEs increased over time, the difference for the group with lower-paying characteristics (the first in each pair) increased even faster (the third column). The one complication is the comparison of provinces. Industrialized Liaoning had higher wages in 1995 but lower wages in 1999: because of the collapse of much of its heavy industry, real wages in its LMEs fell. Second, of the four groups, wage growth was least rapid for workers with lower-paying characteristics in LMEs in each case (columns 4 and 5).

*Table 12.8* Predicted wages of particular groups of workers (in 1995 yuan)

| | *1995* | | *1999* | |
|---|---|---|---|---|
| | *PME (1a)* | *LME (1b)* | *PME (2a)* | *LME (2b)* |
| Female | 5,733 | 4,650 | 8,261 | 5,216 |
| Male | 7,081 | 5,465 | 9,833 | 6,402 |
| | (1.24) | (1.18) | (1.19) | (1.23) |
| Primary school | 5,791 | 4,585 | 7,419 | 4,718 |
| College level | 8,529 | 6,518 | 12,721 | 8,224 |
| | (1.47) | (1.42) | (1.72) | (1.74) |
| Urban collective | 5,385 | 4,540 | 6,213 | 5,044 |
| Private sector | 8,706 | 5,203 | 10,035 | 6,164 |
| | (1.62) | (1.15) | (1.62) | (1.22) |
| Unskilled | 5,427 | 4,421 | 7,480 | 4,768 |
| Professional | 7,374 | 6,061 | 10,808 | 6,901 |
| | (1.36) | (1.37) | (1.45) | (1.45) |
| Manufacturing | 6,420 | 5,085 | 8,239 | 5,416 |
| Financial sector | 7,781 | 6,378 | 11,948 | 8,819 |
| | (1.21) | (1.25) | (1.45) | (1.63) |
| Liaoning | 6,154 | 5,129 | 8,033 | 4,696 |
| Jiangsu | 5,981 | 4,286 | 10,006 | 6,247 |
| | (0.97) | (0.84) | (1.25) | (1.33) |

Notes:
1 Being based on estimated equations in which the dependent variable is the logarithm of annual earnings, the predicted mean wage of each group is its geometric mean and not its arithmetic mean.
2 The figure in parentheses shows the wage of the second of each pair expressed as a ratio of the first.

## 12.8 Conclusions

Enterprise reform in urban China had involved greater managerial autonomy, including more decentralized wage-setting. In principle this could have produced a more competitive labour market, in which the 'law of one price' increasingly prevailed. However, that process was hampered by two factors. One was a lack of labour mobility among urban workers. Had employees of low-paying firms been willing and able to transfer to high-paying firms, the resultant adjustments in labour supply should have generated market forces bringing wages closer together. The other factor was the structure of managerial incentives. Even in the late 1990s it was not necessary for firms to be profit-maximising, and they were apparently willing to hand over some of the profits to their workers.

The combination of low labour mobility and profit-sharing behaviour may explain why there was a considerable difference in (standardized) mean wages between profit-making and loss-making firms in 1995. The wage ratio grew substantially between 1995 and 1999, in which year the wage difference between highly profitable and just profitable firms was also large. The loosening of labour market policies over the four years – e.g. greater managerial powers on wage and

*Table 12.9* Relative predicted wages of particular groups of workers

| | PME/LME | | | 1999/1995 | |
|---|---|---|---|---|---|
| | *1995 (1a)/(1b) =(1c)* | *1999 (2a)/(2b) =(2c)* | *1999/1995 (2c)/(1c)* | *PME (2a)/(1a) =(3a)* | *LME (2b)/(1b) =(3b)* |
| Female | 1.23 | 1.58 | 1.28 | 1.44 | 1.12 |
| Male | 1.30 | 1.54 | 1.18 | 1.39 | 1.17 |
| Primary school | 1.26 | 1.57 | 1.25 | 1.28 | 1.03 |
| College level | 1.31 | 1.55 | 1.18 | 1.49 | 1.26 |
| Urban collective | 1.19 | 1.23 | 1.03 | 1.15 | 1.11 |
| Private sector | 1.67 | 1.63 | 0.98 | 1.15 | 1.18 |
| Unskilled | 1.22 | 1.57 | 1.29 | 1.38 | 1.08 |
| Professional | 1.23 | 1.57 | 1.28 | 1.47 | 1.14 |
| Manufacturing | 1.26 | 1.52 | 1.21 | 1.28 | 1.07 |
| Financial sector | 1.22 | 1.35 | 1.11 | 1.54 | 1.38 |
| Liaoning | 1.20 | 1.71 | 1.43 | 1.31 | 0.92 |
| Jiangsu | 1.40 | 1.60 | 1.14 | 1.67 | 1.46 |

Notes:
1 Derived from Table 12.8.
2 Note that (2c)/(1c) is identical to (3a)/(3b).

employment levels, and the cracking of the 'iron rice bowl' that had tied workers to firms – might be expected to have reduced labour market segmentation. By contrast, our evidence suggests that labour market segmentation among firms was strong and became stronger over the period. Blecher (2002: 286–93) conducted interviews with Chinese workers and found them to be well aware that their wages depended on the economic health of their employer. Workers generally felt that this was unfair, but they tended to accept the unfairness as inevitable or to blame their enterprise managers rather than the system or the government. Profit-related wages may not have political consequences, but they are a stumbling block on China's path to an efficient competitive labour market.

We also found that profits were distributed to workers in different ways in the two years. In 1995 the workers who gained most from being employed in profit-making firms were those with longer employment experience (which is difficult to separate from longer tenure with the firm) and those in state-owned and private, as opposed to urban collective, enterprises. It appears that more experienced, longer-serving workers were particularly rewarded. This relationship had disappeared by 1999. In that year, only the intercept term was important, implying that all workers received roughly the same (proportionate) increase in wages on account of having profit-making employers. This development suggests that managers chose to adopt a more neutral, less discriminating stance in sharing profits, consistent perhaps with the need to satisfy and motivate all their workers.

The relationship between profits and wages contributed to a widening of wage inequalities during the period of study. Not only were the employees of loss-making firms paid less than those of profit-making firms in 1995 but also their wages grew less rapidly over the subsequent four years, and among them it was particularly the unskilled workers with low-paying characteristics who fell behind.

We have shown that firm profitability is extremely important in understanding wages in urban China. Less progress was possible in identifying the underlying processes and causation. Our interpretation was that managers, if they have profits, are willing to share them with their workers, and that some loss-making firms may be unable to pay even contracted wages. In attempting to measure the causal effect of profits on wages, we had to deal with potential selection bias and simultaneity bias. The extreme immobility of labour and the results of our tests indicate that selection bias is not a problem. We were less sure about simultaneity bias, and the direction of any such bias was not predictable. Although SOE workers are likely to be well informed about their employer's profitability, it is possible that some workers' assessments of firm profitability are influenced by their wages. Two pieces of evidence favoured the rent-sharing explanation. First, our test could not reject the exogeneity of profits in the wage equation. Second, as the iron rice bowl cracked in the late 1990s, the threat of lay-off should have become an additional disciplinary device, so reducing the equilibrium efficiency wage, whereas the sensitivity of the wage to profits actually rose between 1995 and 1999. Nevertheless, the possibility remains that pay is at least partly governed by standard efficiency wage considerations and thus influences profits.

In any case, it is plausible in the Chinese conditions that failure to share profits can lead to the withdrawal of cooperation by workers. Given this threat, the efficiency wage is a positive function of profits: profit-sharing and efficiency wage effects are intertwined, and their separation would be artificial. This intertwining reflects the distinctive characteristics of the Chinese work unit (*danwei*). To some extent it remains a social institution with a set of managerial objectives and worker attitudes that set it apart from an enterprise in the Western sense.

Previous Chinese studies of this issue concerned the early reform period and had to rely only on enterprise-level data. By contrast, our study relates to the mid- and late 1990s and our data on individuals have made possible an analysis of the relationship between profits and wage structure as well as wage level. However, we have little enterprise-level information; nor could we discern whether firms adjust wages differently to increases in profits and in losses, or whether they treat urban-registered 'insiders' differently from rural-registered migrant 'outsiders', as argued by Knight, Song and Jia (1999). The importance of the wage–profit relationship calls for more research, using new surveys containing rich matching data sets on both individual workers and their employing firms.

## Notes

The chapter was written while Li Shi was visiting the Department of Economics, University of Oxford. The financial support of the Ford Foundation and the UK Department for

International Development is gratefully acknowledged. A shortened version of this chapter appeared under the title 'Wages, firm profitability and labor market segmentation in urban China' in *China Economic Review*, Vol. 16, 2005. Reproduced with permission from Elsevier.

1 For instance, Maddala (2001) 369–71).
2 This account of the efficiency wage model is adapted from Layard *et al.* (1991: 151–61).
3 See *The Outline of Enterprise Management in the Ninth Five-Year Plan*, issued by the State Economic and Trade Commission, February 1996.
4 The instrument is significant at the 5 per cent level in the first stage equation and the first stage residual has a *t*-value of under 0.5 in the second stage equation. A systematic search for identifying instruments was made, but – the (past) allocation of workers to (current) profit-making or loss-making firms being a fairly random process – no other variables could be found.
5 Derived as $\exp(\beta) - 1$, where $\beta$ is the coefficient.
6 Beijing and Jiangsu average sixth and Henan and Gansu seventeenth in the marketization index for China's provinces created by Fan *et al.* (2001).
7 Parents' party membership was also tried as an exclusion restriction variable in the 1999 selection model, but its coefficient was not significant in the probit equation.
8 The standard decomposition methodology of Oaxaca (1973) is used, viz. applying the PME coefficients to LME mean characteristics to calculate what LME workers would earn if paid according to the PME wage function. The alternative decomposition–applying the LME coefficients to PME mean characteristics to calculate what PME workers would earn if paid according to the LME wage function – yields very similar results.
9 This definition of the intercept gives economic meaning to the arbitrary division of the contributions of the intercept and coefficients. The omitted variables are female, lower middle school education, unskilled occupation, non-party membership, urban collective ownership, manufacturing sector and Liaoning province. See Tables 12.1 and 12.3.

## References

Bewley, T.F. (1999) *Why Wages Don't Fall in a Recession,* Cambridge, MA: Harvard University Press.

Blanchflower, D., Oswald, A. and Garrett, M. (1990) 'Insider power in wage determination', *Economica*, 57: 143–70.

Blanchflower, D., Oswald, A. and Sanfrey, P. (1996) 'Wages, profits and rent-sharing', *Quarterly Journal of Economics*, 111: 227–51.

Blecher, M.J. (2002) 'Hegemony and workers' politics in China', *The China Quarterly*, 170: 283–303.

Christophides, L. and Oswald, A. (1992) 'Real wage determination and rent-sharing in collective bargaining agreements', *Quarterly Journal of Economics*, 107(3): 985–1002.

Fan, G., Wang, X. and Zhang, L. (2001) 'Marketization index for China's provinces', Beijing: National Economic Research Institute, mimeo.

Groves, T., Hong, Y., McMillen, J. and Naughton, B. (1994) 'Autonomy and incentives in Chinese state enterprises', *Quarterly Journal of Economics*, 109(1): 183–209.

Hay, D., Morris, D., Liu, G. and Yao, S. (1994) *Economic Reform and State-Owned Enterprises in China, 1979–1987*, Oxford and New York: Oxford University Press.

Howitt, P. (2002) 'Looking inside the labor market: a review article', *Journal of Economic Literature*, 40(1): 125–38.

Hussain, A. and Zhuang, J. (1994) 'Impact of reform on wage and employment determination in Chinese state enterprises, 1986–1991', London School of Economics, Programme of Research into Economic Transformation and Public Finance: EF/12, November.

Jefferson, G., Singh, I., Hu, A. and Wang, B. (1999) 'Wage and employment behavior in Chinese industry', in Jefferson, G. and Singh, I. (eds), *Enterprise Reform in China: Ownership, Transition, and Performance*. Oxford and New York: Oxford University Press for the World Bank, pp. 171–96.

Knight, J., Song, L. and Jia, H. (1999) 'Chinese rural migrants in urban enterprises: three perspectives', *Journal of Development Studies*, 35(3): 73–104.

Krueger, A. and Summers, L. (1987) 'Reflections on the inter-industry wage structure', in Lang, K. and Leonard, J. (eds), *Unemployment and the Structure of the Labor Market*, New York: Basil Backwell.

Krueger, A. and Summers, L. (1988) 'Efficiency wages and the Inter-industry wage structure', *Econometrica*, 56(2): 259–93.

Layard, R., Nickell, S. and Jackman, R. (1991) *Unemployment: Macroeconomic Performance and the Labour Market,* Oxford: Oxford University Press.

Maddala, G.S. (2001) *Introduction to Econometrics*, 3rd ed., Chichester: John Wiley.

Nickell, S. and Wadhwani, S. (1990) 'Insider forces and wage determination', *Economic Journal*, 100: 496–509.

Oaxaca, R. (1973) 'Sex discrimination in wages', in Ashenfelter, O. and Rees, A. (eds), *Discrimination in Labor Markets*, Princeton, NJ: Princeton University Press.

Teal, F. (1996) 'The size and sources of economic rents in a developing country manufacturing labour market', Economic Journal, 106: 963–76.

Ward, B. (1958) 'The firm in Illyria: market syndicalism', *American Economic Review*, 48(4): 566–89.

Zhuang, J. and Xu, C. (1996) 'Profit-sharing and financial performance in the Chinese state enterprises: evidence from panel data', *Economics of Planning*, 29(3): 205–22.

## Appendix 12.A: Wage functions of workers in firms with and without profit, 1995

| | *Workers in PMEs* | | | *Workers in LMEs* | | |
|---|---|---|---|---|---|---|
| | *Mean* | *Estimate* | *t-value* | *Mean* | *Estimate* | *t-value* |
| Intercept | 1.000 | 7.541 | 125.84*** | 1.000 | 7.571 | 93.50*** |
| *sex1* | 0.536 | 0.143 | 6.04*** | 0.521 | 0.124 | 4.06*** |
| *we* | 19.737 | 0.070 | 16.05*** | 20.159 | 0.046 | 7.49*** |
| $we^2$ | 482.165 | −0.001 | −12.73*** | 489.981 | −0.001 | −5.51*** |
| *ed1* | 0.049 | 0.178 | 2.95*** | 0.026 | 0.015 | 0.15 |
| *ed2* | 0.130 | 0.032 | 0.76 | 0.121 | 0.050 | 0.93 |
| *ed3* | 0.145 | 0.033 | 0.87 | 0.126 | −0.022 | −0.42 |
| *ed5* | 0.371 | −0.081 | −2.66** | 0.399 | −0.080 | −2.15** |
| *ed6* | 0.047 | −0.271 | −4.63*** | 0.061 | −0.190 | −2.82*** |
| *own1* | 0.784 | 0.202 | 6.88*** | 0.742 | 0.144 | 4.18*** |
| *own3* | 0.017 | 0.370 | 4.13*** | 0.006 | −0.005 | −0.02 |
| *occ1* | 0.187 | 0.161 | 3.84*** | 0.176 | 0.121 | 2.24** |
| *occ2* | 0.023 | 0.257 | 3.12*** | 0.018 | 0.007 | 0.06 |
| *occ3* | 0.063 | 0.240 | 4.27*** | 0.055 | 0.091 | 1.19 |
| *occ4* | 0.138 | 0.087 | 2.21** | 0.164 | −0.046 | −0.91 |
| *occ5* | 0.310 | 0.085 | 2.68** | 0.327 | −0.006 | −0.15 |
| *occ7* | 0.043 | 0.095 | 1.58* | 0.049 | −0.013 | −0.18 |
| *par1* | 0.194 | 0.055 | 1.73* | 0.207 | 0.051 | 1.25 |
| *sec1* | 0.032 | 0.044 | 0.68 | 0.018 | 0.107 | 0.96 |
| *sec3* | 0.049 | −0.065 | −1.22 | 0.038 | 0.051 | 0.67 |
| *sec4* | 0.054 | 0.010 | 0.20 | 0.055 | −0.011 | −0.16 |
| *sec5* | 0.170 | −0.092 | −2.78** | 0.178 | −0.018 | −0.42 |
| *sec6* | 0.033 | −0.125 | −1.93* | 0.022 | 0.025 | 0.25 |
| *sec7* | 0.032 | 0.046 | 0.71 | 0.022 | 0.071 | 0.72 |
| *sec8* | 0.008 | 0.387 | 3.10*** | 0.004 | −0.064 | −0.28 |
| *sec9* | 0.012 | −0.222 | −2.10** | 0.006 | −0.308 | −1.59* |
| *sec10* | 0.046 | −0.317 | −5.74*** | 0.044 | −0.236 | −3.30*** |
| *prov1* | 0.151 | 0.320 | 8.50*** | 0.073 | 0.445 | 6.92*** |
| *prov3* | 0.206 | 0.187 | 5.36*** | 0.228 | 0.337 | 7.22*** |
| *prov4* | 0.144 | −0.174 | −4.53*** | 0.126 | −0.037 | −0.69 |
| *prov5* | 0.196 | 0.078 | 2.22** | 0.315 | 0.048 | 1.10 |
| *prov6* | 0.071 | −0.218 | −4.40*** | 0.089 | 0.040 | 0.67 |
| Adjusted $R^2$ | 0.275 | | | 0.214 | | |
| *F*-value | 33.20 | | | 12.00 | | |
| Mean of dep. variable | 8.599 | | | 8.376 | | |
| No. of observations | 2,629 | | | 1,253 | | |

Note: ***, ** and * denote statistical significance at the 1%, 5% and 10% level, respectively.

## Appendix 12.B: Wage functions of workers in firms with and without profit, 1999

| | *Workers in PMEs* | | | *Workers in LMEs* | | |
|---|---|---|---|---|---|---|
| | *Mean* | *Estimate* | *t-value* | *Mean* | *Estimate* | *t-value* |
| Intercept | 1.000 | 7.839 | 116.93*** | 1.000 | 7.365 | 77.53*** |
| *sex1* | 0.549 | 0.102 | 4.44*** | 0.547 | 0.128 | 4.02*** |
| *we* | 19.716 | 0.045 | 9.45*** | 20.817 | 0.055 | 7.95*** |
| $we^2$ | 468.988 | −0.001 | −6.38*** | 502.843 | −0.001 | −5.82*** |
| *ed1* | 0.062 | 0.308 | 5.80*** | 0.038 | 0.340 | 3.91*** |
| *ed2* | 0.196 | 0.154 | 4.36*** | 0.141 | 0.133 | 2.46** |
| *ed3* | 0.145 | 0.075 | 2.06** | 0.128 | 0.052 | 0.99 |
| *ed5* | 0.291 | −0.052 | −1.74* | 0.377 | −0.044 | −1.13 |
| *ed6* | 0.015 | −0.118 | −1.30 | 0.030 | −0.213 | −2.33** |
| *own1* | 0.783 | 0.252 | 7.07*** | 0.758 | 0.157 | 3.80*** |
| *own3* | 0.102 | 0.388 | 8.05*** | 0.061 | 0.226 | 3.07*** |
| *occ1* | 0.210 | 0.221 | 5.80*** | 0.171 | 0.185 | 3.46*** |
| *occ2* | 0.019 | 0.060 | 0.68 | 0.017 | 0.224 | 1.78* |
| *occ3* | 0.087 | 0.177 | 3.54*** | 0.065 | 0.083 | 1.14 |
| *occ4* | 0.152 | 0.101 | 2.61** | 0.122 | 0.176 | 3.17*** |
| *occ5* | 0.299 | 0.105 | 3.24*** | 0.342 | 0.107 | 2.66** |
| *occ7* | 0.013 | 0.028 | 0.28 | 0.008 | 0.072 | 0.43 |
| *par1* | 0.267 | 0.070 | 2.46** | 0.246 | 0.098 | 2.38** |
| *sec1* | 0.037 | −0.020 | −0.34 | 0.072 | 0.211 | 3.43*** |
| *sec3* | 0.072 | −0.007 | −0.16 | 0.047 | 0.017 | 0.24 |
| *sec4* | 0.155 | 0.222 | 6.69*** | 0.068 | 0.318 | 5.18*** |
| *sec5* | 0.111 | 0.077 | 1.95* | 0.105 | 0.018 | 0.33 |
| *sec6* | 0.137 | 0.269 | 7.72*** | 0.062 | 0.128 | 2.02** |
| *sec7* | 0.037 | 0.155 | 2.53** | 0.032 | 0.036 | 0.41 |
| *sec8* | 0.019 | 0.336 | 4.08*** | 0.008 | 0.439 | 2.61** |
| *sec9* | 0.010 | 0.105 | 0.93 | 0.004 | −0.096 | −0.39 |
| *sec10* | 0.031 | −0.020 | −0.29 | 0.035 | −0.042 | −0.50 |
| *prov1* | 0.163 | 0.431 | 11.94*** | 0.089 | 0.565 | 8.89*** |
| *prov3* | 0.181 | 0.292 | 8.20*** | 0.157 | 0.321 | 5.90*** |
| *prov4* | 0.173 | 0.026 | 0.73 | 0.200 | 0.094 | 1.80* |
| *prov5* | 0.155 | 0.103 | 2.80*** | 0.225 | 0.202 | 4.05*** |
| *prov6* | 0.109 | −0.037 | −0.89 | 0.159 | 0.107 | 1.97** |
| Adjusted $R^2$ | 0.295 | | | 0.258 | | |
| *F*-value | 29.84 | | | 15.91 | | |
| Mean of dep. variable | 9.053 | | | 8.604 | | |
| No. of observations | 2,136 | | | 1,329 | | |

Note: ***, ** and * denote statistical significance at the 1%, 5% and 10% level, respectively.

# 13 Social capital, unemployment and women's labour market outcomes in urban China

*Linda Yueh*

## 13.1 Introduction

Since economic reforms were introduced in 1978, with earnest implementation in urban areas during the mid-1980s, China has moved from a planned to a more market-oriented economy. Accompanying the gradual transition towards greater marketization is a general increase in inequality of income, including the incomes earned by men and women (Bian 1994; Khan and Riskin 1998; Knight and Song 1999; Yao 1999; Gustafsson and Li 2000). One factor that may determine success in an imperfect labour market could be *guanxi*, the Chinese variant of social capital.

Social capital is thought to have an economic role. We present a brief section on social capital with a focus on *guanxi*. Then, we develop a model of social capital in which the decision to invest is a function of time and resources expended, with a focus on gender differences. The form of the capital is likely to be dependent on the community under study; however, we posit that the decision to invest in relationships is generalizable beyond urban China. Finally, we seek to analyse its economic returns, specifically with the labour market, and thus we model but do not estimate the consumption component or non-economic returns to social capital.

## 13.2 *Guanxi* in China

An aspect of Chinese society that remains important before and after 1978 – in economic as well as in non-economic life – is *guanxi* (see, e.g., Bian 1994; Chang and Feuchtwang 1996).[1] *Guanxi*, the relationships that an individual has and maintains in a social network, is used synonymously with social capital.[2] Meals or gifts are common and effective methods to cement personal relationships or cultivate *guanxi* (see Yang 1994 for a sociological study of the flow of gifts in urban China; see also Yan 1996 for a similar study of gifts and reciprocity in rural China).

In certain respects, the *guanxi* practised in China appears to be affected by the institutional framework, including the lack of a comprehensive legal structure, the inconsistent enforcement of laws, risk minimization in an uncertain political–economic–social environment, risk spreading through pooled resources in an economy characterized by labour and material shortages, and information sharing in imperfect markets (Bian 1994; Yang 1994; Chang 1999; Knight and Song 1999).

Market imperfections in China likely contribute to the use and cultivation of *guanxi* as an informal strategy. However, Chinese communities in places with established institutions continue to rely on *guanxi,* thereby suggesting that the use of social capital is not merely in reaction to the lack of formal institutions. The benefits of transaction cost reduction may play a role in motivating investment in *guanxi* regardless of the specific context, but the environment is expected to affect the form of the capital.

There appear to be gender differences in acquiring *guanxi*. In her sociological study of the practice of *guanxi* in urban areas, primarily Beijing, Yang (1994) finds that women are unable to practise *guanxi* effectively because of fear of gaining a bad reputation. Women intellectuals and cadres are more involved in practising *guanxi* than those in the working class. Women may be excluded from *guanxi*-enhancing activities, such as drinking and banquets, decreasing their ability to develop contacts with men who tend to hold positions of influence.

The widespread use of *guanxi* suggests that there are positive returns that justify its costs. A portion of the returns is likely to be non-economic; however, some may be economic. A 1996 social anthropological study of a village in rural China finds that cultivating *guanxi* is akin to "fattening" a pig in which the profit is less than the cost of fattening the pig, but the possible future return of this favour warrants the action (Chang 1999). One economic return may take the form of generating job opportunities that improve employment outcomes. In urban China, Bian (1994) argues that *guanxi* was a determinant of employment success even in a system of allocated jobs.[3]

If there are gender differences in social capital, then the relationship between *guanxi* and employment outcomes suggests there may be differential opportunities available to those who invest in relationships. Opportunities can reduce transaction costs in imperfect markets (aiding the job-search process and thus facilitating labour mobility) and also increase efficiency on the job (contributing to productivity and successful self-employment). It is difficult to differentiate among these effects, but social capital might be one cause of gender differences in imperfect labour markets.

## 13.3 Optimal lifetime investment in *guanxi*

The model that follows is derived from well-known human capital models (Schultz 1961; Becker 1993 [1964]) and views investments in *guanxi* or social capital as a cost–benefit decision that takes into account present expenditures in terms of time, physical (e.g. monetary and in-kind gifts) as well as non-physical resources (e.g. emotions, attachments), as evaluated against the present value of future expected benefits in the form of economic and non-economic returns (see Uphoff 2000[4]). The economic returns could be a contact leading to a job and non-economic might be the utility of having many friends or maintaining good rapport among relatives. The focus will be to model the rate of economic returns to investments to the stock of social capital[5] or *guanxi*,[6] defined simply as interpersonal relationships (see also Krishna 2000[7]).

Akin to the human capital models, the investment costs in social capital consist of the direct and opportunity costs of the investment, as well as risk and liquidity premiums (Becker 1993 [1964]). The cost of the investment can be monetary or non-monetary, and can be both. The risk premium is large since it is uncertain whether returns are likely from investing in relationships. Finally, social capital, again like human capital, is highly illiquid because it cannot be used as collateral for a loan or other such security and would warrant a high liquidity premium.

We assume that a person will live $n$ periods. Her utility, $U_g$, depends on her consumption over time of commodities, as in

$$U_g = U_g(C_1, \ldots, C_n) \tag{13.1}$$

where $C_g$ is the amount of the commodity consumed in period $g$. The commodity, $C_g$, is produced at home with inputs consisting of her market goods and time. Let the composite market goods used in period $g$ be $x_g$, and the composite amount of time combined with $x_g$ be $t_{c_g}$. Then,

$$C_g = f(x_g, t_{c_g}), \qquad g = 1, \ldots, n \tag{13.2}$$

where $f$ is the production function in period $g$.

A person's time can be allocated among labour market activity (e.g. wage employment [work]), non-market consumption activity (e.g. reading [leisure] or cooking a meal [home work]) or social activity (e.g. chatting with friends or giving gifts [investing in social capital]). She produces social capital by investing some of her time and goods to cultivate relationships. The rate of change in her capital equals the difference between her rate of production and the rate of depreciation on her stock. This is represented by

$$o_g = f(t_{s_g}, x_{s_g}) \tag{13.3}$$

where $o_g$ is the output of social capital in the $g$th period, and $t_{s_g}$ and $x_{s_g}$ are the time and goods inputs, respectively. As a simplification, let the composite amount of time combined with $x_{s_g}$ be $t_{s_g}$.[8] For simplicity, $f$ is the same in all periods.

The stock of social capital is given by

$$S_{g+1} = S_g + o_g - \varphi S_g \tag{13.4}$$

where $S_{g+1}$ is the stock of social capital at the beginning of the $g + 1$ period, $S_g$ denotes the stock of social capital at the beginning of the $g$th period, and $\varphi$ is the rate of depreciation. Depreciation is positive in each period, $\varphi > 0$, and depends on the chance of reciprocation in every relationship.[9] For instance, if a relationship terminates so that the contact is no longer part of the social network, then $\varphi$ captures the rate of decrease in the person's stock of social capital.[10]

Each person maximizes the utility function (13.1), subject to the production constraints in (13.2), (13.3) and (13.4), and to the following time and goods (budget) constraints:

$$t_{c_g} + t_{w_g} + t_{s_g} = t, \qquad g = 1, \ldots, n \tag{13.5}$$

$$\sum_{g=1}^{n} \frac{(x_g + x_{s_g})}{(1+d)^g} = \sum_{g=1}^{n} \frac{(w_g t_{w_g} + v_g)}{(1+d)^g} \tag{13.6}$$

where $x_{s_g}$ is expenditure on social capital investment, $x_g$ is expenditure on market goods, $x_{s_g} + x_g$ is the expenditure on goods that must equal income in present value terms, $d$ is the interest rate, $w_g$ denotes the wage in period $g$, $v_g$ is the amount of non-labour income in period $g$, $s_g$ is the payment per unit of social capital in period $g$, $t_{c_g}$ and $t_{w_g}$ respectively represent the amount of time spent in consumption and work, while $t_{s_g}$ denotes the time spent investing in social capital in $g$, and $t$ is the total time available. Assuming non-zero values, the first-order optimality conditions are

$$\left(\frac{\partial U_g}{\partial C_g}\right)\left(\frac{\partial f}{\partial x_g}\right) = \lambda\left[\frac{1}{(1+d)^g}\right], \qquad g = 1, \ldots, n \tag{13.7}$$

$$\left(\frac{\partial U_g}{\partial C_g}\right)\left(\frac{\partial f}{\partial t_{c_g}}\right) = \lambda\left[\frac{w_g}{(1+d)^g}\right], \qquad g = 1, \ldots, n \tag{13.8}$$

$$0 = \lambda\left[\frac{w_g}{(1+d)^g}\right] - \sum_{N=g+1}^{n}\left[\frac{S_N t_{w_g}}{(1+d)^N}\right]\left(\frac{\partial S_N}{\partial t_{s_g}}\right) \tag{13.9}$$

where $\lambda$ is a Lagrangian multiplier equal to the marginal utility of wealth.

In equilibrium, equation (13.7) shows that the marginal utility of consumption of market goods depends on the interest rate, time preference and substitution between goods and time. The marginal utility of an additional hour of consumption, as seen in equation (13.8), is additionally affected by the wage. The path of these marginal utilities depends on the elasticities of substitution between goods and time in consumption and production. Regarding investment in social capital, equation (13.9) expresses the equilibrium condition that the present value of the marginal cost of investing in social capital equals the present value of future returns. Following Becker's solution, recall that we simplified the input into the production of social capital as a composite of time and market goods. Thus, the theoretical cost is forgone earnings, which is equal to the shadow price of time. In actuality, the shadow price of time consists also of the cost of market goods, so that the investment cost is forgone earnings plus expenditures. The return is equal to the shadow price of an hour of work or wages ($w_g = s_g S_g$). Therefore, the investment in social capital tends to decline with age for two reasons, one on the returns side and one on the cost side. The number of remaining periods will decrease with age so there will be fewer periods to enjoy the returns. Moreover, the cost of investing will tend to increase with age, i.e. as $S_g$ rises, forgone earnings will rise assuming an increasing age–earnings profile up to the age of the peak wage rate.

If women have more home work obligations, then they have less time (more constrained by equation (13.5)) and as secondary earners have fewer monetary resources (more constrained by equation (13.6)). In equilibrium, as seen in equations (13.7) and (13.8), they can afford fewer market goods and also have less time with which to invest in social capital. As a result, women invest less than men when they equate the marginal cost and returns per equation (13.9) and will have less social capital.

## 13.4 Returns to social capital in the labour market

The supply of labour to a firm is affected by job opportunities. Opportunities are viewed as options beyond the current job, such as alternative wage employment, non-employment or self-employment. Even under perfect information, there exist transaction costs such as the costs of job search that cause the supply of labour to be upward-sloping with respect to a firm. Social capital reduces frictions, lowers search costs, and thus generates returns in the form of favourable job opportunities.

We use a simple labour supply function to show how social capital affects the labour supplied to a firm. Labour supplied to a firm is a function of the firm-specific production function and the average wage in the industry faced by each group of labour, which is in turn affected by transaction costs and thus social capital.

A labour supply function takes the following form:

$$E(h_{i,k}|w_{i,k}) = E(h_{i,k}|w_{i,k}, h_i > 0) \times \Pr[h_{i,k} > 0|w_{i,k}, E(w_i)] \qquad (13.10)$$

where the *i*th individual will supply hours, $h_{i,k}$, to the *k*th firm conditional on the wage offered, $w_{i,k,}$ and the probability that he will supply a positive number of hours to this firm, which is conditional on both the offered wage and E($w_i$), his expected average wage offers that are not specific to the *k*th firm.[11]

The first expression in equation (13.10) captures an individual's decision at the intensive margin in choosing between work and leisure, and the second term regards participation and employment choices at the extensive margin (see Heckman 1993). We modify the equation to model the hours of labour supplied to a firm, which affects the interpretation of the second term. If equation (13.10) is the decision of an individual to supply labour *to a firm*, then the second term is also influenced by job search and social capital.

Assuming similar preferences regarding work and leisure for men and women in the first term, we expect that the group with lower search costs (larger value of the second term) will have more elastic labour supply functions (larger left-hand-side value, indicating more change in hours per unit change in the wage). The conditional expectation reflects the importance of the expected wage distribution facing an individual when she decides at the extensive margin to continue to supply hours to a firm or to undertake job search. Therefore, the extensive margin decision is whether a worker stays with the current firm or leaves for another firm, non-employment or self-employment. It becomes a matter of opportunities available to a worker and his degree of mobility that determines his search costs.

We argue that the greater share of home work causes women to have more familial obligations and additional mobility constraints, higher reservation wages and less investment in social capital. When the labour supplied is to the market as a whole, women are typically found to have more elastic labour supply curves because they choose more frequently not to participate in the labour market because of the greater share of home work (an additional use of time) than men and are secondary earners (more non-labour income), and thus have higher reservation wages. Opting out of the labour market generates zero hours supplied and thus greater responsiveness of hours to wage changes; therefore, a relatively more elastic labour supply. Our formulation models hours of labour supplied to a firm, so that the reservation wage argument is part of the decision to supply labour to a firm. Even with a greater likelihood of opting out of the labour market, this can be offset by a less favourable set of alternative wage offers outside a given firm. Women with fewer choices will change the labour they supply to a firm to a lesser extent than men. The relatively less elastic labour supply of women will cause them to experience less favourable employment outcomes than men. Social capital can exacerbate the outcomes if the opportunities generated by this form of capital reduce frictions more for men than women.

## 13.5 Hypotheses for testing

We hypothesize that women, with less social capital, will have fewer opportunities in an imperfect labour market and are less able to reduce the frictions causing the labour they supply to a firm to be upward-sloping. The group with the relatively less elastic labour supply curve to a firm – women – will experience labour market discrimination. Women, on account of not being the primary income earners in the household and bearing more household responsibilities, will have less time and resources to invest in social capital than men. Moreover, women will earn less income than men with equal productive characteristics and find re-employment more difficult after experiencing unemployment.

## 13.6 The models for estimation

We first estimate income functions for the combined sample and the sub samples of men and women that include social capital. We investigate whether there are different returns to these variables for men and women. The logarithm form of annual income gives the following expression for the $i$th individual:

$$\ln w_i = \alpha_0 + \alpha_1 \boldsymbol{Z}_i + \alpha_2 S_i + \alpha_3 D_i + u_i \tag{13.11}$$

where $\mathbf{Z}_i$ is a vector of personal characteristics, $S_i$ is social capital, $D_i$ are city dummy variables designed to capture city-specific effects within urban China, and $u_i$ is the error term. Earned income is only observed for those individuals who worked for pay. Thus, given the possibility of heteroscedasticity induced by selection bias into wage employment and the clustering effect of using a household data set to estimate individual income functions, we compute robust standard errors that are also adjusted for clustering at the household level.

The second approach is another test of the importance of social networks and social capital in the job-search process. We investigate whether *guanxi* affects the probability of re-employment after experiencing unemployment. We specify a logit equation in which the dependent variable, *R*, is successful re-employment. For person *i*, this is given by

$$\Pr(R_i = 1) = \beta_0 + \beta_1 \mathbf{Z}_i + \beta_2 S_i + \beta_3 D_i + u_i \tag{13.12}$$

where $\mathbf{Z}_i$ denotes the vector of personal characteristics, $S_i$ denotes social capital, $D_i$ are the city dummy variables and $u_i$ is the error term. If women have less social capital and are less likely than men to become successfully re-employed, then this will provide support for our principal hypothesis.

## 13.7 Data

The data set we use to test our hypotheses is the 1999 CASS survey. The total sample size is 4,000 urban households, 2,500 of which were NBS sample households and the remainder are from a representative sampling frame begun in 1999 that includes urban residing households without urban *hukou*. In addition, independent samples are drawn of 500 households surveyed in which a member had experienced unemployment and of 800 migrant households.

The survey covers six provinces and thirteen cities. To establish the basic hypothesis that the group with less social capital will experience labour market disadvantage, survey data are needed that generate measures of social capital and employment outcomes. The author had the opportunity to design the relevant part of the questionnaires concerning social capital.[12] These were geared towards providing original measures of *guanxi* and linking these variables with labour market outcomes for men and women in urban China. Our questions asked respondents to provide information regarding the time, and the monetary and non-monetary resources, that they invested in relationships. Together with the data on income and employment, it is possible to estimate returns to investments in social capital. The author's part of the survey provides the first original data set designed to measure an investment-based approach to social capital. Appendix 13.A reports the relevant questions on *guanxi*.[13]

Our sample is the separately drawn 500 households – the men and women who experienced some form of unemployment in the five years from the end of 1994 to the end of 1999. This sample was chosen because this group of individuals has had the occasion to conduct job search and explore the use of social capital within the labour market. The 1,691 persons who experienced unemployment come from

695 households. These households averaged 3.24 persons; there are 734 men (43.41 per cent) and 957 women (56.59 per cent). Considering the working-aged among them (97.99 per cent of the sample), there are 1,657 in total: 710 men (42.84 per cent) and 947 women (57.16 per cent). Mean income for working-aged men and women is 4,599 yuan. Men have higher mean income than women (5,673 yuan versus 3,800 yuan).[14]

## 13.8 Results of hypothesis testing

In this section, we present the results of our hypothesis testing concerning the stock of social capital as well as the returns to this variable with respect to the earned income and re-employment prospects of men and women. We explore whether women suffer from economic discrimination on account of labour supply differences associated with social capital.

### *13.8.1 Stock of social capital*

Table 13.1 presents the social capital variables for the working-aged population. We find that men have 6.21 contacts while women have 5.35 contacts, and the means are significantly different. The medians are not, indicating that the conclusions we draw are based on the upper part of the distribution. With respect to the means, we conclude that men have larger social networks than women in both samples.

Then, we compute social capital by proxying the time and monetary and non-monetary resources invested in relationships that comprise an individual's social network. The variable for time is a scaled response of time spent by the respondent with a contact over the past month. Monetary investment is the gift variable, which is the value of gifts given over the past year. Closeness serves as a proxy of non-monetary investment in a contact. We recognize that this can be interpreted as a stand-alone indicator of the amount invested in a relationship. However, given the importance of the expenditure and time aspects of social capital, the measure of closeness can be viewed as a proxy for psychological or emotional energy expended on a contact. Therefore, to approximate total investment in relationships in a social network, an index variable of these three proxies provides the best measure of the stock of social capital.[15]

The time measure ranges from 1 to 6, where 1 indicates that the respondent did not spend any time with a contact in the past month (assuming the last month is not atypical). A response of 6 indicates that the respondent spent at least some time each day with the contact. We find men, on average, spend slightly more time with each contact than women (2.84 for men, as compared with 2.82 for women). The difference in means is not statistically significant.

The second variable measures monetary resources invested in contacts, proxied by gifts given in yuan in the past year. Men tend to give, on average, slightly higher mean values of gifts per contact than women (186 RMB for men as compared with 180 RMB for women). In terms of annual gifts, men gave less than women (501 RMB as compared with 508 RMB).[16] Again, these differences in means are not statistically significant.

*Table 13.1* Social capital for the working-aged population

| *Variables* | *Male* | *Female* | *Total* |
|---|---|---|---|
| *Social network* | | | |
| Mean | 6.2090** | 5.3541** | 5.7193 |
| Median | 4.0000 | 4.0000 | 4.0000 |
| Standard deviation | (17.9194) | (8.3247) | (13.2997) |
| Minimum | 0.00 | 0.00 | 0.00 |
| Maximum | 400.00 | 200.00 | 400.00 |
| Sample size | 598 | 802 | 1400 |
| *Closeness* | | | |
| Mean | 4.5792 | 4.5689 | 4.5729 |
| Standard deviation | 0.8395 | 0.8681 | 0.8568 |
| Minimum | 1.00 | 1.00 | 1.00 |
| Maximum | 5.00 | 5.00 | 5.00 |
| Sample size | 378 | 604 | 982 |
| *Time spent* | | | |
| Mean | 2.8423 | 2.8289 | 2.8341 |
| Standard deviation | 1.4333 | 1.2856 | 1.3441 |
| Minimum | 1.00 | 1.00 | 1.00 |
| Maximum | 6.00 | 6.00 | 6.00 |
| Sample size | 372 | 587 | 959 |
| *Mean value of gifts* | | | |
| Mean | 185.5296 | 179.9758 | 182.0313 |
| Standard deviation | 281.404 | 356.7722 | 330.6347 |
| Minimum | 0.00 | 0.00 | 0.00 |
| Maximum | 2,000.00 | 5,000.00 | 5,000.00 |
| Sample size | 208 | 354 | 562 |
| *Total annual gifts* | | | |
| Mean | 500.5077 | 508.4463 | 505.5082 |
| Standard deviation | 729.2628 | 975.7832 | 891.8385 |
| Minimum | 0.00 | 0.00 | 0.00 |
| Maximum | 4,360.00 | 15,000.00 | 15,000.00 |
| Sample size | 208 | 354 | 562 |
| *Social Capital I (Closeness*Time*Value of gifts)* | | | |
| Mean | 4.147 | 3.9913 | 4.0486 |
| Standard deviation | 7.5779 | 7.6908 | 7.6429 |
| Minimum | 0.00 | 0.00 | 0.00 |
| Maximum | 49.68 | 100.00 | 100.00 |
| Sample size | 138 | 347 | 549 |
| *Social Capital II (Closeness*Time*Value of gifts as a proportion of income)* | | | |
| Mean | | | |
| Standard deviation | 0.9329* | 0.4770* | 0.6526 |
| Minimum | 7.7085 | 1.2077 | 4.8731 |
| Maximum | 0.00 | 0.00 | 0.00 |
| Sample size | 100.00 | 14.21 | 100.00 |
| | 171 | 273 | 444 |

Source: The 1999 CASS Survey.

Note: ** indicates that the means for men and women are significantly different at the 5% level, and * at the 10% level, in a two-tailed test using a *t*-test and an ANOVA test.

The third variable is a self-reported measure of closeness. The scale is from 1 to 5 and proxies non-monetary or emotional resources invested in a contact, where a 5 represents the highest value of closeness. Men have invested a little more deeply – though not significantly – in each contact than women (4.58 versus 4.57).

Men, on average, invest slightly more time, monetary and non-monetary resources than women in the contacts in their social networks. However, the means of these three variables are not significantly different as between men and women. There are potentially multiple formulations of social capital using these components. It is also possible to create an index of two of the three components of social capital, i.e. time and closeness. Consistent with our model, we combine all three components into a social capital stock variable that is an index of time spent and monetary and non-monetary resources invested in all contacts in a social network. The stock is the product of time spent, closeness and gifts summed over the number of contacts in a social network. Gifts are normalized so that the minimum value is 1 yuan. Otherwise, a value of zero for gifts would negate the other investments of time and non-monetary resources. For the gifts variable, there are several possible configurations, such as actual value, as a proportion of income, by quintiles, in logarithms, etc. Several variations are tried and two are reported in Table 13.1. Social Capital I is an index of time spent, closeness and the actual value of annual gifts given to contacts in a social network. Social Capital II is an index of time, closeness and annual gifts given to contacts computed as a proportion of income. Both are rescaled to lie between 0 and 100.[17] The difference in means is significant for Social Capital II but not Social Capital I. For all formulations, including Social Capital I and II, men have larger stocks of social capital than women. Therefore, we find some support for the first part of our hypothesis.

To empirically test the returns to this variable in the labour market, we choose the first formulation (Social Capital I) that uses the actual value of total gifts given to contacts because it provides the most information and directly corresponds to the measure in our theoretical model. Moreover, Social Capital II is thought to be endogenous to an income function. Social Capital I is found to be exogenous to this model according to the Durbin–Wu–Hausman test, so we can estimate with some confidence its effects on employment outcomes. Thus, our measure of social capital is determined by factors other than those measured in a household income and consumption survey. Locale, neighbourhood and other associative factors may hold explanatory power as to why people invest in relationships.

### *13.8.2 Returns to social capital*

Our analyses are limited to estimating economic returns to social capital as it encapsulates the capital inherent in social networks.[18] We test for two forms of returns in labour markets; the first pertains to earned income. Table 13.2 investigates the determinants of income for all working-aged employed individuals, while Table 13.3 reports separate income functions for men and women.[19]

We include a set of control variables including age, age squared, Communist Party membership, ownership sector of the employer, occupation, years of education and

*Table 13.2* The determinants of income for all employed individuals

| *Dependent variable: log of annual income* | *Coefficient (t-statistic)* | | *Mean value or percentage (standard deviation)* |
|---|---|---|---|
| | *(1)* | *(2)* | |
| Intercept | 7.9049 | 7.4417 | |
| | (9.585)*** | (5.720)*** | |
| *Social capital* | — | 0.0340 | 4.0486 |
| | | (2.400)** | (7.6429) |
| Interaction term of social capital with gender | — | −0.0265 | 2.5227 |
| | | (−1.662)* | (6.4076) |
| *Personal characteristics* | | | |
| Gender | −0.3355 | −0.3190 | 0.5715 |
| | (−5.361)*** | (−2.618)*** | 0.4950 |
| Age | 0.0383 | 0.0592 | 38.8105 |
| | (0.947) | (0.922) | (7.6631) |
| Age squared | −0.0003 | −0.0005 | 1564.943 |
| | (−0.621) | (−0.563) | (584.122) |
| Communist Party member | −0.0739 | −0.2468 | 0.1045 |
| | (−0.708) | (−1.391) | (0.3060) |
| Years of education | 0.0102 | −0.0143 | 10.026 |
| | (0.717) | (−0.606) | (2.2937) |
| Years of employment experience | −0.0094 | −0.0156 | 18.0607 |
| | (−1.233) | (−1.285) | (8.0582) |
| Ownership sector of employer | 0.0722 | 0.073 | 1.6764 |
| | (3.041)*** | (1.803)* | (1.4886) |
| Occupation | −0.0204 | 0.0088 | 6.6818 |
| | (−1.465) | (0.376) | (2.3586) |
| *Cities* | | | |
| Beijing | 0.4836 | 0.1809 | 0.0978 |
| | (2.633)*** | (0.739) | (0.2971) |
| Shenyang | 0.3428 | 0.6064 | 0.0682 |
| | (1.454) | (1.515) | (0.2522) |
| Jinzhou | 0.3300 | 0.1426 | 0.1032 |
| | (1.770)* | (0.713) | (0.3043) |
| Nanjing | 0.2790 | 0.2882 | 0.0591 |
| | (1.543) | (1.267) | (0.2360) |
| Xuzhou | −0.0810 | 0.1170 | 0.0610 |
| | (−0.421) | (0.587) | (0.2393) |
| Zhengzhou | −0.0335 | 0.2289 | 0.0736 |
| | (−0.171) | (0.877) | (0.2612) |
| Kaifeng | −0.1873 | −0.1037 | 0.0682 |
| | (−0.940) | (−0.468) | (0.2522) |
| Pingdingshan | −0.0177 | −0.1302 | 0.0314 |
| | (−0.085) | (−0.582) | (0.1744) |
| Chengdu | −0.0162 | 0.1575 | 0.1038 |
| | (−0.091) | (0.704) | (0.3051) |
| Zigong | −0.0036 | 0.5677 | 0.0833 |
| | (−0.019) | (1.463) | (0.2764) |

(Continued)

*Table 13.2* (Continued)

| *Dependent variable: log of annual income* | *Coefficient (t-statistic)* | | *Mean value or percentage (standard deviation)* |
|---|---|---|---|
| | *(1)* | *(2)* | |
| Nanchong | −0.0849 | −0.2405 | 0.0652 |
| | (−0.456) | (−1.124) | (0.2469) |
| Lanzhou | 0.1707 | −0.1487 | 0.1171 |
| | (0.881) | (−0.425) | (0.3216) |
| Inverse Mills ratio | −0.8255 | −0.8733 | |
| | (−14.3961)*** | (−7.6242)*** | |
| Wald $X^2(20)$ | 91.10*** | — | |
| Wald $X^2(22)$ | — | 57.60*** | |
| Log-likelihood | −1,598.326 | −561.4671 | |
| Mean of dependent variable | 8.2875 | 8.2875 | |
| No. of observations | 769 | 280 | |

Source: The 1999 CASS Survey.

Notes:

1 Omitted dummy variables for equation (1) are: male, non-Communist Party members, urban collective sector, individuals who are not home-owners, and Pingliang. For equation (2), they are: male, non-Communist Party members, urban collective sector, individuals who are healthy, single and have drive, and Pingliang.

2 The exclusion restriction for equation (1) is positive and significant at the 10% level. It is a dummy variable that equals 1 for those who own their homes, including homes purchased at preferential prices. Individuals who can raise capital to buy their homes or be able to negotiate preferential prices may have some ability to cope with changing financial circumstances, since home ownership became a necessity when the housing allocation from the employer was abolished at the end of 1998. This ability to cope may not increase income *per se*, but this sort of drive can affect selection into employment. For equation (2), it is a variable capturing having poor health, being married and having no drive, which is significantly negative at the 10% level. It is a dummy variable that equals 1 for those who are in poor health, are married and have no drive, according to a question that assesses whether an individual has motivation to work to become better off economically. The survey question asked: 'Do you agree or disagree with the following statements – In order for yourself to maintain a stable household standard of living in the long run? (a) Just want to follow the crowd.' An answer of 'Agree' is taken to proxy an individual's lack of drive and assigned a value of 1. A value of 0 indicates having drive.

3 *** denotes statistical significance at the 1% level, ** at the 5% level and * at the 10% level.

4 Heteroscedasticity-consistent robust standard errors adjusted for clustering at the household level are computed.

employment experience, as well as cities in each estimation.[20] We focus on the gender dummy variable and the social capital variable. Table 13.2, equation (1), is a base specification in which the variable of social capital is not included. We see in Table 13.2, equation (1), that female gender decreases income by 28.5 per cent.[21]

Social capital is included in equation (2) of Table 13.2 and is significantly positive at the 5 per cent level. A unit of social capital increases income by 3.4 per cent. Comparing someone with an average amount of social capital (stock of 4.05[22]) with someone without any, the premium is 13.8 per cent. The interaction term of social capital with gender is significant and has a negative coefficient of 0.0265, equivalent to –10.7 per cent. This indicates that a woman with an average stock of social capital will receive a much smaller income premium (3.1 per cent) than a man with an average stock of social capital. Again, female gender reduces income by 20.6 per cent.

When we estimate the determinants of income for men and women (Table 13.3), social capital has a significant and positive effect for men but not women. Social capital increases income for men by 3.21 per cent per unit (Table 13.3, equation (2)). For women, social capital has a positive coefficient, but is not significant (Table 13.3, equation (5)). Comparing a man with average stock of social capital (stock of 4.15) with a man without any, there is a positive income premium of 13.3 per cent.

We conclude that social capital has different effects on income for men and women. There are returns to social capital for men but not women. To explore the effects of the clear gender differences in returns to these variables, we contemplate some counterfactuals.

If a woman with an average stock of social capital (3.99) has the returns of a man (a coefficient of 0.0321 on social capital for men), she would receive a positive income premium of 12.8 per cent. If she also has the average stock of social capital of a man (4.15), the premium would be 13.3 per cent. This is again considered in light of the pure effect of gender that decreases income by 20.6 per cent, standardizing for other characteristics. These simulations suggest that if women were to earn returns to social capital, then the positive returns could improve the income of women.

Therefore, we find positive income premiums associated with social capital together with striking gender differences in its returns. Our simulations show that, standardizing for other characteristics, if women earn the returns of men to social capital, they could improve their income. These findings are consistent with our theoretical arguments that these variables might provide different opportunities for otherwise similarly productive individuals. We have evidence of gender inequality in earned income that is consistent with differences in social capital.

### *13.8.3 Probability of re-employment*

Virtually every variable is insignificant in Table 13.4, including gender. Although the social network and social capital variables are insignificant, there are differences in the predicted probabilities of re-employment when they are included in the logit estimations.[23]

We find that there is a 42 per cent probability of re-employment after experiencing unemployment (equation (1), Table 13.4). When we include social networks in equation (2) of the same table, they have a very small and negative marginal effect. This suggests that social networks do not have a positive effect on re-employment.

Unlike social networks, social capital increases the probability of becoming re-employed (Table 13.4, equation (3)). The probabilities of re-employment for

*Table 13.3* The determinants of income for employed men and women

| *Dependent variable: log of annual income* | *Coefficient (t-statistic)* | | | | | | *Mean value or percentage (standard deviation)* | |
|---|---|---|---|---|---|---|---|---|
| | *Men* | | | *Women* | | | *Men* | *Women* |
| | *(1) Probit* | *(2) Corrected MLE* | *(3) Uncorrected OLS* | *(4) Probit* | *(5) Corrected MLE* | *(6) Uncorrected OLS* | | |
| Intercept | −7.9107 | 6.1106 | 2.9942 | −1.0627 | 5.3607 | 5.3834 | | |
| | (−2.511)** | (2.840)*** | (1.169) | (−0.467) | (3.550)*** | (3.360)*** | | |
| *Social capital* | −0.0221 | 0.0321 | 0.0279 | −0.0051 | 0.0048 | 0.0048 | 4.1470 | 3.9913 |
| | (−1.311) | (3.422)*** | (3.086)*** | (−0.471) | (1.100) | (1.037) | (7.5779) | (7.6908) |
| *Personal Characteristics* | | | | | | | | |
| Age | 0.3689 | 0.1142 | 0.2330 | 0.0251 | 0.1204 | 0.1198 | 39.0732 | 38.6135 |
| | (2.573)** | (1.166) | (2.028)** | (0.213) | (1.511) | −1.415 | (8.2149) | (7.2201) |
| Age squared | −0.0057 | −0.0006 | −0.0024 | −0.0006 | −0.0015 | −0.0015 | 1,594.107 | 1,543.078 |
| | (−3.258)*** | (−0.476) | (−1.644) | (−0.377) | (1.485) | (−1.389) | (634.8775) | (542.2838) |
| Communist Party member | 0.2120 | −0.2197 | −0.0412 | 0.1983 | 0.0263 | 0.024 | 0.1608 | 0.0623 |
| | (0.618) | (−1.043) | (−0.191) | (0.552) | (0.122) | (0.105) | (0.3676) | (0.2418) |
| Years of education | 0.1313 | −0.0621 | −0.0160 | 0.0296 | 0.0142 | 0.014 | 10.0848 | 9.9820 |
| | (2.347)** | (−1.737)* | (−0.385) | (0.671) | (0.53) | (0.5) | (2.4300) | (2.1630) |
| Years of employment experience | 0.0894 | −0.0629 | −0.0374 | 0.0259 | 0.0058 | 0.0056 | 18.6179 | 17.6452 |
| | (2.725)*** | (−2.825)*** | (−1.220) | (1.253) | (0.501) | (0.467) | (8.6629) | (7.7026) |
| Ownership sector of employer | −0.0018 | 0.0512 | 0.0448 | −0.0995 | 0.0523 | 0.0531 | 1.875 | 1.5359 |
| | (−0.019) | (0.879) | (0.696) | (−1.708)* | (1.163) | (1.121) | (1.5136) | (1.4554) |
| Occupation | −0.0952 | 0.0902 | 0.0627 | 0.0415 | −0.0192 | −0.0194 | 6.3544 | 6.9253 |
| | (−1.660)* | (2.555)** | (1.552) | (1.120) | (−0.789) | (−0.767) | (2.3761) | (2.3170) |
| Poor health* married*no drive | −1.3617 | — | — | — | — | — | 0.0296 | — |
| | (−1.995)** | | | | | | (0.1695) | |
| Help with home work | — | — | — | 0.117 | — | — | — | 0.9609 |
| | | | | (1.879)* | | | | (1.4769) |

| *Cities* | | | | | | | | |
|---|---|---|---|---|---|---|---|---|
| Beijing | 1.6595 | 0.2366 | 0.7136 | 0.6585 | 0.4635 | 0.4585 | 0.0915 | 0.1024 |
| | (2.025)** | (0.795) | (2.627)*** | (1.451) | (1.983)** | (1.850)* | (0.2886) | (0.3034) |
| Shenyang | −0.3279 | 1.7419 | 1.4205 | −0.0138 | −0.0078 | −0.0065 | 0.0563 | 0.0771 |
| | (−0.466) | (3.535)*** | (2.410)** | (−0.031) | (−0.027) | (−0.021) | (0.2307) | (0.2669) |
| Jinzhou | 0.0502 | 0.5314 | 0.2917 | 0.161 | 0.0084 | 0.0076 | 0.0972 | 0.1077 |
| | (0.099) | (1.635) | (0.938) | (0.497) | (0.047) | (0.041) | (0.2964) | (0.3102) |
| Nanjing | 1.3667 | 0.5091 | 0.9728 | 0.8600 | 0.5800 | 0.5737 | 0.0465 | 0.0686 |
| | (2.123)** | (1.762)* | (4.577)*** | (1.861)* | (2.666)*** | (2.499)** | (0.2107) | (0.2530) |
| Xuzhou | 1.3174 | 0.3640 | 0.6458 | 0.9373 | 0.5248 | 0.5178 | 0.0577 | 0.0634 |
| | (2.210)** | (1.257) | (2.569)** | (2.264)** | (3.352)*** | (3.181)*** | (0.2334) | (0.2437) |
| Zhengzhou | 0.417 | 0.1717 | 0.1218 | 0.0199 | 0.2385 | 0.2388 | 0.0662 | 0.0792 |
| | (0.705) | (0.550) | (0.429) | (0.048) | (0.951) | (0.898) | (0.2488) | (0.2702) |
| Kaifeng | 0.2614 | −0.1193 | −0.2253 | −0.2090 | 0.0320 | 0.0329 | 0.0718 | 0.0655 |
| | (0.491) | (−0.364) | (−0.750) | (−0.550) | (0.163) | (0.158) | (0.2584) | (0.2475) |
| Pingdingshan | 0.7983 | 0.5761 | 0.7359 | 0.5275 | 0.0099 | 0.0052 | 0.0197 | 0.0401 |
| | (0.998) | (1.136) | (1.287) | (1.280) | (0.071) | (0.036) | (0.1391) | (0.1964) |
| Chengdu | 0.8002 | 0.1707 | 0.2824 | 0.7175 | 0.5684 | 0.5626 | 0.1085 | 0.1003 |
| | (1.334) | (0.511) | (0.898) | (1.761)* | (2.866)*** | (2.719)*** | (0.3112) | (0.3006) |
| Zigong | 0.2447 | 0.6428 | 0.5039 | −0.1338 | 0.6054 | 0.6068 | 0.0901 | 0.0752 |
| | (0.313) | (1.433) | (1.174) | (−0.283) | (1.910)* | (1.810)* | (0.2866) | (0.2639) |
| Nanchong | 1.1186 | 0.1930 | 0.4649 | 1.0174 | 0.1156 | 0.1082 | 0.0761 | 0.0578 |
| | (1.758)* | (0.488) | (1.257) | (2.547)** | (0.637) | (0.593) | (0.2653) | (0.2334) |
| Lanzhou | 0.4269 | 0.4049 | 0.5757 | 0.1904 | −0.5145 | −0.5159 | 0.1394 | 0.0981 |
| | (0.721) | (1.342) | (2.828)*** | (0.391) | (−0.872) | (−0.828) | (0.3466) | (0.2977) |

(Continued)

*Table 13.3* (Continued)

| *Dependent variable: log of annual income* | *Coefficient (t-statistic)* | | | | | | *Mean value or percentage (standard deviation)* | |
|---|---|---|---|---|---|---|---|---|
| | *Men* | | | *Women* | | | *Men* | *Women* |
| | *(1) Probit* | *(2) Corrected MLE* | *(3) Uncorrected OLS* | *(4) Probit* | *(5) Corrected MLE* | *(6) Uncorrected OLS* | | |
| Inverse Mills ratio | — | −0.8001 (−6.5792)*** | — | — | 0.0159 (0.1463) | — | 0.8652 (0.5798) | 0.5950 (0.2388) |
| $R^2$ | — | — | 0.3896 | — | — | 0.1741 | | |
| Pseudo-$R^2$ | 0.2247 | — | — | 0.0832 | — | — | | |
| $X^2$ (21) | 51.99*** | — | — | 32.16* | — | — | | |
| Wald $X^2$ (7) | — | 18.84*** | — | — | — | — | | |
| Wald $X^2$ (20) | — | — | — | — | 60.59*** | — | | |
| $F$(20, 91) | — | — | 4.99*** | — | — | — | | |
| $F$(20, 187) | — | — | — | — | — | 2.45*** | | |
| Log-likelihood | −89.6904 | −152.385 | — | −177.1323 | −370.7839 | — | | |
| Mean of dependent variable | 0.3538 | 8.4862 | 8.4862 | 0.3892 | 8.1324 | 8.1324 | | |
| No. of observations | 168 | 92 | 92 | 295 | 188 | 188 | | |

Source: The 1999 CASS Survey.

Notes:

1 Omitted dummy variables are: non-Communist Party members, urban collective sector and Pingliang.

2 The exclusion restriction for men is a variable that captures being in poor health, being married and having no drive. For women it is a variable that is the degree of home work obligations. It is a composite of childcare responsibilities, the number of generations in a household greater than one, whether an individual is married and the number of persons in the household.

3 *** denotes statistical significance at the 1% level, ** at the 5% level and * at the 10% level.

4 Heteroscedasticity-consistent robust standard errors adjusted for clustering at the household level are computed.

*Table 13.4* Binomial logit analysis of the likelihood of re-employment for men and women

| *Dependent variable: Re-employed = 1 (439) Unemployed = 0 (632)* | *Coefficient (t-statistic)* | | | *Mean value or percentage (standard deviation)* |
|---|---|---|---|---|
| | *(1)* | *(2)* | *(3)* | |
| Intercept | −3.2526 (−1.455) | −4.3992 (−1.753)* | −3.1067 (−0.793) | 0.4099 (0.492) |
| *Social network* | — | −0.0145 (−0.625) | — | 5.7193 (13.2997) |
| Interaction term with gender | — | 0.0272 (0.839) | — | 3.0707 (6.8365) |
| *Social capital* | — | — | 0.0458 (0.875) | 3.9630 (7.5175) |
| Interaction term with gender | — | — | −0.0348 (−0.639) | 1.3134 (4.7636) |
| *Personal characteristics* | | | | |
| Gender | 0.0013 (0.007) | −0.0470 (−0.184) | 0.0624 (0.189) | 0.5715 (0.4950) |
| Age | 0.1554 (1.400) | 0.1843 (1.505) | 0.1426 (0.757) | 38.8105 (7.6631) |
| Age squared | −0.0017 (−1.208) | −0.0021 (−1.330) | −0.0008 (−0.359) | 1564.943 (584.122) |
| Years of education | −0.0336 (−0.890) | −0.0190 (−0.464) | −0.0569 (−0.862) | 10.0260 (2.2937) |
| Communist Party member | 0.2726 (1.018) | 0.2360 (0.828) | 0.0125 (0.031) | 0.1045 (0.3060) |
| Poor health | −1.0852 (−3.988)*** | −0.9952 (−3.438)*** | −1.1801 (−2.745)*** | 0.0851 (0.2791) |
| Head of household | 0.2893 (1.574) | 0.2956 (1.513) | 0.5449 (1.804)* | 0.4043 (0.4909) |
| Experience | −0.0144 (−0.737) | −0.0065 (−0.302) | −0.0527 (−1.679)* | 18.0607 (8.0582) |
| Work unit sector | 0.0920 (1.546) | 0.0932 (1.442) | 0.1621 (1.640) | 1.7142 (1.3181) |
| Occupation | −0.0317 (−0.897) | −0.0565 (−1.504) | −0.0584 (−0.974) | 6.6818 (2.3586) |
| Drive | 0.4435 (2.763)*** | 0.4137 (2.382)** | 0.3686 (1.408) | 0.4359 (0.4961) |
| *Cities* | | | | |
| Beijing | −0.4697 (−0.964) | −0.1007 (−0.179) | −0.6492 (−0.853) | 0.0978 (0.2971) |
| Shenyang | −0.2848 (−0.584) | 0.1034 (0.184) | −0.1496 (−0.210) | 0.0682 (0.2522) |
| Jinzhou | 1.2409 (2.599)*** | 1.6499 (3.023)*** | 1.1398 (1.871)* | 0.1032 (0.3043) |
| Nanjing | 0.8060 (1.610) | 1.2858 (2.249)** | 0.5689 (0.794) | 0.0591 (0.236) |
| Xuzhou | 0.3456 (0.685) | 0.7084 (1.237) | (0.1913) (0.289) | 0.0610 (0.2393) |
| Zhengzhou | −0.6083 (−1.124) | 0.0248 (0.041) | −0.8446 (−1.160) | 0.0736 (0.2612) |
| Kaifeng | −0.462 (−0.905) | 0.0515 (0.089) | −0.6250 (−0.952) | 0.0682 (0.2522) |
| Pingdingshan | −1.8160 (−2.605)*** | −1.2935 (−1.721)* | −1.4082 (−1.729)* | 0.0314 (0.1744) |

(Continued)

*Table 13.4* (Continued)

| *Dependent variable: Re-employed = 1 (439) Unemployed = 0 (632)* | *Coefficient (t-statistic)* (1) | (2) | (3) | *Mean value or percentage (standard deviation)* |
|---|---|---|---|---|
| Chengdu | −0.8055 | −0.2782 | −0.6976 | 0.1038 |
| | (−1.450) | (−0.425) | (−0.700) | (0.3051) |
| Zigong | −0.3575 | 0.3409 | 0.1076 | 0.0833 |
| | (−0.624) | (0.543) | (0.119) | (0.2764) |
| Nanchong | −0.8632 | −0.2911 | −0.5226 | 0.0652 |
| | (−1.458) | (−0.444) | (−0.654) | (0.2469) |
| Lanzhou | −0.5423 | −0.0443 | —(1) | 0.1171 |
| | (−0.963) | (−0.071) | | (0.3216) |
| Pseudo $R^2$ | 0.1157 | 0.1180 | 0.1450 | |
| Wald $X^2$ (24) | 109.52*** | — | — | |
| Wald $X^2$ (25) | — | 94.72*** | 51.11*** | |
| Wald $X^2$ (26) | — | — | — | |
| Log-likelihood | −493.739 | −426.9363 | −202.8226 | |
| Predicted probability of re-employment (2) | 42.20% | 41.85% | 47.23% | |
| Marginal effect of social networks (3) | — | −0.0033 | — | |
| Marginal effect of social capital | — | — | 0.0113 | |

Source: The 1999 CASS Survey.

Notes:

1 Lanzhou was dropped as it predicts failure perfectly.

2 This is the predicted probability of becoming re-employed estimated at the mean values of the independent variables.

3 This is the slope or marginal effect of a variable estimated at the mean values of all independent variables (see Greene 1997 [1993]: 873–80). The formula is $[e^{\beta' x}/(1+e^{\beta' x})^2]\beta$, where $\boldsymbol{\beta}'$ denotes the coefficients of the vector of independent variables, **x**, evaluated with respect to the coefficient, $\beta$, on either the social network or social capital variable.

4 Omitted dummy variables are: male, non-Communist Party members, urban collective sector, not household head, healthy individuals, individuals who lack drive, and Pingliang.

5 *** denotes statistical significance at the 1% level, ** at the 5% level and * at the 10% level.

6 Heteroscedasticity-consistent robust standard errors adjusted for clustering at the household level are computed.

someone with an average amount of social capital (stock of 3.96) and someone without any are 51.7 per cent and 42.8 per cent, respectively. Although insignificant, there is a positive effect on the likelihood of re-employment associated with social capital but not social networks. We now estimate the probabilities of re-employment for men and women separately.

As in the combined sample (Table 13.4), not many variables are significant in Table 13.5, including social networks and social capital. Among other variables that are significant, there are some that may imply additional social network or social capital effects. These are father's Communist Party membership, which increases the probability of re-employment for men, while themselves being a party member helps women. Communist Party membership is likely to be a form of cultivating contacts and accords with the definition of social capital used by Putnam, Leonardi and Nanetti (1993) in which social capital is measured by the number of associational memberships. The nature of Communist Party membership is difficult to disentangle and is open to several possible interpretations. It is also possible that Communist Party membership is a signal to employers that an individual has ambition or another unmeasured characteristic that is desirable, especially in the state-owned sector. Other significant determinants are poor health, which decreases the probability of re-employment for men, and drive, which increases the likelihood of re-employment of women. We concentrate our analyses on our measures of social networks and social capital.

Men have a 43 per cent probability of becoming re-employed, while the probability is just slightly lower for women at 42 per cent (equations (1) and (4) in Table 13.5). Social networks have a small and negative marginal effect on the likelihood of re-employment for men (Table 13.5, equation (2)). For women, the marginal effect of social networks is similarly small, but positive in equation (5) (Table 13.5). The effects of social networks are negligible when we compute the probabilities of re-employment for someone with an average-sized network and someone without any.

In contrast, social capital has a positive and small effect on the probability of re-employment when comparing someone who has invested and someone who has not invested in this form of capital. From Table 13.5, equation (3), men with mean social capital (stock of 4.15) have a probability of re-employment of 54.3 per cent, while men without any social capital have a probability of 53.5 per cent. Comparing women with average social capital (stock of 3.99) to women without any stock of social capital, the predicted probabilities of re-employment are 45.5 per cent and 43.4 per cent, respectively. Although insignificant in the logit estimations, having an average stock of social capital appears to increase the likelihood of re-employment more for women than for men, e.g. by approximately 2 per cent for women and 1 per cent for men.

Consider the counterfactual of a woman having more social capital, i.e. if she has the average social capital of men (stock of 4.15) and her returns, her predicted probability of re-employment is 45.5 per cent. This suggests that despite having higher returns, women have a lower predicted probability of re-employment than men for the same amount of social capital. Thus, social capital helps women more than men in job search, but there are other impediments to becoming successfully re-employed for women. These could be due to taste or statistical screening or labour supply differences. Thus, we find support for the hypothesis in that women have a lower probability of becoming re-employed than men in our estimations of the likelihood of re-employment after experiencing unemployment.

Further, with the understanding that these variables are insignificant, social capital increases the probability of re-employment, while the effect of an average-sized social network is negligible. This provides evidence that is contrary to what is known as the folk theorem in the social network literature, likely traced to the 'strength of weak ties' theory advanced by Granovetter (1995 [1974]). The

*Table 13.5* Binomial logit analysis of the likelihood of re-employment for men and women in separate samples

| *Dependent variable:*<br>*Re-employed* = 1<br>*Unemployed* = 0 | *Coefficient (t-statistic)* | | | | | |
|---|---|---|---|---|---|---|
| | *Men* | | | *Women* | | |
| | | *N* = *182*<br>*N* = *262* | | | *N* = *257*<br>*N* = *370* | |
| | *(1)* | *(2)* | *(3)* | *(4)* | *(5)* | *(6)* |
| Intercept | −6.8628<br>(−1.930)* | −8.364<br>(−1.880)* | −9.787<br>(−1.228) | −2.893<br>(−0.819) | −4.351<br>(−1.170) | 1.611<br>(0.301) |
| *Social network* | — | −0.0248<br>(−0.559) | — | — | 0.0018<br>(0.070) | — |
| *Social capital* | — | — | 0.0582<br>(0.700) | — | — | 0.0111<br>(0.591) |
| *Personal characteristics* | | | | | | |
| Age | 0.2702<br>(1.595) | 0.2784<br>(1.407) | 0.365<br>(0.864) | 0.1407<br>(0.831) | 0.232<br>(1.281) | −0.0082<br>(−0.032) |
| Age squared | −0.0023<br>(−1.100) | −0.0019<br>(−0.770) | −0.0026<br>(−0.495) | −0.0018<br>(−0.845) | −0.0031<br>(−1.341) | 0.0007<br>(0.217) |
| Communist Party member | −0.1253<br>(−0.343) | −0.0575<br>(−0.141) | −0.379<br>(−0.567) | 0.8365<br>(1.909)* | 0.7603<br>(1.697)* | 0.7005<br>(1.134) |
| Years of education | −0.0268<br>(−0.436) | −0.0127<br>(−0.188) | −0.1198<br>(−0.968) | −0.026<br>(−0.471) | −0.018<br>(−0.304) | −0.0575<br>(−0.629) |
| Poor health | −2.2084<br>(−4.020)*** | −2.0371<br>(−3.476)*** | −2.818<br>(−3.171)*** | −0.6155<br>(−1.753)* | −0.5135<br>(−1.373) | −0.4418<br>(−0.844) |
| Experience | −0.0629<br>(−2.073)** | −0.081<br>(−2.107)** | −0.1022<br>(−1.313) | 0.0042<br>(0.156) | 0.0124<br>(0.435) | −0.046<br>(−1.092) |

| | | | | | | |
|---|---|---|---|---|---|---|
| Work unit sector | 0.0431 | −0.0110 | 0.2462 | 0.1053 | 0.1316 | 0.1648 |
| | (0.4390) | (−0.100) | (1.078) | (1.319) | (1.577) | (1.321) |
| Occupation | −0.0229 | −0.0694 | 0.0615 | −0.0484 | −0.0591 | −0.0851 |
| | (−0.354) | (−0.920) | (0.397) | (−1.138) | (−1.322) | (−1.297) |
| Drive | 0.3646 | 0.4511 | 0.2704 | 0.5030 | 0.4963 | 0.5614 |
| | (1.298) | (1.443) | (0.511) | (2.432)** | (2.241)** | (1.637)* |
| Head of household | 0.3265 | 0.4369 | 1.1205 | 0.5923 | 0.5473 | −0.2149 |
| | (0.940) | (1.068) | (1.538) | (1.787)* | (1.543) | (−0.398) |
| Father is a Communist Party member | 0.7079 | 0.9932 | 0.7417 | −0.1683 | −0.2218 | 0.4071 |
| | (2.176)** | (2.632)*** | (0.932) | (−0.691) | (−0.878) | (1.161) |
| Mother is a Communist Party member | 0.3786 | 0.4891 | 0.0532 | −0.7536 | −0.6064 | −0.6035 |
| | (0.728) | (0.759) | (0.056) | (−1.648)* | (−1.260) | (−0.953) |
| Number of household members | 0.3004 | 0.2737 | 0.4502 | −0.0408 | −0.1703 | −0.5307 |
| | (1.640) | (1.133) | (1.184) | (−0.250) | (−0.999) | (−2.129)** |
| Home-owner | −0.1930 | −0.2670 | 0.0643 | −0.3083 | −0.3083 | 0.2983 |
| | (−0.559) | (−0.672) | (0.105) | (−0.724) | (−0.691) | (0.479) |
| *Cities* | | | | | | |
| Beijing | −0.7423 | 0.0788 | −1.3590 | −0.3212 | −0.1028 | −0.3284 |
| | (−0.758) | (0.0540) | (−0.645) | (−0.531) | (−0.163) | (−0.360) |
| Shenyang | 0.0326 | 0.6831 | −0.0182 | −0.2238 | −0.0132 | 0.0524 |
| | (0.033) | (0.459) | (−0.011) | (−0.371) | (−0.021) | (0.064) |

(Continued)

*Table 13.5* (Continued)

| *Dependent variable:*<br>*Re-employed* = 1<br>*Unemployed* = 0 | *Coefficient (t-statistic)* | | | | | |
|---|---|---|---|---|---|---|
| | *Men* | | | *Women* | | |
| | | *N* = *182*<br>*N* = *262* | | | *N* = *257*<br>*N* = *370* | |
| | *(1)* | *(2)* | *(3)* | *(4)* | *(5* | *(6)* |
| Jinzhou | 1.9205 | 2.7731 | 0.7206 | 1.2816 | 1.3927 | 1.2386 |
| | (1.829)* | (1.859)* | (0.432) | (2.187)** | (2.297)** | (1.795)* |
| Nanjing | 0.9193 | 1.9226 | −0.4292 | 1.0222 | 1.2541 | 1.4863 |
| | (0.921) | (1.278) | (−0.255) | (1.643) | (1.918)* | (1.737)* |
| Xuzhou | 0.3791 | 1.4883 | −0.1361 | 0.5843 | 0.5739 | 0.4134 |
| | (0.382) | (1.011) | (−0.082) | (0.948) | (0.899) | (0.523) |
| Zhengzhou | 0.0143 | 1.2813 | −1.3560 | −0.8179 | −0.5912 | −0.2458 |
| | (0.014) | (0.821) | (−0.806) | (−1.157) | (−0.788) | (−0.285) |
| Kaifeng | −0.5885 | 0.4903 | −1.1212 | −0.0508 | 0.0397 | −0.1486 |
| | (−0.596) | (0.333) | (−0.690) | (−0.081) | (0.061) | (−0.190) |
| Pingdingshan | −1.1485 | −0.1797 | −1.5897 | −2.0475 | −1.902 | −1.6815 |
| | (−0.921) | (−0.102) | (−0.847) | (−2.160)** | (−1.985)** | (−1.589) |
| Chengdu | −1.4252 | −0.0547 | −(1) | −0.3173 | −0.0153 | 0.2177 |
| | (−1.323) | (−0.035) | | (−0.422) | (−0.018) | (0.160) |
| Zigong | −0.5388 | 0.8623 | 2.5104 | 0.0336 | 0.3893 | 0.078 |
| | (−0.480) | (0.554) | (1.331) | (0.046) | (0.512) | (0.078) |
| Nanchong | −1.1783 | −0.0058 | 0.1535 | −0.0918 | 0.0775 | −0.3905 |
| | (−1.102) | (−0.004) | (0.075) | (−0.116) | (0.096) | (−0.433) |
| Lanzhou | −1.0707 | 0.1243 | −(1) | 0.1185 | 0.3739 | −(1) |
| | (−0.967) | (0.081) | | (0.163) | (0.494) | |

| | | | | | | |
|---|---|---|---|---|---|---|
| Pseudo $R^2$ | 0.1888 | 0.2116 | 0.2652 | 0.1258 | 0.1266 | 0.1475 |
| Wald $X^2$ (25) | — | — | 36.18* | — | — | — |
| Wald $X^2$ (26) | 54.86*** | — | — | 62.97*** | — | 37.04* |
| Wald $X^2$ (27) | — | 53.27*** | — | — | 54.02*** | — |
| Log-likelihood | −172.8993 | −142.734 | −58.3168 | −292.5829 | −259.0181 | −131.7623 |
| Predicted probability of re-employment (2) | 42.95% | 42.11% | 53.91% | 41.58% | 41.97% | 44.44% |
| Marginal effect of social networks | — | −0.0056 | — | — | 0.0004 | — |
| Marginal effect of social capital | — | — | 0.001 | — | — | 0.0026 |

Source: The 1999 CASS Survey.

Notes:
1 Chengdu and Lanzhou were dropped as they predicted the outcome of failure perfectly.
2 This is the predicted probability of becoming re-employed estimated at the mean values of the independent variables.
3 Omitted dummy variables are: non-Communist Party members, urban collective sector, not household head, healthy individuals, individuals who lack drive or own their homes, whose parents are not Communist Party members and Pingliang.
4 *** denotes statistical significance at the 1% level, ** at the 5% level and * at the 10% level.
5 Heteroscedasticity-consistent robust standard errors adjusted for clustering at the household level are computed.

hypothesis is that the breadth, rather than the closeness of contacts, is important in finding a job. Our evidence suggests that social capital (the depth of ties) and not social networks (the breadth of ties) matters for re-employment.

## 13.9 Conclusion

We explored gender inequality within the labour market and tested the hypotheses concerning the employment outcomes for men and women when their respective amounts of social capital are considered. Our theory posits that social capital generates returns in the form of opportunities in the labour market. By providing employment options, individuals with social capital can decrease some of the frictions in imperfect markets and have more elastic labour supply curves. Thus, the group with the relatively less elastic labour supply with respect to a firm will suffer from discrimination, i.e. holding productive characteristics constant, they will earn less income after experiencing unemployment. We now assess the cumulative evidence to determine whether the labour market outcomes of men and women in urban China are consistent with our hypotheses.

We find that women have less social capital when measured in a combined index form than men. This may be due to their bearing a greater share of home work (i.e. less time to invest in relationships). The evidence is that men spend slightly more time on average than women with each contact. Women will also have less income with which to invest in social capital and we find that they have a smaller mean value of gifts than men. More home responsibilities, such as childcare, also mean fewer non-monetary resources. Men, on average, are also found to be slightly closer to their contacts than women.

The two forms of labour market outcomes we examine are earned income and re-employment. Through counterfactuals, that is, if women were to have the returns of men to social capital, they would earn income premiums of about 13 per cent. Also, even though social capital increases the likelihood of re-employment more for women than men (2 per cent versus 1 per cent), men have higher probabilities of becoming re-employed than women. The evidence shows that social capital, and to some extent social networks, can improve earned income and re-employment prospects. The better labour market outcomes of men, moreover, might be correlated with men having larger social networks and more social capital than women.

Our findings are potentially consistent with several explanations for gender inequality within labour markets. The significantly negative coefficient on the female gender variable in the income functions may be attributable to a taste for discrimination against women, some form of statistical screening, or labour supply differences not accounted for by social capital. Nevertheless, social capital tends to be significant and positive along with the female gender dummy variable. This can be interpreted as support for the notion that social capital garners economic returns in at least two respects. The first is that there are efficiency gains, so a worker with social capital – perhaps by reducing the transaction costs of getting things done on the job – is more productive and is rewarded by a positive income premium. In none of our estimations of income functions is social capital associated with a negative coefficient. A second effect is that by generating employment opportunities that are not related to productivity on the job, social capital reduces the frictions impeding mobility that characterize an imperfect labour market. In this way, social capital affects the labour supplied to a firm. We cannot rule out alternative, more conventional explanations. Nevertheless, our evidence suggests that social capital provides employment opportunities so increasing the elasticity of labour supplied to firms, and thus raises wages and decreases frictions associated with job search.

In conclusion, it is possible that women and men with equal productive characteristics will experience differential treatment in the labour market if they have different amounts of social capital. These outcomes may be explained by the opportunities associated with economic returns to these variables. They further provide support for discrimination to be economically motivated in imperfect labour markets. The gender income inequality in the current reform period in urban China might, at least in part, be explained by the differential opportunities available to men and women that are more apparent in a more market-oriented system.

These findings further suggest that the labour market is as yet undeveloped with respect to labour mobility. To the extent that social capital decreases transaction costs rather than increases efficiency, there are frictions with respect to matches between firms and workers that can be reduced with the development of a mature labour market in which hires and earnings are based less on contacts and more on productivity. Possible interventions could include increasing the array of job opportunities, more transparent hiring procedures and multiple ways of decreasing search costs, such as fewer institutional restrictions on movement.

## Notes

The support of the UK Department for International Development and the George Webb Medley Fund is gratefully acknowledged. The author wishes to thank John Knight and Ken Mayhew for their comments. We are also indebted to Li Shi and the members of the Institute of Economics, Chinese Academy of Social Sciences, for their assistance in making the survey possible. A version of this chapter was presented at the Workshop on Urban Poverty in China held in Oxford in August 2001 and was published as Discussion Paper No. 83 in the Discussion Paper Series at the Department of Economics, University of Oxford. Any errors are the author's.

1 In China, *guanxi* refers to social capital, while *guanxiwang*, literally translated as a web of *guanxi*, means social networks. In other Chinese communities, such as Taiwan, Hong Kong and the overseas diaspora, *guanxi* typically refers to both social networks and social capital.
2 We focus on individual-level social ties, but recognize the importance of firm-level connections.
3 Bian (1994) argues that *guanxi* was used most heavily in periods when government control of jobs was the least rigid, especially in the late 1980s, but it was always prevalent. Work units were characterized by differential resources and state labour agencies had the authority to control labour supply and demand. Thus, individuals used *guanxi* to gain favourable assignments.

4 Uphoff (2000) finds in a study of Sri Lanka in the 1980s that farmers who cooperated in irrigation projects stated that although they benefited personally, they were motivated also by helping others less fortunate than themselves. He also argues that the outcome was Pareto optimal since all were helped and no one was harmed by distributing water more efficiently.

5 Following the completion of this model, we read an independently formulated and similar approach by Glaeser, Laibson and Sacerdote (2002). Both models change direction from the existing approaches to social capital by focusing on the individual decision to invest and are based on Becker's human capital formulation. There are some differences, including our definitions. Glaeser, *et al.* (2002: 4) define individual social capital as 'a person's social characteristics – including social skills, charisma, and the size of his Rolodex – which enable him to reap market and non-market returns from social interactions with others'. Our definition is more measurable. Social capital is defined as the relationships that an individual has (stock) and maintains in a social network (flows). A social network is defined simply as the number of persons with whom an individual has relationships and with whom he or she interacts from time to time.

6 This conception differs from the models of Granovetter (1995 [1974]) and Boorman (1975) in that, rather than assuming that tie or contacts is a dichotomous variable (either strong or weak), we posit that it is a continuous variable with multiple degrees of intensity. This will also allow us to model the investment decision considering rates of return instead of as probabilities of returns (see e.g., Boorman (1975: 220–27). This point was also recognized in Boorman (1975: 243–4): 'Throughout the present model, we have assumed exactly two types of ties – strong and weak. An obviously more realistic approach would be to treat the strength of a tie as a continuous variable.'

7 Krishna (2000) argues that social capital should not be a deterministic concept but one in which it is possible through purposive action to enhance the flows of even a fixed stock. For instance, Krishna (2000: 73, 75) defines social capital as a 'category for various kinds of social assets that yield streams of benefits. These assets comprise the stock of social capital, while the benefits constitute the flow' and further states that '[t]rust and cooperation, which form the core of social capital, exist in some form in all societies'.

8 Empirically, our input is a composite index of time, closeness and gifts, which mirrors the theoretical formulation.

9 A game-theoretic formulation of cooperation to produce returns to social capital could be explored as an extension of this model.

10 There can be some debate as to the appropriate depreciation rate. One issue has to do with location-specific social capital. We maintain that in the same way as firm-specific human capital depreciates at a faster rate than general human capital with job change, the same can occur with social capital if an individual moves. These are shocks in a sense, but our general solution holds.

11 We model the labour supplied to a firm rather than to the market as a whole. Thus, non-labour income, which is considered in labour supply functions with respect to the market as it affects the reservation wage, is implicit in the labour supply function with respect to a firm. The reason is when a worker leaves the firm – he may opt out of the market or take other employment – if the offered wage is less than the reservation wage or if the offered wage is less than expected wage minus search costs. In either event, the worker leaves the firm.

12 Fieldwork was undertaken by the author during the survey administration in February–March 2000 and follow-up interviews were conducted in August–September 2000.

13 In the interest of brevity, the entire survey questionnaires are not attached.

14 Before we turn to our hypothesis testing, there is a data issue concerning earned income that warrants discussion. In our earned income functions we use the logarithm

of annual income as the dependent variable, excluding those observations for which there was only non-wage income, which allows us to correct for sample selection in the usual manner. The rationale for using annual income instead of wages is two-fold. First, the returns that we estimate will represent the welfare implications associated with total income. The advantage for our purposes is that we capture returns to the total income of an individual who invests in social capital, i.e. in terms of transfers and other support. Second, because we do not have data on hours worked, we cannot standardize for hours. Thus, the use of wages as the dependent variable may not accurately reflect rates of return. The same problem exists when we use annual income. It is mitigated by the fact that nearly 90 per cent of the sample worked in state-owned enterprises (SOEs) or urban collectives, where hours are standardized at 40 hours per week. Our approach corresponds to those of other researchers using these sets of data from 1988, 1995 and the current 1999 survey. Wages constitute approximately 47 per cent of income due to social securities and other forms of support received by those who have experienced unemployment. When we include all employment income, we find that work-related income (e.g. self-employed income and other employment income) comprises approximately 78 per cent of total income. Thus, approximately 80 per cent of annual income is composed of earned income.

15 There is a downward bias in our measure of the stock of social capital because there is an upper limit of 10 persons for whom details are given within each respondent's social network. This bias should not be substantial as the mean number of contacts within a social network is between 5 and 6 persons. However, there are differential response rates to the social capital question: more women than men responded (response rates are 75.44 per cent for women and 63.71 per cent for men). We find 381 men reported some details on 3.61 contacts (with a standard deviation of 2.65), while 605 women reported on 4.02 contacts (with a standard deviation of 2.87). However, this measurement error did not significantly affect the social capital variable, as men have a larger stock of social capital than women.

16 This measure is likely skewed by a few high-value outliers for women. For instance, one female respondent gave total annual gifts of 15,000 yuan, all of which were to her parents or parents-in-law. We do not know the reason for the gifts, but they may indicate a medical emergency or other expenditure that, although valid, does not necessarily correspond to typical investment in these relationships. When we remove these outliers for women, the mean is higher for men. We leave in these observations but further investigate their impact through different formulations of the social capital variable. It turns out that even if the outliers are included, men have a larger stock of social capital than women.

17 Social Capital I is rescaled by a factor of 1,560 to lie between 0 and 100. A change by a factor of 1,560 in the product of gifts, time and closeness would generate a unit change in social capital. Social Capital II is rescaled by a factor of 4.72 to lie between 0 and 100; thus, a change by a factor of 4.72 would change social capital by one unit.

18 Social networks were found not to be a significant determinant in the estimations for the combined sample, so we focus on social capital exclusively in the earned income estimations. It is insignificant but reported in the second set of re-employment estimations in order to compute the probabilities.

19 We use the natural logarithm of annual income as the dependent variable and alternatively refer to income and earnings or wages in discussing our results.

20 The specifications and effects of the control variables are standard and we do not discuss them in detail unless otherwise warranted. Briefly, age, age squared, years of education, years of employment experience, work unit ownership sector and occupation are continuous, and Communist Party membership and cities are dummy variables. The work unit ownership sector variable is ranked by mean income, where the lowest value is associated with SOEs and urban collectives is the omitted category. The occupation term is ranked starting with professionals to unskilled labour.

21 Selection into wage employment include age, Communist Party membership, years of education and work experience, which increase the likelihood of entering into wage employment, while age squared decreases the likelihood. Female gender and work sector have no effect on selection into employment. The implication is that being a woman and ownership sectors do not significantly reduce the selection into wage employment (unreported probit estimations for equations (1) and (2), Table 13.2).

22 Recall that social capital is an index variable of time and monetary and non-monetary resources, which was rescaled by a factor of 1,560 to lie between 0 and 100. A mean value of 4.05 requires expenditures on gifts of 6,318 yuan (£530) if time and closeness were at their respective minimum, and 211 yuan (£18) if time and closeness were at their respective maximum. A unit increase in social capital will require expenditure on gifts of 1,560 yuan (£131) if time spent and closeness were at their minima, whereas an expenditure of 52 yuan (£4) will increase social capital by one unit if the time spent and closeness were at their maxima.

23 We also estimated a logit specification for the likelihood of re-employment that includes the value of gifts given directly in appreciation for job assistance and found it to be insignificant (unreported equation).

## References

Becker, G.S. (1993) [1964] *Human Capital,* Chicago: University of Chicago Press.

Bian, Y. (1994) *Work and Inequality in Urban China,* Albany, NY: State University of New York.

Boorman, S.A. (1975) 'A combinatorial optimization model for transmission of job information through contact networks', *Bell Journal of Economics*, 6(1): 216–49.

Chang, X. (1999) ' "Fat pigs" and women's gifts: agnatic and non-agnatic social support in Kaixiangong village', in West, J., Zhao M., Chang, X. and Cheng, Y. (eds), *Women of China: Economic and Social Transformation*, Basingstoke: Macmillan.

Chang, X. and Feuchtwang, S. (1996) *Social Support in Rural China (1979–1991): A Statistical Report on Ten Villages*, London: China Research Unit, Department of Sociology, City University.

Glaeser, E.L., Laibson, D. and Sacerdote, B. (2002) 'The economic approach to social capital', *Economic Journal*, 112: 437–58.

Granovetter, M. (1995) [1974] *Getting a Job: A Study of Contacts and Careers*, Chicago: University of Chicago Press.

Greene, W.H. (1997) [1993]. *Econometric Analysis*, London: Prentice-Hall.

Gustafsson, B. and Li, S. (2000) 'Economic transformation and the gender earnings gap in urban China', *Journal of Population Economics*, 13(2): 305–29.

Heckman, J.J. (1993) 'What has been learned about labor supply in the past twenty years?', *American Economic Review,* 83(2): 116–21.

Khan, A.R. and Riskin, C. (1998) 'Income and inequality in China: composition, distribution and growth of household income, 1988 to 1995', *The China Quarterly*, 154: 221–53.

Knight, J. and Song, L. (1999) *The Rural–Urban Divide: Economic Disparities and Interactions in China*, Oxford: Oxford University Press.

Krishna, A. (2000) 'Creating and harnessing social capital', in Dasgupta, P. and Serageldin, I. (eds), *Social Capital: A Multifaceted Perspective*, Washington, DC: The World Bank.

Putnam, R.D., Leonardi, R. and Nanetti, R.Y. (1993) *Making Democracy Work*, Princeton, NJ: Princeton University Press.

Schultz, T.W. (1961) 'Investment in human capital', *American Economic Review,* 51(1): 1–17.

Uphoff, N. (2000) 'Understanding social capital: learning from the analysis and experience of participation', in Dasgupta, P. and Serageldin, I. (eds.), *Social Capital: A Multifaceted Perspective*, Washington, DC: The World Bank.

Yan, Y. (1996) *The Flow of Gifts: Reciprocity and Social Networks in a Chinese Village*, Palo Alto, CA: Stanford University Press.

Yang, M.M. (1994) *Gifts, Favors and Banquets: The Art of Social Relationships in China*, Ithaca, NY: Cornell University Press.

Yao, Y. (1999) 'Rural industry and labour market integration in eastern China', *Journal of Development Economics*, 59: 463–96.

## Appendix 13.A: Survey questions on *guanxi*

### *Questionnaire for the unemployed/xiagang (laid off), the 1999 CASS Survey*

37. Please list 10 relatives (including family members), friends and acquaintances within your *guanxi* network with whom you exchange gifts. Answer the following 21 questions for each person.

| Name | | | | | | | | | | |
|---|---|---|---|---|---|---|---|---|---|---|
| 37a | | | | | | | | | | |
| 37b | | | | | | | | | | |
| 37c | | | | | | | | | | |
| 37d | | | | | | | | | | |
| 37e | | | | | | | | | | |
| 37f | | | | | | | | | | |
| 37g | | | | | | | | | | |
| 37h | | | | | | | | | | |
| 37i | | | | | | | | | | |
| 37j | | | | | | | | | | |
| 37k | | | | | | | | | | |
| 37l | | | | | | | | | | |
| 37m | | | | | | | | | | |
| 37n | | | | | | | | | | |
| 37o | | | | | | | | | | |
| 37p | | | | | | | | | | |
| 37q | | | | | | | | | | |
| 37r | | | | | | | | | | |
| 37s | | | | | | | | | | |
| 37t | | | | | | | | | | |
| 37u | | | | | | | | | | |

37a) Their relationship to you

1. Spouse
2. Child
3. Grandchild
4. Parent
5. Parent-in-law
6. Grandparent

7. Sibling
8. Other relative
9. Friend
10. Classmate
11. Fellow villager
12. Neighbour
13. Colleague
14. Other

37b) Gender: 1. Male 2. Female
37c) Age (Years)
37d) Employment status

1. Employed
2. Off-duty
3. Retired
4. Youth waiting for a job assignment
5. Laid off from SOE
6. Internal retired
7. Unemployed
8. Homemaker
9. Full-time student
10. Disabled
11. Other

37e) Ownership of work unit (choose from the same selections as listed in question 8)
37f) Industrial sectors of work unit (choose from the same selections as listed in question 11)
37g) Their occupation (choose from the same selections as listed in question 13)
37h) If they are professionals and cadres, what are their professional titles and ranks

1. Senior title
2. Middle title
3. Junior title
4. Technician level
5. Bureau chief level and above
6. Division chief level
7. Section chief level
8. Section member

37i) Their educational level

1. College or above
2. Professional school
3. Middle level professional school (technical school, vocational school)
4. Upper middle school
5. Lower middle school
6. Primary school
7. Less than primary school

37j) Are they Communist Party members? 1. Yes 2. No
37k) What are their incomes approximately (yuan)?
37l) How familiar are you with them?
1. Not familiar 2. Not very familiar
3. Fairly familiar 4. Familiar 5. Very familiar

37m) If you did not have a job, can you ask them to help you find a job? 1. Yes 2. No
37n) Did they help you to find a job in fact? 1. Yes 2. No
37o) If 'Yes', did they find a job for you in their work unit? 1. Yes 2. No

37p) If ‘Yes’, the job that you got with their help is: 1. Your current job
2. Your previous job 3. Other

37q) Did they make use of their connections when helping you to find a job?
1. Yes 2. No

37r) Did you give them any gifts to express your appreciation around the time of the assistance?
1. Yes 2. No

37s) If ‘Yes’, how much were your gifts worth (yuan)?

37t) What was the value of your gifts to each of them in the past year (yuan)? (Please estimate the monetary value of all goods and cash gifts)

37u) How many times did you get together with them in the past month (including meals, chatting, going to movies, watching TV, and other activities)?
1. None 2. One or two times 3. Once a week
4. Two or three times a week 5. Almost every day 6. At least once a day

# Index

For Product Safety Concerns and Information please contact our EU representative GPSR@taylorandfrancis.com
Taylor & Francis Verlag GmbH, Kaufingerstraße 24, 80331 München, Germany

www.ingramcontent.com/pod-product-compliance
Lightning Source LLC
LaVergne TN
LVHW011111300926
849160LV00008B/351